W9-ASM-657

COACHING
matters

Leadership and Tactics of the NFL's Ten Greatest Coaches

BRAD ADLER

Brassey's, Inc.

WASHINGTON, D.C.

Library of Congress Cataloging-in-Publication Data

Adler, Brad, 1960–
    Coaching matters : leadership and tactics of the NFL's ten greatest coaches / Brad Adler.— 1st ed.
        p. cm.
Includes index.
    ISBN 1-57488-613-4 (hardcover : alk. paper)
    1. Football coaches—United States—Biography. 2. Football—Coaching.
I. Title.

GV939.A1A35 2003
796.332'07'7—dc21

                                                              2003010443

Printed in the United States of America on acid-free paper that meets the American National Standards Institute Z39-48 Standard.

Brassey's, Inc.
22841 Quicksilver Drive
Dulles, Virginia 20166

Text design by Pen & Palette Unlimited

First Edition

10 9 8 7 6 5 4 3 2 1

CONTENTS

LIST OF PHOTOGRAPHS

ACKNOWLEDGMENTS

I would like to thank the following people for their faithful assistance in the production of this book: the folks at Brassey's, especially Chris Kahrl, Kevin Cuddihy, and Emily Costello; Eddie Epstein, whose advice and insight during the formative stages of this undertaking were of great import; and Bob Broomall, whose expertise in polishing the manuscript was invaluable. I would also like to thank my family for the love and encouragement they have given me over the years: my mother, Lucille, my father, Ira, my sister, Robin, my brother, Roy, my nephews, Jeffrey and Sean, and my dog, Cindy. I cherish each of them and can always count on their support.

INTRODUCTION

A professional football coach's job description can be summarized in one word: *win*.

The way in which a coach chooses to traverse the course towards winning is his choice. He is free to develop and implement any system he deems worthy. He can devise strategies that he believes will accentuate the abilities of his athletes. He can deploy his players in any fashion that he sees fit. But the truly elite coaches, the ones who win consistently and totally endear themselves to the men they direct, all seem to have special attributes that transform them from mere "managers" into gifted leaders who maintain the uncanny ability to mold minds, shape futures, and energize human beings to levels of unthinkable distinction.

As you may have ascertained, the title of this book has a dual meaning. Coaching does *matter*—to a much greater degree than most people realize. But so does the manner in which "coaching matters" are handled. For it is entirely possible that a coaching candidate qualifies as a tactically sound fundamentalist; however, if that same individual cannot successfully convey his systems and schemes, advantageously apply his strategies and techniques, and ultimately earn the respect and devotion of his players, then the *manner* in which he operates is insufficient to produce a prosperous outcome. It is this dynamic which is often the most underappreciated and overlooked aspect of the coaching process. And its meaningfulness relative to the identification and classification of talented head coaches is immense.

Hopefully, this book will give people a clearer understanding of the methods and leadership skills necessary for coaches to earn victories in the National Football League. At that point, they may also discover a newfound appreciation for the truly elite head coaches.

Chapter 1

THE QUOTE

My very close friend, ex-sports executive and author Eddie Epstein, and I still laugh hysterically at the mere mention of it. O. A. "Bum" Phillips's fifteen-word assessment of his counterpart and nemesis Don Shula, head coach of the Miami Dolphins during Phillips's tenure as coach of the NFL's Houston Oilers from 1975 through 1980: "He can take 'hisins' and beat 'yourins,' or he can take 'yourins' and beat 'hisins.'"

Believe it or not, these fifteen words crudely but adequately summarize the basis for this book and its fundamental assertion.

Certainly, a scholar with a formal education could more eloquently articulate the mastery with which Don Shula commanded and directed his football teams, but somehow, at its rudimentary best, Bum Phillips said it all. And though Shakespeare, as well, may have put it in a somewhat more polished fashion, Phillips's appraisal of one of professional football's most highly acclaimed and recognized coaching icons bluntly captures the frustration, angst, and yet ultimate respect that most counterparts have, or had, for their most successful and hated coaching rivals.

It didn't matter if "hisins" were a bunch of misfit, woebegone outcasts, or if "yourins" were a pathetic group of unathletic, has-been geriatrics—Don Shula was going to take either team and beat you—consistently! In fact, if it were physically possible to have coach Shula play you or any other "mere mortal" of the coaching brigade, with the same players playing for both teams at the same exact time, he would *still* beat you—consistently.

Why?

The answer is quite simply and emphatically that great coaches will ultimately win regardless of the talent or conditions that surround them.

And therein lies the foundation of this book.

Great coaches appear to transcend the game itself and can seemingly impose their irrepressible will to win on any given situation, eventually producing victory irrespective of outside influences or luck. In effect, that's what makes them great coaches.

One predominant, mutual characteristic will evidence itself in regard to these leaders of men: They have to do it their way. They must be in a position to fundamentally control their own destiny, and they often feel the need to make, or be consulted on, every major decision within their organization.

In this book, I will investigate, in detail, the personalities, routines, and strategies of ten of the greatest coaches in NFL history. I will then scrutinize their idiosyncrasies and techniques in an attempt to identify the traits, characteristics, and tactics most frequently associated with their success. And not only do I plan to examine the impact and correlation between all of their attributes and practices relative to winning, but I also intend to analyze the way in which their methods are applied. In the process, I will strive to prove several assertions. First, that the head coach is the most consequential member of a football organization. Second, as stated above, that great coaches will ultimately win regardless of the talent or conditions that surround them. Third, that the manner in which a head coach communicates his concepts and utilizes his systems and techniques are just as important, if not more so, than the quality of the strategies and procedures themselves.

To begin this analysis, the first task will be to select an appropriate group of coaches to study. Therefore, an interpretation of the term "great coach" is essential. Since winning is the most important evidence of superior performance in sports, it seems clear that the best way to identify outstanding coaches would be to employ a set of numerical requirements based on victory totals, championships, and longevity. Though I will not entirely restrict myself to the following standards, the ensuing criteria will serve as a guideline for my selection procedure, thereby greatly limiting any personal biases that I could inadvertently bring to the process. The only binding restriction that I will enforce is that the majority of each coach's career must have been served after the 1950 All-American Football Conference/NFL merger. Beginning in 1950, free substitution was permanently adopted in the NFL. This allowed athletes to specialize as offensive or defensive players without being disqualified from further participation upon leaving the game. The impact on the league was enormous, and, in combination with the new merger, the landscape of professional football was forever changed. Consequently, it makes sense to begin my investigation at that precise point in time. The basic qualifications will be as follows:

1. A minimum winning percentage of .600.

> In any professional sport, a winning percentage of .600 usually indicates above average performance. For example, in the present-day NFL, a 10–6 record (the closest rounded equivalent of a .600 winning percentage) will almost certainly advance you to the playoffs. In fact, one has to go back to 1991 to find a team that went 10–6 or better and did not qualify for postseason

play. And though a single season of .600 football does not distinguish a team or coach as extraordinary, a career winning percentage of .600 does. Not many coaches with careers of meaningful length have achieved that standard.

2. A minimum career of ten complete seasons or at least 150 games.

   This excludes the three- or four-year "wonders," coaches who prospered for a short period of time, perhaps based on other uncontrollable circumstances which were to his advantage, such as benefiting from the opportunity to use a former coach's personnel and systems.

3. At least *two* conference championship victories, one of which must have resulted in an NFL championship (an NFL title game win before 1966) or a Super Bowl triumph.

   This criterion serves to ensure that our list is truly indicative of championship caliber coaches. Using this guideline does not diminish the accomplishments of coaches such as Bud Grant, Marv Levy, or Dan Reeves, each of whom appeared in four Super Bowls without winning one. Many a coach would sell his soul to achieve such status. However—though it may seem somewhat harsh—the ultimate goal in any sport is to win championships. Consequently, in this context, these individuals cannot be considered *truly* elite coaches and will not qualify for this endeavor.

As of February 2003, the aforementioned requirements produced the following list of coaches: Paul Brown, Joe Gibbs, Mike Holmgren, Tom Landry, Vince Lombardi, George Seifert, Don Shula, and Bill Walsh.

After scrutinizing the list, however, I felt compelled to make one arbitrary exclusion and allow three other exceptions for coaches who did not otherwise meet the criteria. Though I believe George Seifert to be a good coach—his stint with the Carolina Panthers notwithstanding—I made the decision to exclude him due to the fact that he inherited a Super Bowl–winning club from Bill Walsh in 1989 and that he greatly benefited from the 49ers' spendthrift policies of the early- to mid-1990s. In regard to the exceptions, I believe it was absolutely necessary to include the following three men: Chuck Noll, John Madden, and Bill Parcells.

Noll led the Steelers to four Super Bowl titles in six years, and, just as significantly, was at the helm as Pittsburgh ended nearly four decades of mediocrity to become an NFL power. Even though his career winning percentage is only .566, I felt this study would lose credibility if he were excluded.

John Madden coached ten complete seasons, won a world championship, enjoyed a lifetime winning percentage of .750, and never had a losing year. But although he won a Super Bowl, he failed to win the equivalent of *two* conference championships. Madden's .750 winning percentage (103–32–7) represents the highest of any coach in history with more than 100 games. And though George Allen has a somewhat comparable lifetime record (116–47–5, .705), Allen never won a world championship, did not have quite as high a winning percentage, and had a vastly inferior postseason record of 2–7, as opposed to Madden's 9–7. John Madden must be included as well.

Bill Parcells very quickly transformed three habitual losers into championship contenders. He won two Super Bowls with the Giants, led the Patriots to a Super Bowl berth, and brought the Jets to an AFC championship game. And though his lifetime winning percentage (.579) is below the standard, the magnitude of his career achievements are too great to overlook.

Several other coaches who were close to qualifying but were not included warrant mention. Mike Shanahan, current head coach of the Denver Broncos, has a career winning percentage of .601 (89–59) and two Super Bowl victories. He fell just short, however, of the ten complete seasons/150 games requirement. Bill Cowher, Pittsburgh Steelers' head coach since 1992 and owner of a .622 career winning percentage (109–66–1), was eliminated based on the fact that he has only one conference championship (1995) on his postseason resume. Jimmy Johnson won two Super Bowls with Dallas. However, both his career winning percentage (.555) and games/seasons coached (144/9) were below the standard. Mike Ditka won a Super Bowl and had an outstanding .631 winning percentage in Chicago through eleven seasons, but he had only one championship (his Super Bowl victory in 1986). Ditka's career serves as an excellent example for the validity of my selection criteria. Upon leaving the Bears after the 1992 season, he would have been ineligible because he never won another championship (remember, two is the minimum), not even a conference crown. When he retired from the New Orleans Saints after his disastrous 1999 campaign, Ditka's winning percentage of .560 was also insufficient to qualify (even if he had won another championship). And though Ditka was indeed a very good coach, I do not believe that most football historians and experts would classify him in the same category as the very best that ever walked the sidelines. Therefore, it appears that the combination of a .600 winning percentage, 150 or more games or ten seasons, at least two conference championships, and one world championship or Super Bowl, constitutes both a sound and logical basis for selection guidelines.

So the final roster includes the following coaches, listed alphabetically: Paul Brown, Joe Gibbs, Mike Holmgren, Tom Landry, Vince Lombardi, John Madden, Chuck Noll, Bill Parcells, Don Shula, and Bill Walsh.

Before we examine these coaches, however, a quick historical survey of the NFL will reveal how the landscape has changed during the past fifty years. This survey will provide us with a more realistic perception of the challenges faced by coaches in different eras and offer a better understanding of the strategies and tactics they employed.

Chapter 2

THE NEW NFL

The hierarchy of any business must continually evaluate its products and modify its policies and strategies in response to changes in its industry. In professional football, this means that coaches and general managers must constantly assess their players and their methods. Times change, and certain tactics that worked in the past may no longer bear the fruits of success.

In 1977, a new concept was introduced to the NFL: free agency. Though extremely suppressive, this option allowed players a small degree of independence and a limited opportunity to explore employment possibilities with other clubs. Until that season, player movement was restricted so that the team that held the player's original draft rights could essentially keep that individual until he retired—even if some other organization was willing to pay him more money or give him more playing time.

In 1993—when the NFL loosened its free-agency guidelines—this unique form of player freedom blossomed into a full-fledged assault on the owners' pocketbooks and created the need for a multitude of new strategies and management philosophies. Athletes, desiring more playing time, money, and notoriety, immediately began to solicit offers from other teams. Player movement from team to team became so prevalent that organizations had to instantly revise their franchise-building philosophies of the past. No longer could coaches, general managers, and scouts count on two or three good drafts to keep their clubs well stocked for a four- to six-year period. And players themselves began to think twice about signing long-term contracts, which could shut them out of what would certainly become a seller's market.

Accurate personnel evaluation became even more important when organizations began losing key players annually. The days when teams like the Baltimore Colts or Miami Dolphins could stash away a veteran like Earl Morrall as their backup quarterback were over. No longer could the Oakland Raiders give a young, inexperienced quarterback like Ken Stabler that extra year or two in which to develop a deft touch in the professional passing game. Teams had to correctly identify their most capable players and endeavor to sign them to long-term contracts before they became eligible for free agency.

To further complicate and muddle the labor picture, a salary cap was instituted in 1994. In exchange for the more liberal free-agency specifications established the previous season, players forfeited the luxury of uncapped earnings when their aggregate salaries reached a certain percentage of gross revenues (approximately 63 percent). Teams could no longer spend as much money as they deemed necessary. Every club would be restricted in relation to the total, aggregate amount of its salaries—a hard cap on player expenditures.

When the smoke cleared, both players and owners apparently received what they wanted. The players obtained free agency, and the owners secured a salary cap. Everything seemed harmonious. The new system, though, was far from perfect.

In past years, NFL franchises built their rosters and evaluated their personnel with the goal of placing the best players on the field. As the game headed into the salary cap era, however, many clubs soon discovered that they could not afford to put their best players on the field. This financial "crisis" was certainly not due to a lack of money but rather to the restrictions of the league's spending threshold.

Each team in the NFL gets to spend the same exact amount of money on player salaries, unlike teams in Major League Baseball (MLB) or the National Hockey League (NHL), where clubs are free to spend any amount they deem necessary. For the 2002 season, the NFL cap number was approximately $71 million, roughly $1.34 million per person (if it were distributed evenly among all fifty-three players). Each year, however, it grows increasingly more difficult for teams to regenerate their talent base when they are fighting the personnel battle on two fronts (free agency and cap restrictions). Teams wish to retain their best players, yet these athletes often cost more money than the clubs have at their disposal. Consequently, many organizations find themselves in the unenviable position of having to sacrifice talent for dollars in order to remain within the parameters of the league's spending regulations.

The combination of free agency and the salary cap created a new league where players seek out teams with money to spend and franchises pursue the most talented players at the most reasonable prices. After decades of roster stability from season to season, the "new" NFL promised fast and furious player movement—from one club to the next—with players chasing dollars and franchises chasing bargains. The ground rules have changed forever. Dynasties appear to have become a thing of the past, a three- or four-year "run" being the most that any sane prognosticator dare conceive. For with winning comes prosperity, and with prosperity comes money, and with money come salary cap issues. As teams ascend to the pinnacle of success, so do the salary figures commensurate with champions. And sooner or later, the piper has to be paid.

Every team strives to win the Super Bowl. Every team is limited in regard to their salary investments. But the teams that make the playoffs and win the championships find themselves in a position of having to compensate their athletes accordingly. Therefore, it is quite obvious why the Dallas Cowboys and San Francisco 49ers—two

organizations with incredibly successful legacies and huge pressure to win—succumbed to the "cap crunch." These two franchises, pillars of the NFL, were consistent
winners during the initial stages of the salary cap era (the mid-1990s) and then
became victims of the system. Certainly, both squads could have managed their situations in a somewhat more efficient manner. Are you listening Jerry Jones and Carmen
Policy? Nevertheless, in their defense, the insidious, divisive nature of the cap greatly
increased the probability of their demise.

It seems clear that the teams which invest the most money in salaries generally
have a better chance for success in the NFL. The more money a team spends, the easier it is for them to keep their own good players and sign the best free agents. And
though every team is essentially limited to the same amount of money in regard to
salary expenditures, the Cowboys and 49ers were the first to figure out that they could
circumvent the league's salary cap restrictions—thereby affording themselves the ability to spend more money—by guaranteeing free agents deferred cash. This promise of
large sums of deferred dollars made the deals much more lucrative than most of the
other contracts those free agents could have signed at the time—and a vast majority
of the money did not count against the team's salary cap until several years later. Since
both the Cowboys and 49ers wished to continue their success but were forced to pay
their athletes high salaries commensurate with their achievements, the only alternative they had—other than to release their best players—was to create cap room by defer-
ring their expenditures into the future. Dallas (1993–1998), San Francisco (1993–1998),
Jacksonville (1996–1999), and Baltimore (2000–2001) all spent money indiscriminately
in this fashion and won. However, the process never ceases. The more you win, the
more you ultimately need to spend to sustain your success as player after player
demands to be compensated for the team's accomplishments. Inevitably, whenever
teams win (whether or not they were frugal leading up to that point), they are forced
to spend much more money to keep their players. A vicious circle develops. In order
to win consistently, teams have to spend money. As they spend money, they eventually
encounter cap problems. When they encounter cap problems—which all successful
teams eventually do—they can't spend, so they lose (Dallas 1999–present, San Francisco 1999–2000, Jacksonville 2000–present, Baltimore 2002–present). Teams invariably rise and fall in relation to their salary cap situations. Though it's certainly not
impossible, I'm sure most football analysts admit that it would take a Herculean effort
to perpetuate a winning scenario under this system.

In the end, you might think that the current salary cap system and its uniform
spending plan should work out in a positive and equitable manner—which would be
good for the league—but it doesn't. It creates a negative impact in three major ways.

First, the system is actually inequitable. The present plan inherently handicaps
the good clubs while benefiting the inept franchises. The only ways to replenish your
roster from year to year in the NFL are via the annual draft of college players, veteran
free agents (who sometimes cost big bucks), and undrafted free agents. At one time, if
coaches and/or general managers demonstrated the prowess to systematically select,

develop, and refine the best players available, then their teams had a good chance to consistently win football games. And for years, that's how it worked in the league. However, the implications of the free agency/salary cap era have changed the rules. Now, in return for their masterful ability to distinguish talent better than their competitors, the outstanding coaches and general managers—the men who run the good teams— receive a nice, sweet reward: After their precocious athletes have demonstrated their skills to the rest of the league, the good teams lose those players to the inept franchises.

Any NFL player, subject to contractual agreements, can become a restricted free agent after three seasons in the league. At that point, his original team has the ability to match any contract offer for the player and still retain his rights. After four years, however, players can become unrestricted free agents, at liberty to negotiate and sign with whomever they choose. When an outstanding player becomes an unrestricted free agent, almost every team has interest in his services. A bidding war ensues, and invariably the winning organizations find themselves in a subordinate position relative to the salary cap and the availability of funds. Since the consistent losing franchises seldom, if ever, produce high-quality talent on their own, the incompetent teams usually have an abundance of money (cap space) with which to work and a distinct advantage when it comes to signing free agents. It becomes nearly impossible for the good teams to keep a majority of their better players because of the nature of the system. Sure, the inept clubs get "burned" sporadically when they sign an overrated free agent—or even a skillful free agent at an exceptionally inflated price—but that usually does little to diminish their arsenal of dollars, nor does it preclude them from occasionally signing a player worthy of his cost. As the saying goes, "Even a blind squirrel finds an acorn once in a while." And though the poor teams are usually not the first choice of many top-of-the-line free-agent prospects, it is also true that money talks, and sooner or later—if enough dollars are contributed to the till—the losing history of the club becomes a secondary consideration, and a top team loses a good player to a poor team.

The end result is that the good franchises quite literally wind up as scouts for the lesser teams in the league. It's as if the NFL has issued a mandate: "Since some of you (the perennially inferior teams) cannot seem to keep up with the rest of the group, we will assist by giving you some hints as to which players can actually play." It turns into a constant recycling project for the good teams and the good coaches: Find the talent. Cultivate the talent. Benefit from the talent—for a few seasons. Surrender that talent to teams (losing clubs) with money to spend. Then find more talent, and so on.

Consistency in victory becomes a function of which teams can continually draft the better players, because this infuses a club with good, young athletes at a fraction of a veteran's price tag. And even though first-round selections earn huge, up-front bonuses, all draftees are protected from unrestricted free agency for four years after the draft. The trouble, however, is that it usually takes a few years for rookies to develop into productive players, and then, of course, they too become "free."

The second negative impact of the present system is that it promotes extensive roster turnover. Fans no longer know the players without a program. There is little, if any, consistency from year to year regarding team rosters because the cap crunch forces clubs to release players in droves. The athletes become less and less familiar to the fans, and this eventually creates apathy.

Lastly, the current policy produces what I like to call "roller-coaster" football—clubs winning for a short while, then losing for a similar period. This creates extremely inconsistent results on an annual basis, and tends to inhibit the formation and per-petuation of the rivalries that helped make the NFL the most dominant sports entity in the world. Rivalries evolve when teams remain proficient for extended periods of time and meet in several crucial, competitive, emotional games. But with teams habit-ually in transition—good for two or three years and terrible for a few years thereafter—it becomes nearly impossible to develop passionate competition with anyone. As rivalries fade and teams become more and more unpredictable, fans grow intolerant, and enthusiasm for the game diminishes.

Ultimately, many NFL salary cap lessons have been learned since 1994, especially from the experiences of both the 49ers and Cowboys, each of whom endured desper-ate periods with approximately $20 to $25 million in "dead money" immediately fol-lowing their spendthrift eras. Dead money is cash (including deferred money) that organizations have guaranteed to players who are no longer on the team. For exam-ple, the 2000 49ers were forced to account for $15 million allocated for ten players who were released before the 2000 season (Steve Young, Chris Doleman, Lawrence Phillips, Gabe Wilkins, et cetera). That $15 million counted against San Francisco's salary cap figure of approximately $65 million and could not be used to sign players—that's con-sidered dead money! Believe me, NFL teams did take the cap lessons to heart. The 2001 and 2002 free agent signing periods were among the worst (from a player's stand-point) in history. Many players could not even field a respectable offer. And though the 49ers, Cowboys, and other teams certainly deserve some blame in regard to the fate bestowed upon them (for attempting to circumvent the cap by continually deferring payroll), the fact remains that the system is flawed. Every year several teams (mostly winning clubs) face the possibility of "cap death." Clearly, the NFL needs to reexamine its current policies. Players are growing weary of the monetary constraints dictated by the cap, franchises are growing impatient due to the constant struggle to win and remain within the system's boundaries, and the fans are becoming restless in regard to the incessant turnover of personnel and the wild fluctuations in team performance. I can't imagine these developments are what the NFL expected, and I don't believe it is what the majority of fans truly enjoy. Something has to change, quickly, or the NFL risks labor unrest and fan disenchantment.

A more liberal, equitable, and fan-friendly salary cap system should be adopted. The more football savvy organizations—the teams that initially discover and cultivate the talent—deserve at least some leverage with which to retain the athletes that they have developed. Perhaps exemptions could be adopted that allow teams to re-sign their own free agents at 10 to 15 percent over the cap, without penalty, a hybrid NBA-type system. This would help stabilize rosters and eliminate some of the inconsistency in team performance—two of the major problems that plague the system. Hopefully, a practical compromise can be reached in the near future. When paying customers become disillusioned, troubled times will almost certainly ensue. Just ask Major League Baseball.

In terms of coaching, the point of the matter is that as times change, coaches must change, and so too must the standards by which coaches are evaluated. Winning consistently in the twenty-first century appears to be a much more difficult proposition than it was during much of the past fifty years. But in order to prove this hypothesis and to intelligently evaluate coaches from a historical perspective, you need an accurate depiction of the circumstances prevalent in each era.

For the purpose of equitably comparing and contrasting the challenges faced by successful NFL coaches both before and during the free agency/salary cap period, it would seem that an examination of two of the NFL's premiere all-time franchises—the Green Bay Packers of the 1960s and the San Francisco 49ers of the late 1980s and '90s—would perfectly suit our needs. The goal of this endeavor will be to measure and differentiate the roster turnover on these outstanding teams. This will allow us to comparatively assess the difficulties coaches had with regard to retaining players and sustaining victory during those eras.

The Green Bay Packers were considered to be the most formidable team of the 1960s. Their remarkable run started with a humble beginning, the 1959 season, when they earned seven victories versus five losses. From 1960 to 1969, the Packers, under the inimitable Vince Lombardi for eight of those seasons, compiled a record of 96–37–5, for an astounding .714 winning percentage and five NFL titles. As the years passed, they were always able to bring their best players back into the fold, just like every other team of that period.

The San Francisco 49ers' teams of the 1980s and '90s are perhaps the most comparable team to the Packers of the 1960s. From 1981 to 1998, the 49ers also won five titles and suffered only one losing season. Since the goal here is to examine roster turnover on a successful team during the free agency/salary cap era, the most appropriate ten-year span to investigate for the 49ers is very probably 1989 (the year after their third Super Bowl victory) through 1998. The NFL's precursor to modern free agency, a system called "Plan B," began in 1989. The combination of the current free agency system and salary cap restrictions started with the 1993 and 1994 seasons. Consequently, this ten-year interval provides us with a good portion of the salary cap era as well as being representative of free agency. During this stretch (which included two more Super Bowl victories), the 49ers compiled a record that would make even the Packers proud, 123–37, for an absolutely ungodly winning percentage of .769. San Francisco, though, seemed to have much more difficulty retaining their players from season to season.

To truly understand the changes created by the NFL's new policies in the latter part of the twentieth century, you need look no further than tables 2-1 and 2-2. They compare the personnel turnover rate between the two premiere teams.

Table 2-1. Green Bay Packers (1960–1969 rosters)

Year	Percentage of New Players from Previous Year
1960	28.2%
1961	21.1%
1962	13.5%
1963	27.5%
1964	25.0%
1965	17.5%
1966	22.0%
1967	20.9%
1968	29.8%
1969	20.0%
10-year average turnover:	22.6%

Table 2-2. San Francisco 49ers (1989–1998 rosters)

Year	Percentage of New Players from Previous Year
1989	29.0%
1990	24.1%
1991	37.0%
1992	36.8%
1993	29.5%
1994	42.1%
1995	33.0%
1996	33.3%
1997	32.1%
1998	43.9%
10-year average turnover:	34.1%

SOURCE: Statistics based on *Total Football*'s and *Pro Football Weekly*'s rosters and organizational information presented by both teams.

To the untrained eye, the above figures probably don't jump off the page. However, to a seasoned statistician, the numbers are amazing. A 34.1 percent average turnover rate as compared to a rate of 22.6 percent represents 51 percent more personnel changes per season, on average.

The Packers teams of the 1960s averaged approximately forty players per year and experienced an average yearly turnover of 9.04 players. The 49ers teams of the 1980s and '90s averaged about fifty-five players per year and experienced an average yearly turnover of 18.8 players.

To put this in perspective, had the 49ers been permitted the luxury of a personnel turnover rate equivalent to that of the Packers, they would have lost an average of only twelve players per season as opposed to nineteen. They would have been able to retain almost 13 percent more of their entire roster. Conversely, if the Packers had been burdened with personnel turnover rates as unforgiving as those that the 49ers faced, the Packers would have suffered the additional attrition of five more players per season, for an average turnover rate of fourteen versus their real figure of nine. And remember, the Packers had only about forty players on their roster at the time.

In 1962, there were only five new Packers players (13.5 percent of their thirty-seven-man roster) as compared to the year before—an incredible statistic relative to the modern game. Green Bay won another title that year, just as they had in 1961. In 1963, the number of new faces swelled to eleven (27.5 percent of their forty-man roster), a figure that was a whopping 120 percent more than the turnover heading into

1962. Even disregarding the additional roster spots allocated that year (forty versus thirty-seven, meaning that three extra players *had* to be signed), new players accounted for 21.6 percent of the team versus 13.5 percent the year before (a full 60 percent more than the 1962 club). Guess what? You got it. The Packers did not win the title that season, and they lost their conference as well. Though they finished with a fine record, 11–2–1, they were not quite good enough to repeat as champions.

San Francisco's 1989 Super Bowl–winning roster included seventeen new players (29 percent of the team). And remember, this was before the advent of *true* free agency and the salary cap. In the peak free agency/salary cap years of the mid- to late-1990s (1994–1998 in our study), the numbers increase to an average turnover rate of 36.9 percent, which would equate to approximately twenty new players each season. If we take this pattern to its final extreme and include the 49ers teams of 1999 and 2000— when free agency and the cap severely impacted their situation—the numbers become quite staggering. The 1999 San Francisco 49ers endured a 50 percent turnover rate (thirty-one of sixty-two roster spots), while the 2000 club finished at 46.4 percent (twenty-six of fifty-six). It's no wonder that San Francisco suffered through 4–12 and 6–10 seasons those last two years.

There should be no doubt that contemporary NFL head coaches must deal with a different, more severe set of rules and regulations—details that tend to inhibit the prolongation of victory. Nothing compares to these roster turnover numbers when attempting to determine the true impact and significance of salary cap restrictions and free agency relative to the angst and consternation that they create for the men charged with the responsibility of successfully running the franchises. Keeping an accomplished roster intact from one year to the next is now nearly impossible. The monumental changes in the NFL between the eras of the 1960s, '70s, and '80s as compared to the 1990s, are, in some ways, as enormous as the difference between the automobile and the airplane.

Clearly, the landscape of professional football has effectively been altered. In the modern era, teams cannot expect to keep a successful group of players together indefinitely. No longer can organizations expect the harvest of three or four outstanding drafts to fuel their clubs for the next eight to ten years. The new system creates an extremely difficult challenge for coaches in regard to maintaining franchises at or near the apex of success for any extended period of time. Conversely, it has become much easier to revamp and retool losing organizations in a quick, decisive fashion. Using the proper mix of draft, free agent, and coaching strategies, clubs can sometimes restructure their situation in one off-season. Ultimately, the inequities of the system have created a contemporary league where the emphasis is on short-term struggles for prominence, as opposed to the more long-range plans of attack that were in vogue in the past.

Appropriate, prudent coaching evaluation must also change accordingly. And though few may be certain as to the proper standards that should govern the assessments that will surely follow, it seems quite obvious that a more suitable method of appraisal must be employed to accurately reflect coaching performance in the "new" NFL.

Chapter 3

PAUL BROWN

No other person in history had as great an influence on the game of professional football as Paul E. Brown.

Paul Brown was born on September 7, 1908, in Norwalk, Ohio. Before his tenth birthday, his father, Lester, a railroad dispatcher, was transferred to Massillon, Ohio, about sixty miles southeast of Norwalk. There, Paul Brown attended Massillon (also known as Washington) High School and participated in track, basketball, baseball, and, his first love, football. A slightly built youngster with the spirit of a tiger—which, ironically, was the nickname of the Massillon High team for which he played—Brown was a solid if unspectacular high school quarterback. After graduating from Massillon in 1926, he attended Ohio State University in Columbus, Ohio. Due to his diminutive stature (145 pounds), however, the Ohio State football program would not allow him to participate. So Brown transferred to Miami University in Oxford, Ohio, where he enjoyed both the college life and an opportunity to play the sport he so dearly loved. He started for two seasons with the Redskins, playing several positions including quarterback, running back, punter, and return specialist. Miami recorded a 13–4 record during Brown's career.

Upon graduating from Miami in 1930, Brown—an extremely gifted student—inquired about the opportunity to continue his studies at Oxford. Not "Oxford" as in Oxford, Ohio, but rather Oxford, England. He had qualified for a prestigious Rhodes Scholarship. But the Depression had begun, and money was tight. Consequently, rather than dash across the world into unfamiliar surroundings and an unknown future, Brown and his newlywed wife, Katy, moved to Annapolis, Maryland, where he was recommended for a teaching and football coaching position at Severn Preparatory School.

After two years in Maryland, Brown acquired the mandatory educational credits to satisfy the state teaching requirements in his home state of Ohio. His former mentor and ex-Massillon coach, Dave Stewart, sent a letter of recommendation on his behalf to the president of the Ohio school board. In 1932, Paul Brown became the new head coach of the Massillon Tigers, his former high school.

Massillon High had won only one game the year before Brown took control. The football program was $37,000 in debt, and their three-thousand-seat stadium was usually half empty during games. By the time Brown left the school nine years later (in 1940), they had won eighty games, lost only eight, averaged an incredible 18,000 fans per contest, and had a brand-new twenty-one-thousand-seat football facility named after a gentleman whose name would adorn an even larger, more well-known stadium in the state of Ohio in the not too distant future—Paul Brown.

In 1941, Brown turned his attention to college football. Ironically, Ohio State, the university that hadn't considered Brown worthy of their program several years earlier, was now clamoring for the young coaching mastermind to bail them out of the doldrums. The Buckeyes had fallen on hard times and, shamed by a 40–0 massacre at the hands of archrival Michigan in 1940, they decided that a change was in order. At the age of thirty-three, Brown became the youngest head coach in the history of the Big Ten conference.

One of the first changes Brown made at Ohio State was to limit the squad's practice time. Under Francis Schmidt, Ohio State's former head coach, a typical practice was about three hours. Most other college football teams of that era worked out three hours a day as well. Paul Brown, however, condensed his practice sessions to eighty to ninety minutes. "Any time a practice exceeds an hour and twenty minutes, a player's attention span and learning capacity quickly diminish," Brown said. "Players also get tired standing around for long periods and begin holding back."

In 1941, Brown's first season as coach, Ohio State lost only one game, a 14–7 defeat at the hands of the Northwestern Wildcats. The Wildcats' tailback (quarterback of the day) was a fellow by the name of Otto Graham. Paul Brown never failed to recognize a great football player when he saw one, and Graham caught Brown's attention during that game. "I never forgot Otto's tremendous peripheral vision," Brown said, "and his ability to run to his left and throw far across the field with such strength and accuracy." Little did the two men know at the time, but they would soon become acquainted as members of the same professional football organization.

Brown led Ohio State to an 18–8–1 record from 1941 to 1943, highlighted by a national championship in 1942.

After the 1943 season, Brown joined the service and landed a coaching position with the Navy's Great Lakes team just outside of Chicago. The Great Lakes squad played many of the outstanding college teams of the day, and the highlight of Brown's tenure was a 1944 game versus none other than Ohio State—which Great Lakes lost, 26–6. Brown coached and served as a naval officer (battalion commander) at Great Lakes for two years (1944–1945), compiling a 15–5–2 record. After the war ended, Brown had every intention of returning to Ohio State. He had been promised his head coaching position back as soon as his naval obligations were completed. But Ohio State had been extremely successful during Brown's absence. They were using the players he recruited, and their interim head coach had been handpicked by Paul him-self—Carroll Widdoes. Though the administration at Ohio State claimed to be ready and willing to honor its commitment to reinstall Brown as head coach, Brown sus-pected that they preferred to keep Widdoes, so he decided to take a gamble and enter the world of professional football.

The All-American Football Conference (AAFC) was the inspiration of Arch Ward, sports editor of the *Chicago Tribune*. Ward's plan was to create competition for the National Football League, which would hopefully lead to a baseball-like situation where there was an American and National league. In February of 1945—though tech-nically still in the service—Brown signed a coaching contract with the new league that paid him a retainer while he worked out his naval discharge. The AAFC agreed to compensate him $25,000 per year and awarded him 5 percent ownership of the new franchise in Cleveland, Ohio. According to Brown, the most significant part of the con-tract—aside from the small equity position which eventually made him a multimil-lionaire—was that it provided him with the authority he needed to become successful. "Most important to me," he said, "I had complete control of the team's operation, with total freedom to sign players and coaches."

The new league did not begin play until the 1946 season, giving Brown adequate time to work out his affairs with the Navy. In the meantime, however, Cleveland needed to build an administrative infrastructure to begin assessing, and ultimately signing, players. To that end, Brown hired another Ohio coach he knew, John Brickels, to act as a general manager of sorts, at least until Brown could devote more time to the organi-zation.

Brickels and Brown (sounds like a law firm) spent many evenings on the phone discussing players. Brown's strategy was simple: "I felt sure about the players I coached or played against," he said. "With players I did not know, or had never seen, I got iron-clad recommendations from football people whose opinions I respected, to make sure the player was my kind of person."

Brown's ideal player was one of impeccable character and intellect. His concep-tion of building a successful football team was based on his determination that the game was as much about people as it was about strategies, tactics, and motivational techniques. He contended that if you placed the best *individuals* (not necessarily the most talented football players) in the most advantageous positions, winning would almost come naturally. A Paul Brown "individual" was one who was totally devoted to winning football games and was willing to sacrifice his entire lifestyle in order to achieve that ambition. He had to possess an unselfish attitude and never put personal consid-erations ahead of the organization's goal of championship football. In addition, Brown greatly valued a player's learning capacity. "Everywhere we did our testing, we found that players with low intelligence progressed only so far," he said. "Knowing a man's capacity to learn before we drafted him helped us calculate his potential." In Brown's system, this intelligence-level measurement was even more important than it was with other teams.

Brown's offensive philosophy was predicated on detail and repetition. He required each player to know the entire playbook—from cover to cover—including the unusual demand that they be familiar with the responsibilities of players at positions other than their own. Brown felt that if the players were aware of all functions on a given play, there was a much better chance for a successful outcome. "In every training camp, I applied the basic laws of learning—seeing, hearing, writing, then doing, again and again," he said. "All the players diagrammed the complete play and wrote their individual assignments in detail in their playbooks. We wanted them to know the play's complete concept, not just their individual parts." Learning the playbook in this manner was not a simple task, but it was, nonetheless, a mandatory prerequisite for all team members. If a prospective athlete had outstanding physical skills but lacked the intelligence to grasp Brown's complex system, he was bypassed.

Brown's unique talent-assessment procedures set the standard for all professional football scouting departments in the 1950s and '60s. He was one of the first coaches to advocate serious preparation for the college draft. Typically, Cleveland created hundreds of files and player rankings of those athletes eligible for selection, while other teams often utilized nothing more than old game programs or football magazines. This gave Cleveland a huge edge when teams were forced to make instantaneous decisions on the merits of potential draftees as the process unfolded.

From an athletic standpoint, Brown coveted speed for skill players and bulk strength for linemen. He theorized that if a skill player was fast, he could overcome many other deficiencies, such as being short or slender. With his linemen, he felt somewhat the opposite. While many contemporary NFL scouts believe that you can enhance a player's strength with off-season conditioning programs, Brown believed that the best linemen were the ones who were naturally strong and could devastate their opponents at the point of attack. The nuances of pass blocking and foot movement, Brown thought, were much easier to teach and faster to develop than having to wait for the player to acquire the muscle mass necessary to drive people off the line of scrimmage.

When appraising an individual's physical stature, Brown insisted that his scouts,whenever possible, view a player in shorts to note his body type and muscle structure. This evaluation technique eventually became standard operating procedure in the NFL and is still utilized each year at the league's annual scouting combine in Indianapolis. If a lineman was very productive in college but lacked the prototypical size and bone structure of an NFL lineman, he was downgraded. Every once in a while, though, Cleveland's scouts would make an exception for an athlete the staff called a "player." These individuals did not possess the physical characteristics that the organization believed were necessary to perform at a premium level in professional football, but they produced at a consistently high rate in college, making plays that seemed to belie their natural abilities. Usually, these players possessed great instincts for the game and overcame their physical liabilities with a savvy, intuitive style of play.

Brown was always mindful of the subconscious temptation to upgrade a player's value just because he filled a particular need for the team. Conversely, he was always wary of the possibility of unintentionally downgrading a player because he played a position where the team was already solid. The foundation of his drafting system was based on a selection method that categorically distinguished between players, regardless of the team's particular needs in any one given season. "If we rated a particular center as a third- or fourth-round choice, we didn't select him in the first or second round, even though we might have needed a center," Brown said. "We tried to select the best player available and hoped it would strengthen us at a particular position." The exception was at quarterback, where Brown always took a chance on a player that was rated a little lower than others still on the board in order to secure a potentially gifted signal caller for use several years down the road. "A quarterback is a unique property in professional football," Brown always said. And the remarkable utilization of a quarterback's talents in Brown's system clearly justified the early selection of a gifted passer.

There was no college draft in the AAFC before the first season of play (1946), so the player acquisition process was essentially a free-for-all, with the idea being to sign the best players in a quick, decisive manner—beating other clubs (some NFL teams included) to the punch. Since many teams' scouting staffs were not formed in time to evaluate players during the 1945 season, and because there were no televised games or reliable game films to accurately assess the available talent, most of the signings were based on prior relationships (as Brown preferred), where players and coaches were familiar with each other's talents and character. In many ways, this made the league more appealing, developing a regional tone and promoting fierce rivalries between teams featuring local heroes.

While Brickels was busy running the team's operation from Cleveland, Brown made one visit to a player in close proximity to his naval base in Chicago. Otto Graham, the multitalented back from Northwestern who had made an indelible impression in Brown's mind while in college, was finishing his flight training at nearby Glenview Naval Air Station. Graham had been drafted by the Detroit Lions in the first round of the 1944 NFL draft, but because he was in the service, the Lions had not even contacted Graham before Brown's visit. Otto was making seventy-five dollars a month in the Navy. Cleveland offered him a $250-per-month retainer until he was discharged and agreed to pay him a salary of eighty-five hundred dollars his first season. Graham eagerly signed the contract. Cleveland acquired several players with the promise of a retainer while they were still in the service. Among them were Lou Groza (kicker and tackle), Lin Houston (lineman), Lou Saban (linebacker), and George Young (defensive end).

With the season fast approaching, the AAFC's Cleveland Browns (a name chosen by the public as a tribute to their head coach) headed to training camp in Bowling Green, Ohio. The first day of training camp began with a two-hour lecture from Paul Brown on the Cleveland Browns' system. For the next thirty years, Brown made the same exact speech to begin each season. There were never any football matters discussed, just protocol and team priorities. Everyone left the meeting with a categorical understanding of their responsibilities relative to the organization. They were there for one purpose—to be successful football players on a winning team. The club required and expected their total and uncompromising dedication to football.

On the practice field, Brown's basic method of operation during training camp was to have his offense implement two new plays per day. In the morning, the squad executed the fundamental elements of a running play, and in the afternoon they followed with the routine of a passing play. The progression of the system was always precise and consistent. The plays evolved based on their complexity. The first running play was a simple handoff up the middle. Next came the off-tackle variety, moving out from the center gradually while stressing the fundamental blocking techniques associated with each maneuver. This gave the team a firm understanding of the essence of each play from the standpoint of blocking tactics and player movement. As the plays expanded to end runs and pitchouts, the blocking schemes changed from straight on, blow-your-man-out drive blocks, to more athletic, open-field blocks on linebackers and defensive backs. "The more carefully these basic plays were presented, the better the team's entire structure would be," said Brown.

The first passing plays always utilized full protection, limiting the patterns to ends only. This gave Brown the opportunity to convey the precise details of his unusual pass blocking system. Since the NFL's inception in the 1920s, teams approached pass blocking in much the same manner as run blocking. Linemen would simply charge forward and attempt to push the opponent out of the way. As passing took on a more prominent role, this strategy became counterproductive. Often, defensive linemen expecting a pass would simply dodge the oncoming charge of the offensive linemen—realizing that no back would be coming through the hole created by their sidestep—and then rush towards the quarterback, unabated. Brown, therefore, devised a clever blocking scheme in which his offensive linemen were instructed to step backward and redirect defenders, literally "blocking" the defense's path to the quarterback, who would stand in the middle of what would come to be known as the "pocket" of protection. This process furnished Cleveland with the most effective pass blocking techniques in professional football at the time, affording their quarterbacks more time to deliver the ball. After the full-protection pass plays and blocking schemes were introduced, Brown progressed to the next set, which included passes to the backs. Finally, special formations where there were four or five potential receivers in the pattern were added.

When mistakes were made, or when Brown noticed a player executing his responsibilities in a lazy fashion, he would almost never yell or scream at the individual. He preferred to calmly advise the player as to the proper method and/or motivation necessary to carry out the play. If necessary, Brown would call a player in for a private meeting, during which time he would further explain the routine or the effort expected of the individual.

On defense, Brown stressed the fundamentals of tackling more than any other phase of the game. He believed that if his players were efficient form tacklers, this could mitigate against other potential deficiencies in their play. Every practice and every game was preceded by a drill that emphasized the correct form of a proper tackle.

Defensive players would pair off and take turns performing the rudimentary essentials of a tackle—in slow motion—on their partner. One player would move into the other's body, place his shoulder in his partner's waist area, and with his head up, looking straight forward, he would lift his partner off the ground and gently drive him into the turf. The players took turns, and on each successive attempt would get a little closer to full speed. This technique also served to warm up the players, gradually exposing them to the fierce hitting they would encounter once the game started.

Paul Brown's practices were as innovative as the rest of his procedures. He was the first coach to introduce specialized instruction during practice sessions. Prior to the mid-1940s, teams exclusively utilized eleven-on-eleven, full-squad drills to prepare for games. Brown changed that, employing individual coaches to supervise specific units of the team. Cleveland often divided into smaller groups to concentrate on the techniques associated with a particular position. "He broke down practice into individual areas," said former NFL coach Sid Gillman. "Paul was an organizational genius. Everybody knew, when they hit the field, what they were going to do. He had position coaches. I don't know that anyone had position coaches before Paul Brown."

The length of Brown's professional practice sessions did not differ much from those of his amateur days, rarely extending beyond ninety minutes. He recalled that his teams probably practiced less than any of their opponents, always concluding their critical preparation in an expedient manner. In addition, Brown never burdened his coaching staff with a demanding schedule requiring extraordinary hours. He felt that the drain of excessive hours would fatigue everyone and ultimately be counterproductive. "I never believed in working into the wee hours of the night," he said. "I personally functioned and thought more clearly when I was well rested, and I think a coaching staff does, too." And since Brown's coaches were full-time, year-round employees—contrary to the rest of the league in the 1940s and '50s—they were generally much more prepared than their adversaries, eliminating the necessity for an extended work week. In regard to the productivity of modern NFL head coaches who claim to consistently work ninety-hour weeks, Brown said, "I always wondered how much they really accomplished during all those hours."

On September 6, 1946, the Cleveland Browns opened their first season in the AAFC with a resounding 44–0 defeat of the Miami Seahawks before 60,135 fans at Cleveland's Municipal Stadium. At the time, the crowd was the largest in the history of professional football for a regularly scheduled event. The game marked the beginning of an era as dominant as anyone had ever witnessed, as Cleveland became the home of pro football's most highly acclaimed team for years to come. The Browns didn't taste defeat until the eighth game of the 1946 season and finished their initial foray into professional football with a 12–2 record.

Cleveland defeated the New York Yankees in the inaugural AAFC championship game 14–9. Cleveland had beaten the Yankees during the regular season twice, 7–0 and 24–7. And though it took late heroics from Otto Graham to seal the victory for the Browns in the title game, Cleveland was without a doubt the much superior club. In fact, Cleveland's statistical command over the entire AAFC that year was astounding. They were particularly devastating throwing the football. The Browns led the league in almost every major passing category, including the outrageously dominant figure of 9.6 yards-per-pass-attempt, a total that was 43 percent greater than the league average (6.7), and almost 40 percent better than their next closest competitor's figure of 6.9 (tables 3-1 through 3-4).

The Cleveland Browns became king of the AAFC, winning every championship in the league's four-year history (1946–1949). They compiled an awesome record of 47–4–3 (.898) and a 5–0 postseason mark. In 1948, the Browns went 14–0 and defeated Buffalo 49–7 in the championship game. They were the first professional team to complete a season as an undefeated and untied champion. But because the NFL does not recognize AAFC statistics, the 1972 Miami Dolphins remain the sole owner of that dis-

Table 3-1. Cleveland Browns, 1946 (AAFC)

Category	
Points	423*
Points against	137*
Yards	4273*
Yards against	2933
Average per rush	4.1
Average per rush against	3.0
Completion pct.	51.9
Completion pct. against	41.8*
Average per pass	9.6*
Average per pass against	4.4*
Passes intercepted	7*
Opponent passes intercepted	41*

*Led league

Table 3-2. Leading Rushers, 1946 (AAFC)

Player	Team	Attempts	Yards	Average
Spec Sanders	NYY	140	709	5.1
Norm Strandlee	SF	134	651	4.9
Vic Kulbitski	BUF	97	605	6.2
Marion Motley	Cle	73	601	8.2
Edgar Jones	Cle	77	539	7.0

Table 3-3. Leading Passers, 1946 (AAFC)

Player	Team	Att	Comp	Pct	Yards	YPA	TDs	INTs
Glenn Dobbs	Bkn	269	135	50.2	1886	7.01	13	15
Otto Graham	Cle	174	95	54.6	1834	10.50	17	5
Charley O'Rourke	LA	182	105	57.7	1250	6.90	12	14
Frankie Albert	SF	197	104	52.8	1404	7.13	14	14
Bob Hoernschemeyer	Chi	193	95	49.2	1266	6.56	14	14

Table 3-4. Leading Receivers, 1946 (AAFC)

Player	Team	Number	Yards	Average	TDs
Dante Lavelli	Cle	40	843	21.8	8
Alyn Beals	SF	40	586	14.7	10
Saxon Judd	Bkn	34	443	13.0	4
Fay King	Buf	30	466	15.5	6
Elroy Hirsch	Chi	24	347	12.9	3

tinction in the record books. Paul Brown called the 1948 club the best team to ever put on pads. And though the stats could sway one to believe that the 1946 or 1947 Cleveland teams may have been superior, perhaps the AAFC was a better overall league in 1948, mitigating against the ungodly statistical dominance evidenced in the earlier years.

Unfortunately, the AAFC had two major problems, directly related to one another, that eventually caused its demise. Each year the Browns would win, and each year the league grew one step closer to bankruptcy. The AAFC had very little competitive balance and consequently was losing its fan support. The Browns' domination caused interest in other cities to wane. While Cleveland, San Francisco, Los Angeles, and New York (which was merged with Brooklyn in 1949) were solid—both on the field and financially—the remaining clubs struggled. As early as 1948, several teams had already folded, and Arch Ward had begun talks with the National Football League about a potential merger. The NFL, however, was not terribly interested. But when the NFL began to experience problems of its own in 1949—such as losing a franchise in Boston, and seeing the Pittsburgh Steelers and Green Bay Packers begin to feel monetary pressure—it had a sudden change of heart.

In 1950, after almost two years of protracted negotiations, the AAFC's preeminent asset, the Cleveland Browns, was merged into the NFL along with the San Francisco 49ers and the Baltimore Colts. The other four remaining AAFC squads were disbanded, and their players were drafted by the thirteen NFL teams. NFL Commissioner Bert Bell decided that a showdown between the AAFC's champion and the NFL's champion, the Philadelphia Eagles, in Pennsylvania, would be the consummate beginning to what would surely be a glorious decade for professional football.

Earle "Greasy" Neale was the Eagles' head coach, under whom Philadelphia had won back-to-back NFL championships in 1948 and 1949. They finished 11–1 in 1949 and had shut out the Los Angeles Rams 14–0 in the NFL title game. On offense, Philadelphia featured future Hall of Famer Steve Van Buren, one of the NFL's truly great running backs. Van Buren had eclipsed the one-thousand-yard mark several times, and enjoyed a 4.7-yard average per carry up to that point in his career. Due to their ferocious ground attack—which led the NFL and amassed almost 400 yards more than their closest competitor—the Eagles seldom passed the football. When they did, however, quarterback Tommy Thompson was very effective. The Eagles averaged an exceptional 8.1 yards per pass attempt in 1949 (the league average was 6.5) and were the only NFL team to accumulate more passing touchdowns than interceptions (18–14). From top to bottom, the Philadelphia Eagles were a formidable football team.

NFL coaches and players were convinced that AAFC teams were not nearly talented enough to compete with their elite brand of professional football. And they were certain that the Cleveland Browns—as successful as they had been in the "inferior" league—would be trounced by the NFL champion Eagles, especially since Philadelphia utilized Earle Neale's innovative 5–2–4 (five linemen, two linebackers, four defensive backs) defense, which had proven effective against the passing game.

The basic NFL defense of the 1940s was the 5–3–3. Philadelphia's configuration added an extra defensive back in place of a linebacker, which, most experts believed, was the perfect scheme to foil Cleveland's incredibly successful passing attack. Earle Neale, in particular, was extremely confident that Philadelphia would stymie the Browns' offense and easily defeat Cleveland. Trouble was, he and everybody else underestimated the abilities of Paul Brown, who had devised a counterstrategy to negate the Eagles' tactics and actually implode their defense from the inside out.

Brown decided to exploit the vulnerable middle of the Eagles' defense. With only two linebackers, Brown figured that if he could coax one or both of those players to the outside, he would then be able to connect on short patterns across the middle of the field and give his fast, talented wide receivers plenty of room to turn them into long gains. "We decided to neutralize the linebackers by putting our left halfback, Rex Bumgardner, in motion, and starting each play in a double wing formation (two wide receivers to one side) to force single coverage," Brown said. "That meant that Russ Craft, their cornerback, would have to cover Dub Jones man for man, which was nearly impossible." In addition, there were instances when Brown had two backs flare out to opposite sides—taking the linebackers with them—leaving the middle of the field unguarded and vulnerable to the crossing patterns they wished to employ. In either case, Philadelphia was caught with one or both linebackers in the flat area (short outside) and an opening in the middle of the field, creating ideal conditions for the Cleveland receivers to abuse the Eagles' man-for-man coverage. Brown, who through another of his innovative tactics was the first coach in professional football to call his team's plays (via the use of a substitution system which shuttled Cleveland's offensive guards), orchestrated the perfect play-calling sequences to effectively exploit Philadelphia's weaknesses.

Cleveland whipped the hell out of Philadelphia that day, 35–10. The Browns outgained the Eagles 487–266, including 346 yards in the passing game. The vaunted Eagles' defense—a unit that led the NFL in 1949 and permitted just twelve points per game over the course of the previous two seasons—was outplayed, outcoached, and anything but outstanding.

After the game, a contrite Neale talked about the lasting impression that Cleveland quarterback Otto Graham left in his mind. He marveled at Graham's ability to stand in the pocket, wait for the most opportune moment, and then instinctively place the ball in the perfect spot for a completion. "I tried for ten years to get my quarterbacks to do that, but they just didn't have the knack," he said. "I never saw a passer who hung on to the ball out there the way Graham does. Anyone who can put the ball up there for a guy to catch just a yard before stepping out of bounds, or put it right in his hands the moment the defender is beaten, is great."

Earle Neale had just witnessed the future of the National Football League, about fifteen to twenty-five years before its time. Paul Brown's progressive offensive philosophy—in harmony with ingenious passing tactics that were ridiculed before they were accepted—reshaped the foundation of professional football and forever transformed

Legendary Cleveland Browns coach Paul Brown pumps his fist as his team approaches the line of scrimmage behind him. Brown introduced the idea of timing patterns to the NFL with great success.

the game from a simple, strength-based, smash-mouth endeavor into a more scientific, finesse-type game, which accentuated the athletic skills and instincts of its players as much as, if not more than, their brute strength.

Brown's passing philosophy was based on precision and synchronization. Cleveland's quarterbacks and receivers were the first ones who were taught timing patterns. A timing pattern required the passer and receiver to be in perfect rhythm, each knowing the precise moment the ball should be thrown and where it should go. When it worked—and it often did—opponents were utterly amazed and almost defenseless. As Earle Neale indicated after the game with the Browns, for Graham to have the ability to perfectly place the ball at the spot of the receiver at the exact moment the defender was beaten was a thing of beauty, impossible to defend.

What Neale and other coaches and players of the day did not realize was that it wasn't so much the incredible ability of Graham and the Cleveland pass catchers as it was Paul Brown's revolutionary system of timing patterns. Graham was awesome, no doubt, and the Browns' receivers were very talented as well; but it was the mechanics of the scheme just as much as, if not more than, the talents of the players that made the tactic so effective. Cleveland receivers ran specific patterns of predetermined distance and/or duration and then cut, or came back for, the quarterback's pass, which—due to the precise timing of the play—was already on its way. "I think we were the first team to ever develop this type of pass pattern," Brown said, "an exercise in true precision because Otto had to throw the ball before the receiver looked for it or came back to meet it." Brown later explained that this tactic gained more notoriety when utilized by the Colts with "Weeb" Ewbank in the late 1950s. Ewbank, a Cleveland assistant, learned the concept from Paul Brown, of course. And quarterback Johnny Unitas and wide receiver Raymond Berry garnered the recognition when the Colts won consecutive NFL championships in 1958 and 1959.

Berry's success proved a point about both Brown's timing pattern system and the somewhat overrated aspect of speed in a receiver's repertoire. Berry, a twentieth-round selection out of SMU in 1954, was one of the slowest wide receivers in the league. But he had fabulous hands and possessed the unique ability to run precise patterns that befuddled defensive backs. As a result, he excelled in the NFL, ultimately reaching the Hall of Fame. "I always maintained that a receiver getting open wasn't just a matter of speed, but a matter of technique and knowing how," Brown said.

Another eventual Hall of Famer, quarterback Otto Graham, was the key to the Browns' offense. He had a unique blend of talents, including the more obscure abilities—intelligence, timing, cunning, and anticipation. These skills allowed him to capitalize on the strengths of the offense and at the same time limit his errors, which could cause interceptions. Eliminating errors was especially important to Paul Brown. "Football is a game of errors," he always said. "The team that makes the fewest errors in the game usually wins." Though other quarterbacks of that era could have succeeded in Paul Brown's system, few could have exploited the potent offensive concept as much as Graham. In addition to the aforementioned attributes, Graham also possessed unrivaled accuracy and dedication, the latter of which was an instrumental factor in his success. "Everyone marveled that Otto could work so well with our receivers," Brown said, "but he had learned to anticipate their movements by watching their shoulders. The intricate timing was a result of their work together for hours after the team had finished practicing each day."

It's interesting to note that Paul Brown had not always been a proponent of the passing game. While with Ohio State and Great Lakes, Brown concentrated on the running game to achieve victory. He recalled a sound whipping, however, at the hands of the Brooklyn Dodgers—in an AAFC exhibition game in 1946—that changed his mind. In that game, Brooklyn's quarterback, Glenn Dobbs, marched the Dodgers down the field with the aid of a quality passing attack, taking a large lead over the Browns while Cleveland tried to respond with their running game. "I had never run into a passing attack like that before," Brown confessed. "I became convinced that a team could not succeed in pro football by concentrating too much on the running game to the near exclusion of the passing attack." Brown then exhibited one of the truly essential qualities of any great coach—the ability to adapt his methods to keep pace with the game's latest and most advantageous tactics.

The Browns progressed to the end of their first NFL season as the dominant team in the league. They finished with a 10–2 record, tied for the lead in the American Conference with the New York Giants. Interestingly enough, it was the Browns' defense that actually defined the team in their first season. The Browns surrendered only 144 points—just three more than the Eagles—good enough for second in the NFL. But there were other important defensive categories where the Browns' excellence was apparent (table 3-5).

Cleveland beat the New York Giants in a playoff contest in 1950 for the right to host the Los Angeles Rams in the title game. The Rams had beaten the Chicago Bears in a National Conference playoff game to advance. Ironically, the Rams had moved from Cleveland in 1946, paving the way for the AAFC to place a team in Cleveland and use Municipal Stadium for its games. The Rams were an even more adept offensive club than the Browns, amassing awesome offensive totals during the regular season. Los Angeles scored 466 points, an NFL record that stood until 1981. They scored a hundred more points than their closest competitor. They had offensive explosions of

Table 3-5. Cleveland Browns, 1950 Team Defensive Statistics (13 teams)

Category	Number	League rank
Points	144	2
Rushing yards	1573	4
Average per rush	3.5	3
Passing yards	1581	1
Average per attempt	5.4*	1
Interceptions	31	T-1

*Almost 20 percent better than the league average of 6.7

70, 65, and 51 points in three contests during the season, and averaged almost forty points per game. The Rams gained a vast majority of their yardage through the air, primarily utilizing two quarterbacks, Norm Van Brocklin and Bob Waterfield, and wide receiver Tom Fears, who caught a league record eighty-four passes for 1,116 yards that season. All three players ultimately became Hall of Famers.

One of the greatest games of all time started out ominously for the Browns. On the first play from scrimmage, halfback Glenn Davis—known more for his pass-catching skills than his running ability—scored on an eighty-two-yard pass from Waterfield. Cleveland was stunned but responded with a brilliant offensive display of their own, scoring on their initial drive via a thirty-one-yard strike from Graham to Dub Jones. The relentlessness of the Rams' offense, however, quickly evidenced itself on the ensuing Los Angeles possession. A forty-four-yard pass from Waterfield to Fears highlighted an eight-play drive that resulted in another Rams' touchdown, restoring Los Angeles' lead, 14–7.

Paul Brown employed the same strategy for the championship game that he had utilized against the Eagles earlier in the season. When the Browns flared a back out in the flat, the Rams' linebackers followed, creating an opening in the middle of their defense. This allowed Cleveland's wide receivers to exploit the middle of the field against one-on-one coverage. Graham took full advantage, completing easy passes just beyond the line of scrimmage to wide-open targets. Just before the half, Browns' wide receiver Dante Lavelli, a future Hall of Famer, caught one of these tosses—one of the dozen he snared in the game—and took it in for a twenty-six-yard touchdown. Cleveland missed the extra point, however, and trailed 14–13 at the intermission.

Early in the second half, Graham hooked up with Lavelli for another touchdown, this one a thirty-nine-yard strike which gave the Browns a 20–14 advantage. To their credit, the Rams were far from finished. They took a 21–20 lead when running back Dick Hoerner scored on a one-yard run, capping a seventy-one-yard march. And with the aid of a fumble by Cleveland fullback Marion Motley on the first play after the kickoff, they increased their lead to 28–20.

The fourth quarter often determines champions. Like Johnny Unitas later that decade and John Elway a half century after, Otto Graham took charge and led the Browns to destiny's door with a scintillating performance in crunch time. And though Graham's entrance into the fraternity of champions was delayed at the threshold, he eventually gained admittance.

After Cleveland intercepted a Rams' pass, Graham directed a perfect drive that featured five straight completions to Lavelli and an acrobatic, fourteen-yard catch by Rex Bumgardner in the corner of the end zone. The Rams' lead was cut to 28–27. On the ensuing series, Waterfield was intercepted by linebacker Tommy Thompson, giving the Browns a chance to regain the lead. Graham once again moved Cleveland quickly down the field and had them in position to attempt an easy field goal should their drive stall short of a touchdown. But with just three minutes left, disaster struck. Graham was hit and fumbled on the Rams' twenty-two-yard line, and Los Angeles recovered. Graham was distraught, believing that he would be solely responsible for the impending Cleveland loss. Paul Brown—himself anguished by the unforeseen mishap—gallantly consoled and encouraged his young quarterback. "Don't worry Otto, we'll get the ball back and win this thing yet," he said, though deep in his mind even he doubted his oral conviction. But Cleveland's defense, which had been reeling early in the contest, stiffened just when the Browns desperately needed it. Cleveland forced a Los Angeles punt and gave Otto Graham a chance at redemption.

Los Angeles knew they were in trouble. Graham and Lavelli had ripped their defense to shreds most of the game, and now Graham had a personal score to settle—with himself. With the NFL championship hanging in the balance and less than two minutes remaining on the clock, Cleveland had a first and ten at their own thirty-two-yard line trailing by a single point. On the first play, Graham took advantage of the defensive formation and ran the perfect play, a quarterback draw. Between the linemen rushing Graham and the remaining defensive players dropping into coverage, there was a huge opening in the middle of the field, and he gained fourteen yards to the forty-six. Paul Brown's innovative style and comprehensive game planning had paid off once again. During a play in the 1946 season, Graham and Motley collided on what was supposed to be a trap play. As the defense charged in after Graham, Otto handed off to Motley in an instinctive, desperation-type maneuver. The play ended up in a large gain. "We didn't think much of it at the time," Brown explained, "but looking back at the game film, Otto said, 'I think that could become a play,' so we developed the blocking assignments and techniques which went with it." Ultimately, Brown devised both running back and quarterback draw plays and instructed Graham to look for the most opportune defensive formations in which to utilize them.

The Rams frantically tried to solve the Otto Graham "mystery" on that final drive, even double-teaming Lavelli to make certain that Graham could not hook up with his favorite target. But Graham connected on three short completions (two to Bumgardner) that resulted in the ball resting at the Los Angeles eleven-yard line with twenty seconds remaining. The kick went into the record books as a short sixteen-yard Lou Groza field goal to win the game 30–28, but if you ask any of the Browns' players, the ball is still sailing through the uprights more than fifty years later.

For the game, Graham completed twenty-two of thirty-three passes for 298 yards with four touchdowns and only one interception. Paul Brown put it best, some time later, by saying, "Otto was magnificent, operating with the poise and confidence that not only buoyed our players, but tolled a knell the Rams' defense must have heard every time he took the center snap." Rams' quarterback Bob Waterfield finished with similar numbers to Graham, eighteen completions in thirty-one attempts for 312 yards. However, Waterfield accounted for just one touchdown while suffering five interceptions.

When it was over, Bert Bell proclaimed it as "the greatest game I've ever seen." For Paul Brown, it was both the culmination *and* vindication of his career at the same time. He had won the biggest football prize on earth—the NFL title—to go along with his four AAFC titles and a college championship. And he had achieved this success

Table 3-6. NFL Title Games 1950–1957

Year	Winning team	Losing team	Score
1950	Cleveland	Los Angeles	30–28
1951	Los Angeles	Cleveland	24–17
1952	Detroit	Cleveland	17–7
1953	Detroit	Cleveland	17–16
1954	Cleveland	Detroit	56–10
1955	Cleveland	Los Angeles	38–14
1956	New York	Chicago	47–7
1957	Detroit	Cleveland	59–14

with what was considered to be a second-string team from a second-rate league, with a peculiar, second-class offensive system.

In 1951, Cleveland reaffirmed its worthiness by registering the NFL's finest regular season record (11–1), thus advancing to another title contest. Ironically, they faced Los Angeles once again, this time succumbing to the Rams 24–17. The loss marked the first championship game setback for Paul Brown and Cleveland in six attempts.

Cleveland's title game appearances in 1950 and 1951 were the first two of seven the team made in the decade of the fifties. From 1950 through 1957, the Cleveland Browns were as acclaimed a football team as the *New York Times* is a newspaper. They appeared in every title game but one (1956), winning three and losing four (table 3-6).

The 1953 season was almost a very special one for the Browns. Cleveland began the year with a 27–0 route of the Packers and subsequently reeled off ten more consecutive victories to afford themselves a chance at immortality. They headed into Philadelphia for the season finale with an 11–0 record and an opportunity to become the NFL's first undefeated, untied champion. But hopes deteriorated quickly. Cleveland blew a seventeen-point lead against the Eagles and eventually lost the game, 42–27.

Apparently unnerved by the defeat, the Browns performed very poorly in the championship game in Detroit against the Lions two weeks later. Otto Graham played with an injured finger on his throwing hand and endured one of the worst games of his career. Paul Brown replaced him in the second quarter. Backup quarterback George Ratterman did not fare much better, though, and in the second half Graham reentered the contest. Incredibly, after a futile team passing effort which totaled only nine yards on three completions in sixteen attempts, the Browns led 16–10 with four minutes to play.

At that point, Detroit had the ball on their own twenty-yard line. Lions' end Jim Doran—normally a defensive player—entered the game on offense for the first time, replacing injured wide receiver Leon Hart. Doran was a physical player and sometimes quite underhanded. He began coaxing Browns' defensive back Warren Lahr into heated exchanges of elbows and verbal assaults. Then, as part of his master plan, Doran faked an elbow to Lahr. As Lahr positioned himself to retaliate, Doran swept by him en route to the end zone. Detroit quarterback, future Hall of Famer Bobby Layne—who called for the improvised play in the huddle—hit Doran with a perfect thirty-three-yard touchdown pass that gave the Lions the lead with just 2:08 remaining in the contest. Detroit's resulting 17–16 championship game victory marked the third time in a row that Paul Brown was defeated by coach "Buddy" Parker's Detroit Lions.

"What a season," Parker said after the game. "This one is for the players. The game means $2,424.10 each." A large lump-sum total for those days.

Paul Brown and the Cleveland dressing room were quite somber, as one would suspect. "It was the toughest game we've ever lost," Brown said. "I doubt if any team ever lost a tougher one."

The loss to Detroit in the championship game notwithstanding, the 1953 Browns were an awesome offensive football club. They may have been the most effective passing unit in history. They were the last NFL team to average greater than ten yards per pass attempt (10.1), a figure which calculated to the phenomenal total of more than 55 percent greater than the NFL average of 6.5. In addition, the Browns' remarkable accomplishment of 63 percent pass completions—as compared to the league norm of just 47.3 percent—amounted to 33 percent better than average and would equate to the staggering rate of 77.5 percent completions if calibrated to NFL standards in the year 2001. Furthermore, the club's total of only nine interceptions in 303 attempts (2.97 percent), was almost 59 percent better than the NFL average of 7.17 percent, an achievement directly attributable to the precision skills of Otto Graham and the adept coaching techniques of Paul Brown.

As fate would have it, Paul Brown got another shot at the Lions in 1954. Both teams had clinched their respective conferences before the last game of the year. In an ironic twist to the story, the very last game of the NFL's regular season (played December 19, during the intended off-week between the end of the regular season and the title game) matched the Browns and the Lions, in Cleveland, the result of their earlier meeting having been cancelled due to a Cleveland Indians World Series game at Municipal Stadium. It was a meaningless game, and both teams were "vanilla" with their tactics, not keen on tipping their hand before the "real" contest the following week. Once again, the Lions snatched victory in the final seconds, when Bobby Layne threw a last-minute touchdown pass to secure a 14–10 decision. Although the game was inconsequential, some of the Browns' players and coaches had to believe they were snakebitten in their efforts to overcome Detroit and Buddy Parker. The Lions at the time were 4–0 against Cleveland and, no matter the circumstances, it seemed that Detroit could always conjure up some sort of miraculous finish to overtake the Browns. Things got so tense that big Doug Atkins—all 6′ 8″, 260 pounds of him—wanted to physically attack 5′ 10″, 185-pound teammate Warren Lahr after Lahr once again experienced the ignominy of allowing the Lions' winning score in the last minute of the precursor to the championship game.

Paul Brown saved a couple of tricks for the Lions in the title game. Cleveland's speedy young wide receiver, Ray Renfro, was purposely overlooked in the Browns' scheme the previous week. Renfro had been injured on and off during the year, and though Brown knew he was healthy enough to play the last regular season game, he refrained from incorporating Renfro into the game plan in order to surprise Detroit in the championship game. To augment this strategy, Brown devised a new play utilizing Renfro's speed and targeting a weakness he had detected in the Detroit secondary.

Brown had picked up on a tendency of Lions' defensive back Bill Stits. Stits, it seemed, almost always played close to the line of scrimmage when the Browns configured themselves in the basic T-formation (an alignment with no receivers split wide). Brown was convinced that Stits could not cover Renfro (who ran a 9.4 hundred-yard dash) man for man from such a close position. He subsequently contrived a play that was designed to take advantage of the expectation that Detroit—unaware of both Renfro's availability and capability—would elect to have Stits cover him man for man in this situation. Brown's strategy was to place Renfro in the backfield, essentially utilizing him as a flanker, and then send him down the middle of the field while the tight ends occupied the safeties. Stits, with what would hopefully be single coverage on the speedier Renfro, would have little chance to defend the play.

The plan worked beautifully. Detroit (three-point favorites in the game) was completely unprepared for a healthy Renfro and never considered anything but single coverage on the fleet wideout. Otto Graham collaborated with the youthful receiver for touchdown passes of thirty-one and thirty-five yards, both of which were the result of a clever Paul Brown strategy that combined a little subterfuge with a lot of film study. The Browns' defense played its part in the victory by intercepting Layne six times and recovering three fumbles. The stunned Lions fell badly, 56–10. Paul Brown and Cleveland had exacted sweet revenge and convincingly won another NFL championship in front of almost 44,000 delighted Browns fans at Municipal Stadium.

In a storybook ending to the 1955 season, the Browns won their third NFL championship, thrashing the Rams 38–14 before a record crowd of 87,695 at the Memorial Coliseum in Los Angeles. Otto Graham, who had unofficially retired after the 1954 season, returned for a final year in response to the urging of Paul Brown. Graham was chosen the game's most valuable player. He threw for two scores (a fifty-yard bomb to Lavelli and a thirty-five-yard toss to Renfro), ran for two more, and completed fourteen of twenty-five passes for 202 yards on the day.

Sid Gillman, in his first season as the Rams' head coach, decided to employ a zone defense with four deep backs and a single middle linebacker for the championship encounter. It was a forerunner of the modern-day 4–3 alignment. Paul Brown made the defense look like Swiss cheese, however, riddling the middle of the field with wide-open crossing patterns made possible by his usage of the double wing formation and fullback motion. "The middle linebacker [in their zone] always flowed with the fullback," he said, "so we sent our fullback one way and threw to the opposite area." Once Los Angeles realized Cleveland's tactics, they switched to a man-for-man defense and, according to Brown, "forgot" why they had used the zone in the first place—to offset the Browns' superiority in single-coverage situations. Otto Graham and his receivers—Lavelli, Jones, and Renfro—decimated the outmanned Rams' secondary thereafter.

As good as the Browns' offense was, the defense was even better. Cleveland intercepted *seven* Rams' passes (second most in championship game history) and recovered

Table 3-7. Cleveland Browns, 1955
Team Defensive Statistics (12 teams)

Category	Number	League rank
Points	218	1
Rushing yards	1189	1
Average per rush	3.4	2
Passing yards	1775	2
Average per attempt	5.5*	1
Completion pct.	39.0†	1
Total yards	2964‡	1

*Almost 17 percent better than the league average of 6.6
†Almost 19 percent better than the league average of 47.9
‡380 yards better than their closest competitor

one fumble. During the course of the 1955 season, the Browns' defense was extraordinary. They finished first or second in the NFL in almost every significant defensive category, in many cases well ahead of their closest competitor and far below the league's average yield (table 3-7).

When most football analysts examine Paul Brown's career, they generally focus on his offensive achievements. After all, Brown brought more creative and decisive offensive strategies to the NFL than any other coach in history. The unfortunate aspect of this tendency is that his teams' defensive exploits have largely been ignored. Cleveland's defensive supremacy was certainly not limited to the 1950 (see previous statistics) and 1955 seasons. As a matter of fact, Paul Brown's defensive units were easily the most dominant of the decade and deserve recognition among the greatest in the history of the NFL (table 3-8).

From 1950 to 1957 (eight years), Cleveland led the NFL in points allowed an amazing six times. They also led the league in yardage allowed four times during that period. Only once in eight years were the Browns worse than second in either of these extremely important defensive categories.

Among the Browns' foremost defensive stalwarts were defensive linemen Len Ford and Bill Willis, both of whom became Hall of Famers. Ford was a remarkable athlete. At 6' 4", 245 pounds, he was both strong and agile. In fact, he caught sixty-eight passes as an offensive end in the AAFC for two years (1948–1949), averaging an astounding 17.5 yards per catch. Ford eventually earned his living as a fearsome defensive end in the NFL, terrorizing quarterbacks and ball carriers with his tremendous speed and athleticism. He was a unanimous all-star from 1951 to 1955. Willis, who also played some middle linebacker, was probably the quickest defensive lineman in

Table 3-8. Cleveland Browns' Defensive League Ranking

	1950	1951	1952	1953	1954	1955	1956	1957
Points allowed	2	1	2	1	1	1	1	1
Yardage allowed	2	2	1	6	1	1	1	2

NOTE: Rankings out of 13 teams in 1950, 12 in other years

the NFL during the 1950s. He often penetrated opponents' backfields before the quarterback had taken two steps. Part of Willis's success was attributable to his intelligence. When questioned by Paul Brown as to how he was able to anticipate the snap count, Willis indicated that he watched the center's fingers intently, and when they tightened around the football he knew the snap was on its way. Other star defenders for Cleveland included lineman Don Colo, linebackers Tommy Thompson and Tom Catlin, and defensive back Warren Lahr.

After the 1955 season, Cleveland had been in the NFL for six years. They had earned three championships and played in every title game since their admittance into the league. Instead of questioning the merits and methods of Paul Brown and his band of "renegades," other NFL teams began to copy every shrewd "gimmick" that Cleveland devised.

In 1956, Cleveland was dealt several serious blows. First and foremost was the retirement of Otto Graham—this time, for good. Second, flanker Dub Jones, Cleveland's sure-handed speed merchant who was on the receiving end of so many of Graham's tosses, also retired. Lastly, the team lost several key players to military service that season. The Browns' resultant 5–7 record placed them fourth in the NFL's Eastern Conference and kept them out of their league's championship game for the first time in eleven years, dating back to the 1946 season in the AAFC. As consolation for their poor season, Cleveland was awarded a chance to select higher in the 1957 NFL draft.

With the fifth pick in the first round, Paul Brown selected a kid from Syracuse, and not just because he liked his last name, Brown. *Jim* Brown was a big (6′ 2″, 232 pounds), bruising back with speed and power, whom Cleveland had ranked high on their draft list. Now that Cleveland had three Browns—Paul, Jim, and the team—it made things much more complicated, especially for authors like myself.

Interestingly, each of the first seven picks in the 1957 NFL draft enjoyed very productive careers. In fact, it may not be an overstatement to rate this group as the best "first seven" of any draft in history (table 3-9).

Paul Brown later admitted that, if the Pittsburgh Steelers had not taken Len Dawson just before Cleveland's selection, he would have taken the Purdue quarterback instead of Jim Brown. Paul Brown had Dawson rated slightly ahead of Jim Brown,

Table 3-9. 1957 NFL Draft

Team	Player	College	Position	Career
Green Bay*	Paul Hornung	Notre Dame	Back	Hall of Fame
Los Angeles	Jon Arnett	USC	Back	10 years[†]
San Francisco	John Brodie	Stanford	QB	17 years[†]
Green Bay	Ron Kramer	Michigan	End	10 years[†]
Pittsburgh	Len Dawson	Purdue	QB	Hall of Fame
Cleveland	Jim Brown	Syracuse	RB	Hall of Fame
Philadelphia	Clarence Peaks	Michigan St	Back	9 years[†]
Baltimore	Jim Parker	Ohio State	Tackle	Hall of Fame

* Bonus pick
[†] Enjoyed a distinguished career, garnering at least one All-Pro season

and Cleveland was in the market for a quarterback to replace Otto Graham. Paul Brown was still fuming from a 1948 AAFC league-mandated decision to force Cleveland to surrender the rights to future Hall of Fame quarterback Y.A. Tittle to the Baltimore Colts. In order to assist the struggling Colts, who were added to the AAFC in 1947, the Browns were instructed to renounce their rights to the promising quarterback. Now, some nine years later, in the NFL, Cleveland was paying the price for that transaction.

Hoping to ease some of the pressure from the loss of Graham and the disappointment of missing out on Dawson, Cleveland took quarterback Milt Plum, from Penn State, with their second-round selection in 1957. Plum eventually developed into a capable quarterback, but he was forced into action in crucial situations in his rookie season, much sooner than both he and Paul Brown anticipated.

Jim Brown was forced into immediate action, as well. Coach Brown, however, knew that, unlike his rookie quarterback, his brawny running back was up to the challenge. Paul Brown loved big backs and preferred to feature them in his offense whenever possible. He felt that the powerful running style of a large back intimidated and demoralized defenders; and, since he often utilized his backs for pass protection, bigger was usually better. Paul Brown revered fullback Marion Motley in particular. Motley was an instrumental factor in the Browns' drive to glory from 1946 through 1953, table 3-10. In Brown's opinion, he was one of the most underrated players ever to play the game of football.

Of Motley, Brown said, "Marion was a great runner and a great blocker; no one ever got near Graham when Marion was nearby." Motley was a unique fullback for his era. At 6' 1", 232 pounds, he was big and strong enough to block defensive ends one on one and fast enough to run away from linebackers and even some defensive backs. And when the burly running back broke into the secondary on a running play, I'm quite sure many defensive backs wished they were somewhere else. After Motley's departure following the 1953 season, there was a huge void in the Cleveland backfield.

Table 3-10. Marion Motley's Rushing Performance

Year	Att	Yards	Average	TDs
		AAFC		
1946	73	601	8.2	6
1947	146	889	6.1	9
1948	157	964	6.1	7
1949	113	570	5.0	8
		NFL		
1950	140	810	5.8	4
1951	61	273	4.5	1
1952	104	444	4.3	3
1953	32	161	5.0	0
1955*	2	8	4.0	0

*With Pittsburgh

Paul Brown was confident that Jim Brown could fill that void in his rookie year of 1957, and the first-round pick from Syracuse did not disappoint. While he was never the blocker Motley was, Jim Brown became the NFL's all-time leading rusher and a proficient pass receiver as well. In his first season, he gained 942 yards, averaged 4.7 yards per carry, and led the Browns to a 9–2–1 record and the Eastern Conference title.

Injuries, however, ruined Cleveland's title chances in 1957. Quarterback Tommy O'Connell, who was acquired in 1956, had taken over for Graham and was having a banner season (table 3-11).

But O'Connell broke his ankle late in the year, and Milt Plum was thrust into action. Plum, like most rookies, struggled mightily and forced the Browns into becoming a one-dimensional rushing team, with all of their hopes pinned on Jim Brown in the postseason.

Cleveland's title game opponent, once again, was the Detroit Lions. Detroit had defeated San Francisco in a playoff game to earn the Western Conference crown and the right to host the Browns in the 1957 championship event. Paul Brown knew that overcoming Detroit—which had beaten Cleveland during the regular season, 20–7—would be a difficult proposition. He did not know, however, that it would be a nearly impossible task. In bizarre fashion, Milt Plum suffered a severe hamstring injury after slipping on some ice just three days before the game. The injury rendered him useless for the title contest. O'Connell was not completely healed from his ankle injury and was so rusty from inactivity that Brown doubted he could have a positive impact on the game. So Cleveland could do nothing but give Jim Brown the ball and hope for a miracle.

The miracle never materialized. Detroit quarterback Tobin Rote—himself filling in for the injured Bobby Layne—had a career day in the championship encounter, tossing four touchdown passes and amassing 296 yards versus the Browns. Detroit gained revenge for their humiliating loss to Cleveland in 1954 by trouncing the Browns 59–14. After the game, Brown smiled for the reporters. "I'm philosophical about it; the ball was just going to bounce that way, and it did," he said, in reference to the injuries sustained by his team. He also praised the Detroit crowd, as their constant noise led to many Browns' mix-ups in signal calling.

In 1958, Milt Plum assumed the majority of Cleveland's quarterbacking responsibilities. Though he was still in the learning stage—entering just his second season—he acquitted himself rather well. Let's take a look at Plum's career numbers in table 3-12.

Paul Brown admitted that Plum's lack of arm strength and his resultant inability to stretch a defense mitigated against his effectiveness. But it is extremely interesting to note the remarkable success that Plum enjoyed in Cleveland—under the tutelage of

Table 3-11. Tommy O'Connell's 1957 Passing Performance

Year	Att	Comp	Comp%	Yards	YPA	TD	INT	Rating
1957	110	63	57.3	1229	11.17	9	8	93.3

Table 3-12. Milt Plum's 1957–69 Passing Performance

Year	Att	Comp	Comp%	Yards	YPA	TD	INT	Rating	
				Cleveland					
1957	76	41	53.9	590	7.76	2	5	60.7	Rookie season
1958	189	102	54.0	1619	8.57	11	11	77.9	
1959	266	156	58.6*	1992	7.49	14	8	87.2	
1960	250	151	60.4*	2297	9.19*	21	5	110.4*	
1961	302	177	58.6	2416	8.00	18	10	90.3	
				Detroit					
1962	325	179	55.1	2378	7.32	15	20	68.2	
1963	77	27	35.1	339	4.40	2	12	18.7	
1964	287	154	53.7	2241	7.81	18	15	78.5	
1965	308	143	46.4	1710	5.55	12	19	51.2	
1966	146	82	56.2	943	6.46	4	13	47.8	
1967	172	86	50.0	925	5.38	4	8	54.5	
1968	12	5	41.7	49	4.08	1	1	46.9	
1969	9	3	33.3	37	4.11	0	0	47.0	
Total	2419	1306	54.0	17536	7.25	122	127	72.2	

*Led league

Paul Brown—as opposed to the outright washout he became later in his NFL career. Plum's career was a statistical anomaly, his numbers in Cleveland and Detroit so disparate that they appear to be the stats of two different quarterbacks. In fact—and this is no stretch—had Plum enjoyed four or five more seasons under the direction of Paul Brown, we might be examining the career statistics of a Hall of Fame quarterback as opposed to those of a journeyman. Unfortunately for Plum, he was traded to Detroit before the 1962 season and was subsequently benched.

The example of Milt Plum's career further substantiates the theory that Paul Brown's ingenious offensive system, in conjunction with his peerless game-planning abilities, could greatly enhance the effectiveness of his players, many times enabling them to defeat more talented adversaries.

Cleveland finished the 1958 campaign with a 9–3 record, tied with the New York Giants for the Eastern Conference title. Rookie Bobby Mitchell, a seventh-round draft pick, had a fabulous season. He averaged more than six yards per carry and totaled more than twelve hundred all-purpose yards. Mitchell lasted until late in the draft because of fumbling troubles in college. But Brown investigated the problem by speaking with Mitchell's college coach and came away convinced that the difficulty was more in the ball exchange with the quarterback than a ball protection dilemma while running. While every other team shied away from drafting Mitchell, Brown selected a diamond in the rough. In the ensuing years, Mitchell and Jim Brown combined to form an awesome one-two punch for Cleveland's offense.

In their 1958 playoff encounter with New York at Yankee Stadium, the Browns' offense sputtered badly. The Giants limited Cleveland to only seven first downs and eighty-six total yards for the entire game. New York, meanwhile, gained more than three hundred yards on the day. The only touchdown of the contest came when Charlie Conerly, the Giants' quarterback, ran ten yards with a lateral from running back Frank Gifford in the first quarter. Kicker Pat Summerall then added a twenty-six-yard field goal in the second period to end the scoring and give the Giants a well-deserved 10–0 victory. New York advanced to the 1958 NFL championship game the next week, succumbing to Johnny Unitas and the Baltimore Colts in a 23–17 overtime contest that is generally regarded as the greatest game in pro football history.

Cleveland compiled a 7–5 record in 1959 and followed that with an 8–3–1 mark in 1960, both times placing second in the Eastern Conference. At that point, Paul Brown had accumulated eleven division titles, three second-place finishes, and one fourth-place finish in his fifteen-year career dating back to the AAFC.

In 1961, Art Modell purchased the Cleveland Browns from local businessman David Jones for approximately $4 million. That transaction marked the beginning of the end of the Paul Brown era in Cleveland. Modell was a "hands-on" owner and made sure that everyone in the organization, Brown included, understood that he (Modell) would make most of the team's decisions. According to Paul Brown, as explained in his book, *PB: The Paul Brown Story,* Modell told him in no uncertain terms, "This team can never fully be mine as long as you are here, because whenever anyone thinks of the Cleveland Browns, they think of you. Every time I come to the stadium, I feel I am invading your domain, and from now on there can only be one dominant image."

Cleveland finished the 1961 season with an 8–5–1 slate, good enough for a third-place conference finish. But in 1962—after Brown engineered what, in hindsight, turned out to be the disastrous trade of Bobby Mitchell (future Hall of Famer) for rookie Ernie Davis (who was diagnosed with leukemia two days after the swap and never played a down in the NFL), and after Cleveland again finished the season in third place with a disappointing 7–6–1 record—Modell fired Brown. Many years later, Modell called it "the biggest mistake I ever made."

As it turned out—and isn't this often the case?—the firing was probably the best thing that ever happened to Paul Brown and his family, at least from a financial standpoint. They wound up in nearby Cincinnati, Ohio, with an American Football League expansion team in 1968. And because Brown was the controlling partner of a group that invested $14 million for the "Bengals"—two years before a prearranged merger with the NFL took place—he had full command of the franchise. In an interesting sidebar to the story, since Brown had unofficially retired from coaching after being relieved of his duties in Cleveland, by the time Cincinnati took the field in 1968, their coach had already been inducted into the Pro Football Hall of Fame. Brown gained entrance into Canton in 1967, five years after he left Cleveland.

Paul Brown never won another championship, but he did manage to take an expansion club and turn it into a contender within three seasons. The Bengals finished 3–11 in their first AFL season of 1968, 4–9–1 in their second AFL season of 1969, and then broke through with an 8–6 record and a Central Division title in their first NFL season of 1970. In the contemporary "free agency" world of the NFL, Cincinnati's accomplishment of winning a division in just their third season of existence would not be considered a tremendous feat. But in 1970, with an inexperienced team from the supposedly inferior AFL and no quality free agents to enlist, Paul Brown's achievement was remarkable. The Bengals succumbed in the 1970 playoffs to the eventual Super Bowl champion Baltimore Colts 17–0. That defeat, however, did little to discourage Cincinnati fans and players from basking in the glory of their surprise success.

In 1971, Paul Brown made a shrewd decision which benefited the Bengals' organization for years to come. After discovering the virtues of an unknown signal caller named Ken Anderson, from obscure Augustana College in Illinois, Brown invested a third-round selection in the 1971 NFL draft on him. The extremely bright, dedicated, strong-armed quarterback became the backbone of the Cincinnati franchise for the next sixteen years, long after Paul Brown retired. Anderson led the NFL in passer rating four times and twice in total passing yards.

Another of Brown's astute determinations in Cincinnati was the choice of Bill Walsh as an assistant coach in 1968. Brown and Walsh collaborated to devise clever augmentations for Brown's already ingenious attack, including the first known implementation of scripted (preplanned) plays into an offensive game plan. Walsh eventually followed in Brown's footsteps by becoming perhaps the most innovative head coach of the late twentieth century. He developed his own unique version of Paul Brown's passing system and subsequently won three Super Bowls with the San Francisco 49ers in the 1980s.

After the 1975 season (his eighth with Cincinnati), at the age of 67, Paul Brown retired from coaching. Tired and worn out from twenty-five years as a professional head coach, and becoming more and more disgruntled with the changing face of NFL football—which, towards the end of his career began to include player strikes, frequent salary disputes, and less and less loyalty between players and franchises—Brown decided to call it a career. He went out in grand fashion, however. The Bengals concluded the 1975 season at 11–3 (their best record ever to that point), finishing in second place in the Central Division to the eventual Super Bowl champion Pittsburgh Steelers. In the playoffs, they gave the vaunted Oakland Raiders everything they could handle before suffering a heartbreaking 31–28 loss. And though Cincinnati's final game ended in defeat, their coach, Paul Brown, went out a winner, as did every athlete who ever played under his command.

Paul Brown's basic coaching philosophy was a simple one: "Everything we do must be in terms of our team and of doing our best," he said. The *team* was everything. Brown believed that the best teams were first and foremost made up of quality people. He was convinced that with diligence, wisdom, and teamwork, an assemblage of average players formulated from high-character individuals could—while working in unison as a close-knit crew—achieve much greater success than a group of all-star *individuals* who were incapable of functioning in harmony.

After gathering the "proper" players, Brown invoked an intense, demanding coaching style, advocating a disciplined, intelligent approach to winning football games. He was certain that all individuals—even the most rambunctious, high-strung athletes—worked best when subjected to a structured and orderly training routine that accentuated a player's mental abilities as well as his physical skills. This consummate foundation, Brown believed, would bring forth the best in his players even under the most adverse circumstances. Brown then engaged a masterful system predicated on innovative techniques, impeccable tactics, and flawless execution. Though football is an emotional game, Brown never believed in hot-tempered discourse or loud motivational implorations to invigorate his athletes. Instead, he preferred to thoroughly prepare his teams for success, relying on his comprehensive coaching skills to instill a confident, winning attitude into his players' psyches, the result of their exceptional training. Winning, Brown concluded, would then come naturally, without the need for impassioned verbal encouragement.

Paul Brown's overall influence on professional football was extensive. His impact on the passing game, however, was revolutionary. The professional passing game of the modern era is directly traceable to the foundation Brown laid in the 1940s and '50s. He created a precise, synchronized passing attack that redefined the game of football. Ironically, he seldom if ever conducted his teams with a pass-first mentality. In five different seasons from 1950 to 1960 (eleven years), the Cleveland Browns attempted the fewest passes in the NFL. On five other occasions during that same time frame, they attempted the second- or third-fewest passes in the league. In total, the Browns finished last, next to last, or third from last in total passing attempts in ten of those eleven seasons. Yet, during that era, Cleveland gained notoriety as one of the most prolific passing teams in the history of the NFL. How was this possible?

Quite simply, the Browns' success was due to their remarkable passing efficiency, or, more accurately, their consistently high yards-per-attempt (YPA) figures. Other than interception percentage (in which the Browns also excelled), YPA is the most decisive statistic relative to the forward pass. Cleveland finished first or second in the NFL in YPA an astounding eight times from 1950 to 1960, including their incredible achievement of 10.1 in 1953. And since their YPA numbers were usually much greater than those of their competitors (the Browns gained an average of 2.5 more yards per pass attempt than the league norm during their five most efficient seasons of that period), Cleveland was often able to produce more yardage on far fewer passing attempts than their rivals. The Browns were so proficient in this area that they recorded the awesome achievement of four top-five placings (out of twelve or thirteen teams) in total passing yardage during the aforementioned seasons in which they finished at or near the bottom of the league in total attempts. In fact, several teams attempted as many as 125 to 150 more passes than Cleveland during each of those years and still finished with fewer total passing yards than the Browns.

The Browns' stunning aerial success was clearly the result of their prudent though maximal exploitation of the forward pass and not simply the consequence of numerous attempts and gaudy yardage totals, which often do not equate to victory. Cleveland won more games and had more championship game appearances than any other team of their era, accomplishments largely attributable to the exquisite orchestration of a remarkable passing system by an incomparable head coach. Paul Brown dominated the NFL by utilizing the passing game in the most beneficial fashion, and his teams have the championship records to prove it.

The scope of Cleveland's aerial supremacy during the 1950s is often underestimated by modern-day NFL connoisseurs. Comparison with a more contemporary offensive powerhouse may help to change that recollection. The St. Louis Rams of 1999–2001, guided by superb quarterback Kurt Warner and brazen head coach Mike Martz, are generally regarded as the most explosive and accomplished passing team of the last twenty years in the NFL. They compiled a 37–11 record and appeared in two Super Bowls (winning one) during their three-year stretch of dominance. They also led the NFL in passing yardage and YPA during those years. The Rams' YPA average for those three seasons was 9.0. The league maintained a 6.8 standard during that same period. These figures gave St. Louis a 32 percent advantage over the average NFL team for those years. The Cleveland Browns compiled a 9.4 YPA average during their five most-productive seasons from 1950 to 1960, while the league average calculated to 6.9. This gave the Browns an enormous 36 percent advantage over the average team of their era, even greater than that of Warner's Rams teams. Under the supreme guidance of Paul Brown, the Cleveland Browns were one of the most talented passing teams the game has ever witnessed.

Interestingly enough, Cleveland was also an extremely talented pass *defending* team during Brown's tenure. In addition to the defense's superior yardage rankings and point totals reported earlier in this chapter, Cleveland led the NFL in yards per pass attempt allowed an incredible six times from 1950 to 1957. Although Paul Brown's defensive tactics are not as noteworthy as his offensive modifications, his teams' defensive results were extraordinary.

One of the most meaningful achievements for an NFL coach is realized when his methods and tactics are emulated throughout the league, both during and after his career. When contemporaries begin to implement many of the techniques and routines established by one of their peers, it is a foregone conclusion that the architect of the system attained a high level of distinction. In addition, when many of a coach's former players become outstanding coaches in their own right, incorporating the same procedures and programs that they learned from their former mentor as trademarks of their own coaching philosophies, that too is a worthy indicator of success. By the early 1960s, almost every team in the NFL had incorporated segments of Paul Brown's passing philosophy into their offense. And by the end of that decade, three Paul Brown disciples—each of whom eventually gained Hall of Fame recognition—had entered the NFL's coaching fraternity.

Don Shula, whom Brown drafted in 1951, retired from coaching after the 1995 season as the NFL's all-time leader with 328 coaching victories. He also won two Super Bowls. Chuck Noll, who was drafted by Brown in 1953, led the Pittsburgh Steelers to an unprecedented four Super Bowl victories in the 1970s. And "Bud" Grant, who played under Brown at Great Lakes in 1945, accumulated 158 lifetime victories, a .620 winning percentage, and four Super Bowl appearances during his coaching career in Minnesota. All three men exhibited an extensive Brown influence in their coaching repertoires. They stressed a team-first mentality, discipline, preparedness, attention to detail, intelligence, and fundamentals, all winning with alarming regularity. And don't forget Bill Walsh, who also became a Hall of Fame coach by winning three Super Bowls in San Francisco in the 1980s. Walsh probably applied more Paul Brown techniques than any of Brown's disciples, including the development of a brand-new offensive attack based on his mentor's passing schemes which he learned while a member of the Cincinnati Bengals' coaching staff. Walsh did his part in furthering the Brown tradition by teaching and instructing his *own* disciples in the same manner—a whole host of whom have gone on to glorious NFL coaching careers. Paul Brown, in essence, became the football equivalent of Northern Dancer as a racing stallion. He was the preeminent "sire of sires"—coaching the superior coaches of the future.

Paul Brown died in 1991. He was eighty-two years old. His career coaching statistics are exceptional. His teams won 213 games, had eleven title game appearances, won seven championships (including three in the NFL), and earned the equivalent of fourteen division titles. Brown's career winning percentage in professional football was .667. His teams won titles in the state of Ohio in high school, college, and the professional ranks. And the Cincinnati Bengals' new stadium, built in 2000, was named after their original coach and owner. Paul Brown was to Ohio football what Babe Ruth was to baseball.

When Chuck Bednarik, former great Eagles' center and linebacker, was inducted into the Pro Football Hall of Fame, he looked out into the audience, spotted Paul Brown, and said, "Paul Brown is the greatest coach who ever lived." Though Bednarik's coach, Earle Neale, whom he had chosen to be his presenter, was sitting in the audience as well, Bednarik still singled out Brown as the best coach he had ever seen. And while it may not have been the politically correct thing to do, Bednarik was never known to care if anyone thought he was being obtuse. It was just the way Bednarik truly felt, having exhausted himself on many an occasion in a vain attempt to beat the *best there ever was.*

Paul Brown brought the game of football to a higher level. He proved that intelligence, planning, and craftiness could overcome brute strength and physical force— even in a game predicated on violence. He emphasized honor, discipline, integrity, and the team above all other elements of the sport. If the NFL—and athletic competition in general—had more coaches and leaders like Paul Brown, the games and the players would likely be much more enjoyable than they are today.

Paul Brown's Coaching Capsule

Category	Numbers
AAFC	
Seasons	4
Wins	47
Losses	4
Ties	3
Winning pct.	.898
Pct. >/< avg. Super Bowl–winning coach (.601)*	+49.4%
World championships†	4
World championship game appearances†	4
World championship pct. (champ/seasons)	100%
Losing seasons	0
Pct. of losing seasons	0%
Playoff record	5-0
Playoff winning pct.	1.000
Average wins per 16 games (a current season)	14.4
Average losses per 16 games	1.6
NFL	
Seasons	21
Wins	166
Losses	100
Ties	6
Winning pct.	.621
Pct. >/< avg. Super Bowl–winning coach (.601)*	+3.3%
World championships†	3
World championship game appearances†	7
World championship pct. (champ/seasons)	14.3 %
Losing seasons	4
Pct. of losing seasons	19.0%
Playoff record	4–8
Playoff winning pct.	.333
Average wins per 16 games (a current season)	9.9
Average losses per 16 games	6.1

NOTE: Ties count as a half-win and a half-loss in calculating percentages.
*See Epilogue
†Super Bowls or NFL championships 1920–1965.

Combined AAFC and NFL record: 213–104–9 (.667); postseason 9–8 (.529)

(continued next page)

Paul Brown's Coaching Capsule (continued)

3 Years after Brown

City	Years	Record	Pct	Brown's Career Pct
				.621
Cleveland	1963–65	31–10–1	.750	
Cincinnati	1976–78	22–22–0	.500	

Yearly records

Year	Team	Wins	Losses	Ties	Playoffs
AAFC					
1946	Cle	12	2	0	1–0*
1947	Cle	12	1	1	1–0*
1948	Cle	14	0	0	1–0*
1949	Cle	9	1	2	2–0*
Totals		47	4	3	5–0
NFL					
1950	Cle	10	2	0	2–0†
1951	Cle	11	1	0	0–1
1952	Cle	8	4	0	0–1
1953	Cle	11	1	0	0–1
1954	Cle	9	3	0	1–0†
1955	Cle	9	2	0	1–0†
1956	Cle	5	7	0	
1957	Cle	9	2	1	0–1
1958	Cle	9	3	0	0–1
1959	Cle	7	5	0	
1960	Cle	8	3	1	
1961	Cle	8	5	1	
1962	Cle	7	6	1	
1968	Cin	3	11	0	
1969	Cin	4	9	1	
1970	Cin	8	6	0	0–1
1971	Cin	4	10	0	
1972	Cin	8	6	0	
1973	Cin	10	4	0	0–1
1974	Cin	7	7	0	
1975	Cin	11	3	0	0–1
Totals		166	100	6	4–8

*Won AAFC championship
†Won NFL title

Chapter 4

VINCE LOMBARDI

I f there was ever a man who was born to coach professional football, it was Vince Lombardi.

Vincent Thomas Lombardi was born on June 11, 1913, in Brooklyn, New York. He was the eldest of the family's five children. Harry Lombardi, Vince's father, was a butcher of Italian descent. He was a hardworking gentleman with a domineering personality, traits he would instill in his son. Early in Vince's childhood, his father advised him that hard work was the ticket to success in life. "Before you can do what you want to do, before you can exist as an individual, the first thing you have to accept is duty, the second thing is respect for authority, and the third is to develop a strong mental discipline," his father told him. These words became the foundation on which Vince would base his philosophy of life.

As a child, Lombardi was both smart and athletic. He maintained a B-plus average in his studies and excelled in both basketball and football. Unfortunately, Cathedral Prep, his first high school—an institution intended for boys who aspired to become priests—did not have a football team. So Lombardi concentrated on basketball and earned a spot on the varsity team in his junior year. After three years at Cathedral, Lombardi decided to forego his plans to enter the priesthood and left the school. He subsequently enrolled at St. Francis Prep to complete his final year of high school. Due to his reputation as a great football player earlier in his youth, he received a scholarship from St. Francis. He was an immediate sensation on the gridiron at both halfback and guard, and earned All-City honors at the conclusion of the season.

New York City's Fordham University presented Lombardi with an opportunity to further both his education and football pursuits by offering him a scholarship in 1933. He played offensive and defensive guard for the Rams, and though he did not receive much playing time until his senior year, he became one of the famous "Seven Blocks of Granite"—a moniker used to describe the extraordinary defensive achievements of Fordham's line during the 1936 season.

Lombardi graduated from Fordham *magna cum laude* in 1937, earning a degree in business. He took a job with a finance company in 1938 but quit after one year in order to pursue a degree at Fordham's school of law. In his spare time (little that there was), he played semipro football for the Wilmington (Delaware) Clippers.

Due to below-average grades and a lack of desire to become an attorney, Lombardi left law school in 1939. He assumed a teaching and coaching position at Saint Cecilia High School in Englewood, New Jersey. In consideration of a seventeen-hundred-dollar annual pay check, he taught Latin, algebra, chemistry, and physics while coaching basketball, baseball, and—you guessed it—football.

In 1947, Lombardi left the high school ranks to ply his football coaching techniques with the freshmen squad of his alma mater, Fordham University. One year later, he joined the varsity as an assistant coach. In 1949, Lombardi took a position as an assistant coach at one of the country's premier college football programs, that of the United States Military Academy at West Point. There he learned the nuances of the game from the legendary college coach Colonel Earl "Red" Blaik. Blaik stressed the fundamentals of the game. "Blocking, tackling, and execution," he said would consistently win football games.

Lombardi got his big break in 1954, when he left Army to assume what was ostensibly the offensive coordinator's position with the NFL's New York Giants, under the direction of Jim Lee Howell. Vince's defensive counterpart on that Giants' team was none other than Tom Landry—future coach of the Dallas Cowboys—who was entering his next to last season as a player but the first year of his designation as player-coach in charge of the Giants' defense.

Lombardi and Landry had unique positions as assistant coaches in New York. They both retained complete control over the players on their side of the ball. Howell was more an administrator than a head coach, so both Lombardi and Landry were charged with all responsibilities regarding the offensive and defensive structure of the team. This experience would serve both men well later in their careers, in that they were already performing many of the duties associated with the head coaching position even though they were technically still assistants. With a premium staff directing their fate, the Giants were transformed from a 3–9 club in 1953 to a 7–5 team in 1954.

It was with the Giants that Lombardi's legacy as a great coach and teacher would truly begin. Lombardi relished the role of teacher. He especially loved to demonstrate the fundamentals of blocking and tackling as well as basic movement and technical responsibilities pertaining to play design. Lombardi at the blackboard diagramming plays was a sight to behold. The inflection of his raspy, passionate voice and the constant pounding of the chalk against the board when stressing a critical maneuver were awe inspiring. "The right tackle moves *first*, he blocks the defensive tackle *here*," Lombardi would say as he pounded the chalk against the board. "The guard *waits* a split second, *he waits*, got that, *he waits*." Lombardi pounded the chalk louder and louder every time he reiterated the guard's delay in movement. "Otherwise, the whole play is ruined!" Later, on the practice field, Lombardi took each play and ran it through like he did in the classroom, with just as much vigor and enthusiasm, further implanting the routine into the minds of his players. "He drove us crazy," halfback Frank Gifford said. But the process worked to perfection. Rarely did a New York Giants offensive player fail to perform the play as it was outlined on the blackboard.

Lombardi's move from college football to the professional ranks was not free of turmoil. There was a transition period in which he learned the more subtle aspects of coaching necessary to succeed in the NFL. Lombardi's style and disposition was predicated on a fiery, demonstrative, take-charge spirit and attitude—something that bore positive results with still-impressionable college athletes but not something particularly appealing to some of the older, more worldly professional players.

At one of the Giants' first practices, Lombardi began to teach quarterback Charlie Conerly a play that had been successful for him in college, at Army. It was an option play where Conerly had a choice to either give the ball to the fullback off tackle or fake the handoff and run around end himself. Conerly, a seven-year veteran who was never a talented runner—even when he was younger—was utterly contemptuous of the play and of Lombardi's insistence that the Giants install it in their game plan. In practice, each time Conerly faked the handoff, he would get summarily smashed into the ground by one of the Giants' defensive linemen. Eventually, Conerly refused to run the play—even changing the call when it was sent in from the sideline during scrimmages. "You want to run the goddamn play," a disgusted Conerly said as he walked past Lombardi, "you run it."

Inevitably, the dispiriting challenge of interacting with some players whom he perceived as egotistical and closed-minded took its toll on Lombardi, and his resoluteness and determination waned. "How can I teach and improve the team if players refuse to adhere to my guidelines?" he often wondered to himself. Several other incidents similar to the Conerly episode led the rookie coach down the road of uncertainty, manifesting itself with a period of introspection where Vince contemplated quitting professional football and returning to work for his friend and confidant, "Red" Blaik, at Army.

But soon Lombardi realized that with intelligent people—in all walks of life—you had to earn their respect and trust before they would categorically welcome your ideas. He rationalized that in professional football, where players were more experienced and more involved with the game than in college, there sometimes needed to be a give-and-take relationship, as opposed to the dictatorial setting pervasive in the amateur ranks. He learned to accept suggestions and ideas from players, especially grizzled veterans who had been around forever. Thereafter, Lombardi developed a rapport with many of the Giants' key players, including Conerly.

Being an intelligent, inquisitive individual with a progressive mind, Lombardi began to develop an affinity for the tactical side of professional football. He became adept at matching strategies with counterstrategies and quickly established an aptitude for tactical methodology. After a dismal 2–5 start to the 1955 season, Coach Howell grew impatient with New York's play. He asked each of his assistants for suggestions on how to improve the club. Lombardi had an idea. He and the Giants' line coach, Ed Kolman, had conceptualized a scheme that cannibalized part of the single-wing formation and inserted it into the T-formation package. The eventual product would utilize single-wing blocking with T-formation rushing. Ostensibly, this enabled the Giants to double-team opponents at the point of attack—with the unbalanced line of a single-wing—but in performing the play from a T-formation, it also allowed New York the wherewithal to fake the run when the defense adjusted to the maneuver and throw a pass from the same alignment. The Giants went 4–0–1 in their last five games after implementing the concept and averaged twenty-seven points per game as compared to the nineteen they had scored before the change. "What a difference it made," said Howell of Lombardi's strategy.

With the aid of an outstanding coaching staff, New York was able to string together six straight years of winning football. The Giants became NFL champions in 1956 and were runners-up in both 1958 and 1959. This success paved the way for Lombardi's first head coaching position.

In 1959, Lombardi left the championship-caliber establishment of the New York Giants for a five-year contract to coach one of the NFL's most woeful organizations, the Green Bay Packers. Lombardi loved New York and had developed a sincere friendship with Giants' owner Wellington Mara, but the Packers offered him a guaranteed five-year contract for thirty-six-thousand dollars per season and total control of the organization. It would have been foolish to decline.

The Packers' last winning season dated back twelve years to 1947. From 1948 to 1958, the Packers' aggregate record amounted to 37–93–2, for a .288 winning percentage. The Green Bay franchise, at that point, might have been better off disenfranchised. Fan support—especially when the Packers traveled to Milwaukee for some of their home games—was atrocious, and interest in the city of Green Bay itself was not much better.

Upon taking over the team, Lombardi told the Packers, "Dancing is a contact sport, football is a hitting sport," intimating that they would be expected to "physically invest themselves" to meet the requirements of his training regimen. He then proceeded to inform the group that he demanded their full attention, complete dedication, and unquestioned obedience from training camp throughout the entire season. In return for their sacrifices, he promised prosperity—winning football seasons and championships—the latter of which, Lombardi knew, would not come easily.

The first obstacle Lombardi needed to overcome in Green Bay was the defeatist attitude of his players, particularly their lack of pride and determination. But Lombardi had an incredible talent to lead and inspire men, which often resulted in the revitalization of their spirits and the restoration of their tenacity, making the difficult task of invigorating the depressed Packers much easier. In order to facilitate this attitude change, however, Lombardi needed to convince the players of the merits of his tactics and philosophies, which would subsequently generate faith in his program and allow Lombardi to maximize the players' potential. Once this was accomplished, Lombardi was able to develop a loyal group of "mercenaries" willing to do whatever was necessary to win. During his reign, his players were often overheard to say, "If he [Lombardi] tells you to go to hell, you look forward to the trip."

In one of his first training camp lectures, Lombardi said, "We're going to have a football team, and we're going to win some games. And you know why? Because you're going to have confidence in me and my system. By being alert you're going to make fewer mistakes than your opponent. By working harder you're going to out-execute, out-block, out-tackle every team that comes your way. I've never been a losing coach, and I don't intend on starting here." Lombardi went on to state that things would be done his way or no way at all. He told players that if they believed in him, he would turn them into winners—both on and off the football field. He indicated that there would be certain regulations instituted. He would expect a disciplined, professional group of athletes and would demand nothing less than 100-percent effort—both mentally and physically—from each and every man in his charge. In conclusion, Lombardi explained, "You can stay here and pay the price for winning, or else you can get the hell out." This speech enlivened the despondent team. Linebacker Bill Forester got so keyed up that he could hardly sleep that night. Quarterback Bart Starr recalled thinking, "Where have you been all my life?"

The next day, Max McGee, Packers receiver, recounted Lombardi's very candid admission. "He came over to me and looked relieved. He said he'd been nervous as hell about giving that speech. He was afraid the whole squad might leave. But no one did."

Vince Lombardi had an extremely authoritative personality. He was assertive by nature and always strove to be at the forefront of any situation. In almost every circumstance in his adult life—sports related or not—Lombardi pursued the power to command and control people, to be in charge. This passion to lead reflected an inner strength borne of his security in the knowledge that he had expended *every* effort to prepare himself—both mentally and physically—for the opportunity to supervise. And his belief in the benefits of extensive preparation manifested itself in his fundamental approach to football. Lombardi's basic methods and principles were grounded in the theory that if two people, or two teams, were evenly matched in talent, technique, knowledge, and discipline, then the better-conditioned athlete(s) would have the advantage.

Training camp for a Vince Lombardi team was pure hell. It involved rigorous physical exercise, monotonous repetition, long hours, and a total, uncompromising devotion to football. Army boot camp would have been a picnic compared to the arduous tedium that every Packers player would have to endure, season after season. Fundamentals, discipline, and hitting—hard-hitting, day in and day out—that was a Lombardi training camp.

In sharp contrast to the contemporary NFL, training routines employed in the 1950s and 1960s were much more grueling. Many teams in the new millennium do not even begin practice until late July, approximately five weeks before the season begins. And practice schedules and training camp standards are much more relaxed and tolerant. Much of the difference has to do with the financial aspect of sports in the modern era; still, the prevailing opinion of coaches has seemed to change in the last few decades. The football seasons grew longer—sixteen games as opposed to the twelve to fourteen in Lombardi's era—the injury rates increased, and the monetary commitment to the players escalated, subsequently fashioning the trend towards less strict, more moderate training methods.

Lombardi would have had none of it. "I don't say these things because I believe in the brute nature of man, or that men must be brutalized to be combative," he said. "I believe in God, and I believe in human decency. But I firmly believe that any man's finest hour, the greatest fulfillment of all he holds dear, is that moment when he has worked his heart out in a good cause and lies exhausted on the field of battle—victorious."

Packers assistant coach Phil Bengston may have described a typical Lombardi training camp as well as anyone when he said, "No one was permitted to dog it. Soon, almost all of us were able to survive. Nobody vomited after the first couple of days."

Lombardi training camps were designed to tax athletes to their fullest capacities. He wanted to assess his football players under duress—to see what kind of mental and physical fortitude they possessed. Observers would later characterize Lombardi's methods as character-building sessions, but that was inaccurate. "I don't build character," he said. "I eliminate the people who don't have it." Lombardi wanted to witness and assess the players' instincts and reactions under the worst of conditions. He rationalized that if they could withstand the pressure and physical punishment of his training camp, then anything they encountered after that would seem like a walk in the park.

It was not out of the ordinary for players to lose ten to twenty pounds during a nine-week Lombardi summer camp. One of Vince's favorite exercises was referred to as a "grass drill." Later, it would commonly become known as "Green Bays." Players would run in place in an exaggerated motion, and at the leader's command—usually Vince himself—they would drop to the ground, chest first, and pop right back up, again running in place. After just one minute total exhaustion would set in, and Vince would be forced to relent and give them a break.

It was commonplace in a Green Bay training camp for players to view film of practice sessions—often edited versions produced by Lombardi and his coaches—to learn the specifics of certain techniques. The players would watch as the coaches critiqued the tapes, detailed the correct methods for each procedure, and explained why that precise maneuver was necessary for success in each situation. Wide receiver Gary Knaflec had been with the Packers for five years before Lombardi became the coach. Though Knaflec was 6' 4", 217 pounds—big for a wide receiver—he was a terrible blocker. After watching film and practicing for several days, Knaflec finally synchronized the correct blocking techniques for his position. "I didn't even know I *could* block, I had never done it," he said.

One of Lombardi's strictest training camp regulations was that players had to be in bed by the 11 P.M. curfew. Lombardi was so inflexible on this point that he actually fined running back Jim Taylor twenty-five dollars one evening because Jim was sitting on the *edge* of his bed—in socks and shorts—when the clock struck eleven. He asked Jim what time it was and Taylor responded that it had just turned eleven. "Then why aren't you in bed?" Lombardi inquired.

After the shock—both physical and mental—of the first Lombardi preseason camp in Green Bay dissipated, the Packers were set for the 1959 season. Coming off a 1–10–1 year and having been outscored 382–193, the Packers' faithful would have offered effusive praise for their new coach if the team even approached a .500 season. Privately, Lombardi thought that it would be a successful season if the club won four games.

September 26, 1959, marked the commencement of the coaching career of one of the game's true immortals. And, of course, it was a victorious beginning. Quarterback Bart Starr had not enjoyed a stellar training camp and would begin the season as the team's backup signal caller. Lamar McHan, a veteran of six years in Chicago—and a newcomer to the Packers—began the year as the starter even though he had not fared much better in the exhibition season. Lombardi's rationale was that Starr, having been in Green Bay for three seasons, exemplified the losing history of the club to that point, and Lombardi thought the team needed a change.

The Chicago Bears, the "Monsters of the Midway," invaded Green Bay with none other than George "Pappa Bear" Halas—perhaps the greatest coach in league history to that point—at the helm. The Bears were the most formidable team in the NFL, having suffered just three losing seasons in the past twenty-three years. They were heavy favorites to trounce the Packers on Opening Day, 1959. But the times, they were a-changin'.

Green Bay's physical offensive and defensive lines were the difference in the game. The Packers outgained the Bears by more than one hundred yards, 277–171. A fumbled punt return recovered by Green Bay center Jim Ringo was the key play of the contest, as Lombardi's troops scraped and clawed their way to a gutsy 9–6 win on that windy autumn day in Green Bay. The victory so inspired the players that they carried Lombardi off the field on their shoulders and proceeded to win their next two contests as well, over Detroit and San Francisco. The Packers, 3–0. Say it ain't so! Was this the same team that had toiled in squalor for more than a decade?

It may have been the same players, but it was not the same team. Vince Lombardi had instilled a newborn confidence and attitude that smacked of brashness and boldness, one that actually gave the team the audacity to believe that they were good.

Speaking of smack, that's exactly what the Los Angeles Rams, Baltimore Colts (twice), New York Giants, and Chicago Bears (this time in the Windy City) did to the Packers in quick succession subsequent to Green Bay's 3–0 start. But the Packers persevered and managed to salvage a more than respectable season by winning their remaining four games. In the process they returned the favor to both the Rams and the Colts and concluded the season at 7–5—their first winning record in twelve years.

A winning football team in Green Bay was almost incomprehensible, especially with a rookie head coach. The city was ecstatic. Explanations abounded, but the players knew. "It's really Lombardi," said running back Don McIlhenny. Lamar McHan agreed. "I've never seen a man with such tremendous knowledge of football." Bart Starr added, "We went into games as well prepared and as well organized as it was possible to be."

To improve the Packers in the off-season, Lombardi made a trade with the Cleveland Browns to acquire a former fifteenth-round draft pick, defensive end Willie Davis. In exchange, the Packers sent wide receiver A.D. Williams to Cleveland. Davis added another athletic, physical player to the Green Bay front wall. He had a fairly productive career as well, ultimately entering the Hall of Fame in 1981. Williams lasted one year with the Browns, catching just one pass. He was completely out of football in 1962. Not a bad exchange.

Green Bay started the 1960 season with a loss to the Bears, 17–14. Starr had been chosen as the starter at quarterback but was unceremoniously replaced in the second game by McHan. The team proceeded to win that game and the next two contests as well. However, during the season's fifth game, against the Steelers in Pittsburgh, Lombardi replaced the ineffective McHan and would never again waver on his choice of a starting quarterback. The Packers finished the season with an 8–4 record, which, lo and behold, was good enough to edge Detroit and San Francisco for the Western Conference crown and catapult Green Bay into their first championship game appearance since World War II (1944).

The Philadelphia Eagles beat the Packers in the 1960 championship game, 17–13. It was the first and last time that Vince Lombardi would lose a championship contest. Interestingly enough, Green Bay almost managed to pull it out at the end. The Eagles—who trailed 13–10 late in the game—scored on a five-yard Ted Dean touchdown run with 5:21 remaining. The Packers—behind future Hall of Famer Bart Starr—then drove to the Eagles twenty-two with only eight seconds remaining. On the last play of the game, Starr threw a pass to Jim Taylor, who was tackled by the Eagles' own Hall of Famer, linebacker Chuck Bednarik, at the eight-yard line as time ran out.

Though the Packers lost the championship game, there was no doubt that pro football was *back* in Wisconsin.

From 1929 through 1939, Green Bay had been the pro football "capital of the world." Earl "Curly" Lambeau (no relation to "Curly" Howard of the Three Stooges) led the Packers to five NFL titles in that eleven-year span, with only one losing season (1933). "Maybe the 'new' Packers, dare we dream, could even win a title themselves," fans conjectured. Alas, Packers fans would have to settle for something else. For under Vince Lombardi, Green Bay would garner *five* titles in just seven seasons—the fastest five-title run in the history of the NFL, and one that may never be surpassed.

The Packers finished at 11–3 in 1961 and won their second Western Conference crown in a row. In the championship game, they pummeled the New York Giants into submission, 37–0, for their first title in seventeen years. Green Bay outgained the "G-men" 345–150, for more than twice as many total yards. But the fact that the Packers destroyed the Giants should not have surprised as many experts as it did. Though the

Packers had beaten New York by only three points in their regular season meeting, 20–17, a quick glance at the statistics proved that Lombardi had assembled the far superior squad.

The 1961 Packers outgained their opponents by slightly more than five hundred yards that year, 4,852 to 4,324, but that wasn't nearly as meaningful as their averages per play. Green Bay dominated the entire NFL in this category, to the tune of a 5.0 yard rushing average and an 8.2 average per pass attempt. Conversely, their defense permitted averages of only 4.1 and 6.4 respectively. On the whole, Green Bay gained an average of 6.2 yards per play, while their adversaries could manage only 5.2. That amounted to a 19 percent advantage—far and away the best in the league.

The Giants also outgained their opponents by more than five hundred yards, 4,882 to 4,361. But New York was outgained per attempt on the ground 4.2 to 4.0, while their air superiority was only 7.3 to 6.7, translating to a rather mundane average advantage per play of 5.6 versus 5.4 (less than 1 percent). The Lombardi-led Packers were clearly the dominant team.

In 1962, Green Bay assembled one of the finest teams to ever grace a football field. Eleven future Hall of Famers were on the squad: defensive back Herb Adderley, lineman Willie Davis, offensive lineman Forrest Gregg, running back Paul Hornung, defensive lineman Henry Jordan, linebacker Ray Nitchke, center Jim Ringo, quarterback Bart Starr, fullback Jim Taylor, defensive back Willie Wood, and their exceptional head coach, Vincent Thomas Lombardi. Though this group played together for several seasons, none would be quite comparable to 1962. The Packers finished with a 13–1 record. They outscored their opponents by a mere 267 points (415–148)—almost triple their output—for an average advantage of 30–11 each game. And though Green Bay was actually outgained by the New York Giants in the 1962 championship game, the Packers' defense held the Giants to just seven points, as Green Bay prevailed 16–7.

For the year, Green Bay outgained their opponents 5,081 to 3,615, for an average per play advantage of 6.1 versus 4.8 (approximately 27 percent). And their rushing touchdown superiority is legendary—36–4—representing complete physical annihilation of opponents, exactly the way Lombardi wanted it (table 4-1).

The years 1963–1964 were "lean" for Lombardi's Packers. They managed *just* nineteen victories against seven losses and two ties and finished in second place each season.

Turmoil and commotion punctuated the 1963 season. Just after the 1962 season ended, a rumor began circulating that star halfback Paul Hornung was involved in an

Table 4-1. Green Bay Packers, 1962

	Rushing				Passing			
	Att	Yards	Avg	TDs	Att	Yards	Avg	TDs
Packers	518*	2460*	4.7*	36*	311	2621	8.4	14
Opponents	404	1531	3.8	4*	355	2084*	5.9*	10*

* Led league

Vince Lombardi shares a chuckle with Paul Hornung, *5,* Bart Starr, *15,* and Jim Taylor, *31.*

illegal betting scheme, conveying specific information regarding NFL contests and possibly even wagering on his own games. Another NFL star, Detroit Lions' defensive tackle Alex Karras, was also implicated in a similar case. On April 17, 1963, NFL Commissioner Pete Rozelle made a decision to suspend Hornung for the entire year. Lombardi was devastated. He had trusted Hornung, like all of his athletes. He had warned him of the consequences and perils of gambling and being associated with the "wrong" element. "I thought a great deal of Paul," Lombardi said. "He always gave me one-hundred percent in football. Paul made the mistake of thinking that the rules were made for everyone but him."

Hornung's failure to meet his coach's demand of putting the team first greatly troubled Lombardi. He later admitted it was his deepest disappointment as a head coach. One of Lombardi's greatest strengths was that he always knew his players— really knew them. In the book *Run to Daylight,* author W.C. Heinz asked Lombardi for candid assessments of the Packers' players, the makeup of the men as both people and football players. The book, which is a classic, notes Lombardi's appraisal of Hornung as follows: "[He] can take criticism in public or anywhere. You have to whip him a little. He had a hell-with-you attitude, a defensive perimeter he built around himself when he didn't start out well here. As soon as he had success, he changed. He's still exuberant, likes to play around, but serious on the field. Always looks you straight in the eye. Great competitor who rises to heights." It sounds like a CIA file on a notorious criminal or head of state. So detailed, so poignant, so personal and incisive a "dossier" that you can truly appreciate the motivation and effort that Lombardi expended, somewhat from a personal viewpoint, but more from a business approach. He was keen on finding a player's strong and weak personality traits and exploiting them at the appropriate time to advance the fortunes of the organization. In the end, Hornung's "hell-with-you" attitude cost him a year of his livelihood, much money in the near and distant future, and the trust and confidence of a friend and coach.

George Halas's Bears won the NFL's Western Conference championship in 1963, and Don Shula and the Colts grabbed the title in 1964. Think about that for a moment. George Halas was not included in this study since he coached the majority of his career before 1950. But his record of 318–148–32, .671, with six NFL championships, would easily have qualified.

Lombardi, Halas, and Shula, *all in one seven-team conference.* My, how times have changed. When else would someone be able to note the achievements of three Hall of Fame coaches—who appear in almost everyone's top-five list of all-time greats—in a single sentence, relative to a single season, applicable to the equivalent of a single NFL division. And to boggle your mind even further, consider that George Allen, another Hall of Famer, joined the conference in 1966, as coach of the Rams. The only time Lombardi, Halas, and Shula should be grouped together might conceivably be in a Hall of Fame sculpture or statue—football's equivalent of Mount Rushmore—but not all in one (seven-team) conference. Between Lombardi, Halas, and Shula, their aggregate record includes 742 wins, a .680 winning percentage, and thirteen NFL Titles in twenty-two attempts! What a shame, two of them had to lose every year!

In one of the most entertaining seasons of the decade, the 1965 Packers attempted to "right the ship" and reestablish their NFL dominance. Heading into the last week of the season, the Packers stood at 10–3 and could clinch the conference title with a win in San Francisco against a 49ers team that they had beaten earlier in the year 27–10. The Baltimore Colts were right behind the Packers in the conference race, at 9–3–1, and would face the lowly Los Angeles Rams in their last game. The Colts would play first, as their game was slated for Saturday, December 18. The contest was close, but Baltimore bested Los Angeles 20–17. And though the Colts certainly had a chance to win the conference, no one really thought the Packers would yield in San Francisco the following day.

Much to the chagrin of Vince Lombardi, the Packers *did* yield—that is, they didn't win. The contest ended in a 24–24 tie, which enabled the Colts to gain back the crucial half game they needed. Both teams finished at 10–3–1, and a playoff would be held in Green Bay on December 26 to decide the conference champion.

Unfortunately for Baltimore, both of their quarterbacks, Johnny Unitas and Gary Cuozzo, were injured, so Colts' halfback Tom Matte—a former quarterback at Ohio State—was forced into action as the Colts' signal caller. With the plays taped to his wrist, Matte desperately attempted to produce points for a shorthanded Colts' offense. Though his final passing stats for the game were terrible (5–12, for forty yards), and the Colts' only touchdown came on a fumble return, Matte—along with a stingy Colts defense—kept Baltimore in the game for the entire sixty minutes. Ironically, Packers quarterback Bart Starr was injured during the contest as well. Reserve quarterback Zeke Bratkowski played most of the game for Green Bay, accounting for almost 250 passing yards. In the end, only a controversial twenty-five-yard field goal by Packers kicker Don Chandler, in overtime, allowed Green Bay and Lombardi to prevail. The contested kick was judged to be just inside the right upright. In reality, as shown on replays (which were not permitted in those days), the kick was *not* good, as it was unquestionably wide of the goalpost. The call was not a simple one for the referees to determine, as the ball reached a trajectory that brought it over the goalposts in height and made the referees' judgment much more difficult. It is interesting to note that the NFL later raised the uprights to eliminate the possibility of this type of controversy in the future. In any case, the Packers edged the Colts 13–10 in one of the most memorable games in NFL history. And they earned the right to face the Cleveland Browns in the NFL championship game the next week.

The Packers trounced Cleveland in the 1965 title game 23–12, as Green Bay completely manhandled the outclassed Browns. Hornung and Taylor combined for 201 rushing yards, and the Packers outgained Cleveland 332–161. "This team had more character than any other team I've had," Lombardi said after the game. In what would be the last *true* NFL title game in history—the Super Bowl would begin the next season—Green Bay was crowned league champion for the third time in five years.

The Super Bowl marked the beginning of a sports tradition the likes of which may never again be duplicated. In 1966, the NFL and the AFL agreed on merger plans to be implemented for the 1970 season, with the NFL absorbing all ten teams from the rival league. Three NFL teams (Baltimore, Pittsburgh, and Cleveland) would switch over to the newly created conference, the AFC, and there would be a brand-new, twenty-six-team NFL. A new championship game would also be created. The winners of both conferences, the AFC and NFC (the remaining original NFL teams), would meet in a final game which would later come to be called the Super Bowl.

By the next-to-last week of the 1966 season, Green Bay had clinched their conference with an 11–2 record. Their final game of the year would be a meaningless encounter against the Los Angeles Rams, in California. The team, however, had reacted poorly—Lombardi thought—to the fact that they had clinched the title early, and practices were horrible that week. "You fellows don't have any pride," Vince yelled. "All you have is shame. You're a disgrace to the National Football League. If the Rams beat you, you'll never come back. You fellows are a championship team, but you must have been lucky to get where you are." The players, who were quite jovial before the verbal assault, were in disbelief. They thought they had *won* the championship—that they had played well. Now, here's this "lunatic" yelling and screaming at them over practices for a game that didn't even matter.

Although the players had trouble understanding Lombardi's logic for pushing them to the limits to defeat a weak opponent in a meaningless game, it was just another of Lombardi's ploys to motivate them—to get them to perform with maximum effort each and every time they took the field. If players took "breaks" during the season, it was a signal, Lombardi thought, that they had let their guard down and possibly lost their edge. This was something that the coach could not and would not allow to happen. Consistent, one-hundred-percent effort was a fundamental characteristic of any Lombardi team, and the Packers wouldn't be permitted to relax just because they had clinched the conference crown and were facing an inferior opponent.

Lombardi was always masterful at motivating his players and often elicited production levels greater than those each man believed himself capable of. To perform these "miracles" of persuasion, Lombardi's primary "coercive" mechanism was his naturally confrontational personality, which instilled fear in many of his athletes. This anxiety often evoked a behavioral change in the players, sufficient enough to persuade them to become totally committed to their coach and his methods—as opposed to challenging him and risking the wrath and fury of his contempt. "He motivated *me* out of fear," said Allen Brown, tight end from 1966 to 1967, who was continually frightened at the possibility of being confronted by Lombardi and subsequently cut, traded, or embarrassed in front of his teammates for any mistakes he committed.

In the locker room before the "big game" against the lowly Rams in 1966, Lombardi had one final word of wisdom for his troops. "You'll be cheating yourselves, your coaches, your teammates, and the city of Green Bay if you don't give one-hundred per-cent to win this game," he said. "I know we don't have any cheaters on this team."

Green Bay ultimately defeated Los Angeles 27–23 and finished the season with a 12–2 record. "Sometimes, I think no game we ever played for Coach Lombardi gave him as much satisfaction as the one we didn't have to win but did," said Bart Starr.

In addition to the motivational aspects of his tirade before the Rams game, Lombardi had also concluded that it was a perfect opportunity to scold the team for the purpose of correcting some deficiencies that had recently become apparent, even though the Packers had won four games in a row leading up to that contest.

Lombardi always endeavored to critique his club most harshly after *victories,* when things were going well. While part of this policy was designed as a motivational tool—to battle complacency—another vitally important aspect to the theory was Lombardi's belief that attempting to lecture a team after a *loss* could be extremely counterproductive. When a team was reeling, fresh off of a defeat, Lombardi believed that players were more likely to take offense to reprimands and belittlement from their own coaches. They could perceive it as more punishment—similar to that which the opposition had just inflicted in the game. Therefore, whenever possible, Lombardi preferred to address problems when the squad was feeling good—after a winning streak. This way, with everyone in excellent spirits, the team would likely be more willing to tolerate the abuse and gain useful insight from the criticism, as opposed to resenting it.

In the 1966 NFL championship game, the Packers bested the Cowboys and Tom Landry 34–27 for the right to play in the first-ever Super Bowl. History could not have written a better script for the inaugural "game of games." Vince Lombardi and the Green Bay Packers—names synonymous with championship football—would be the main attraction at the Memorial Coliseum in Los Angeles, California, on January 15, 1967. The Kansas City Chiefs, led by the venerable Hank Stram, would be the opponents. Lombardi was confident that the upstart Chiefs would be no match for his more experienced and NFL-tested Packers. As usual, though, he implored his team not to expect an easy win. Lombardi harped on the Chiefs' physical style and their imposing defense, which were very real assets. Kansas City's entire defensive unit was superb, perhaps one of the finest in the history of professional football. And though few people from the NFL took the Chiefs seriously at the time, they started eight all-stars, three of whom would become Hall of Famers: middle linebacker Willie Lanier (Hall of Famer), defensive end Aaron Brown, defensive tackle "Buck" Buchanan (HOF), linebacker Bobby Bell (HOF), defensive tackle Curley Culp, cornerback Emmitt Thomas, safety Johnny Robinson, and cornerback Jim Marsalis.

The Packers' strategy, as devised by Lombardi, was to exploit the Chiefs with a short passing game. Lombardi believed that anytime a defense utilized two linebackers inside their defensive ends, they were vulnerable to outside pass patterns. Kansas City employed a 4–3 defense, utilizing just one inside linebacker. However, when the offense shifted into certain formations, the Chiefs would play one of their outside linebackers in a stacked position—just behind one of their defensive ends—in an area where they would have difficulty covering a properly executed outside pass pattern. Lombardi ordered Starr to throw the ball often, even in short yardage situations—an unusual tactic for the normally conservative Packers. Starr, who would become the game's MVP, wound up completing sixteen of twenty-four passes for the impressive total of 250 yards, including two touchdowns. During the season, Green Bay had averaged twenty-three passing attempts per contest. But considering that the game was all but over early in the third quarter—and that Green Bay was just trying to run the clock out with a ground attack thereafter—the fact that the Packers *still* attempted more passes than they did on average meant that Lombardi's aggressive game plan probably dictated the increase. Green Bay won by the score of 35–10, becoming the first-ever Super Bowl champions.

The Packers of 1966 were quite the statistical marvels. They more than doubled their opponents in points, 335–163, and they averaged almost one full yard more per pass attempt than the second most prolific passing team in the league, the Dallas Cowboys (8.9–8.1). This achievement established Green Bay at a level of performance an astonishing 29 percent higher than the NFL average (6.9). In addition, the Packers defense grabbed twenty-eight interceptions (second best in the league), while the offense sustained just five interceptions of their own. The next best team in the league suffered almost three times as many pickoffs (fourteen). The NFL's interception rate in 1966 was 5.2 percent. Bart Starr—playing without the aid of an efficient running game (the Packers averaged only 3.5 yards per carry)—still managed to escape the turnover bug by tossing only five errant passes in 318 attempts (1.6 percent). As a result, Green Bay compiled an interception percentage that was an incredible 70 percent lower than average. Green Bay's superiority didn't end there. The Packers' 8.9 yards per pass attempt was almost 51 percent superior to their opponents' 5.9. To put that in perspective, it would be the equivalent in dominance to a running back who averaged 4.5 yards per carry versus one who averaged 3.0—a remarkable difference. The Chiefs, though they played well, never really had a chance.

In 1967, the Packers attempted to become the first team since the NFL playoff system was introduced in 1933 to win three straight league titles. Several teams had carved out back-to-back championships, but none had emerged with three titles in a row. The 1967 season marked the beginning of a new era in the NFL. In addition to the newly implemented Super Bowl, the league divided into four divisions, two in each conference—as opposed to just two conferences. Division winners would meet in a playoff game for the right to gain entrance into the "NFL Championship" contest, with the winner of that game representing the league in the Super Bowl. Green Bay struggled in the regular season, amassing a very un-Packers-like mark of 9–4–1. They did manage, however, to win the Western Conference's Central Division by two games over the Bears.

In the Packers' first conference championship playoff game under the new format, they faced the Los Angeles Rams, who two weeks earlier had bested Green Bay in the last minute of play, 27–24. This time would be different. Though the Rams had compiled an 11–1–2 record—and outscored their opponents by more than two hundred points on the year (398–196)—Green Bay stymied Rams quarterback Roman Gabriel and smothered Los Angeles 28–7.

Next were the Dallas Cowboys (in the NFL championship game), a team anxious for revenge after succumbing to the Packers in their 1966 playoff encounter. Dallas had won the Capitol Division and then ripped Cleveland 52–14 in the 1967 Eastern Conference championship. They were primed for another shot at the defending Super Bowl champion Packers.

The "Ice Bowl" is legendary. The atmosphere, the emotions, the weather, the matchup—all created the elements for a historic epic. And the game was uncharacteristically every bit as good as its buildup. In frozen conditions that would have made a penguin cry (wind chills of minus fifty degrees and a game-time temperature of minus thirteen), the Packers jumped out to a 14–0 lead as Bart Starr connected with Boyd Dowler for two first-half touchdowns. Dallas rallied when Starr was hit and fumbled, and the Cowboys' George Andrie scooped it up and ran seven yards for a score. Before the half ended, the Cowboys narrowed the gap to four when Danny Villanueva booted a twenty-one-yard field goal.

As the teams wrestled back and forth throughout the third quarter, one sensed that it would take something dramatic to win this monumental struggle. And then it happened. Dallas quarterback Don Meredith handed Dan Reeves the ball and he started to run left. After three or four steps, he pulled up and glanced downfield to see the Packers' cornerback and safety closing on the line of scrimmage to stop the run. Reeves—a running back who had played quarterback in college at South Carolina and had thrown for two touchdowns during the regular season—then lofted a feathery pass to wide receiver Lance Rentzel. Rentzel caught the ball, pivoted, and ran in for the score. On the very first play of the fourth stanza, Dallas had hit the jackpot with a fifty-yard, halfback-option pass. Reeves would later say that it (the option call) seemed like the only thing to do in those deteriorating conditions—for everyone was having trouble cutting on the "frozen tundra of Lambeau Field."

The Packers were in trouble. With only 4:50 remaining, trailing 17–14, their hopes for a third straight title in the balance, and the weather conditions deteriorating, Bart Starr, Vince Lombardi, and the champion Packers prepared for what they believed would be their last gasp.

"The Drive" started at the Green Bay thirty-two-yard line. After two quick first downs, which moved the ball to the Dallas forty-two, Packers running back Donny Anderson was thrown for a devastating nine-yard loss. Anderson soon redeemed himself, however, when he became the recipient of two consecutive Bart Starr passes that created a first down at the Cowboys' thirty with 1:35 left to play. The pivotal play—which allowed the Packers to enter into easy field goal range to tie the game—came from fullback Chuck Mercein. "I noticed that the Cowboys' linebackers had been taking straight drops as opposed to angled drops towards the sideline," Mercein said. "I figured that if I could get to the outside, I would have a chance for a big play." Mercein grabbed a Bart Starr pass, ran outside Dallas linebacker Dave Edwards, and made it all the way down to the Cowboys' eleven-yard line for a first down. From there, Mercein and Anderson drove the ball inside the Cowboys' two-yard line, giving the Packers another first down. Green Bay subsequently attempted two more running plays, which could only draw them three feet closer. Then—with only sixteen seconds remaining on the clock and facing a third-and-goal from the one—Bart Starr called the Packers' final time-out.

Lombardi and Starr conferred on the sidelines during the brief stoppage in play allotted for the time-out. The Packers had to deal with several issues. First, should they just kick the field goal on third down and take their chances in overtime? Second, could they possibly call a running play and still have time to line up for a fourth-down attempt if it didn't work, realizing that they were devoid of time-outs and couldn't stop the clock? Third, if they did try a play, what would it be?

"We thought they would throw," said Dallas coach Tom Landry. "We thought they probably would go on an option—a rollout run or pass—so they could stop the clock [with an incompletion or by running out of bounds, thus allowing for another play] if it didn't work."

As the saying goes, "Sometimes it's better to be lucky than good." Green Bay attempted a quarterback sneak.

A quarterback sneak!

With a time-out remaining, or more than thirty seconds still on the clock, that strategy would have been appropriate. But since Green Bay was out of time-outs, if the Packers did not get the touchdown, the game would be over—and so would the Packers' season. The mass of humanity unpiling from the third-down attempt would never have been able to gather themselves and get set at the line of scrimmage in only ten or eleven seconds. And the Packers' field goal team would certainly not have had time to deploy.

Either the football gods were rooting for the Packers, or, perhaps, they too were frozen above the neck that day.

Green Bay called "thirty-one-wedge," a play actually designed to be run by the full-back, Chuck Mercein. When Starr called the play in the huddle, he did not mention that he was going to keep the ball himself, preferring to have the offensive line think it would be a handoff. Starr thought the blocking would be better if the line believed they had to open a hole for a conventional running play instead of a quarterback sneak.

In any event, the play worked, and the Packers won the game as Starr plowed into the end zone behind the blocks of center Ken Bowman and right guard Jerry Kramer. Dallas defensive tackle Jethro Pugh—the player against whom the sneak was run—was 6'6", a bit tall for a defensive tackle. Both Bowman and Kramer were 6'3". They were able to double-team Pugh and gain the necessary leverage to lift him far enough out of the way to allow Starr to squeeze through for the score.

"I couldn't see going for the tie and making all of those people in the stands suffer through sudden death in this weather," Lombardi said later. "That's why we gambled for the touchdown." This statement was made by the same man to whom the single most significant sports quote in history is often attributed: "Winning isn't everything, it's the only thing." The only thing *other* than keeping fans warm during championship games, I guess.

"We didn't have any time-outs left," Lombardi further explained, "so we had to gamble that Starr would make it. I had the field goal team ready on the sidelines in case we didn't, but I'm not sure they would have had time to run out on the field and get the kick off."

The quarterback sneak was apparently Starr's idea. Green Bay running back Donny Anderson had slipped on the previous two handoffs and could gain little if any momentum going towards the goal line. The action at the end of the game was confined to Lambeau Field's southern end zone, and the scoreboard's shadow had kept the ground near the goal line in the shade—it was frozen solid. After the second Anderson attempt, Starr decided that a sneak would be the Packers' best option.

Here was Lombardi's assessment of Bart Starr in *Run to Daylight.* Pay close attention to the last few remarks: "Tense by nature, because he's a perfectionist. I've never seen him display emotion outside of nervousness. Modest. Tends to be self-effacing, which is usually a sign of lack of ego. You never hear him in the locker room telling 'I' stories. He calls me 'sir.' Seems shy, but he's not. He's just a gentleman. You don't criticize him in front of others. When I came here he lacked confidence and support. He still lacks daring, and he's not as creative as I'd like him to be, but a great student of the game."

His "starr" quarterback—the one who lacked daring and creativity—decided it would be best to take the dare of a lifetime, to gamble and do the unexpected in one of the biggest games in history! Maybe Heinz got Lombardi's characterization of Starr backwards, or perhaps Lombardi was wrong in his evaluation. But maybe, just maybe, Lombardi's assessment was right on target—that Starr was indeed a great student of the game, and that he knew exactly what play to call.

"I told Coach Lombardi there was nothing wrong with the plays we ran, the backs just couldn't get their footing," Starr says. "I said, 'Why don't I just keep it?' All he said was just run it and let's get the hell out of here. That's all he said to me." There was, apparently, never a word mentioned as to what would happen if the play didn't work. Both Starr and Lombardi must have concluded—unbeknownst to the other—that there would be no time for another play, anyway.

"I don't think it was a smart play," said Cowboys halfback Dan Reeves, now the head coach of the Atlanta Falcons. "But maybe that's why Lombardi won all those championships and I haven't won any."

"I just wish it had failed," said Cowboys assistant coach Ermal Allen after the game. "You think there would have been a few million words written about that? Then we'd see how smart he [Lombardi] felt."

Allen, of course, was right. And even though he was angry and upset—the result of having just been beaten in a monumental struggle—his consternation relative to the play call was understandable. Though we may never know the actual truth behind the decision, we do know it was a play that very few coaches would have called. A better strategy would have been to take the less risky approach—run a play that could stop the clock—and give yourself the opportunity to try a fourth-down play or kick the field goal. Attempting a running play in the middle of the field was not going to afford you those options. Maybe Lombardi and Starr forgot that they were out of time-outs. Or maybe they wanted to surprise the Cowboys by doing the unthinkable. Nevertheless, in the end, they don't ask *how*, they ask *how many*. The Packers won the game, and with it racked up another Green Bay championship. At this point, the particulars only matter for the Monday-morning quarterbacks—like me.

Cameron Snyder, former football correspondent for the *Baltimore Sun*, may have put it best when he said, "A southerner from Alabama [Bart Starr] with nerves as cold as the weather on this coldest day in National Football League history, gambled an unprecedented third straight championship and a possible winners' share of $735,000 on a quarterback sneak... and won, 21–17."

The Packers went on to defeat the Oakland Raiders in a somewhat anticlimactic Super Bowl II, 33–14. Bart Starr won game MVP honors by completing thirteen of twenty-four passes for 202 yards, including a sixty-two-yard strike to Boyd Dowler for a touchdown. Green Bay had become the first team in NFL history to deliver three consecutive championships—a record that is unmatched to this day.

Starr's exemplary two-hundred-plus-yard passing performances in key games—including both Super Bowls—had become indicative of the changing face of professional football. As the game progressed throughout the 1960s, the passing game was taking on a greater significance. Paul Brown's Cleveland teams had proven that a precision aerial attack could augment and even improve a team's running game, making offenses multidimensional and more difficult to defend.

Vince Lombardi had always subscribed to the "win at all costs" mentality that he believed was necessary to become a champion in the National Football League. His squads were consistently among the most physically dominant, the most well conditioned, and the most well prepared. The Packers would rarely if ever find themselves in a situation where they were disorganized or caught off guard. There was no doubt that Lombardi loved the physical aspect of football more than any other part of the game. He craved ferocity and loved nothing more than witnessing his teams literally crush opponents into submission. Naturally, the running game was his chief weapon. The Packers were famous for Lombardi's "Green Bay Sweep," an end run supported by multiple pulling offensive linemen and the fullback, establishing a brutal, intimidating presence at the point of attack. It was the basis for their entire offensive system during the majority of the Lombardi years. And in the late 1950s and early '60s, when the NFL was largely a running league—as evidenced by the play calling (see table 4-2)—that strategy proved decisive. But as the passing game evolved in the mid- to late-1960s, Lombardi realized that he would have to change his offensive philosophy in order to keep pace with the league, and that he would need to devise an appropriate strategy to exploit the new trend.

Table 4-2. Play-Calling Statistics, 1959–67

Year	Teams	NFL			Packers		
		Runs	Passes	Percent of Passes	Runs	Passes	Percent of Passes
1959	12	4901	3714	43.1	421	268	38.9
1960	13	5091	4114	44.7	463	279	37.6
1961	14	6106	5292	46.4	391	306	43.9
1962	14	6064	5356	47.2	518	311	37.5
1963	14	6112	5415	47.0	504	345	40.6
1964	14	6080	5436	47.2	495	321	39.3
1965	14	6031	5407	47.3	432	306	41.5
1966	15	6509	6108	48.4	475	318	40.1
1967	16	6868	6451	48.4	474	331	41.1

The NFL's percentage of passing plays increased by 12.3 percent (43.1 to 48.4 percent) from 1959 through 1967. But Lombardi and the Packers increased their passing percentage by only half as much, approximately 6 percent (38.9 to 41.1 percent).

The statistical indicators that point towards the Packers' apparent reluctance to change their offensive methods in the "new" passing era may appear valid, but they would be misunderstood without knowledge of mitigating factors which tend to compensate for the seeming lack of offensive progress by Lombardi's teams.

First of all, it is true that Lombardi preferred to run the football. And the fact that the Packers were a winning team tended to diminish the urgency which they may have otherwise felt relative to opening up their playbook and becoming more risky offensively. Second, it logically follows that losing teams (clubs that are usually behind on the scoreboard) are likely to pass much more often than teams like Green Bay, who often prefer to play conservatively and run the clock when they possess the lead. Those facts not withstanding, Lombardi did not see fit to capitalize on the passing epidemic simply by increasing the number of throws his team attempted, as the Packers were always near the bottom—many times last—in the league in that category (see table 4-3).

Instead, Lombardi took advantage of the fact that the Packers were considered to be such a dominant force running the football that teams would often stack their defenses to stop their ground attack. Notice in table 4-4 how Green Bay's average per carry and league rank plummeted after 1964.

Lombardi noticed that defenses were relentlessly creeping toward the line of scrimmage. This was making it much more difficult for his running backs to produce as they had in the past and making it just as troublesome to succeed with shorter passing plays, which were usually attempted five to seven yards beyond the line of scrimmage—directly into the tightly grouped defenders. Consequently, Lombardi believed that Green Bay could victimize opponents with an opportunistic, though judicious, downfield passing game.

Table 4-3. Green Bay's League Ranking by Number of Passes Attempted

Year	Passes	Rank	No. Teams
1959	268	11	12
1960	279	11	13
1961	306	14	14
1962	311	14	14
1963	345	13	14
1964	321	14	14
1965	306	14	14
1966	318	15	15
1967	331	15	16

Table 4-4. Packers' Yards per Rushing Attempt

Year	Average	League Rank
1959	4.5	4th
1960	4.6	3rd
1961	5.0	1st
1962	4.7	1st
1963	4.5	2nd
1964	4.6	2nd
1965	3.4	10th
1966	3.5	13th
1967	4.0	5th

Green Bay began to throw passes deeper into the opponents' secondary—just beyond the reach of the tightly grouped defenders—where there was much softer coverage and fewer potential tacklers. The resultant increases in the Packers' average per pass attempt and completion figures after 1964—when their running game was stymied—as compared to the NFL passing averages, which were essentially decreasing during that same time frame—proves that Green Bay executed their strategy perfectly, and that their surge was not simply the product of a league-wide passing ascent. (See table 4-5.)

Lombardi and the Packers did not change their offensive *style* as much as their league counterparts did at the time. What they did alter was their offensive (passing) *philosophy*, relative to deeper patterns and longer throws. Green Bay did not throw the ball as frequently as opponents; but when they did pass, they generally threw the ball farther down the field and with greater success. Their opponents were not winning with the consistency of the Packers, so their major strategic adaptations were fashioned out of the necessity to win more games and were therefore more risky. The Packers, on the other hand, just needed to modify their existing offensive concepts to stay dominant. By consistently ranking at or near the top of the league in yards per attempt, Green Bay was one of the most effective passing teams of that era.

Table 4-5. Packers' Passing Statistics Compared to League

Year	Packers Avg Per Attempt	NFL Avg Per Att	NFL Rank	Packers Avg Per Comp	NFL Avg Per Comp	NFL Rank
1959	7.3	7.2	7/12	15.3	14.5	3/12
1960	7.1	7.2	6/13	14.5	14.4	8/13
1961	8.2	7.5	4/14	14.1	14.3	8/14
1962	8.4	7.9	2/14	14.0	14.8	10/14
1963	7.9	7.7	5/14	15.1	15.0	4/14
1964	7.7	7.2	3/14	13.3	13.9	11/14
1965	8.2	7.5	3/14	15.1	14.5	5/14
1966	8.9	6.9	1/15	14.7	13.4	4/15
1967	8.3	6.9	1/16	15.2	13.6	4/16

Statistically, the conservative Packers may have benefited from the passing explosion more than any other team in the league, despite their lack of overall passing attempts. It was a tribute to Lombardi, Starr, and the coaching staff that the run-loving Packers could flawlessly adjust their attack and capitalize on the league's new offensive trend. Lombardi adapted perfectly to the changing times of the 1960s NFL, and his teams have the records and championships to substantiate that assertion.

In 1968, Vince Lombardi decided to step away from the playing field and took the position of Green Bay's general manager. During his coaching career, Lombardi was considered one of the shrewdest talent evaluators in the league, often acquiring latent talent for inadequate players or stars well past their prime. He was responsible for bringing aboard the likes of Bill Quinlan, Lew Carpenter, Fuzzy Thurston, Lee Roy Caffey, Willie Davis, Henry Jordan, Don Chandler, Carroll Dale, and many others. And though he was not quite as marvelous in the NFL draft, he did make several picks that would prove to be outstanding as well: defensive back Herb Adderley, in 1961 (Hall of Famer); linebacker Dave Robinson, in 1963 (all-star); running back Donny Anderson (who gained more than seventy-five hundred yards rushing and receiving in his nine-year career), in 1965; defensive end Lionel Aldridge, in 1963 (all-star); and even quarterback Daryle Lamonica (who signed with Buffalo of the AFL and later became an all-star for the Oakland Raiders), in 1963.

Green Bay hoped Lombardi could perpetuate their quest for championships by providing the Packers with a bevy of talented athletes every season. However—as Green Bay fans soon recognized—Lombardi the coach was much more effective than Lombardi the general manager. Lombardi himself quickly grew weary of his management position and was itching to get back on the sidelines. He realized that he was most effective on the field, not in an office.

The Packers fell to a record of 6–7–1 in 1968, under the direction of Vince's former defensive coordinator, Phil Bengston. After the season, realizing that the team was playing poorly, that he was suffering with an off-the-field management job, and that his presence was probably detracting from Bengston's authority, Lombardi felt that his situation had became untenable. In February of 1969, Vince Lombardi asked for and was granted a release from his contract with the Green Bay Packers. He was now free to negotiate with other NFL clubs.

A deal with the Washington Redskins had already been worked out before Lombardi's official release from Green Bay. Washington offered Vince two things the Packers could not—equity in the team (the Packers were a public franchise with investment restrictions) and the challenge of resurrecting another losing franchise, something that was of great attraction to Lombardi. On February 6, 1969, Lombardi took the job as head coach of the moribund Washington Redskins.

The last time Washington had a winning season was 1955. Thirteen years of frustrating, monotonous, losing football had turned the Redskins into a sorry collection of professional football players who had grown accustomed to defeat. During their thirteen years of misery, Washington had four different head coaches: Joe Kuharich, Mike

Nixon, Bill McPeak, and Otto Graham. Their overall record for the period was 57–105–10, for a .360 winning percentage.

Although Lombardi had successfully implemented a downfield passing scheme in Green Bay, he was still a proponent of the run-first mentality. In Washington, though, he drastically changed his offensive approach. He knew the Redskins were not nearly as talented as the worst team he had in Green Bay and that they were a very poor rushing team. In deference to his win-at-all-costs credo, Lombardi cast his lot with Redskins' future Hall of Fame quarterback Sonny Jurgensen rather than depend on the substandard Washington ground attack. The result was that the 1969 Redskins attempted more passes than rushes, 444–377, and they compiled the extraordinary statistic of 61.9 percent completions—almost 18 percent better than the league average of 52.6. Jurgensen led the NFL with 3,102 passing yards.

Needless to say, Lombardi won in Washington. He immediately changed the entire complexion and attitude of a second losing franchise, just as he had done in Green Bay. The Redskins finished at 7–5–2 that season and actually had hopes for a championship in 1970.

Unfortunately, Lombardi took ill shortly thereafter and would never again grace an NFL sideline. He died of complications from intestinal cancer on September 3, 1970. The entire league was anguished over the death of one of its icons. On July 30, 1971—just ten months after his passing—Vince Lombardi was enshrined in the Pro Football Hall of Fame.

The Packers, Redskins, and their 1960s counterparts played in an age with some of the greatest coaches of all time: George Allen, Blanton Collier, Tom Landry, Paul Brown, George Halas, and Don Shula. And one needs to remember that there were only twelve to fifteen teams for the majority of that era. But the Packers would take a backseat to no one in the coaching category. In fact, Lombardi won more NFL championships than any of those all-time greats. Lombardi was, by any standards, the consummate coach. He was demanding of his athletes, demanding of his coaches, demanding of himself, and ultimately demanding of victory. He never stopped learning, never stopped teaching, and never *ever* stopped long enough to lose.

During his career, Lombardi constantly attempted to incorporate new strategies and implement new schemes. And not just offensive and defensive schemes. One time, before a big game with George Halas's Chicago Bears, he even tried a little subterfuge. He changed his team's jersey numbers (a legal maneuver at the time) in order to confuse the Bears. Vince Lombardi needed to win football games. And however he had to— always within the rules—he would do it better and more often than anyone else.

Lombardi was as well-known for his quotes as he was for his coaching prowess. He was a highly paid lecturer and guest speaker at many business meetings and professional gatherings.

In *Strive to Excel*, by Jennifer Briggs, Lombardi was once quoted as saying:

Running a football team is no different than any other kind of organization— an army, a political party, or a business. The principles are the same. The object is to win—to beat the other guy. Maybe that sounds hard or cruel. I don't think it is.

It is a reality of life that men are competitive, and the most competitive games draw the most competitive men. That's why they are there—to compete, to know the rules and objectives when they get in the game. The object is to win fairly, and squarely, by the rules, but to win.

And winning is something no one did better than Lombardi. An unprecedented three straight NFL titles, five world championships (including the first two Super Bowls), and the equivalent of six division titles in just ten seasons.

Lombardi's career in professional football was marked by an unparalleled urgency to succeed, a highly desirable characteristic which he deftly transferred to his players. He instilled courage, fortitude, and the will to win in each and every one of his disciples. More than anything else, however, Vince Lombardi taught his players to strive for distinction, never to fear failure, and to expend immense effort to make themselves better—not just as football players, but as people as well. "Success is not in never falling," he would say, "but in getting back up when you fall."

Remarkably, more than thirty years after his passing, Lombardi's influence is still felt by many of his former players and colleagues. The typical Lombardi protocol of "You don't do things right once in a while, you do them right all the time," still rings true in their minds and influences their lives and decision-making policies on a daily basis. Many Packers players of the Lombardi era became enormously successful businessmen, some even millionaires. One of them was defensive end Willie Davis, who owns several radio stations in California and Wisconsin. "I adopted a lot of Lombardi's philosophy and wisdom in everything I do, every day," he said. "I believe that how we played the game of football was instrumental to us winning. And in the business world I found great confidence in thinking, 'Boy, I'm doing this the way Vince Lombardi would have done it.'"

Lombardi touched the lives of so many people it's hard to condense the slew of complimentary quotes down to a few. However—among his friends, disciples, coworkers, and players—none may have benefited more from his philosophies than defensive end Lionel Aldridge. Aldridge developed a debilitating form of schizophrenia after his career which nearly led to his demise. He lost his job, became homeless, and was at the lowest point a human being could tolerate before he turned his life around with the help of his spiritual nature and Vince Lombardi's sustaining guidance. "If I could just tell him one thing," Aldridge said, "I would just say, 'Thanks for giving me the space to share your life for a while.'"

Hall of Fame quarterback Bart Starr said, "The heart of Vince Lombardi's philosophy as a coach was that every player on his team be committed to excellence—to do his best, to use his God-given talents to the fullest, to win games. For Lombardi, there was no other way for his team to succeed. It was a philosophy Lombardi taught his players to apply, not just to achieve success on the football field, but to achieve success in life.

He told us, 'The quality of any man's life is in direct proportion to his commitment to excellence.'"

Hall of Fame fullback Jim Taylor categorized his coach this way: "He did what was required to keep us moving to a higher level. What he said then still pushes me to a higher level today. He could size people up and know what they would respond to, kind of like a psychologist or therapist. Today I can still hear him—talking about the will to win or how fatigue makes cowards of us all. He brought clichés to reality. He trained the mind to push the body. So much, he said, really wasn't about football at all, it was about character and being better. It could apply to anything."

Sam Huff—an NFL Hall of Fame linebacker whose career path coincided with Lombardi's both in New York and Washington—had a very simple yet insightful recollection of his former mentor. "It's almost a shame that he became a football coach," he said, "because he would have been a huge success in whichever field he endeavored to conquer."

Upon Lombardi's death, former mentor Earl Blaik—whom Lombardi once called the best coach he ever knew—said, "Vince Lombardi epitomized twentieth-century America by his devotion to his family and dedication to his church and country. He was recognized as a strong-willed man whose extraordinary success in life came from a seriousness of purpose and hard work. This, coupled with a remarkable intellect, made him the peer of his profession. He was volatile, sometimes gruff, but a lovable, loyal friend who somehow seemed indestructible."

Vince Lombardi *was* indestructible, because while he is no longer with us in life, he is indeed with us in spirit. Those who were fortunate enough to know the man—to truly understand him and appreciate his talents—would be forever and always changed for the betterment of their lives. "He had a covenant with greatness, more than any man I have ever known," said Edward Bennett Williams, Washington Redskins president in 1969, when Lombardi worked for that club. "He was committed to excellence in everything he attempted."

Lombardi's legacy is one of hard work, perseverance, intestinal fortitude, and victory. He preached honesty, integrity, and commitment to the players he directed. He embodied the characteristics of superior leadership as much or more than any man in the history of professional sports. Vince Lombardi was a "football coach's football coach." And there can be no doubt that he was destined for greatness in life, no matter which domain he ultimately chose to master.

Vince Lombardi's Coaching Capsule

Category	Numbers
Seasons	10
Wins	96
Losses	34
Ties	6
Winning pct.	.728
Pct. >/< Avg. Super Bowl-winning coach (.601)*	+21.1%
World championships†	5
World championship game appearances†	6
World championship pct. (champ/seasons)	.50
Losing seasons	0
Percentage of losing seasons	0%
Playoff record	9-1
Playoff winning percentage	.900
Average wins per 16 games (a current season)	11.6
Average losses per 16 games	4.4

NOTE: Ties count as a half-win and a half-loss in calculating percentages.
*See Epilogue
† Super Bowls or NFL Championships 1920–1965.

3 Years Before and After Lombardi

City	Years	Record	Percentage	Lombardi's Career Pct
				.728
Before				
Green Bay	1956–58	8–27–2	.243	
Washington	1966–68	17–22–3	.440	
After				
Green Bay	1968–70	20–21–1	.488	
Washington	1970–72	26–15–1	.619	

Yearly Records

Year	Team	Wins	Losses	Ties	Playoffs
1959	GB	7	5	0	
1960	GB	8	4	0	0–1
1961	GB	11	3	0	1–0*
1962	GB	13	1	0	1–0*
1963	GB	11	2	1	
1964	GB	8	5	1	
1965	GB	10	3	1	2–0*
1966	GB	12	2	0	2–0†
1967	GB	9	4	1	3–0†
1969	WAS	7	5	2	
Totals		96	34	6	9–1

*NFL Champions
† Won Super Bowl

Chapter 5

TOM LANDRY

I f you polled ex-players or coaches about the characteristics and personality of Tom Landry, the word most often associated with the man would undoubtedly be "stoic." The *American Heritage Dictionary* defines the word as meaning indifferent, or unaffected by pleasure or pain; impassive. On the sidelines during a game, Landry never displayed his feelings. Whether his team was ahead by thirty or behind by thirty, the neatly attired, conservative, thinking-man's football coach inevitably expressed little if any emotion. In fact, if any clue at all could be discerned from his facial dispositions, a person would likely have determined that Landry's teams were losing contests at a rate tantamount to that of the opponents of the Harlem Globetrotters. Quite astounding for a man who retired with 250 victories—third most in NFL history—and a winning percentage of over .600.

Thomas Wade Landry was born on September 11, 1924, in Mission, Texas. His father was an auto mechanic and a volunteer fireman. Landry suffered from two traumatic experiences in his early childhood. He was struck by a car and almost killed, and he developed a speech impediment that most likely accounted for his shy, introverted tendencies.

In high school, Landry excelled in football, leading his Mission High team to a 12–0 record and a regional state championship as a passer, runner, and punter. He received a scholarship from the University of Texas, and he enrolled there in the fall of 1942. As a student in Austin, Landry joined the army reserves, and as World War II escalated, he was called to active duty in 1943.

Landry became a pilot for B-17 bombers during the war. On one memorable mission over Czechoslovakia—a bombing run targeting German occupied areas of the country—Landry's plane began to run low on fuel. The crew made it out of the heavy area of flak that they encountered as they dropped their payload on the target; however, soon after heading back towards France and the English Channel, the aviators knew they would have to ditch. Landry, all of twenty years old, was dropping bombs on Nazi Germany and being asked to land planes in the backyards of eastern Europe. As luck would have it, Landry and his crew landed safely in a clearing, clipping off one wing and smashing the first several feet of the cockpit. Everyone, though, walked away from the crash, and the mission had been a success.

In 1946, Landry returned to the University of Texas, where he later starred for the Longhorns' football team as a quarterback, halfback, and defensive back. After studying engineering and graduating from Texas the semester after his football career ended (1949), Landry and his wife, Alicia, headed for New York City.

Landry had been selected by the New York Giants in the eighteenth round of the 1947 NFL draft. But he would not play for the Giants until the 1950 season. Instead, he played the 1949 season for the All-American Football Conference's (AAFC) New York Yankees, who were owned by the baseball team bearing the same name. After Landry's first season in the AAFC, the league was absorbed into the NFL. He wound up playing for the Giants, but *not* because he was drafted by them in 1947.

The AAFC players on teams other than Baltimore, San Francisco, and Cleveland (teams that were kept intact and merged into the new league) were drafted by the NFL with regional considerations observed. The New York Giants selected Landry, again, along with several other Yankees players. Landry played six years in the NFL (1950–1955), all with New York. Although he punted and occasionally played quarterback and running back, Landry was primarily a defensive back. Known for his jarring hits (some of which may have been considered late) and ball-hawking abilities—he had thirty-one interceptions in his career—Landry quickly rose to prominence in the league. He was named All-Pro in 1954. That same year, Landry's coaching career officially began. In retrospect, however, he had already been coaching for quite some time.

Steve Owen had been the Giants' head coach since 1931. Under his leadership, the Giants were very successful, winning more than 150 games in twenty-three years. Owen's unorthodox style was basically to give his players a general idea of the concepts he wanted to employ, then let them figure out the best way to execute the strategies during the week of practice. But as professional football moved into the late 1940s the game was changing, becoming much more sophisticated and complex. There were numerous ramifications with each new tactic, and players had to be educated on the best way to apply the strategy. Owen's nonchalant coaching manner—which had sufficed in the past—would be inadequate in the 1950s NFL.

Owen scouted the highly anticipated NFL season opener in 1950 between the league's reigning champion Philadelphia Eagles and the AAFC's four-time champion Cleveland Browns. New York was scheduled to play Cleveland two weeks later. After the game, Owen was amazed at how easily Cleveland had decimated Philadelphia's defense en route to their 35–10 victory.

The prevailing defense in the NFL at the time was the 5–3–3 (five defensive linemen, three linebackers, and three defensive backs). Philadelphia, however, had become somewhat famous for a modified version of that defense, as developed by their head coach Earle "Greasy" Neale. The Eagles' alignment replaced one of the linebackers with a fourth defensive back, creating a 5–2–4 setup. Before the game with Cleveland, Neale proclaimed that his scheme (with the extra defensive back) would be perfect to foil the Browns' potent aerial game. The defense obviously failed. In fact, it played right into the hands of Cleveland's head coach and master tactician, Paul Brown.

Cleveland's passing game relied heavily on timing patterns (a brilliant Paul Brown innovation) and crossing patterns. Timing patterns were precise, synchronized pass routes that enabled the quarterback to throw the ball before the receiver turned to look. Crossing patterns were designed to take advantage of a receiver's speed by sending him across the field in man-for-man coverage. The elimination of the third linebacker in Philadelphia's defensive arrangement made the Eagles especially vulnerable to Cleveland's crossing patterns. Cleveland receivers waited for their running backs (heading into the flat on opposite sides of the field) to draw Philadelphia's two linebackers to the sidelines. When the linebackers obliged, the middle of the gridiron was left completely uncovered. At that instant, the Browns' ends dashed across the field catching easy, short passes with no defenders in their path.

After witnessing Cleveland's massacre of Philadelphia and contemplating potential strategy, Owen concluded that a 6–1–4 defensive configuration would be the best alternative in an attempt to neutralize the Browns' attack. In his usual manner, he walked up to the chalkboard and briefly diagrammed the positional movements of the defenders in his new scheme. He then walked out of the room. The players were quite confused, having never seen that type of defense before. Uncharacteristically, Landry found himself rising up out of his chair and heading towards the board to begin a detailed explanation of what Owen desired from the defense. "We had never played that defense before," Landry said, "and I knew someone had to get up and explain it. I'd never done anything like that before [taking control of the meeting], but I just got up, went to the blackboard, and began to explain the defense in detail."

Landry's coaching career began with that blackboard session back in 1950. In fact, Landry later said, "I learned much of my coaching from playing under him [Owen], because I [constantly] had to work out the details of what he meant." Landry illustrated to the Giants' defense that Owen intended to have them form what looked like a 6–1 defense but in reality was more like a present-day professional football 4–3, a defense that Landry himself later advanced with the Cowboys. The strategy called for the two ends in the front six to drop into pass coverage much more frequently than rushing the quarterback. This would create double-team situations on the Browns' wide receivers. At the same time, the presence of the middle linebacker would fortify the center of the field. The four defensive backs would essentially form an "umbrella" pattern in the secondary, a format which was the precursor to the zone defense of the 1960s.

When the teams met on October 1, 1950, the defensive tactics worked to perfection. Cleveland and their future Hall of Fame quarterback, Otto Graham, were caught off guard. "We had a great day against the Browns that day," Landry said. "Graham didn't complete a pass in the first half against us. Certainly, that's one of the games I'll always remember." Not only did Graham fail to complete a single pass that half, but he also threw three interceptions. In the second half, Paul Brown adjusted to have Graham try to take advantage of the two ends dropping into coverage. Owen then countered by blitzing the ends and rushing Graham, confusing him even more. The Giants won the game 6–0, and Tom Landry's "coaching career" was off to an auspicious beginning. Landry the "teacher" had conveyed the essence of Owen's defensive strategy in complete detail, with no ambiguities, and the shutout of the NFL's premier offense was the proof.

Though New York defeated Cleveland and Paul Brown in their 1950 meeting, Landry learned a lot from the eminent head coach. "I can't say that I patterned my coaching style or philosophy after any one coach," he said, "but it is easy for me to point to the one man whose coaching played the biggest role in shaping both my football strategy and the kind of coach I became. That man was Paul Brown."

One lesson Landry learned from Brown was the limited effect that emotion had on the outcome of football games. Many coaches inspired their players into frenzied enthusiasm before encounters in hopes of gaining a critical edge. Brown, however, would have none of it. Though passion could be beneficial, Brown knew that it was simply a state of mind. It was not going to make a dramatic difference during a game and certainly wouldn't sustain a club throughout the course of a season. If one team's players were better, and/or they had the superior strategy, there would be very little the opposition could do to overcome that advantage. To depend on players to consistently achieve a higher emotional level than that of their opponents in order to win football games would surely be foolhardy, and sometimes counterproductive, Brown concluded. Landry himself recalled emotional moments during his playing career when he became more concerned with exacting revenge against a particular player rather than winning the game.

Paul Brown's logic and tactics crystallized in Landry the idea that football wasn't necessarily a game dominated by the most spirited, toughest, or strongest players. It was more a game of systems, technique, and teamwork, especially as the game evolved in the 1950s. "Paul Brown and his Cleveland teams changed the game into more of a science," Landry said. "They were a precision unit, and to have success against them you had to devise your own countermeasures of precision football." This philosophy would form the foundation for Tom Landry's theories and strategies over the next thirty years.

Just before the 1954 season, the New York Giants fired Steve Owen and brought in former player Jim Lee Howell to coach the club. As part of the deal with owner Tim Mara, Howell was permitted to hire two assistants who would manage the offense and defense while Howell concentrated more on administrative duties. Howell quickly sought out Landry to become player-coach of the defense.

The Giants' defensive unit improved immediately under Landry. In fact, New York permitted almost one hundred fewer points in 1954 than they did in the previous season (277–184). In 1955, the year Landry retired as a player, the Giants came within six points of leading the NFL in points allowed. Shortly thereafter, Landry designed a scientific play-recognition system—light years ahead of its time—that helped the Giants' immensely talented middle linebacker Sam Huff develop into a Hall of Famer.

Landry had come to believe that one of the most important aspects of defensive football was the ability of the defenders to know where the offense was going to attack. To that end, he devised an absolutely ingenious method of discerning an offense's strategy based on the position and movement of certain players. He called these hints "keys." In countless hours of viewing game films, Landry noticed that, by concentrating on his keys, he could often tell what play was being run the instant after the ball was snapped.

"Teams in those days only had a couple basic offensive formations; we called them red and brown," he said. "If a team set up in the red formation and the halfback went one way, you could expect one or two possible plays. If the fullback went the other direction you could expect one or two other plays." The offensive alignments and movement were limited enough that most defensive players had to learn only a few simple keys in order to have a general idea of the upcoming play. Sam Huff and the New York Giants exploited Landry's exquisite scheme and devastated NFL offenses for years to come.

Landry's counterpart with the Giants—the modern day equivalent of the team's offensive coordinator—was none other than Vince Lombardi. The triumvirate of Howell, Landry, and Lombardi became the best coaching staff in the NFL during that era, and maybe the best in league history. They led the Giants to an NFL championship in 1956 and title game appearances in 1958 and 1959.

In 1960, Landry interviewed for the position of head coach of an NFL expansion team, in Dallas. At the same time, however, Bud Adams—owner of the Houston franchise in the newly formed AFL—indicated an interest in the native Texan. Ultimately, Landry decided to stay in the NFL, and he accepted an offer from millionaire owner Clint Murchison, Jr., to become the first ever head coach of Dallas's NFL franchise.

Landry was very used to the surroundings in New York, where almost every player was an all-star. In Texas, it would be a situation in which almost every player would be a journeyman or a rookie, and Landry knew to expect a long hard road to success.

There was much tumult surrounding the initial player-acquisition ground rules for the newly designated Dallas Rangers. Millionaire Lamar Hunt had been lobbying the NFL to allow him to start a new franchise in the Dallas area for several years. When the league kept delaying a decision to expand, Hunt took matters into his own hands and started a rival organization—the American Football League—scheduled to begin play in 1960. With competition for the huge Texas football market, the NFL moved with haste. Dallas was formally admitted into the league in January of 1960 and would be owned by Murchison. They would play the 1960 season, but without the benefit of an opportunity to select players in the NFL draft, which, due to the anticipated battle for college players between the newly formed AFL and the NFL, had been moved up to November 1959. But Murchison, with the able assistance of George Halas—head coach and owner of the Chicago Bears—was proactive and took a gamble by signing two excellent college players, quarterback Don Meredith and running back Don Perkins, to personal services contracts during the five-month period when the NFL was deciding whether or not to admit a Dallas team, and well before the November draft.

In the league's expansion draft, Dallas was allowed to pick thirty-six players, taking a total of three athletes from each of the other twelve teams in the league. The existing clubs were permitted to protect twenty-five players, thereby exposing their remaining eleven members for selection. Each time a team lost a man, it was afforded the opportunity to recall another unprotected player. The Rangers were given twenty-four hours to make their choices.

The logistics of the expansion draft—given that teams could essentially protect every starting player they employed and that expansion franchises were excluded from participation in the college draft—made life as a member of the 1960 Dallas football organization miserable. It made life as the 1960 Dallas head coach—the man in charge of the whole mess—nearly intolerable. Things were so bad, talent-wise, that Landry had to coax former Redskins quarterback Eddie LeBaron out of retirement, as the coach was unwilling to throw the rookie Meredith to the wolves in his initial season. The good news was that LeBaron did sign with Dallas. The bad news was *also* that LeBaron signed with Dallas. The Cowboys were forced to give the Redskins their number-one pick in the 1961 college draft as compensation. One good thing did happen for Dallas in 1960, though. At the behest of General Manager Tex Schramm, owner Clint Murchison made a last-second decision to change the name of the club to the Cowboys instead of the Rangers. Otherwise, Tom Landry may have spent much of life coaching a baseball team (ha, ha).

Since Landry knew that the Cowboys would have problems winning games, he decided to incorporate another of his ingenious schemes into the team's offense with the hopes of at least making the club exciting to watch and drawing fans away from the AFL's Dallas Texans at the same time. Being one of the driving forces behind the development and implementation of the league's new fancy—the 4–3 defense—and the designer of the now widely utilized system of reading keys to diagnose plays, Landry set out to devise a complex strategy to defeat his own creations and help the Cowboys score points.

"I felt the best way to attack the 4–3 defense we'd established in New York was the multiple offense," he said. "I knew that defense so well I had a good idea of the best way to beat it. To be effective, the defense had to have the jump by recognizing the formation and then knowing what plays could be run from it. I felt if we used multiple sets, shifting from one to another, we could confuse the defense. They [Dallas's opponents] had worked all week on perfecting certain keys, and if we could destroy those keys we might be able to move the ball and have a chance even to win."

The most accomplished innovators occasionally fail in their attempts to push the envelope. And in football, one needs at least *some* talent to pull off even the best of strategies. Since the Cowboys were deprived of skilled athletes—given that they were unable to participate in the college draft and that few good players were available in the expansion draft—even an inspired, resourceful ploy that was likely ten years ahead of its time could not fortify the abused expansion team.

"Our guys were afraid to touch the football, it was so dangerous," Landry recalled of the 1960 campaign. "Eddie LeBaron used to raise his hand for a fair catch before taking the snap from center." Needless to say, the Cowboys' initial season did not go well. The club compiled a record of 0–11–1. They were outscored by an average of 31–15 each game and were last in the league in the following categories: points scored, points allowed, rushing yards, rushing yards allowed, average per rush against, opponent rushing touchdowns, and interceptions. If ever there was a team that defined and personified the term "expansion franchise," it was the Dallas Cowboys.

The Cowboys never won fewer than four games and never finished in last place from 1961–1963. But they also never won *more* than five games and never finished better than fifth (out of seven clubs) in the NFL's Western Division. Things had gotten so bad during the 1962 season that the players didn't even seem to know what plays were being called. Don Meredith called an audible at the line of scrimmage against the Browns. One of the Cowboys guards, Joe Bob Isbell, thought that he was supposed to pull and trap the defensive tackle. The other guard, Andy Cvercko, thought that he was supposed to be the pulling guard on the play. Essentially, it amounted to confusion as to which side of the field the play was supposed to be run. At the snap of the ball, both men headed to the other side of the line, colliding violently right in front of the quarterback and nearly knocking themselves out cold. Eighty thousand Cleveland fans thought it was rather funny. Landry and the two guards had differing viewpoints.

Early in 1964, after four years of dreadful football and a 13–38–3 overall record, Cowboys' fans began clamoring for a coaching change. And with some of the Dallas players characterizing their feelings towards Landry by saying it felt as though they were playing for the Pope—referring to Landry's deeply religious background—the situation reached a critical point. Something had to be done, and General Manager Tex Schramm knew what it was. On February 5, 1964, at the urging of Schramm, Clint Murchison, Jr., *extended* the contract of Tom Landry for a staggering ten-year period. Not many coaches with a record as inferior as that of Tom Landry—a man who had never even approached a winning season in the NFL—have their contracts extended, and certainly not for a decade. Landry later called it "the most significant thing that ever happened to me."

Upon hearing that a press conference was scheduled, Landry and everyone else had expected Murchison to make a change at the coaching position. It came as a total shock to everyone connected to the team that Landry was given an extension. "From then on, I really dedicated myself to be a football coach," Landry said.

The 1964 season brought more heartache for Landry and the Cowboys—a 5–8–1 record and another fifth-place finish. But 1964 was not all bad. Though at the time nobody really knew it, the building blocks for the future began to emerge. The 1964 NFL draft brought the Cowboys three players who would make significant contributions in the coming seasons. Mel Renfro, a defensive back and halfback from Oregon, was selected in the second round. Renfro would eventually excel as both a defensive back and a kick returner. Bob Hayes, a halfback from Florida A&M, was taken as a future pick in the seventh round. He ultimately switched to wide receiver in the NFL and became a major weapon in the Cowboys' offense. And quarterback Roger Staubach, the Heisman Trophy winner from the Naval Academy, was selected as a future pick in the tenth round. Staubach was obligated to perform a four-year tour of duty with the Navy and did not become eligible for the Cowboys until 1969. Despite the late start, he became a tremendous signal caller and a true leader for the Dallas organization.

The draft proved to be a vital instrument in the Cowboys' success. Dallas had already landed a gem in the 1961 draft, defensive lineman Bob Lilly, with a pick they received from the Browns. But in 1963, under the auspices of Schramm, the Cowboys moved into the computer age, becoming the first NFL team to successfully develop a software package for its scouting department. It took several years to fully integrate the software program into the Cowboys' system, but it paid huge dividends down the road.

Everything began to take shape in 1965, or at least that's what Landry and Dallas supporters initially thought. However, after a 2–0 start, the club suffered five straight rudely awakening defeats. Fans were livid, management couldn't have been happy, and Landry knew he had come to a crossroads. His starting quarterback had played dreadfully over the five-game losing streak. After seven contests, Don Meredith's completion percentage was only 38 percent, horrible for a five-year veteran. Rookie backups Craig Morton and Jerry Rhome were inserted at quarterback in game seven (against the Steelers), as Landry had seen enough of Meredith's exploits.

But Landry knew it wasn't all Meredith's fault. The offensive line was putrid, often giving Meredith little or no time in the pocket. And though the quarterback generally takes the blame when things go awry, it was obvious to Landry that the whole team had faded into the abyss. Meredith, being the honorable person that he was, stood up in the locker room after his dismal performance against Pittsburgh and took full responsibility for the team's woes. The media crowded around Landry in the post–Steelers game press conference, anxious for the coach's thoughts on the quarterback position and who would start the next week. "I haven't decided yet," the dejected coach said, "but after today it's safe to say I'm going to be reevaluating our quarterback situation."

"They were the two worst days of my life," Landry said, referring to the Monday and Tuesday after the Pittsburgh game. "We couldn't possibly win with a performance like Meredith had turned in against the Steelers. I had to go with one of the rookies."

But later, Landry's instincts told him differently. He was always wary of starting rookie quarterbacks, fearful of exposing them too soon and ruining whatever chance they may have in the future by shattering their confidence so early. He had done the same with Meredith, always hesitating to use him during his rookie campaign, which is why the club brought in Eddie LeBaron in the first place. "I tossed and turned for two miserable nights," Landry said. Then, on Wednesday, he called Meredith into his office. "He sat down," Landry said of the seemingly unflappable, devil-may-care Meredith, "face somber, ready for the blow he knew had to be coming. I looked at him and said, 'Don, I believe in you. You're my starting quarterback for the rest of the year.'" Meredith began to weep, as did his supposedly unemotional head coach.

There are many times when a coach gives in to the pressure of the situation and makes a change because it appears to be the safe way out—what the public wants. The rationale is that if it's the wrong decision then "everyone was wrong, not just me." That is something Tom Landry would never do, not in a million years. He and he alone made the football decisions in Dallas, and he and he alone would live with the consequences.

Meredith justified Landry's faith in him by having an excellent second half of the year in 1965. He rallied the Cowboys, and the team won five of their last seven contests to finish out the season with a .500 record. Landry was vindicated, and the Cowboys seemed as if they were on the road to success.

Tom Landry was a deeply religious man. He grew up a devout Christian, never yelled, and never swore. When Clint Murchison extended his contract in 1964, Landry said, "I reevaluated what my life purpose was. Being in God's plan, I felt it was a call-ing for me to coach." This quote makes one believe that Landry had contemplated leaving professional football and beginning a career elsewhere, as he apparently had to reconsider his "life purpose" in order to convince himself to remain a football coach. In retrospect, every Cowboys fan of the last thirty years should breathe a sigh of relief that he did reassess his plight. Beginning in 1966, Landry radically changed the fortunes of the Dallas Cowboys.

After a bye in the opening week of the season, Dallas proceeded to win their first four games. They beat New York 52–7, Minnesota 28–17, Atlanta 47–14, and Philadelphia 56–7—for an aggregate whipping of 183–45. And this was a team with a six-year prior record of 25–53–4, for a .329 percentage. Meredith seemed to have a newfound confi-dence. He had an awesome year and was the catalyst for the team (table 5-1).

The Cowboys finished the season at 10–3–1, winning the Eastern Conference crown for the first time. Dallas's success was fortuitous in that 1966 was the first year of the Super Bowl. The winner of the playoff game between the Cowboys and the Western Conference Champion Green Bay Packers—to be played in Dallas—would advance to the NFL's new championship venue.

The vaunted Packers, led by the revered Vince Lombardi, were likely the best team in NFL history to that point. They had won championships in 1961, 1962, and 1965 and were the considerable favorite to take the NFL crown and make history by winning the first Super Bowl. But the Landry-led Cowboys were not going to be a pushover. Landry had resurrected the Dallas franchise and molded it into a menacing

Table 5-1. Don Meredith's 1966 Passing Performance

Year	Att	Comp	Comp%	Yards	YPA	TD	INT	Rating
1966	344	177	51.57	2805	8.15	24	12	87.7

Table 5-2. Dallas–Green Bay 1966 Team Statistics

	Dallas	Green Bay
Points scored	445*	335
Points allowed	239	163*
Rushing touchdowns	24*	18
Rushing touchdowns allowed	6*	9
Average per rush	4.5	3.5
Average per rush against	3.3	3.7
Average per pass attempt	8.1	8.9*
Average per pass attempt allowed	6.1	5.9*
Passing touchdowns	27	18
Passing touchdowns allowed	17	7*
Interceptions (offense)	14	5*
Interceptions (defense)	17	28*

* Led league

foe. Statistically the Cowboys matched up rather favorably with one of the fiercest football teams of the era (table 5-2).

The Cowboys appeared to possess the more potent offensive club, especially on the ground. But the NFL's Western Conference was generally considered to be the tougher of the two conferences at that time, possibly mitigating against some of Dallas's statistical achievements. In any event, the Cowboys presented a talented bunch of hungry athletes aspiring for national prominence, and what better place to gain that notoriety than in a championship game at the expense of the vaunted Green Bay Packers.

Dallas fought back courageously from an early 14–0 deficit, but the champion Packers ultimately prevailed 34–27. Late in the game, the Cowboys had the ball at the Green Bay two-yard line with a chance to tie the score. However, defensive back Tom Brown intercepted a Don Meredith fourth-down pass in the end zone to preserve the Packers' victory. Though Dallas had lost their first ever playoff contest, the game marked the beginning of an era when the Dallas Cowboys were, perhaps, the most dominant team in the National Football League, a team that would come to define the essence of a man who was recognized and respected as one of the foremost innovators and strategic masterminds in the history of professional football, Tom Landry.

In 1967, the Cowboys went 9–5 and won the new Capitol Division of the NFL. Landry's squad met Paul Brown's Cleveland team in the playoffs, in Dallas. The Cowboys controlled the game from the outset, stomping the Browns 52–14. The victory over Cleveland set up a rematch with the Packers in the 1967 NFL championship. This time, the game would be played in Green Bay, where the weather was always a factor in December.

According to Landry's autobiography, Landry's wife, Alicia, took the call. "Good morning. It's 8 A.M. and the temperature is now sixteen degrees . . . *below zero*," said the operator at the Cowboys' hotel in Green Bay.

The Cowboys were in trouble. The Packers were much better equipped to handle the adverse weather conditions—a fact that became obvious when Green Bay surged to a 14–0 advantage early in the second quarter. Dallas, however, stormed back into the game when the Packers made two mistakes late in that same period. Deep in Green Bay territory, Dallas defensive tackle Willie Townes hit Packers quarterback Bart Starr and jarred the ball loose. Defensive end George Andrie scooped up the pigskin and returned it seven yards for a touchdown. The Cowboys converted another Packers fumble into a field goal to pull within 14–10 at the half.

In the second half, the temperature was well on its way to absolute zero, checking in at a balmy twenty below zero with windchills approaching forty below. The Packers' new heating system underneath the field had failed, and the turf was freezing quickly. The contest began to resemble more of a hockey game where the players forgot to bring their skates, as individuals from both sides had their hands (or feet, as it were) full just trying to stay upright. But Dallas somehow managed to turn on the "heat" and launched several drives while the Packers had great difficulty mustering as much as a first down on their possessions. Unfortunately for Dallas, each Cowboys drive ended with no points. A missed field goal and a fumble stymied the Dallas attack. Landry, however, used a little subterfuge to produce points on the initial play of the final quarter.

Still trailing 14–10, Landry instructed Don Meredith to call the halfback option pass to Lance Rentzel, a flanker that Landry had acquired from the Minnesota Vikings before the season started. Rentzel had a questionable reputation in Minnesota, but Landry was willing to take a shot on the former second-round pick from Oklahoma because he was a gifted football player, and the Cowboys needed help at his position. The move paid off, as Rentzel caught fifty-eight passes for a 17.2-yard average and eight touchdowns in 1967. His ninth touchdown came on the next play.

Meredith handed off to Dan Reeves who began to sweep to the left side of the Cowboys' line. As the Packers' defenders came up to meet Reeves—totally unprepared for the possibility that the Cowboys might attempt an option pass in the terrible weather conditions—Rentzel, who was about eight yards downfield, faked a block and ran by the defensive back. Reeves faked his run and pulled up for the toss to his wide-open teammate. Perfection! Green Bay was completely surprised, and Dallas took the lead, 17–14. Landry later explained that Reeves, a right-handed thrower, would usually run the option to his right. So when the moment presented itself, the Cowboys decided to try the play the opposite direction, hoping to catch the Packers off guard. They did, and Dallas was less than one quarter away from the Super Bowl.

A little less than five minutes remained in the game when Green Bay, still trailing by three points, began a drive at their own thirty-two-yard line. The trick was, at that point in the "hockey game," to try and maintain your footing as everyone around you fell down. The Packers, living closer to Canada, were apparently the superior skaters. Two plays were crucial in the twelve-play drive. As several Cowboys slipped and fell, therefore missing tackles, Packers halfback Donny Anderson and fullback Chuck Mercein took short passes and turned them into long gains. The result was a Green Bay first down at the Dallas two-yard line with about fifty seconds remaining.

On first-and-goal, Anderson slipped and could only get about half a yard. On second down, Anderson slipped again but was able to move the ball inside the one. Bart

Starr called the Packers' last time-out with just sixteen seconds remaining and went to the sidelines to deliberate with Lombardi. Green Bay had two major decisions to make during the short break. First, should they just kick the field goal on third down and take their chances in overtime? Second, if they did run a play, exactly what play would they choose? It would almost surely have to be a pass into the end zone or a rollout option—run or pass. The latter would allow them to stop the clock with an incompletion or by running out of bounds. Any other play in the middle of the field would be too risky. If they were stopped short of the goal line and tackled inbounds, the clock would certainly run out before they could line up for a fourth-down try.

Although there is much disagreement as to who said what and why the play was called, the bottom line is that the Packers decided on the most unlikely of the apparent choices. Green Bay attempted a running play in the middle of the field—a quarterback sneak. If the Cowboys stopped them the game would be over. As the play unfolded, Green Bay center Ken Bowman made the key block, leveraging himself to move Dallas tackle Jethro Pugh just far enough to allow Bart Starr to sneak through for the touchdown. Green Bay prevailed 21–17 and went on to win another Super Bowl.

The Cowboys were devastated, searching for answers as to the implausible Lombardi call. To make matters worse, a replay clearly indicated that Packers right guard Jerry Kramer had moved before the snap of the ball. There was no penalty called, however. "In a goal-line situation like that you key the football," Jethro Pugh said later, "and I could visualize Kramer's hand moving just before the ball did. My first thought was, 'We got 'em, he's offsides, and that'll cost them five yards.' I was shocked when I didn't see a flag. I kept looking around for one."

Landry was bewildered yet realistic after the game. "I can't believe that [play] call," he said. "But now it's a great call."

The two championship game losses to the Packers stung the Cowboys' psyche. Unfortunately, there would be more trauma and discomfort in Dallas's future, and the team would need to be emotionally stable in order to handle the setbacks.

In 1968, the Cowboys won their division with a 12–2 record; they felt primed for a "Super" showing in the postseason. It was not to be, however. The Cleveland Browns, aided by home-field advantage, upset Dallas 31–20 in the Eastern Conference championship game. Don Meredith was intercepted several times, and after the game he was so distraught he refused to fly home with the team.

"A whole year shot down in two and a half hours," was how Tex Schramm assessed the carnage. Landry, as expected, was also quite depressed, saying, "This is my most disappointing day as a coach."

If there was a bright side, Dallas was still a young team. And their regular season performance, as measured by their statistical superiority, was certainly indicative of a club with championship potential (table 5-3).

Dallas's defensive accomplishments in 1968 could be attributed to yet another in the long line of Landry innovations. Back when he was coaching the Giants, Landry and Steve Owen instituted the basic structure of the 4–3 defense. Later, Landry

Table 5-3. Dallas Cowboys' League Rankings, 1968 (16 Teams in NFL)

Points	1st
Points allowed	2nd
Rushing yards	2nd
Rushing yards allowed	1st
Average per rush	3rd
Average per rush against	1st
Touchdowns rushing	1st
Touchdowns allowed rushing	1st*
Passing yards	1st

*Tied all-time NFL record (2)

added to its effectiveness by developing his famous "keys" to reading offensive plays. However, the NFL does not allow teams to patent specific concepts, a fact which permits opposing coaches to utilize other teams' strategies and encourages organizations to develop new methods and ideas in order to stay one step ahead of their competition. After many teams adopted all or parts of Landry's 4–3 defense, and after offenses discovered a few weak points in the standard 4–3 alignment, the Cowboys' leader commenced work on a new defensive tactic he hoped would confound his opponents.

The origins of the "flex" defense can actually be traced back to 1964. That year, Landry began to gradually implement a novel strategy for his defensive linemen. In traditional defensive schemes, linemen were asked to either penetrate into the backfield and seek out the ballcarrier or to neutralize their blocker in a head-to-head confrontation. The latter tactic enabled a player to defend two gaps—the spaces to his immediate right and left—where the ballcarrier could run through the line. Both of these procedures were sound, except that they tended to work best for the teams with the biggest, strongest, quickest players—something that the Cowboys usually lacked early in their existence. In the flex defense, no penetration was necessary, and players were never asked to control two gaps. The concept called for defensive linemen to slant and maintain their position in one gap. At that point, they were instructed to wait for the ballcarrier to approach them while the rest of the defense surrounded the play. This gave the less gifted Dallas linemen the advantage of not having to take on more powerful blockers in a point-blank, brute-force matchup while guessing where (in which gap) the back was going to go. Instead, they just needed to occupy a single gap and let the play develop. When properly executed, the flex defense forced the ballcarrier to adjust his route—as there was no hole through which to run—and *then* the defensive linemen reacted to him along with the other defenders. Landry's scheme asked a lot of its middle linebacker, as he would still be responsible for two gaps and was the focal point of the entire defense. But the Cowboys had a great middle linebacker in Lee Roy Jordan, and he was terrific at almost anything he did on the football field. The one drawback to the system was that it was heavily dependent on pursuit and could therefore become susceptible to cut-backs and counterplays.

Underneath the trademark fedora was the brain of a defensive mastermind. After opposing offenses figured out his 4-3 defense, Tom Landry threw the new "Flex" defense at them, spurring the Cowboys on to even more success.

To augment his new strategy, Landry devised a staggered front-four design in which his linemen stationed themselves in an uneven pattern across the line of scrimmage. The right end and left tackle would line up in their conventional places, right up against the helmet of their counterpart offensive lineman. But the right tackle and left end would line up a half yard or so back from the line of scrimmage. This ploy afforded the two offset linemen more time to decipher the play, more space to take advantage of their quickness, better control of their gap responsibilities, and a different look to confuse the offensive blocking assignments.

Since the flex defense and its new techniques were brand new for the players in 1964, it took a few years for the defenders to adapt and let their old instincts fade. However, by 1966 and 1967, the defense started to pay dividends. And by 1968, with even better players and more practice, it was incredibly effective.

Landry's cutting-edge defensive strategies and innovative offensive schemes had shaped the Cowboys and prepared them for success. It was just a matter of time, Landry thought immediately prior to the 1969 season, before Dallas would make that Super Bowl trip at the end of a year. They would have to do so, unfortunately, without the services of quarterback Don Meredith, who retired at the conclusion of the 1968 campaign.

Luckily, Craig Morton, a first-round product of the Cowboys' computer drafting system in 1965, seemed ready to lead an NFL offense. Morton had been groomed in typical Landry fashion, never having been thrust into extensive action before he was adequately prepared. The care taken in the development of Morton paid immediate dividends as the novice starter played very well from the outset of the 1969 season. He threw for twenty-one touchdowns and compiled an 85.4 quarterback rating. Roger Staubach, selected as a future pick in 1964, was back from his naval maneuvers and assumed the role as backup signal caller.

Along with Morton, rookie running back Calvin Hill—a first-round selection from Yale—and veteran wide receiver "Bullet" Bob Hayes enjoyed outstanding seasons in 1969. Hill gained more than 940 yards while averaging 4.6 yards per carry. Hayes, who had already established himself as one of the most effective wideouts in the league, caught forty passes and averaged almost nineteen yards per catch despite missing four games due to injury (table 5-4).

Dallas turned in another dominating regular-season performance in 1969, finishing with an 11–2–1 record and capturing the Capitol Division title for the third consecutive year (table 5-5).

Table 5-4. Bob Hayes's Wide Receiver Performance, 1965–69

Year	Receptions	Yards	Average	TDs
1965	46	1003	21.8*	12*
1966	64	1232	19.3	13*
1967	49	998	20.4	10
1968	53	909	17.2	10
1969	40	746	18.7	4

*Led league

Table 5-5. Dallas Cowboys' League Ranking, 1969 (16 Teams in NFL)

Points	2nd
Points allowed	4th
Rushing yards	1st
Rushing yards allowed	1st
Average per rush	3rd
Average per rush against	3rd
TDs rushing	1st
TDs allowed rushing	1st
Passing yards	3rd

Once more, however, a promising season had a disastrous conclusion. In the conference championship game in Dallas, the Cowboys were again defeated by the Cleveland Browns, 38–14. The game was out of reach by the middle of the second quarter.

Something, it seemed, was amiss with the Dallas Cowboys. Landry himself began to experience self-doubt, desperately seeking to unlock the mystery as to why the Cowboys couldn't quite mesh in the postseason. Although earlier in his tenure he had instituted a quality-control routine for the club—one in which films of each play were reviewed and then critiqued on every aspect of those attempts—Landry was unable to pinpoint the exact cause of the team's problems. "I guess we'll have a complete reevaluation," he said. "When you finish first in the league offensively and third defensively and then it all comes down to nothing, you have to reevaluate. Perhaps there is a reason, something I should have seen but overlooked. I just don't know what it is."

In an attempt to solve his dilemma, Landry secluded himself in his own version of a think tank shortly after the 1969 season. He desperately needed to find out why the team had been unable to capitalize on at least one of the opportunities they had to advance to the Super Bowl in the last four years. He came to two basic conclusions. First, he steadfastly believed that with each playoff loss the tension mounted, making each successive attempt that much more difficult. Until Dallas could win the big game, there was little Landry could do about the subconscious aspect of the problem, except to reassure the players that they were very talented and that they would soon have their day in the sun. The second issue, he believed, was the overall attitude of the team. If the Cowboys were getting complacent and/or weary of the playoff losses of the past four seasons, perhaps that was a major cause for the underachievement of the squad. So Landry set out to ascertain the true mind-set of the Dallas Cowboys, and he needed to be sure the results would not in any way be skewed by the data collection process.

Each player was asked to complete an anonymous survey of the entire organization, from training and practice routines, to the game plans, to the offensive and defensive philosophies, to the discipline of the club and more. "We asked players to define certain words relative to football, like commitment and mental toughness, to tell us what they thought we needed to change to win a championship, and why they believed we lost to the Packers and the Browns," Landry said.

The decision to poll players and reappraise the team's methods would have been thought ludicrous by most, if not all, NFL teams of the era. But Landry was not your ordinary administrator, and he truly believed that the opinions of his athletes mattered, contrary to his image as a "robot" coach. Most players agreed that the club's philosophies were appropriate and dependable. The most common observations were that perhaps the team spent too much time preparing for games, and maybe they needed to be more physical and use less of a big-play/finesse style, that the club needed to change the training methods relative to conditioning and strength, and that there were too many cliques on the team, creating a separation of groups.

So Landry instituted the following changes during the winter months of 1970:

1. He brought aboard former Olympic weightlifting coach Alvin Roy to restructure the team's training program.

2. He appointed Dan Reeves as player/coach to act as a buffer between the players and the coaching staff.

3. He sent out a letter to all players stating that no one was assured of a job and that all positions would be wide open for competition in training camp.

4. He detailed a new "performance standards" method of player evaluation and informed the team that individuals not meeting the appropriate levels would be subject to disciplinary action or release.

In April of 1970, Dallas raised some eyebrows by selecting running back Duane Thomas with their first pick in the NFL draft. The Cowboys were already solid at halfback, as Calvin Hill had performed admirably as a rookie in 1969. Why then did the Cowboys take a shot on Thomas, a player notorious for his temper tantrums and stubborn streaks?

Before the draft, Landry and Dallas scout Red Hickey discussed Thomas in detail. Hickey held back no punches, informing Landry that Thomas was likely the best player available but that he had an attitude that would make Attila the Hun look like a choirboy. He could be the steal of the draft, or a time bomb waiting to explode. When the Cowboys' turn came at the twenty-third spot in the first round, Thomas was still on the board. Since Dallas's computer system supported Hickey's appraisal of Thomas' on-the-field abilities, and with no one else jumping off the scouting page at Landry and his coaches, the Cowboys took a chance on the moody running back.

As the 1970 season was about to begin, Dallas received some discouraging news. Due to a bad shoulder that had not responded as quickly as anticipated after off-season surgery, Craig Morton would be sidelined for at least two games. That meant that Roger Staubach, in only his second year, would have to start at quarterback. The twenty-eight-year-old Navy alumnus was immediately overmatched, and though the Cowboys won their first two contests, it was in spite of Staubach and not because of him. Morton returned in week three, and while he was very rusty, he was better than the inexperienced Staubach. Eight weeks into the season, the Cowboys found themselves at 5–3 but far from the team they had been in the four previous years. Dallas then suffered one of the most embarrassing defeats in team history, a 38–0 shellacking at the hands of the St. Louis Cardinals on *Monday Night Football*.

Landry was shaken. The players were dejected. Dallas was 5–4, three games behind the NFC East–leading Cardinals, and all but eliminated from playoff contention. At that point, the pressure and anxiety that had been building for the last four years finally reached dire proportions, and the mental perspective of the team began to deteriorate rapidly. The myriad of organizational changes that had improved the Cowboys' psychological state at the beginning of the year now seemed to be of little benefit. Morale was extremely low, and if the team's vitality was not restored quickly, Landry risked losing control of the club. In this overwhelming atmosphere of desperation and despair, however, Landry did not panic. He assessed the situation and came up with what he believed was the only viable solution. His vast football experience, covering three decades of competition, had taught him one great lesson in motivation and human nature. "As a general rule," he said, "a coach needs to be most demanding when his team is doing well, because there's a human tendency to ease up when you're winning. When things are going poorly, especially when the effort is there, that's when a team needs encouragement and affirmation more than it needs pressure from the coach. That's the time to back off."

The next practice, Landry shocked the team by telling them, "We're just gonna go out today and play *touch football*." That was it. The Dallas Cowboys, coached by the supposedly stoic and rigid Thomas Wade Landry, were going to loosen up and have fun. "Blasphemous," some said. "Check his pulse. Does he have a temperature?"

So the Cowboys went out on the field and played a good, old-fashioned game of touch football. Defensive players were playing on offense. Huge offensive linemen were playing defensive back. The whole team was having fun, forgetting the present dilemma of the franchise for a few hours. Landry himself, "Mr. No-nonsense," was laughing and enjoying the circus-like atmosphere of practice that day. "The fans, the press, everybody was down on us," said Lee Roy Jordan. "Tom seemed to indicate to us that if we did anything the rest of the year we'd have to do it ourselves. So we got together, *really* got together, and decided everybody was against us and all we had was ourselves."

Landry made only one legitimate football determination that week. He decided to begin calling the plays for Craig Morton, who had been struggling at the time. Always of the belief that Morton was a talented quarterback, Landry decided to lighten the mental load on his signal caller, hoping to improve his performance by having him concentrate solely on executing the offense. It worked. Morton caught on fire, and the team systematically dismantled each and every one of their remaining five opponents, finishing the year at 10–4. The Cardinals—as if they were part of an orchestrated plan to revive the tenuous Dallas franchise—collapsed and folded, falling to third place in the division and finishing their season at 8–5–1. "It [the circumstances surrounding the 1970 season] was the most amazing thing I had ever experienced in my career," Lee Roy Jordan later said.

The Cowboys' defense finished the 1970 season with a string of twenty-three consecutive quarters in which they did not permit a touchdown. The club allowed only fifteen points in the last four regular-season games. The defense became the squad's calling card and was instrumental in the team's postseason fate. In the first NFL playoff game without a touchdown in twenty years, Dallas's defense tackled Detroit quarterback Greg Landry (no relation) for a safety and intercepted a late fourth-quarter pass to secure a 5–0 Cowboys victory at the Cotton Bowl.

Dallas beat the 49ers 17–10 the next week in San Francisco, despite a poor performance by Morton (seven completions in twenty-two attempts for 101 yards). Again, the Dallas defense stifled their opposing quarterback, John Brodie, who threw two interceptions.

Duane Thomas, who had been productive all season—especially when Calvin Hill was sidelined with several minor injuries throughout the year—was dazzling in the playoff win at San Francisco. He carried the ball twenty-seven times for 143 yards and a touchdown. For the season, Thomas averaged well over five yards per carry (table 5-6).

Dallas had finally made it—the Super Bowl! They faced the Baltimore Colts in Miami, Florida, on January 17, 1971. The game matched two of the better defenses in the NFL against each other. The Baltimore defense was especially stingy versus the run, having allowed only 3.7 yards per carry and just six rushing touchdowns all season. This was of great concern to the Cowboys' staff, because even though Craig Morton enjoyed one of his better regular seasons that year, he had been awful in the postseason, and Dallas was anything but a passing team. In fact, the Cowboys threw the fewest passes of any club in the NFL that year (297). True to form, Baltimore was able to limit Duane Thomas to just thirty-five yards on eighteen carries, forcing Dallas to throw the football. In a weird and whacky contest—punctuated by fourteen penalties and ten turnovers—the Colts beat the Cowboys 16–13 on a last-second field goal by Jim O'Brien. Craig Morton continued his terrible postseason performance, completing twelve of twenty-seven attempts for only 127 yards and three interceptions.

The famous Lilly helmet toss that is so vividly captured for posterity at the end of NFL Films' recap of Super Bowl V accurately portrayed the disgust and anguish that the Cowboys felt as the field goal sailed through the uprights. But there was light at the end of the tunnel. Dallas had finally breached their Super Bowl barrier and could now hope that the fate of the Colts, who had redeemed themselves after tasting Super Bowl defeat in 1969, would become that of the Cowboys in the very near future. Landry saw reason for hope as well, citing the way the club had bonded when the Cardinals' debacle threatened the team's confidence in November. He expected big things in 1971, which, at that point in Cowboys' history, meant nothing other than a Super Bowl victory.

Table 5-6. Duane Thomas, 1970 Performance

Attempts	Yards	Average	TDs
151	803	5.3	5

What would a season be if not for a few well-placed roadblocks to guard the path of success?

The time bomb named Duane Thomas began to tick louder in July of 1971. Thomas needed money due to the fact that he had hired an unscrupulous agent out of college and that he had saved little of the salary he earned in his rookie season (about seventy-five thousand dollars). At first, he was a no-show at the Cowboys' Thousand Oaks training camp. Then he demanded that his contract be renegotiated and that a friend be given a tryout by the Cowboys. Dallas refused on both accounts. In a bizarre turn of events, the Cowboys worked out a trade with the New England Patriots and received halfback Carl Garrett and a number-one pick in return for the insubordinate running back. Thomas, however, refused to take a drug test with New England and did not respond well to the Patriots' coaching staff. The trade was later nullified by the league, and Thomas was sent back to Dallas. He did not show up at the Cowboys' facilities, though, until the third game of the season.

The whole time, the Cowboys had even bigger problems. They had Calvin Hill to take Thomas's place, but Craig Morton was still hampered by the sore arm he had dealt with for two seasons, and Landry was not very enamored with the concept of starting the still inexperienced Staubach. During the August preseason games, neither quarterback distinguished himself enough for Landry to choose between them. So Landry took a gamble and decided to alternate the two in the regular season, Morton starting the first game and Staubach the second. Dallas found itself at 2–1 after the third week of the year, but again, neither signal caller had taken the opportunity to wrest the position away from the other.

As the Cowboys prepared for week four, Duane Thomas made an appearance at Cowboys' headquarters. He was ready to honor his initial contract and came to play ball—as best he could, having missed all of training camp and three regular-season games. Landry didn't know how long it would take to get Thomas in condition, but Hill was playing well so there was no emergency.

Or was there?

In the Giants' game that week, Hill went down with an injury, so Landry decided to give Thomas a chance after only a few days of training . Thomas carried nine times for sixty yards. "Duane is just an amazing fellow," Landry said after the game. "He is a great natural runner and just doesn't make many mistakes." Thomas was back for now, but he would soon find trouble again.

Meanwhile, Roger Staubach was fuming. Landry had pulled Staubach in the middle of the Giants' game, and Dallas—led by Morton—came back to gain the victory. After the game, Landry approached Staubach, but before he could utter a word Staubach cut him off by saying, "Coach, just don't say anything. You'll never understand me! What you did by pulling me was uncalled for. You'll just never understand me!"

Landry was stunned by Staubach's confrontational reaction, but Landry had only done what he felt was right for the Cowboys by benching the inconsistent quarterback. On the other hand, Staubach had a point. He was twenty-nine years old, had been promised a chance at the starting job, and had never been given more than a cursory look for a game or so. He wasn't a third-year, twenty-five- or twenty-six-year-old player; he was a third-year player going on thirty. Finally, after a loss to the Chicago Bears in week seven of the 1971 season—a game in which Landry alternated his quarterbacks on each *play*—Landry made a decision. He called Staubach at his home and told him that he would be the starting quarterback for the remainder of the year. "I won't let you down, Coach," Staubach said.

"Both quarterbacks have played well," Landry told the media the following day. "But I will go with Roger just in case some of the indecisiveness about the situation [alternating quarterbacks] is truly upsetting to our team. Roger will make mistakes, but I'm confident he'll do the job and keep improving."

When Staubach took over, Dallas stood at 4–3. In what had become typical Dallas Cowboys' style, the team finished fast, winning their remaining seven games to complete the year at 11–3. They captured the Eastern Division title and firmly established themselves as the team to beat in the NFC. Staubach was simply incredible (table 5-7).

The postseason began with a visit to Minnesota to play the Vikings. Although the Cowboys were outgained 311–183, Dallas survived the contest 20–12. Staubach threw one touchdown pass, and Thomas ran for the other. In the NFC championship game, the Cowboys faced the 49ers again, this time in Dallas. Despite another poor performance by the offense (Staubach passed for only 103 yards), the Cowboys won the game 14–3. Dallas's "Doomsday Defense" picked off three of thirty John Brodie passes and held the 49ers to nine first downs.

The Cowboys celebrated their championship game victory, but it was a modest scene in the clubhouse. As Landry had always preached, "Emotion can cover up a lot of inadequacies, but in the end it also gets in the way of performance." The team could be happy and accept the moment, but they could not let their excitement get the best of their psyches. The Cowboys still had a game to play—a game they *had* to win.

On January 16, 1972, more than eighty-one thousand people turned out for the Miami Dolphins–Dallas Cowboys Super Bowl at Tulane Stadium in New Orleans, Louisiana. Miami, just two years removed from being the laughingstock of the old AFL, had undergone a resurgence led by their inimitable head coach, Don Shula. They featured a run oriented, ball control attack spearheaded by future Hall of Fame fullback Larry Csonka and halfback Jim Kiick. When the Dolphins did pass, a pair of future Hall of Famers, quarterback Bob Griese and wide receiver Paul Warfield, formed one of the finest deep combinations in the NFL. The Cowboys also had a terrific array of offensive talent: Staubach, Thomas, Hill, Hayes, Alworth, and tight end Mike Ditka. Even though the Cowboys' offense had struggled in the playoffs, Dallas's 406 points were by far the most scored in the NFL.

Table 5-7. Roger Staubach's 1971 Passing Performance

Year	Att	Comp	Comp%	Yards	YPA	TD	INT	Rating
1971	211	126	59.7	1882	8.92	15	4	104.8

Table 5-8. Dallas–Miami 1971 Defensive Statistics

	Dallas	Miami
Points	222	174
Rushing yards	1144	1661
Average per rush	3.2	4.1
Rushing TDs	8	10
Completion percentage	49.6	56.7
Passing yards	2660	2293
Average per pass	6.3	6.3
Interceptions	26	17

But the key to the contest would prove to be the defenses. Although Miami had permitted fewer points on the season, 174 versus Dallas's 222, the Dolphins gave up an average of 4.1 yards per carry on the ground while Dallas permitted the NFL–leading total of 3.2. In fact, Dallas's defense was superior in just about every statistical category one could think of *except* points (table 5-8).

The game was never really in doubt. Although the score at the half was only 10–3 Cowboys, Dallas was clearly the superior team from the outset. Miami managed only eighty yards on the ground all game (well below their seasonal average of 174) while the Cowboys thundered to a Super Bowl–record 252 rushing yards and twenty-three first downs. The result was a 24–3 Dallas victory. Duane Thomas, who, as it turned out, was appearing in his last game for the Cowboys, carried nineteen times for ninety-five yards. He was equally effective running inside or outside. Quarterback Roger Staubach played mistake-free football, completing twelve of nineteen passes for 119 yards and two touchdowns. Dallas outgained the Dolphins overall, 352–185. "This game was a tremendous effort," Staubach said. "Our offense played better than it had in the previous two playoff games, and our defense always plays well."

The monkey was off their backs—the Cowboys were world champions! Looking back on the team's preparation for the game, Landry remarked, "You could feel the confidence build during practice. You could see it in our players' eyes. By the time we took the field I had no doubt we'd crossed that last psychological hurdle."

Dallas won ten games in each of the next two seasons (1972–1973) before losing in the NFC championship game both times. The Washington Redskins took conference honors by defeating the Cowboys 26–3 in 1972, while the Vikings toppled Dallas 27–10 the next year. In 1974, the Cowboys experienced their only non-double-digit-winning season in the fourteen-year period from 1968 to 1981, as they compiled an 8–6 slate and missed the playoffs. After that disappointing campaign, the news got even more gloomy. Bob Lilly, Cornell Green, and Walt Garrison all retired, Bob Hayes was traded, and Calvin Hill left the NFL for the newly formed World Football League. The Cowboys were beginning to lose the core of their Super Bowl–winning club, and many experts dismissed the team as a title threat. But Landry and the Cowboys still had a few tricks up their sleeve.

The 1975 draft was one for the record books. They were dubbed the "dirty dozen." Randy White, Burton Lawless, Thomas Henderson, Bob Breunig, Rolly Woolsey, Pat Donovan, Kyle Davis, Randy Hughes, Mike Hegman, Herb Scott, Mitch Hoopes, and Scott Laidlaw represented the crowning achievement of the Cowboys' computer drafting system. Nine of the draftees eventually started, five became Pro-Bowl players in later years, and one, Randy White, ultimately made the Hall of Fame. The Cowboys had reloaded their guns and were primed to wreak havoc on the NFL.

Landry then instituted another of his notable innovations, one that enabled Dallas to take advantage of a concept that was quite remarkable, both *before* and *after* its time. In the early 1960s, Red Hickey—who later joined the Cowboys as a scout—was head coach of the San Francisco 49ers. During his term in San Francisco, Hickey designed a clever offensive alignment similar to Steve Owen's (New York Giants' coach) "A" formation of the 1930s and '40s. The quarterback would line up four to five yards behind the center and receive the snap in a similar fashion to that of a punter. "It made sense to me in obvious passing situations," Landry said. "Instead of snapping the ball under center and dropping back five to seven yards to set up and pass, why not put the quarterback five yards deep and snap the ball to him there? It gives him more time and a better look at the defense." Landry had attempted to incorporate this tactic into Dallas's repertoire in the late 1960s, but Don Meredith was uncomfortable with it. Staubach, on the other hand, loved it. The configuration was known as the "spread" or "shotgun" formation, and after being resurrected by Tom Landry in 1975, it would soon be utilized by almost every team in the NFL.

Armed with a new offensive configuration and the unexpected bounty of an awesome draft, Dallas defied the experts and won ten games in 1975. Everything seemed to come together that season to afford the Cowboys another chance for glory. And though I doubt that God is a football fan, perhaps even the great deity himself was watching that memorable December 28 day in Bloomington, Minnesota, when Dallas got a gift from the heavens.

The Cowboys trailed the Vikings 14–10 with only twenty-four seconds left in the game. On third-and-ten from the fifty-yard line—out of the shotgun formation—Staubach lofted what was sure to be an interception in the direction of wide receiver Drew Pearson. Minnesota's defensive back, Nate Wright, had been stride for stride with Pearson all the way down the field, and safety Karl Kassulke was not far away from the play either. In what Staubach would later describe as his "Hail Mary" pass, Pearson pushed Wright just enough to allow the ball to fall neatly into his hands and dash into the end zone. Replays clearly showed the nudge, but the official closest to the play, Jerry Bergman, either didn't see it or didn't care to see it. In any event, the Cowboys won the game 17–14 and headed for an NFC championship game encounter with the Los Angeles Rams.

Dallas easily defeated Los Angeles, 37–7. Staubach was unstoppable, completing sixteen of twenty-six passes for 220 yards and four touchdowns. The Rams managed just 118 total yards against the Doomsday Defense.

Two weeks later, in Super Bowl X, the Pittsburgh Steelers defeated the Cowboys 21–17. That loss, though certainly disappointing, did little to dampen the spirits of what now was a younger group of athletes who had overachieved, enabling the Cowboys to unexpectedly reach the title game for a third time in six years. Landry and the players were proud of their accomplishments that season, and they had no doubt that they would get another shot at immortality in the near future.

In 1976, the Cowboys won the NFC's Eastern Division with an 11–3 record. It was the club's eleventh consecutive winning season. Dallas's running duties that year were split among Robert Newhouse, Preston Pearson, Doug Dennison, and Charley Young. While all had redeeming qualities, none possessed the talent to be the lead back for a title contender—a fact that was so clearly demonstrated in the team's 14–12 playoff loss to the Rams, when Cowboys runners combined for only seventy-eight yards on twenty-six carries. The team needed a big-time back if they were going to challenge for another championship.

Enter Gil Brandt (at that point a Cowboys' GM), the Seattle Seahawks, and a running back named Tony Dorsett. In the 1977 draft, two running backs were expected to be selected in the first three picks—Ricky Bell, from the University of Southern California, and Dorsett, the Heisman Trophy winner from the University of Pittsburgh. Bell was expected to go first to the Tampa Bay Buccaneers, and Dorsett shortly thereafter. The Cowboys loved Dorsett. But selecting in the twenty-fifth spot of the first round, they knew that it would be impossible to acquire the supremely talented back. So Brandt made a deal with Seattle. Dallas traded their first pick and three second-round selections to the Seahawks in exchange for the second overall choice in the draft. As anticipated, Tampa Bay chose Bell, which left the door open for the Cowboys to select Dorsett. Though he started off slowly, Dorsett eventually made a huge impact in his rookie year.

Robert Newhouse and Preston Pearson received many of the carries early in the 1977 season. Landry, who wanted Dorsett to become more attentive in team meetings and more in tune with the details of the offense, resisted the temptation to start the undisciplined yet highly skilled rookie until the second half of the year. Nonetheless, Dorsett was able to gain 1007 yards on 208 attempts. He averaged 4.8 yards per carry and scored twelve touchdowns.

With a dominating ground attack, a great quarterback, and an outstanding defense, the Cowboys finished 12–2 and won another division title in 1977. Considered to be the NFC favorite to advance to the Super Bowl, Dallas did not disappoint prognosticators. In their first postseason encounter, at Texas Stadium, they manhandled the Chicago Bears 37–7. The Minnesota Vikings were the Cowboys' next victim, in the NFC championship game. A thirty-two-yard pass from Roger Staubach to wide receiver Golden Richards staked Dallas to an early 6–0 lead (the kick was blocked), and a Robert Newhouse five-yard run in the second quarter extended that advantage to 13–0. In the second half, the Cowboys defense limited the Vikings to only 22 rushing yards while forcing several Minnesota fumbles. The visiting Vikings were mauled 23–6, and Dallas earned its fourth NFL title-game berth in eight years.

Led by their dominant defense, which included Harvey Martin, Randy White, Ed "Too Tall" Jones, Charlie Waters, D.D. Lewis, Jethro Pugh, and Thomas Henderson, the Cowboys destroyed the Denver Broncos in Super Bowl XII, 27–10. Dallas more than doubled the Broncos in total yardage, 325–156, and limited Denver to eleven first downs. A spectacular forty-five-yard touchdown pass from Roger Staubach to Butch Johnson midway through the third quarter gave Dallas a seventeen-point advantage and secured the victory. Landry and the Cowboys had captured their second NFL championship.

The next year (1978), Dallas appeared in their last Super Bowl under Tom Landry. After a 12–4 regular-season finish and playoff victories over Atlanta (27–20) and Los Angeles (28–0), the Cowboys met Pittsburgh, again, in Super Bowl XIII. On the strength of a twenty-two-yard scoring run by Franco Harris and an eight-yard Terry Bradshaw–to–Lynn Swann touchdown pass, the Steelers took a commanding 35–17 lead with less than seven minutes remaining in the fourth quarter. But Dallas staged a furious comeback. A seven-yard touchdown pass from Roger Staubach to tight end Billy Joe Dupree with just over two minutes remaining cut the lead to eleven. With only twenty-two seconds left, Staubach again hit pay dirt, this time connecting on a four-yard scoring pass to Butch Johnson. It was too little, too late, however. Pittsburgh recovered the ensuing onside kick and the game was history. The Steelers defeated Dallas 35–31.

From 1979 to 1985, the Cowboys compiled seven more consecutive winning seasons under Landry, establishing an NFL record of twenty straight victorious campaigns dating back to 1966. Unfortunately, the club then suffered three successive losing years, from 1986 to 1988, falling to 3–13 in the last of those seasons. Shortly thereafter, Tom Landry's coaching career came to an abrupt conclusion.

Dallas's original owner, Clint Murchison, had been forced to sell the Cowboys back in 1984, just before he died. His last request to Tex Schramm, who handled the transaction, was that the new owner be committed to the organization's tradition of hands-off ownership. Minority investor "Bum" Bright, who already held a 27 percent interest in the team, became the Dallas Cowboys' new majority stockholder. On February 25, 1989, however—amid a personal financial catastrophe—Bright wound up selling the team to Jerry Jones. On that day, the scream from Clint Murchison's grave could probably be heard at Cowboys headquarters.

Jones immediately instituted a *hands-on* policy, publicly pledging to orchestrate every detail of the Cowboys' future. The day he took over, Jones—in a somewhat undignified manner—dismissed Landry and later replaced him with former Miami Hurricanes' head coach Jimmy Johnson. Though Jones enjoyed initial success by winning three Super Bowls (mostly because of an astute choice of coach in Johnson), that success was short-lived, and the Dallas Cowboys—as of this writing—are one of the NFL's least successful franchises. It seems Jones's hands-on approach and large ego finally became too much of a distraction, even for his lifelong friend Jimmy Johnson. So Johnson—the true architect of the Cowboys' resurrection—left, and Jones (though some of Dallas's ensuing salary cap problems were not entirely his fault) subsequently ran the organization into the ground—hands-on all the way.

Tom Landry's influence in the NFL will be felt for quite some time. And though his statement after being discharged by Jerry Jones was, "People will forget me quick," that was just his modest way of saying good-bye to the game and team he loved so dearly.

In his twenty-nine seasons, Tom Landry's teams won 250 football games, played in five Super Bowls (winning two of them), won thirteen division titles, and had a string of twenty straight winning seasons (1966–1985). Landry was perhaps *the* most innovative coach in the history of professional football—having invented, implemented, or perfected the following concepts: the 4–3 defense, a defensive system of reading keys, the multiple-set offense, the quality control routine, the flex defense, and the shotgun formation. He was inducted into the Pro Football Hall of Fame in 1990.

Former running back Walt Garrison was once asked whether he had ever witnessed a Tom Landry smile. "No," Garrison said, "but I was only there nine years." Landry was commonly known as the emotionless coach who never cared about anything in the world except football. Though his players often joked about the public's perception of their leader, they knew that the man wearing the conservative suits and the fedora was really a devoted, caring husband, father, and football coach who just never displayed his feelings. For it was not a cold, heartless coach who addressed his team after a devastating loss in Pittsburgh in 1965, when it seemed like the whole world was caving in around him. "He cleared the locker room of everybody except the players, then told us how proud he was of our effort," said Bob Lilly. "But he was disappointed with the results [the club had not had a winning season in five years]. 'I may not be here next year,' he said, 'but I want you guys to know I think the world of you.' The he broke down and started crying. That really touched us all. We knew we had to play harder."

It seems that Landry's hard-to-gauge public persona mirrored some of the deceptive though highly effective football tactics that defined his career. His basic offensive game plan utilized multiple alignments specifically developed to confuse defenses that relied on Landry's very own keying method—a system that predicted plays based on formations. His flex defense, with its peculiar configuration and unconventional properties, perplexed adversaries and kept them off balance.

But when it came to his players, Landry needed no creative strategies or disingenuous ploys in order to earn their allegiance and admiration. Landry's athletes respected his vast knowledge of the game and appreciated his dedication to excellence. Convinced he could make them better football players and trusting his instincts as a coach, Landry's players always exhibited one-hundred-percent effort.

Tom Landry took the Dallas Cowboys' franchise from the bottom of the NFL—where they once were the laughingstock of the league—to the penthouse of success, as Super Bowl champions. And he did it with the intelligence of a scientist, the resourcefulness of an escape artist, and the cunning of a general. "I think the whole Cowboys' image came from him," said Roger Staubach at Landry's Hall of Fame induction ceremony in Canton. "I think Tom will always make the Dallas Cowboys more than a football team."

There may never be another Thomas Wade Landry. A man who could so cleverly link the strategies of the past, present, and future into a single philosophy that solidified a franchise and shaped an entire era of the NFL. On February 12, 2000, Tom Landry died. But his name and his legacy will forever hold a place in the annals of the National Football League, especially with the Dallas Cowboys.

Tom Landry's Coaching Capsule

Category	Numbers
Seasons	29
Wins	250
Losses	162
Ties	6
Winning pct.	.605
Pct. >/< avg. Super Bowl–winning coach (.601) *	+0.7%
World championships†	2
World championship game appearances†	5
World championship pct. (champ/seasons)	6.9%
Losing seasons	8
Pct. of losing seasons	27.6%
Playoff record	20–16
Playoff winning percentage	.556
Average wins per 16 games (a current season)	9.7
Average losses per 16 games	6.3

NOTE: Ties count as a half-win and a half-loss in calculating percentages.
*See Epilogue
†Super Bowls or NFL championships 1920–1965

3 Years after Landry

City	Years	Record	Percentage	Landry's Career Pct
				.605
Dallas	1989–1991	19–29	.396	

(continued next page)

Tom Landry's Coaching Capsule *(continued)*

Yearly Records

Year	Team	Wins	Losses	Ties	Playoffs
1960	Dal	0	11	1	
1961	Dal	4	9	1	
1962	Dal	5	8	1	
1963	Dal	4	10	0	
1964	Dal	5	8	1	
1965	Dal	7	7	0	
1966	Dal	10	3	1	0–1
1967	Dal	9	5	0	1–1
1968	Dal	12	2	0	0–1
1969	Dal	11	2	1	0–1
1970	Dal	10	4	0	2–1*
1971	Dal	11	3	0	3–0†
1972	Dal	10	4	0	1–1
1973	Dal	10	4	0	1–1
1974	Dal	8	6	0	
1975	Dal	10	4	0	2–1*
1976	Dal	11	3	0	0–1
1977	Dal	12	2	0	3–0†
1978	Dal	12	4	0	2–1*
1979	Dal	11	5	0	0–1
1980	Dal	12	4	0	2–1
1981	Dal	12	4	0	1–1
1982	Dal	6	3	0	2–1
1983	Dal	12	4	0	0–1
1984	Dal	9	7	0	
1985	Dal	10	6	0	0–1
1986	Dal	7	9	0	
1987	Dal	7	8	0	
1988	Dal	3	13	0	
Totals		250	162	6	20–16

* NFC champions
† Won Super Bowl

Chapter 6

DON SHULA

When "Bum" Phillips uniquely summarized Don Shula's coaching qualifications at the beginning of this book, his quote was born of respect and admiration for a colleague whom he felt was the ultimate adversary.

Phillips coached the Houston Oilers from 1975 to 1980 and the New Orleans Saints from 1981 to 1985. During his career, Phillips met Shula-coached teams on six occasions. In those contests, Phillips won five games. That's right. He was 5–1 against the man whom he claims was one of, if not *the*, best coach ever. And while Bum Phillips enjoyed a modicum of success as a head coach in the NFL, no one would ever confuse him with George Halas. Therefore, we can confidently assume that his glowing compliments of Don Shula were not meant to enhance *his own* credibility as a coach. It's not as if Phillips was later spotted on the sidewalk running up and down the street yelling, "Hey, I beat the greatest coach in the world five out of six times. Which way to Canton?" In fact, few people, including Phillips, probably know that statistic anyway. The reality of the situation was that Phillips had played against Shula, scrutinized his methods, and witnessed countless examples of "Shula magic"—instances where Miami would consistently defeat opponents with better personnel. Phillips valued Shula's talents as only a fierce rival could.

Donald Francis Shula was born on January 4, 1930, in Grand River, Ohio, just outside Painesville. When Shula was a youngster, his family was far from stable economically. Shula's father, Dan, worked several jobs, among them a stint in a nursery and a position with the local fishery.

Upon entering high school, Shula desperately wanted to participate in the football program. Fearing that his mother, Mary, would not condone his football exploits, Don forged her signature on the parent permission form. Shula became an outstanding football and track athlete at Harvey High School and wished to further both his education and athletic career in college.

Though the Shula family lacked the money to finance a secondary education, Don wound up attending college at that well-known Ohio football factory—John Carroll University in Cleveland. Herb Eisele, head coach of the team, offered Shula a scholarship. Eisele, as luck would have it, was friends with legendary coach Paul Brown, who was in the professional ranks with Cleveland in the All-American Football Conference at the time. Eisele frequented many of Brown's coaching clinics, and it was through this relationship that Shula would get his chance to play in the National Football League. Eisele recommended that Brown take a look at Shula and Carl Taseff—both defensive backs at John Carroll. Brown liked what he saw, and Cleveland selected Shula in the ninth round of the 1951 NFL draft and Taseff in the twenty-second round. Shula wasn't completely sure that he wanted to prolong his athletic career, but he eventually decided to take a shot at pro football rather than become a math teacher and football coach at Lincoln High School, in Canton, Ohio. Not to worry, Shula would eventually make it back to Canton.

As a player, Shula was solid, though nothing special. In seven seasons with three different clubs (Cleveland, Baltimore, and Washington), he played in seventy-three games and intercepted twenty-one passes. Don was known for his ferocious hitting, his knowledge of the game, and his relentless desire to succeed, the latter two of which would serve him well in his quest to become a head coach.

After the 1957 season, Shula hung up his cleats and began his coaching career at the University of Virginia. One year later, he moved on to coach for Blanton Collier (Paul Brown's eventual successor in Cleveland) at the University of Kentucky. In 1960, George Wilson—a George Halas disciple—brought Shula back to the NFL, hiring him as a defensive assistant with the Detroit Lions. Ironically, Shula would later supplant Wilson as head coach of the Miami Dolphins in 1970.

At each stop on his coaching tour, Shula took the opportunity to learn strategy and leadership fundamentals from the coaches for whom he served. He paid especially close attention to the two most successful coaches of his playing era. "To me, the two most important people in the NFL were George Halas"—coach of the Chicago Bears—"and Paul Brown," Shula said. "Their two styles were in direct contrast, and I learned from both. From Halas, I learned the handling of men and the toughness and competitiveness of the game. From Paul Brown, I got the teacher-pupil relationship. Paul put the classroom into pro football."

In 1963, after only five years as an assistant, Shula was named head coach of the Baltimore Colts, a team for which he had played four seasons. During the next four decades as a head coach in the NFL, Don Shula was simply awesome.

When Shula took over the Colts in 1963, he was the youngest coach in the National Football League, at age thirty-three. Baltimore had finished with a 7–7 record in 1962, their third straight mediocre season since earning NFL championships in back-to-back years (1958–1959). Under their previous head coach, "Weeb" Ewbank, the Colts—though talented—were floundering and seemed to be playing with little, if any, purpose. Shula, who played with Baltimore from 1953 through 1956 and knew many of the Colts' players, moved quickly and decisively to change the landscape. He immediately instituted a more rigid and disciplined training routine, and, with the assistance of Colts' GM Don Kellet, he began to supplement the Colts roster with new players during the course of the next three seasons.

Shula and Kellet placed twelve new players on the Colts' forty-two-man squad that first year. That restructuring amounted to a 29 percent roster turnover, which, as we know from a previous chapter, represented a high figure for that era of the NFL. Among the new Colts were three draft picks: Bob Vogel, a tackle from Ohio State; John Mackey, a tight end from Syracuse; and Jerry Logan, a safety from West Texas State. All three would become all-stars in the very near future. The Colts improved slightly, to an 8–6 record that season, but with the infusion of fresh players and Shula's more structured and disciplined system, Baltimore seemed to be regaining its championship form.

In 1964, the Colts improved dramatically and wound up with the best record in the NFL, 12–2. Shula's recently drafted newcomers—along with several inexperienced veterans who had not been given an opportunity under Ewbank—combined to inspirit the Colts with youthful enthusiasm as well as enhancing the team's capabilities on the football field. Three seldom-used, younger veterans in particular were masterfully implemented by Shula: running backs Tom Matte and Jerry Hill, and defensive tackle Fred Miller (table 6-1).

Baltimore finished the 1964 season with the league's best offense (30.6 points per game) and defense (16.1) and were the favorites to claim another title against Shula's old boss, Blanton Collier, and the Cleveland Browns. The game was scoreless at halftime, but the Browns broke it open with a seventeen-point third quarter en route to a 27–0 blowout. It would be the first of several disappointments for Shula in championship game settings. Yet, though the shutout loss was disheartening, nobody seemed emotionally devastated by the setback. Everyone in the Colts' organization believed that the team was capable of reaching the title game again in the very near future, especially since Shula had succeeded in eliciting the best effort and ability from each member of the club.

Table 6-1. Tom Matte and Jerry Hill, 1961–64 Running Back Performance

Year	Att	Yards	Average	TDs	Coach
		Tom Matte			
1961	13	54	4.2	0	Ewbank
1962	74	226	3.1	2	Ewbank
1963	133	541	4.1	4	Shula
1964	42	215	5.1	1	Shula
		Jerry Hill			
1961	1	4	4.0	0	Ewbank
1962	Did not play				
1963	100	440	4.4	5	Shula
1964	88	384	4.4	5	Shula

When Weeb Ewbank exited the scene in 1963, Baltimore possessed a talented though aging team. However, Shula's inspired plan to energize the Colts by adding several skilled rookies to the roster, in addition to the incorporation of competent younger veterans who were previously overlooked, worked beautifully, and the team seemed to improve overnight. But Shula did much more than just add new players to the mix in order to revitalize the lackluster squad. He was also instrumental in restoring the production of veterans who, though they were not especially old, were not producing as they had in the past. Whether it was due to tactical or motivational deficiencies, the fact was that many Baltimore players had been underachieving during the previous regime. Shula knew that it was his responsibility to rejuvenate their dormant careers and provide them with every opportunity to display their true abilities. One player in particular who seemed to be stagnating was quarterback Johnny Unitas. It's interesting to note that even a Hall of Fame athlete can greatly benefit from outstanding coaching. Let's take a look in table 6-2 at Unitas's statistics before and after Shula's arrival in Baltimore.

Under Shula, Unitas's statistics improved markedly in almost every major category, especially the two most important: yards per attempt and interceptions. It's little wonder that the Colts' offense also improved dramatically (see table 6-3), suggesting a direct relationship between these variables and scoring.

Table 6-2. Johnny Unitas, Shula versus Ewbank

Year	Att	Comp	Comp%	Yards	YPA	TD	INT	Rating
Coach: Ewbank								
1960	378*	190*	50.3	3099*	8.20	25*	24	73.7
1961	420*	229	54.5	2990	7.12	16	24	66.1
1962	389	222	57.1	2967	7.63	23	23	76.5
Coach: Shula								
1963	410	237*	57.8	3481*	8.49	20	12	89.7
1964	305	158	51.8	2824	9.26*	19	6	96.4
1965	282	164	58.2	2530	8.97*	23	12	97.4

*Led league

Table 6-3. Baltimore Colts, Shula versus Ewbank

Year	Avg. Points scored	Record
Coach: Ewbank		
1960	24.0	6–6
1961	21.6	8–6
1962	20.9	7–7
Coach: Shula		
1963	22.6	8–6
1964	30.6	12–2
1965	27.8	10–3–1

In the 1965 draft, Shula continued to add talented athletes to the club. Middle linebacker Mike Curtis from Duke, center guard Glenn Ressler from Penn State, and defensive end Roy Hilton from Jackson State would each become prime members of the Colts' starting unit in the not-too-distant future. Ironically, Shula made great use of the draft to enrich the Colts with as many as six premium players in the first three years of his tenancy in Baltimore, a process that would reverse itself later in his career.

As the 1965 season neared its conclusion, the Colts and Green Bay Packers were neck and neck for the Western Conference title. Unfortunately for the Colts, catastrophe struck in the last week of the year. Both Unitas and the Colts' backup quarterback, Gary Cuozzo, fell victim to injuries. Neither would be able to play in the team's final game against the Rams. These untimely injuries provided Shula with his first opportunity to demonstrate his versatility as a head coach.

The Colts desperately needed to win their last contest of the season, as they trailed the Packers by one-half game for the conference title. The Rams were far from a dominant team that season (they finished 4–10), but they were good enough to have trounced the Packers three weeks earlier, 21–10. Shula would likely have to sign a new quarterback for the remainder of the season, one who had no concept whatsoever of the Colts' offense. But wait. There was an alternative. Tom Matte, Baltimore's halfback, had been a quarterback in college, at Ohio State. Matte obviously knew the system, and he was an intelligent player. But could Matte *really* direct the Colts' offense? And could he actually succeed, at least enough to give Baltimore a better chance than they would have by bringing in a brand-new quarterback—one who would have his hands full just knowing which way to turn and hand off? Shula gambled that Matte could pull it off. "I changed the game plan to take advantage of Matte's running strength," he said. "Tom didn't know the plays from quarterback, so we ended up writing them on his wristband."

Somehow—miracle of miracles—Matte, Shula, and the Colts beat the Rams, 20–17. And the Packers would only manage a tie with the 49ers which created a playoff between the Colts and Green Bay for the conference title. Matte would again be thrust into the breach, but the Colts would come up short this time—losing 13–10—as a blown call by the officials, who ruled a Packers' field goal to be good when it clearly was not, turned out to be the difference in the game (table 6-4).

Table 6-4. Baltimore Colts–Green Bay Playoff Game, 1965

	Balt	GB
First downs	9	23
Total yards	175	362

Tom Matte:
Rushing   17-57
Passing   5–12–0, 40 yards

It wasn't pretty, and it wasn't quite as productive as one might have hoped for, but the Colts got to the playoff game and almost won. Shula got the most out of his team. He made the best of a desperate situation. In short order, he changed his *entire* offensive game plan to fit the team's dire circumstances, something only the most capable and confident coaches would ever attempt.

Clearly, Don Shula was ready and willing to do everything in his power to win football games. But in order to accomplish his goals, it was imperative that he receive the highest level of production from each and every player under his command. And though Shula possessed unrivaled talents as both a tactician and disciplinarian, his most redeeming attribute may have been as a "football psychologist." His intent with each player was to ascertain their central motivating factor and then enact the precise technique with which to activate their football passion and desires.

When Shula believed in a player, he would utilize whatever methods were possible in order to extract that individual's talent. But he would *never* coddle or baby a player. In fact, sometimes—depending on the individual's constitution—he would provoke and torment him as a form of psychological motivation, then wait to see how the player responded to his challenge.

"In the end, winning and losing doesn't depend on trick plays or using new systems each week," Shula said. "It comes down to a matter of motivating people to work hard and prepare as a team. That's what really counts. In a word, it's called 'coaching.'"

In 1967, the Baltimore Colts selected Charles "Bubba" Smith as the very first pick of the entire draft. Smith—who would later claim fame as a defensive end—was selected as a tackle, not an end. And in training camp he was placed at one of the defensive tackle slots. "My legs were too long to play that position, so most of the time that year I was on the bench," said Smith. "But he [Shula] was so strong willed, he wasn't going to move me to end." It wasn't until Smith generated the nerve to confront Shula that he actually started to play.

In 1968, Smith came into training camp sporting a big Afro hairstyle and love beads. When asked by a reporter if the conservative and authoritative Shula would make him cut the hair, Smith responded, "Is he my barber or my coach?"

Practice began, and Shula and Smith were at odds, constantly testing each other and playing mind games. Smith began to overtly assert himself at every opportunity, hoping to create a situation where Shula and/or the coaching staff would have to give him the chance to earn a starting position. And maybe that's exactly what Shula wanted from Smith. Maybe he wanted Bubba Smith to try and force his way into the Colts' lineup and make believers out of Shula and the team. Perhaps he wanted to motivate Bubba by challenging him. Maybe that would make Smith a better player and, perhaps, a better person in the long run. "You've got to have the courage of your convictions," Shula would say. "Mentally, physically, morally, you've got to have the courage. Somehow, someway, you've got to get the job done." Eventually, everyone realized that Bubba Smith could play, and Shula obviously knew it as well. He had to give Smith his shot. It wasn't long until Smith fought his way into the starting lineup, and, soon there-after, Bubba found his niche as one of the league's best pass-rushing defensive *ends*.

Many years after Smith retired, he was asked about his time with Shula. In one of the funniest quotes I have ever read in relation to pro football, Smith had the "courage of his convictions" to say, "If a nuclear bomb dropped, the only things I'm certain would survive are AstroTurf and Don Shula." It was Smith's offbeat way of compli-menting the career achievements of one of the greatest coaches in history. Because in the end, Shula pushed the right buttons with Smith and helped Bubba develop into the star that he eventually became.

In some instances, a player needed to be handled in a far less confrontational man-ner. Bob Griese—Shula's quarterback from 1970 to 1980 with the Miami Dolphins—was a mild, reserved, contemplative individual. Yelling, screaming, or challenging him in a public fashion would have been quite detrimental to his development—and Shula knew this. So when Shula felt it necessary to admonish Griese, he handled the matter in a different fashion. "I try to fit my feedback to a player's personality," Shula said. "Bob was a very quiet, thoughtful person. He did not respond well to emotional repri-mands. It was better to take him off to the side and talk to him quietly and privately."

Don Shula wanted a certain type of connection with his players in order to facili-tate success. "The relationship I want to establish with my football team is one of mutual respect," he said. "I want my players to respect me for giving them everything that I have to prepare them to play their best. My respect for them has to come from knowing that they are willing to give me all that they have to prepare themselves to be ready to play."

In 1968, the Baltimore Colts dominated the NFL. Earl Morrall, filling in for an injured Johnny Unitas, led the league with twenty-six touchdown passes while com-pleting more than 57 percent of his attempts. The Colts scored 402 points while allow-ing the meager total of 144. In the third Super Bowl in history, Baltimore would face the AFL's New York Jets and their brash young quarterback, Joe Namath.

Baltimore was a twenty-point favorite to pulverize the Jets. Though the AFL clubs were certainly closing the gap with the NFL teams in relation to their talent bases, no one figured the Jets to be able to compete with one of the most formidable teams the NFL had witnessed in the past twenty years. The Jets, however, had different ideas. Namath even went so far as to *guarantee* a New York victory three days before the game.

As the contest began, the Jets' strategy was to attack the Colts' defensive line at its weakest spot—right defensive end Ordell Braase. Fullback Matt Snell consistently pounded the ball at the thirty-six-year-old Braase, spearheading a methodical ground attack that would eventually generate 142 yards. While the Colts were reeling—attempt-ing to compensate at the point of attack—Namath attacked Baltimore's supposedly invulnerable zone pass defense. In an MVP performance, Namath completed seventeen of twenty-eight attempts for 206 yards. Wide receiver George Sauer had a huge game, hauling in eight passes for 133 yards. The turning point of the contest was when Morrall, who played very poorly, overlooked a wide-open Jimmy Orr for a sure touchdown on a flea-flicker play during the second quarter and instead forced the ball into double coverage and threw an interception. The Jets prevailed 16–7 and produced the AFL's first Super Bowl victory—and another heartbreaking loss for Shula and the Colts.

In December of 1969, the Colts beat the Los Angeles Rams 13–7 to finish out the year at 8–5–1. Unfortunately for Colts' fans, that game marked the end of the Don Shula era in Baltimore. In seven very successful seasons with the Colts, Shula earned a record of 71–23–4 for a remarkable .745 winning percentage. His clubs took three trips to the postseason—though each ended in defeat—and the Colts' appearance in Miami, Florida, for Super Bowl III marked the fourth title game in which the franchise had participated in the past eleven years. I guess Shula liked the weather down in Miami, because that would eventually become his new home, as head coach of the Miami Dolphins.

In 1970—the year the NFL and AFL merged—a dispute between Shula and Colts owner Carroll Rosenbloom over how the team should be operated reached its boiling point, and Shula looked for a way out with one of the NFL's new members. He decided to move to the NFL's new conference (the AFC) and became head coach of the Miami franchise. Since Shula was still under contract to the Colts, Baltimore received Miami's number-one selection in the 1971 draft in exchange for allowing Shula to break his agreement with the team. Many observers at the time believed it was a steep price to pay—just for a coach. The draft pick turned out to be a running back from North Carolina by the name of Don McCauley. McCauley played eleven full seasons for Baltimore but never developed into the player the Colts had in mind when they drafted him. Had McCauley been a Hall of Famer, this would still have to rank as one of the most lopsided trades in the history of the league. No knock against McCauley, but in hindsight, even he would likely have made that deal—twice!

Don Shula *had* to be crazy. No mentally stable individual would give up the legendary Baltimore Colts for the lowly Miami Dolphins. Would they?

The Miami franchise that began as part of the American Football League's expansion in 1966 was as dismal an entity as one could imagine. In four seasons, the Dolphins had won fifteen games. Unfortunately, the schedule makers forced them to play forty-one other games as well. Their record was 15–39–2, for a "winning" percentage of .286. To make things worse, Miami would be without their first-round pick in the 1970 NFL draft, which they had traded away to Cleveland. And, let's not forget, the Dolphins had already lost the rights to their first-round pick in 1971 in exchange for that "lunatic" Don Shula.

Can anyone imagine a less enviable situation in which to cast your coaching lot?

Shula and the Dolphins did exactly what was expected of a bunch of misfit, outcast, unprofessional "halloweeners" (people dressed up like football players)—they went 10–4 and went to the playoffs before losing to the Oakland Raiders 21–14. Shula dismissed almost half the team upon his arrival in Miami. The Dolphins' roster in 1970 included twenty-one new players of the forty-seven listed that season—a whopping 45 percent. Shula cleared the deadwood and brought in *his* players, players with a new attitude and a fresh outlook, players with whom he believed he could win. And that's exactly what the Dolphins did—for the next twenty-six years. Under the *lunatic* Shula, they had only two losing seasons in the next quarter of a century. Did someone say genius?

The Dolphins' fans in 1970 must have believed they were dreaming. Don Shula had taken a team that was widely regarded as a perennial joke in the *AFL* and reconstructed them into a powerhouse *NFL* team in just a few short months. "The next thing you know," the bewildered Miami faithful joked, "he'll have them in the Super Bowl."

In 1971, Miami devastated their competition. The Dolphins began the season modestly enough, earning a 1–1–1 record after their first three contests. Then, on the strength of the finest running attack the NFL had seen in several years, the Dolphins reeled off eight straight victories to move to 9–1–1. Larry Csonka, a powerfully built 6′3″, 237-pound fullback from Syracuse University, was the main cog in Miami's awesome attack. When Csonka hit you, it rattled your teeth and the teeth of the guy standing next to you. In his first three seasons in professional football, Csonka had done well—gaining almost two thousand yards and averaging just under 4.3 yards per carry. In 1971 though, Csonka exploded, carrying the pigskin 195 times for 1,051 yards. His 5.4 average that season led the entire NFL by far. And the great thing about Csonka was that he almost never fumbled. In fact, that year he did not turn over the ball once in more than two hundred touches. As a team, Miami rushed for more than twenty-four hundred yards and averaged 5.0 yards each time they handed the ball off—another league-leading mark.

In addition to the Dolphins' success on the ground, quarterback Bob Griese—a four-year veteran from Purdue—enjoyed perhaps his finest season as a professional (table 6-5). Like Unitas before him, Griese's passing statistics improved dramatically during the first three years under Don Shula's tutelage (table 6-6).

Table 6-5. Bob Griese, 1971 Passing Performance

Year	Att	Comp	Comp%	Yards	YPA	TD	INT	Rating
1971	263	145	55.1	2089	7.94	19	9	90.9

Table 6-6. Bob Griese, Passing Performance, Shula versus Wilson

Year	Att	Comp	Comp%	Yards	YPA	TD	INT	Rating
			Coach: Wilson					
1967	331	166	50.2	2005	6.06	15	18	61.6
1968	355	186	52.4	2473	6.97	21	16	75.7
1969	252	121	48.0	1695	6.73	10	16	56.9
			Coach: Shula					
1970	245	142	58.0	2019	8.24	12	17	72.1
1971	263	145	55.1	2089	7.94	19	9	90.9
1972	Injured, fewer than 100 passes							
1973	218	116	53.2	1422	6.52	17	8	84.3

Miami finished the 1971 season at 10–3–1 and secured their first in a long line of AFC Eastern Division titles. Their initial playoff game matched them against the Kansas City Chiefs. In what turned out to be the NFL's longest game ever played, Miami defeated Kansas City 27–24. The epic event took eighty-two minutes and forty seconds to decide. The big play of the game came from the Dolphins' *big* player, Larry Csonka, who broke loose for a twenty-nine-yard run to firmly ensconce Miami in Kansas City territory, at the thirty-six-yard line, midway through the second overtime. Shortly thereafter, Garo Yepremian kicked a history-making thirty-seven-yard field goal, and the Dolphins advanced to meet Shula's old team, the Baltimore Colts, in the AFC championship game in Miami.

Baltimore and Miami had split their regular-season meetings, with Miami winning 17–14 in Florida and the Colts prevailing 14–3 in Baltimore. Miami had the advantage of facing a Baltimore backfield made up of rookies—Don Nottingham and Don McCauley—as the Colts were without the services of their injured starters, Tom Matte and Norm Bulaich. The Dolphins—in what would become typical Miami style in big games over the next few seasons—threw a grand total of eight passes that day. But two of them went from Griese to Hall of Fame receiver Paul Warfield—the first for a seventy-five-yard touchdown and the second for a fifty-yard completion that set up a Larry Csonka plunge into the end zone. Miami beat Baltimore 21–0 and won the right to play the Dallas Cowboys in Super Bowl VI.

"My biggest disappointment," Shula said after the Super Bowl game, "was that we never challenged. They completely dominated." Dallas outgained Miami in total yardage 352 to 185 and soundly defeated the opportunistic Dolphins 24–3. Miami's frustration could easily be detected by the sheer number of passes they attempted, twenty-three. Dallas, under the shrewd direction of Tom Landry, was a team worthy of comparison to Miami—a team that had quickly risen from disgrace to prominence. But Landry and the Cowboys had five years of playoff experience under their belts and were therefore a bit ahead of Miami's timetable.

Any championship game loss is hard to accept, especially when it's your third straight defeat in such circumstances. But Don Shula would not harp on the setback for very long. He had a rule which dictated that he not dwell on *any* game much beyond the next day. And in this instance, since Miami was a relatively young team, had achieved so much in such a very short period, and never really expected to reach the Super Bowl so quickly anyway, it was not as gut-wrenching a defeat as it might have been for a team with aging players and little hope for the future.

Miami's sudden and dramatic improvement surprised many NFL experts. But Shula, who had rapidly turned around the Colts in 1963, was beginning to establish a history of performing unexpected "miracles" with teams that pundits often dismissed. "Determine your players' talents and give them every weapon to get the most out of those talents," he would say in response to a query about the essence of coaching. And no one, it seemed, did it better than Shula. Adversaries soon learned *never* to underestimate the man. Many a season came and went when the Dolphins were thought to be outmanned and outgunned. And many times they were. But they were *never* out-coached. Sooner or later, you knew Shula would *figure it out,* come up big, and win.

One thing that Don Shula figured out early in his coaching career was that there was no detail too small to neglect. Shula lived for details. He also lived for routine and discipline. Every Monday morning, Shula's teams had a meeting. Every Monday morning, Shula would outline every aspect of the entire week's schedule. And even though it never changed—each day, each week, each year—Shula would repeat the routine to the players. It made some people crazy. "Nothing in the routine changed during the ten years that I was there," said Jeff Dellenbach, an offensive lineman from 1985 to 1994. "It was a running joke. Someone would ask, 'Why do we do it this way?' And someone else would say, 'Because that's how they did it in '72 [Miami's undefeated season].'" Who was going to argue any further? Don Shula worked by the book—Shula's book. He always made sure that things were done his way—the *correct* way—and that all of his rules were followed, right down to the last detail.

The *Miami Herald'*s Dave Barry once recounted his nightmare scenario: "You're in the express checkout lane, limit ten items. You have eleven. Running the cash register is Don Shula."

Though he preferred to dot the i's and cross the t's, Shula was not *always* as inflexible as people may remember. "The great thing about Shula was the way he adjusted with the game," said Hank Stram, former coach of the Kansas City Chiefs. "Not many of us ever had his sort of flexibility."

How could a man who plotted out the same routine over and over again for thirty-three years and who insisted in attending to every detail be considered flexible?

Though Shula, like most leaders, preferred to do things according to plan, his teams were always well prepared to alter their tactics or adopt a unique strategy for a specific situation. One of Shula's mandates—which augmented his penchant for flexibility—was total, comprehensive preparation. The key to his system was his demand for players to know their assignments backwards and forwards—so that they would never encounter an instance where they would have to initiate a new strategy and at the same time have trouble remembering their normal responsibilities. "Preparation means everything to me," Shula said. "I'm passionate about my players being ready for anything. If our players are worrying about their assignments, they have a tendency to hold back. They should be so familiar with their assignments that when the game starts they're operating on auto pilot—not thinking, just doing." This dedication to preparation—particularly players' assignment responsibilities—would make it easier for the team to modify their tactics at a moment's notice and still perform at maximum efficiency.

In 1972, the Dolphins were matched against the New York Jets in week four of what would turn out to be their "perfect" season (seventeen wins and zero losses). Miami won the game (of course) 27–17, as Bob Griese passed for 220 yards with a fifteen-for-twenty-seven passing effort. During the game, New York's defense was completely befuddled. Shula and the Miami coaching staff had devised a new strategy which specifically targeted the Jets and their porous secondary—a unit which ranked last in the league. Miami changed their typical run-oriented game plan and deployed a three wide receiver formation during much of the contest. And while this tactic may be commonplace in the present-day NFL, it was anything but prevalent back in 1972.

"We put that in this week," said Griese. "You need anything you can get. We felt it was a good time to use it, and it worked well."

Shula not flexible? He was as flexible as he had to be.

In week five of the 1972 campaign, Griese was injured. He broke his ankle and would be out for the remainder of the regular season. With Griese hurt, thirty-eight-year-old backup quarterback Earl Morrall would have to lead the Dolphins for the rest of the year—and the Miami game plan would have to change accordingly. The younger, more mobile Griese could do things that the older Morrall was incapable of. Griese could run better, had the ability to roll out, and could execute the deep-out without putting extra air underneath the ball (i. e., he had the stronger arm at that point in his career). Shula would have to revise the Dolphins' playbook to fit his new quarterback's style and make the best out of a bad situation. If it meant altering the entire game plan for the rest of the season, then that's what Shula would do—whatever it took to win.

It all reverts back to Shula's proclivity for adopting the best strategy for a particular circumstance. Whether it was his calculated gamble to install Tom Matte at quarterback for the Colts in the most crucial games of the year back in 1965, employing a brand-new, three-wide receiver setup to take advantage of the lowly Jets' secondary in the early part of 1972, or revising his game plan in order to accentuate the strengths of Earl Morrall after Bob Griese's injury, Shula never flinched when change was indicated.

It didn't matter if the change involved adopting a new strategy *during* a game, reevaluating the game plan for a specific opponent the *week of* the game, or completely revising a seasonal strategy—Shula had a system in place which was geared towards promoting the most sensible alternative for the team.

In his book, *Everyone's a Coach*, Shula detailed the logic for makeshift strategies as well as his standard procedure to enact these modifications. "I see no point in sticking with a game plan that's not working," he said. "I also don't believe that the sun rises and falls based on my judgment. I make my assistant coaches responsible for their area and communicating information that develops during the practice week, or the game itself—to help me determine the correct plan of action. Once I've heard the information, I'm willing to make a decision. Part of being ready is being able to shift your game plan at will. I want to be prepared with a plan—and then to expect the unexpected and be ready to change that plan."

The strategy adjustments necessitated by the quarterback change in the middle of the 1972 season were actually quite subtle, and the Dolphins did not miss a beat, finishing the season as undefeated as they had been when Griese left. In looking at the numbers, the Dolphins actually passed *more* with Morrall as opposed to Griese, by about 1.5 passes per game.

Now came the really tough decisions for Shula. Griese was healthy again as the postseason approached. But since Miami was undefeated in nine games with Morrall as the starter, no changes seemed necessary. The playoffs began with a hard-fought victory over the Cleveland Browns, 20–14. In that game, the offensive strategy was conservative; nevertheless, Morrall was ineffective, completing just six of thirteen passes for eighty-eight yards. Fortunately, he had no interceptions. His counterpart, Cleveland's Mike Phipps, wished he could have said the same. Phipps was intercepted five times, which was the key reason the Dolphins prevailed.

During the regular season, Miami averaged 160 yards per game through the air. Though the Dolphins relied on their overpowering running attack to pave the way for their victories, Shula knew that against the better clubs that lay ahead, eighty-eight passing yards would not suffice. Granted, Shula kept Morrall under wraps, but that didn't change the fact that Morrall had played poorly. Since Earl was almost forty years old and his skills had considerably diminished, Shula's pragmatic approach was understandable, but would it continue to pay dividends as the schedule grew tougher?

Pittsburgh was the next opponent, in the "Steel City." The Steelers scored first when Terry Bradshaw fumbled into the end zone and the ball was recovered by Pittsburgh offensive tackle Gerry Mullins for a touchdown. Miami tied the game just before half-time on a Larry Csonka nine-yard catch from Morrall, the key play of the drive being delivered by none other than punter Larry Seiple. Seiple faked a punt from the Steelers' forty-nine-yard line and scampered thirty-seven yards to the twelve, after which Miami tied the game. "No, I didn't tell Seiple to run," Shula said after the game, "but we have an understanding. He can run any time he can make the first down—but he better make it."

Through the first two quarters of the game, Morrall was ineffective again. Though he threw a short touchdown pass to Csonka, he was also intercepted and completed just seven of eleven passes for a mere fifty-one yards. So Shula made the switch, a controversial decision to reinstall Bob Griese in place of Morrall, even though Miami was undefeated through all ten games Earl had started. Morrall was understandably upset, but being the consummate professional, he acted like a true gentleman and a team player. "I wasn't overjoyed," he said. "No, I didn't think I was having a bad game. We weren't getting a good drive going, but we didn't have good field position. No, I'm not going to second-guess the coach. He felt that Bob might get the attack moving, but that doesn't mean I'm overjoyed about it."

Shula had this perspective on the switch. "We hadn't established our offense," he said. "Griese had been working well in practice, so I thought he might get us going."

Get them going he did. Behind the cunning and determination that was Bob Griese, Shula and the Dolphins sustained two long drives in the second half as Miami pulled away from the Steelers and won the game 21–17. "Don came up to me at half-time and said 'You're going in,'" Griese said. "The one thing in this game is, a player has to be ready. If he isn't, then he doesn't belong on this team." Shula was, again, as flexible as he had to be. And in this particular game—due to the controversial quarterback

Shula strove for perfection in everything he did on the football field. "I believe that if you don't seek perfection, you can never reach excellence," he says. From day one in training camp, Shula's goal was to win every single game that he played. Not that he really believed that he would win every game—1972 notwithstanding—but that both he and the team should strive for perfection by, at the very least, *preparing* to win every game. That meant the same rigid practice routine, the same attention to detail, and the same commitment to victory that Shula had always preached.

Shula's motive to seek perfection makes a lot of sense. He rationalizes that if you come up short in your attempt for perfection, you'll still be a formidable team. But if you strive to be just good and come up short, you'll likely wind up an average club. It's a simplistic concept, yet an excellent approach. To put that in a football context, the best analogy I can offer is one where a team strives to get to the goal line only to come up two yards short of their quest. If that team had strived to get five yards into the end zone, they still could have scored even if they finished short of their goal.

To reach *his* goals, Shula preferred to enlist players who were high in character as well as football ability. In fact, Don would sooner pass up the opportunity to acquire a talented player with questionable values and character in order to take a chance on a lesser-skilled player with high moral standards and work ethic. "I've always felt that you win with good people," he said. "To me, character is just as important as ability. Character has to do with how people are put together. It's the correlation between what they believe and how they act."

In *Everyone's a Coach*, Shula fondly remembers two of his greatest character players, "overachievers" Howard Twilley and Nick Buoniconti. "When you looked at Howard, he wasn't big enough and he wasn't fast enough; but he had the biggest heart and the greatest pair of hands in the world," Shula said. "I would put Nick in the same category. Technically, he wasn't big enough, fast enough, or strong enough to play linebacker; but with his great determination, enthusiasm, and love for football, he was one of the best to ever play the game." Both Twilley and Buoniconti personified the character, commitment, and desire that became the trademarks of Shula-coached football teams.

Another supposed trademark of Shula's Miami teams in the 1970s was their affinity for a finesse style of football, both offensively and defensively. And while the defense may have deserved the finesse classification, the offense most assuredly did not.

Shula's offensive units were not constructed or trained to specialize in any one particular style of play; rather, they were designed to be multifunctional, engaging the most suitable strategy to defeat each specific opponent they encountered. Consequently, Shula's offense utilized both finesse *and* power, and his players were schooled to be adept with either phase of the game. The well-rounded Dolphins' "dream team" of 1972 was a shining example of Shula's adjustable approach to successful offensive football. When they needed to be physical, they pounded the ball in the middle of the opponent's defense with Csonka (213 carries for 1117 yards and a 5.2 average) and capitalized on straight-ahead blocking schemes. When circumstances dictated the need for speed and agility, they ran wide and utilized misdirection plays with Mercury Morris (190 carries for one thousand yards and a 5.3 average), applying more subtle blocking techniques. If they desired a combination of styles while mixing in some short passes in the flat, they called upon Jim Kiick (137–521, 3.8, and twenty-one catches) to handle the responsibilities.

Every Shula offense adopted the most appropriate tactics to defeat a particular opponent, whether it was a finesse scheme or a physical strategy. However, due to this versatility, the apparent ease with which they seemed to score on their opponents, the likelihood of "guilt" by association with the team's finesse defense, and—very possibly—Miami's "questionable" AFL origin, the Dolphins' offensive units were generally considered to be more of the deceptive variety, lacking the true power to slug it out in the trenches to sustain their dominance. But make no mistake about it (though many opponents would have indeed contested the validity of this claim *before* they actually played the Dolphins): when Miami desired to be physical, they were as strong and brutal as any team in the NFL, especially with a fellow by the name of Csonka in the backfield. And if the 1972 Dolphins were not convincing enough to prove that Miami could play smash-mouth football and consistently defeat defenses with extraordinary physical talent, the 1973 team—its AFC championship and Super Bowl performances in particular—proved beyond a shadow of a doubt that the Dolphins' offense could battle and brawl with the strongest and most physical clubs in the league.

Coming off of their fabulous 17–0 campaign, Miami was obviously favored to get back to the Super Bowl in 1973. But there was more than a little concern about the team's overall incentive, aggressiveness, and even their dedication, following "perfection." Shula, however, had them ready—marching to a 12–2 record and, for the second straight year, doubling their opponents in the scoring department, 343–150.

In the AFC championship game, the Dolphins would face one of the league's most physically intimidating defenses—the Oakland Raiders. Oakland's defense led the AFC in rushing yards allowed (1470) and yards per carry (3.4) in 1973. They also tied for the NFL lead by permitting a scant five rushing touchdowns all season. Miami's offense proceeded to line up "mano a mano" with the fearsome Raiders and shredded them for a total of 266 rushing yards on fifty-three carries (5.0). The Dolphins scored three rushing touchdowns in that game against a team that had permitted the equivalent of just one rushing score every three games. Needless to say, Miami prevailed, 27–10.

In the Super Bowl, the Dolphins would face another of the league's most physically imposing defenses. The Minnesota Vikings' "Purple People Eaters" were led by All-Pro defensive linemen Alan Page, Carl Eller, and Jim Marshall. Their dominating defensive unit had ruled the NFL landscape for almost seven years. Minnesota had permitted just 168 points in 1973 (second to the Dolphins' 150) and had tied the Raiders and Cowboys for the NFL's fewest rushing touchdowns allowed, with five. A fiercer, more physical complement of defenders there was not in the league.

What would Shula's offensive game plan be against one of the toughest, most formidable defenses of that era? Miami would challenge the Vikings' ferocity head-on, displaying the utmost confidence in their *own* version of power football. The Dolphins' main objective would be to utilize Csonka's strength "up the gut," to establish a daunting physical presence at the line of scrimmage. Thereafter, they would employ end runs and counterplays, the former in an effort to take advantage of Minnesota's anticipated response to try and stop Csonka in the middle of the field, and the latter to expose a flaw that Shula noticed in the Vikings' defense—their propensity to overreact to the motion of each play.

Miami totally dominated the Vikings, 24–7. Csonka had a fabulous day pounding the ball into the teeth of the monster, gaining 145 yards on thirty-three carries. As a team, the Dolphins rushed for a total of 196 yards and once again scored three rushing touchdowns against a defense that tied for the NFL lead by allowing just five scores on the ground *all year.*

The Dolphins' offensive line was superb. "Yep, I've heard we're strictly a finesse team," said a sarcastic Miami offensive lineman, Larry Little. "And it has always made me a little angry. Sure, we can finesse, but today we just took it to them. Straightaway blocking much of the time.

"What we did was run at their strength, Alan Page. We thought the way to beat them was run at him. If we couldn't do that, then we would have had to try something else, or been in bad shape.

"But we came off the ball with the best because we are the best. Finesse, hell."

Little and the Dolphins' offensive line manhandled Page, Eller, Marshall, and the rest of the Minnesota defense all day long. Csonka was unstoppable, and just when it appeared that the Vikings might reverse the trend and fortify the line of scrimmage at the point of attack, Shula instituted a few of the sweeps and cut-back plays he designed to consummate the Dolphins' strategy. "The Vikings were very aggressive all day," Little added. "They overran some plays, and that's why we were able to do so well with the misdirection plays."

Miami's game plan was not just to pound the Vikings ceaselessly and physically attack and confront their ferocious front four. On the contrary, they wanted to mix their plays—as they had done all season—and attempt to keep the Vikings off balance. But Shula decided that the key was to establish the straight-ahead power game first and then implement the misdirection plays and counters, ultimately using the Vikings' overzealousness to the Dolphins' advantage.

The Dolphins had proved their mettle in a battle of titans as their *finesse* offense passed the ball a grand total of *seven* times against the vaunted Vikings' defense. Perhaps the relatively small size of the Dolphins' offensive line helped support the misguided notion that Miami employed a finesse attack. The starters on both of the Dolphins' Super Bowl winning teams (1972 and 1973) were somewhat undersized, even for that era: left tackle Norm Evans, 6' 5", 250; left guard Larry Little, 6' 1", 265;

center Jim Langer, 6' 2", 250; right guard Bob Kuechenberg, 6' 2", 253; right tackle Doug Crusan, 6' 5", 250. Clearly, though, Miami could whip you with raw power and brute force as easily as they could with finesse and technique. And their coach paved the way for their success with brilliantly conceived strategies specifically designed for each opponent they faced. "The underlying factor on our team," said Little, "is that we just have a great coach in Don Shula. And I'm not blowing smoke at him." In the end, Miami had won their second straight Super Bowl, just four years removed from the Wilson-coached AFL doormat they had been in 1969.

Whether it was his incredible penchant for game-planning opponents, his sensational knack for knowing how best to utilize the clock to his advantage, or his patience in waiting for the perfect opportunity to call the unexpected play, Shula, it seemed, was always right. His teams had the uncanny ability to grasp victory from the jaws of defeat. No matter the situation, Shula always seemed to have the edge on his opponents. In fact, the Dolphins led the league in fewest penalties incurred for an amazing nine straight years (1976–1984) and twelve out of twenty-six seasons overall. As Shula always preached, there are no insignificant details, and no advantage is too small to dismiss.

Another avenue Shula used to gain an edge was film study. One of his basic coaching tenets was to try and benefit from every game and every experience in an attempt to expand his own capacities and enhance his teams' abilities. Extensive film analysis of each encounter, Shula discovered, could often expose an obscure detail, which though believed to be of minor consequence by others could actually yield major dividends to the more astute "film critics."

Perhaps a problem as innocuous as a flaw in a formation or a player's stance was detected, either of which could have tipped off the opposition as to Miami's intentions in a given situation and potentially resulted in a game being lost instead of won. The issue was immediately attended to by the Dolphins' coaches. And though it may sound trite and/or meticulous, Shula was often heard to say, "There is no such thing as a small error."

Under Don Shula's guidance, the Miami Dolphins epitomized the word "team" perhaps more than any other franchise the game has ever seen. Shula made certain that every player on the club had a job to do and that every player understood that it was his organizational responsibility to carry out his assignment in the anticipated fashion. Shula and his coaches had gone to great lengths to design a comprehensive system to win football games, and he expected each member of the squad to show respect for those efforts—as well as the labors of his fellow teammates—by sustaining his share of the load. Due to this operational credo, the entire team developed a certain synergy and intensity that enabled them to perform with the workmanlike efficiency of a well-oiled machine as they systematically dismantled every club they encountered. And if a player—in any fashion—compromised the integrity of "the machine," he would have to deal directly with a harsh, unforgiving taskmaster.

Discipline, structure, and loyalty under Shula were never ambiguous concepts. If you did something wrong, you knew about it in a flash. When a player or even a coach upset Shula, they instantly received the "Shula scowl"—that chin-out, steely-eyed glare that made grown men shrivel up like prunes. "I let my emotions out," he said. "I don't mask 'em, I just let 'em go. People can read me very easily. It's part of my personality."

Jim Mandich played tight end for Shula and the Dolphins from 1970 to 1977. He was a second-round draft choice from Michigan in Shula's first year in Miami. In an *NFL Insiders* story, Mandich described his first training camp encounter with Shula in 1970. "He scared the crap out of me," Mandich said. "He had me off balance right from the beginning. I came to camp driving a '62 Valiant with flowers painted all over it. I was wearing love beads and had long hair. I walked into his [Shula's] office and he took one look at me and said, 'You're Mandich? You were the captain of the Michigan football team?'"

Mandich's career started slowly. He caught only one pass in 1970 and just three passes in 1971. "I needed a pretty stern message delivered," Mandich said. "I needed to be told, 'You're really stepping up in class, and it's going to take a lot more effort and commitment than you thought it would take to play in this league.' He [Shula] got the best player out of Jim Mandich that he could get, and that's the essence of coaching." Quite a revelation from a former player with a devil-may-care attitude. Jim Mandich ended his career with 121 receptions, all with the Dolphins. And he won two Super Bowl rings to boot.

Shula's profound influence on his players—both during and after their football careers—is strong evidence that when a leader in any realm is consistent with his methods and successful with his system, his legions will follow him to the ends of the earth. In some cases it doesn't matter if an individual was completely disrespected and denigrated by the leader.

Jim Jensen was selected by the Dolphins as an eleventh-round pick in the 1981 draft. Jensen played quarterback at Boston University. At 6' 4", 215 pounds, Jensen was big enough and versatile enough to play quarterback, wide receiver, running back, or tight end at any given time for the Dolphins. He was also a fabulous special teams player. During Jensen's rookie season, however, he made many mistakes.

"He [Shula] would say things and just about have me in tears," Jensen said. "I almost felt like quitting. It's embarrassing. He calls you every name in the book."

Now, long after his twelve-year tour under Don Shula in Miami has ended, Jensen often finds himself pondering life's uncertainties with the question: "What would Shula do?" Shula! A man who at one time made Jensen's life miserable, but a man who Jensen later came to realize just wanted the best for his team and the most from his players. Do you think Jensen would still, today, be contemplating the actions of a less demanding, less successful coach, perhaps one who coddled and nurtured him and didn't seriously challenge him to be the best he could be? I sincerely doubt it.

One might get the impression—relative to his dealings with Bubba Smith, Jim Mandich, and Jim Jensen—that Shula was inconsiderate and standoffish to his players. To a certain extent that characterization is true. But, unfortunate as it may be, that is the nature of leadership. Sometimes, in order for a coach to motivate athletes and maximize their talents, he has to provoke and confront them. If egos were bruised and someone's pride was hurt in the process, then so be it—that was the cost of victory. Sooner or later, however, players came to realize that Shula—like other highly successful coaches—just wanted to win, and that from time to time he needed to act in a boorish manner in order to achieve the results of a champion. While Shula had his fair share of "encounters" during his career, he made sure that all players were treated equally. Whether you were a first-round pick or a lowly free agent, you were held accountable to the same standards of discipline and given the same opportunity to play. "All he cared about was your ability to play football," said Nick Buoniconti, Hall of Fame linebacker who played for Shula for six years. "He treated everybody the same. If you could play the game you could play for Shula."

In 1982, a lowly eighth-round draft pick named David Woodley attempted to take advantage of the opportunity Shula gave him to direct the Dolphins' offense. After Bob Griese's retirement at the conclusion of the 1980 season, Shula installed Woodley as Miami's starting quarterback. Woodley had struggled mightily during his 1980 rookie season (see table 6-7), but Shula believed the smooth, strong-armed youngster had potential.

Unfortunately, Woodley never lived up to his coach's expectations, and he suffered through another dismal campaign in 1982. The Dolphins, however, enjoyed remarkable success despite their quarterback's inept performance. Miami compiled a 7–2 record during that strike-shortened season and finished second in the AFC (the NFL restructured the conference alignments that year, resulting in the equivalent of one fourteen-team division in each league). Thanks to a stellar defensive unit that finished second in the NFL in points allowed (131), the Dolphins easily defeated New England, San Diego, and the New York Jets in the playoffs and advanced to Super Bowl XVII to face Joe Gibbs's Washington Redskins.

Although Miami's defense made a valiant effort against Washington, Woodley's inadequacies proved too great to overcome. The Dolphins actually led 17–13 heading into the fourth quarter, but a forty-three-yard touchdown run by John Riggins with ten minutes remaining put the Redskins ahead for the first time and ultimately propelled them to a 27–17 victory.

Miami managed just nine first downs in the game, and Woodley was absolutely pathetic, completing just four of fourteen attempts for ninety-seven yards. And if you adjust his statistical summary by eliminating his one successful pass of the day—a seventy-five-yard touchdown to Jimmy Cefalo—Woodley's performance becomes utterly

Table 6-7. David Woodley's 1980–82 Passing Performance

Year	Att	Comp	Comp%	Yards	YPA	TD	INT	Rating
1980	327	176	53.8	1850	5.66	14	17	63.1
1981	366	191	52.2	2470	6.75	12	13	69.8
1982	179	98	54.7	1080	6.03	5	8	63.5

embarrassing: three for thirteen for the almost incomprehensible total of but eighteen yards. Considering Woodley's substandard season, it's a tribute to Don Shula that the 1982 Dolphins even accomplished a winning record, let alone a Super Bowl appearance.

One aspect of Shula's career that would have to be ranked as substandard was his performance in the college draft during his tenure in Miami. Shula essentially had the final say on all of Miami's selections, and most of them were used to select players who were vastly overrated. The ramifications of Shula's poor draft record eerily offer even further proof of the incredible, innate abilities the man possessed as a head coach and leader.

From 1970 through 1990 (the bulk of Shula's tenure with Miami), the Dolphins selected eighteen players in the first round of the NFL draft. The team had no pick in the 1970, 1971, 1973, 1978, and 1986 seasons and had two picks in 1976 and 1989. Of those eighteen picks, only *three* were ever good enough to receive mention on any of the six or seven All-NFL/All-Conference teams as recorded in the reference book *Total Football*. Linebacker/defensive end A.J. Duhe received one first-team designation in 1981, guard Roy Foster received one first-team appointment in 1985, and someone by the name of Marino received nineteen first-team selections in that era (must have been a mistake).

Do the following names ring a bell? Mike Kadish, Don Reese, Daryl Carlton, Kim Bokamper, Larry Gordon, A.J. Duhe, Jon Giesler, Don McNeal, David Overstreet, Roy Foster, Dan Marino (there's that guy again), Jackie Shipp, Lorenzo Hampton, John Bosa, Eric Kumerow, Sammie Smith, Louis Oliver, and Richmond Webb. Of those eighteen players—all selected in the first round of the draft by Shula and the Dolphins—one could accurately assess ten of them (more than half the list) as out-and-out busts. Of the remainder, Marino was, well, Marino. Bokamper, Gordon, Duhe, Foster, McNeal, Oliver, and Webb were all solid performers, but none was a true star. The point is that the Dolphins and Shula stunk it up in the draft department. And whether or not Shula claims that he did indeed have the final say in the matters (and I can't believe he did not, in most cases), no one would classify Donald Francis as the Einstein of the NFL draft.

The selection of Marino in 1983 was obviously the best pick of Shula's career, perhaps one of the best in the history of the NFL draft. Dan was the twenty-seventh player taken in that year's first round. Five quarterbacks were selected ahead of the soon-to-be Hall of Fame signal caller: John Elway, Todd Blackledge, Jim Kelly, Tony Eason, and Ken O'Brien. Under Shula's leadership, Marino became one of those extremely rare quarterbacks to instantly pay dividends to his benefactors, eschewing the "obligatory" two- to four-year learning curve (table 6-8).

The Dolphins were extremely high on Marino from the start. "We had him rated right up there with Elway," Shula said. "We had Elway number one and Marino second. I was surprised to see him still there at twenty-seven [the Dolphins' spot in the first round]. We went in with the idea of taking a defensive lineman, and then—when it looked like Dan might slide to our pick—I made a couple of hurried phone calls, one of which

Table 6-8. Dan Marino's 1983–85 Passing Performance

Year	Att	Comp	Comp%	Yards	YPA	TD	INT	Rating	
1983	296	173	58.4	2210	7.47	20	6	96.0	Rookie season
1984	564*	362*	64.2	5084†	9.01*	48†	17	108.9*	
1985	567	336*	59.3	4137*	7.30	30*	21	84.1	

*Led league
†All-time NFL record

was to Foge Fazio, his coach at the University of Pittsburgh." Fazio highly recommended Marino and referred to him as a "tremendous competitor" and a "super individual."

"That's good enough for me," Shula said. And the rest is history.

What separated Marino from the average quarterback was his uncanny ability to recognize the inherent weakness of any defense and his wherewithal to make intelligent decisions instantaneously under game conditions. "People don't talk enough about the quick decisions Dan made along with his quick release," said Shula. "So a blitzer could get to him, or the heavy rush could be there, but Dan would somehow get rid of the ball and make the play."

In Marino's second season (1984), Miami competed in Super Bowl XIX against the San Francisco 49ers. The Dolphins came out on the short end of a 38–16 score that day, and Marino never made it back to another championship contest during his storied seventeen-year career. But "Dan the Man" retired as the NFL's all-time leader in several passing categories—most notably yards and touchdowns—and the "Don and Dan Show" (Shula and Marino) accounted for 127 victories, seven playoff appearances, and five division titles from 1983 to 1995.

Though Shula had unparalleled success in selecting Marino in 1983 and did well in his drafts with Baltimore from 1963 to 1969, his overall draft record in Miami left much to be desired. Certainly, the Dolphins were handicapped by the fact that they did not select very high in many of those drafts. Nevertheless, over 55 percent first-round busts is a terrible percentage. And other than Marino, not one member of that first-round group ever really distinguished himself as a star player. That type of divisive, counterproductive personnel maneuvering would probably have caused the demise of 99 percent of NFL coaches who have ever lived, not to mention that it would have compromised their chances of approaching even a .500 record. How, then, did Shula acquire capable players and win football games? Like any resourceful leader, Shula exhausted all possibilities in his search for talent and would not rest until a solution to his predicament was found.

Case in point: as a result of their draft problems, Miami was unable to secure a durable, first-rate halfback for the better part of a decade. They tried drafting David Overstreet in 1981 and Sammie Smith in 1989 and even traded for Denver running back Bobby Humphrey in 1992, but nothing worked. And as good as Dan Marino was, he was not good enough to overcome a top-flight defense (which they would invariably meet in the playoffs) that had no respect for the Miami rushing attack. Although Shula must accept much of the blame for the team's poor draft record, he also commands high praise for the production he was able to generate for the Dolphins during this era by discovering the virtues of several obscure players who seemed to possess no more than pedestrian talent.

Before they played for the Dolphins, who had ever heard of Mark Higgs and Bernie Parmalee? I know: your know-it-all neighbor across the street and the Dolphins' fan three doors down will tell you *they knew* who these guys were.

Right!

Higgs was an eighth-round selection of the Dallas Cowboys in the 1988 draft. He made the team as a running back but never toted the pigskin that year. In 1989—as a member of the Philadelphia Eagles—Higgs carried the ball forty-nine times for 184 yards as a backup halfback. And though he appeared to be an adequate replacement for the Eagles, his play was obviously uninspiring, as he was released at the end of the season.

The Dolphins snatched the young running back off the waiver wire, seemingly to perform the same task with Miami that he had in Philly. But Shula saw something encouraging in the diminutive 5' 7", 199-pound running back from Kentucky. Though he played only sparingly in his first season with the Dolphins in 1990 (ten carries for sixty-seven yards), when he did—and when he practiced—Don Shula concluded that the kid had some talent. Hell, that's why Shula brings players aboard in the first place. He and/or someone whose opinion he values notices some ability in a player—however latent or raw it may be—and the Dolphins take a shot on that individual if they get the chance. And Lord knows, the Dolphins always needed help in the backfield.

Miami had drafted running back Sammie Smith in 1989's first round, but it became obvious that he was a poor investment. In 1990, Smith carried the ball 226 times for 831 yards, good enough for a 3.7 average per carry, but insufficient for a number-one pick. He also fumbled eight times in 237 touches for the terrible percentage of 3.4 fumbles for every one hundred carries. Shula hated fumbles! He hated fumbles almost as much as dolphins hate sharks. So Smith was benched and later released.

Enter Mark Higgs, Shula's 1991 "project." Higgs did not average five yards per carry. Higgs did not go on to enjoy a Hall of Fame career. What he did do, however, was produce—at or better than the level of Sammie Smith—and for a hell of a lot less money and aggravation. Higgs gained 905 yards that season and fumbled only three times in 242 touches, or 1.2/100 (an excellent ratio) (table 6-9).

The next season, Higgs duplicated his performance with 256 carries for 915 yards (a 3.6 average) and only five fumbles. And whereas Miami struggled in 1991—finishing at 8–8—they rebounded to forge an 11–5 record and earn a playoff victory in 1992.

Table 6-9. Mark Higgs, 1991 Rushing Performance

Attempts	Yards	Average	TDs
231	905	3.9	4

Shula got the most out of Mark Higgs. A smallish free agent from the basketball school of Kentucky, Higgs was a player of whom Shula could be proud and one with whom he and the Dolphins could win football games—at least until Miami could figure out how the NFL draft was supposed to work.

In 1993, the Dolphins selected Terry Kirby, a running back from Virginia, in the third round. For a middle-round pick, Kirby was adequate, but he was never going to be a satisfactory answer to the starting running-back problem. So Higgs slapped on the pads and gave it his best shot for another season. The results were similar to his past two years (186–693–3.7), and the Dolphins earned a 9–7 record while just missing the playoffs. Although Miami was *still* searching for the "right" back, Shula's instincts to acquire the services of Mark Higgs gave the team a chance to win and made the best of a bad situation.

In 1994, Miami used both Kirby and Higgs, but to a lesser extent. Kirby, as the Dolphins quickly discovered, was mainly a third-down player and would ultimately find his niche in the NFL as a pass-catching back and not as a running threat. Higgs, a smallish player to begin with, had taken a beating for several years as Miami's chief running threat and was beginning to slow down. The Dolphins desperately needed the services of another back.

Enter Bernie Parmalee. I forget which comedian offered this joke, but he put it better than I probably could. "'Bernie Parmalee, who is that?'" he said. "'Sounds like an old Jewish guy living on a pension in Florida.'" Well, the Florida part was right.

Parmalee was an undrafted free agent—a player nobody wanted—whom the Dolphins signed in 1992. In his first two years with Miami, Parmalee carried the ball a grand total of ten times. But, again, Shula saw *something* that endeared him to the former Ball State running back. Parmalee was slightly built, not very fast, not very quick, and not very elusive. Hey! Maybe that's why he wasn't drafted in the first place. But he did have a few attributes, somewhat obscure skills that most coaches and scouts couldn't appreciate relative to his obvious flaws. Except for Shula, that is. Parmalee had great balance, intensity, desire, innate toughness, and instinctive running ability.

Bernie Parmalee—the disregarded, undrafted free agent that every team bypassed—carried the ball 216 times for 868 yards (a 4.0 average) in 1994. He also gave the Dolphins a more versatile starting back than they'd had for the past few years, for he could catch passes out of the backfield as well. He hooked up with Dan Marino thirty-four times that season and between his running and pass-catching talents produced seven touchdowns. Utilizing Parmalee as the team's starting halfback, Miami went 10–6 in 1994 and won a playoff game to boot.

In 1995, Parmalee essentially duplicated his previous year's stats (table 6-10), and the Dolphins finished the season at 9–7 before losing in the first round of the playoffs.

In both the Higgs and Parmalee scenarios, Shula did what he does best: make a bad situation tolerable and coach winning football. He put the players he wanted into the positions that he chose for them. He didn't just happen to have these players or luck out and stumble onto them. He acquired them and put them in a position to succeed. That's

Table 6-10. Bernie Parmalee (first four years of his career, all with Miami)

Year	Rushing			TDs	Receiving		
	Attempts	Yards	Average		Receptions	Yards	Average
1992	6	38	6.3	0	0	0	0
1993	4	16	4.0	0	1	1	1.0
1994	216	868	4.0	6	34	249	7.3
1995	236	878	3.7	9	39	345	8.8

what great coaches do. They somehow figure out a way to put winning football players on the field and manipulate their talents to create success. In this particular instance, relative to the Miami running game, Shula made chicken salad out of chicken shit.

Some people may take a different stance on the matter. If Shula was so good— and such a great football mind—then why could he never seem to obtain a premium running back for the Dolphins? Part of the answer is that, in many prior seasons, Shula *did* have a prime starting back. In a few cases, he had *several* in one year.

From 1970 through 1975, the Dolphins relied on one or all of the combination of Larry Csonka, Mercury Morris, and Jim Kiick, with incredible results. From 1976 to 1978, the Dolphins divided the running game between Benny Malone (whom they drafted in the second round in 1974) and Norm Bulaich, whom they acquired from the Philadelphia Eagles. Both Malone and Bulaich averaged approximately 4.5 yards per carry for the Dolphins during that time. From 1979 to 1985, Miami basically utilized just two running backs. Delvin Williams was acquired from San Francisco and started from 1978 to 1980. Tony Nathan was selected by Shula in the third round of the 1979 draft, and started—at times—from 1981 to 1985. Both were very productive. Williams gained more than twenty-five hundred yards in three seasons, while Nathan averaged 4.8 yards per carry, albeit in a limited number of attempts.

But for the same reason that Brian Billick and the Baltimore Ravens can never seem to find a quarterback, and the Chicago Bears—ever since Jim McMahon departed after the 1988 season—can't seem to do the same, the Dolphins' Achilles' heel in the late 1980s and 1990s was at running back. And *every team* has an Achilles' heel. Except maybe Shula's 1972 Dolphins. Obviously, Shula and the Dolphins' front office were inadequate when it came to assessing the talents of college football players. However, the overwhelming evidence of success which abounds in Shula's thirty-three-year coaching career by far outweighs the trials and tribulations that he incurred along the way. Every coach and every leader, in any realm of society, has problems and deficiencies to overcome. But it is all about how they deal with and surmount these problems that ultimately matters. In the end, only their success or failure is scrutinized.

During the latter stages of his career, Shula could simply have given up, appeased some fans clamoring to see the team's "prized" number-one draft pick, and played the fumbling, bumbling Sammie Smith for several more years after the 1990 season. But if Shula hadn't admitted his draft mistake and hadn't brought in players such as Higgs and Parmalee to augment the Dolphins' backfield, where would Miami have been? They would almost surely have been losers—at least in a few of those seasons between 1991 and 1995. And, hell, the team actually made the playoffs in three of those years. Shula went out and got the players he needed in order to be successful. That's what great coaches do. The always meticulous, always well-prepared Don Shula made certain that every stone was turned and every avenue to success was investigated. He may have struggled in the draft, but he more than compensated with his fabulous ability to discover and deploy effective though uncelebrated talent.

If a few analysts want to give credence to the absurd theory that Shula couldn't have been the great coach people claim he was simply because he could never seem to master the draft and had difficulty adding an accomplished halfback to the Dolphins' roster in the latter part of his career, then so be it. But if you subscribe to that interpretation, then how in the world do you rationalize Miami suffering just two losing seasons in twenty-six years? Did Shula just luck out during an entire quarter century?

Shula himself had one of the most insightful remarks in regard to the luck involved with coaching NFL football when he said, "Sure, luck means a lot in football. Not having a good quarterback is bad luck." No coach—in any sport—just *happens* to get the good players. *They* put them on the field, and in a position to produce victories. If a coach employs an inadequate quarterback for an extended period of time (one with whom he cannot win football games), then that coach alone is solely responsible for the "bad luck" or poor record of the team. Although Shula had difficulty finding a quality running back with the longevity to endure, and although he did not distinguish himself in the draft process, he still put winning players at the proper positions and utilized the talent at his disposal in supreme fashion. And the bottom line is that he won—with alarming regularity.

After the 1995 season, Don Shula retired. During his career, he coached 490 games, almost thirty thousand minutes of football. His overall achievements are scintillating. He wound up as the NFL's all-time winningest coach with a record of 328–156–6, for a winning percentage of .676. He won two consecutive Super Bowls (the 1972 and 1973 seasons with the Miami Dolphins), played in four other Super Bowls (1968 with the Colts and 1971, 1982, and 1984 with Miami), produced nineteen playoff teams, won or tied for thirteen division titles, had but two losing seasons in thirty-three years, became the first coach in history to reach the hundred-win mark in his first ten seasons, was the youngest coach at the time to reach the two-hundred- and three-hundred-win plateaus, and posted the only perfect season—1972 (17–0)—in the history of the entire National Football League. I think most of us would consider that to be an "adequate" career, and considering the aforementioned draft-day blunders, I think we would all consider it mind-boggling. In 1997, Shula was inducted into the Pro Football Hall of Fame.

John Madden, one of Shula's contemporaries, had this to say of the man with whom he engaged in many a tussle. "We had all the great games with Miami, and his teams were always so damn well prepared. I was the kind of coach, if I had something going, I'd do it until you stopped it—except against Shula. Because it wouldn't be there the next time with him. That separated him."

Asked to define coaching, Shula offers this interpretation: "The important thing isn't what the coach knows. The important thing is what the coach can impart to the people he's responsible for. If we win on Sunday, it means the information got through. That's what coaching is—the ability to transmit information." And in Shula's case, the telegraph couldn't transmit information any better.

It's a fabulous achievement for a coach to take over an organization in total disarray and mold it into a winning program—especially when the task is completed in just one year. Don Shula's 1970 Miami Dolphins were an example of such a team. Shula's Dolphins, however, took the additional step of advancing to the Super Bowl in the second year of their new coach's tenure (1971). But the crowning achievement— the pièce de résistance—was realized when the 1972 Miami Dolphins took their immortal step of perfection, resoundingly consummating Shula's transformation of a moribund AFL franchise into the only undefeated champion (17–0) in the history of the National Football League—all in just three short seasons. Taking a distressed group of AFL players and developing them into a team for the ages in such short order is both an unprecedented and extraordinary distinction that sets Don Shula apart from every other coach in the history of the game (table 6-11).

Don Shula was the coach you *least* wanted to play in an important game. His name, his aura, his legacy struck fear in opposing players and coaches. However he had to do it, he was going to beat you, and deep down inside you knew it. He took the two franchises he coached to the pinnacle of success (the Super Bowl), and he did it several times over. Indeed, Don Shula could "take 'hisins' and beat 'yourins,' or take 'yourins' and beat 'hisins.'" Either way, he always won.

Table 6-11. Miami Dolphins' Seasonal Records 1966–1973

Year	League	Record	Points scored	Points allowed	Postseason
Pre-Shula					
1966	AFL	3–11	213	362	—
1967	AFL	4–10	219	407	—
1968	AFL	5–8–1	276	355	—
1969	AFL	3–10–1	233	332	—
Shula's First 4 Years					
1970	NFL	10–4	297	228	L– 1st rd
1971	NFL	10–3–1	315	174	L – Super Bowl
1972	NFL	14–0	385	171	W – Super Bowl
1973	NFL	12–2	343	150	W – Super Bowl

Don Shula's Coaching Capsule

Category	Numbers
Seasons	33
Wins	328
Losses	156
Ties	6
Winning pct.	.676
Pct. >/< avg. Super Bowl–winning coach (.601)*	+12.5%
World championships[†]	2
World championship game appearances[†]	6
World championship pct. (champ/seasons)	6.1%
Losing seasons	2
Pct. of losing seasons	6.1%
Playoff record	19–17
Playoff winning percentage	.528
Average wins per 16 games (a current season)	10.8
Average losses per 16 games	5.2

NOTE: Ties count as a half-win and a half-loss in calculating percentages.
*See Epilogue
[†]Super Bowls or NFL championships 1920–1965.

3 Years Before and After Shula

City	Years	Record	Percentage	Shula's Career Pct
				.676
Before				
Baltimore	1960–62	21–19	.525	
Miami	1967–69	12–28–2	.310	
After				
Baltimore	1968–70	20–21–1	.488	
Miami	1996–98	27–21	.563	

(continued next page)

Don Shula's Coaching Capsule *(continued)*

Yearly Records

Year	Team	Wins	Losses	Ties	Playoffs
1963	Bal	8	6	0	
1964	Bal	12	2	0	0–1
1965	Bal	10	3	1	0–1
1966	Bal	9	5	0	
1967	Bal	11	1	2	
1968	Bal	13	1	0	2–1*
1969	Bal	8	5	1	0–1
1970	Mia	10	4	0	0–1
1971	Mia	10	3	1	2–1†
1972	Mia	14	0	0	3–0‡
1973	Mia	12	2	0	3–0‡
1974	Mia	11	3	0	0–1
1975	Mia	10	4	0	
1976	Mia	6	8	0	
1977	Mia	10	4	0	
1978	Mia	11	5	0	0–1
1979	Mia	10	6	0	0–1
1980	Mia	8	8	0	
1981	Mia	11	4	1	0–1
1982	Mia	7	2	2	3–1†
1983	Mia	12	4	0	0–1
1984	Mia	14	2	0	2–1†
1985	Mia	12	4	0	1–1
1986	Mia	8	8	0	
1987	Mia	8	7	0	
1988	Mia	6	10	0	
1989	Mia	8	8	0	
1990	Mia	12	4	0	1–1
1991	Mia	8	8	0	
1992	Mia	11	5	0	1–1
1993	Mia	9	7	0	
1994	Mia	10	6	0	1–1
1995	Mia	9	7	0	0–1
Totals		328	156	6	19–17

* NFL champions
† AFC champions
‡ Won Super Bowl

Chapter 7

JOHN MADDEN

Fifty years from now, when people talk about John Madden, much of the conversation will likely concern his broadcasting career, his interesting anecdotes, his All-Madden teams, his video game empire, and his amusing Miller Beer commercials. Lest we forget, John Madden was also one of the best coaches in NFL history. He won one hundred games faster than any coach had in history back in 1978, and his lifetime winning percentage of .750 is the highest of any coach with sixty or more victories.

John Madden was born on March 10, 1936, in Austin, Minnesota. At an early age, his family moved west to Daly City, California, just outside of San Francisco. John was an accomplished athlete as a youngster, and he starred in baseball, basketball, and football at Jefferson Union High School. He was such a prolific baseball player that both the Yankees and Red Sox expressed interest in him after high school. Nevertheless, he decided to forgo a professional baseball career to pursue a college education.

Madden's college years were transitory, as he could not decide on a path in life or a school he wanted to attend permanently. He spent time at San Mateo Junior College, the University of Oregon, and Grays Harbor College in Aberdeen, Washington, before finally settling on California Polytechnic, his eventual alma mater. His studies included law and education, and he eventually earned a degree in the latter. On the athletic field, Madden once again excelled in baseball and football. This time, however, when a professional league came calling, Madden was ready to commit.

In 1958, Madden, an offensive lineman, was selected by the Philadelphia Eagles in the twenty-first round of the NFL draft. Unfortunately, he suffered a debilitating knee injury early in training camp that forced him to miss his entire rookie season. It was a traumatic and distressing experience for a young athlete just beginning his career. Madden was devastated, but true to his jovial, happy-go-lucky nature, he did not let it bother him for very long.

Madden rehabilitated his surgically repaired knee early in the morning in the whirlpool at the Eagles' complex at Franklin Field. There, he met Eagles' quarterback

Norm Van Brocklin—a pro football legend and future Hall of Famer—for the first time. Van Brocklin was a diligent student of the game who, like Madden, eventually became an NFL head coach after his playing days ended. "Dutch," as Madden called him, usually made his way to the Eagles' practice facility well before the scheduled practice time, where he would put on the projector and view film of Philadelphia's upcoming opponent. One day, since he and Madden were usually the only ones around at that early hour, Van Brocklin invited John in to watch the films with him. They both sat in the darkened room and discussed the strategies and philosophies of NFL football. Van Brocklin, being a quarterback, would naturally look for the tendencies of the defense—the alignment, the motion of the linebackers, the position of the tackles, or any of a myriad of other indicators that might be a tip-off as to their coverage or scheme. "Every defense is a little bit different," he said. "You've got to attack it a little different." Madden, a wet-behind-the-ears neophyte and all of twenty-two years old, had no idea what Van Brocklin was talking about. As a combination guard/tackle, Madden had been concerned only with his assignment and the overall responsibilities of the offensive line on any given play. It never dawned on him or, for that matter, concerned him (at the time) that there might be clues as to the inclination of the defense based on formations and/or down-and-distance considerations. Madden began to learn the nuances of planning both an attack and a defense based on the tendencies of his opponent. For the first time in his life, especially with a bum knee, John Madden started to seriously consider coaching as a career.

With his knee not responding well to treatment, Madden decided to leave the Eagles in 1959. He headed back to Cal Poly to invigorate his mind, heal his knee, earn his master's degree in education, and sort out his short-term goals in life. In 1961, Madden landed a pro bono coaching job at nearby San Luis Obispo High School, where he had been teaching as part of his master's program. He ran spring football practice for the school as it reassembled a staff that had been released after the previous season. Madden got a break when the coach from a nearby junior college stopped by practice on a recruiting trip. In his book, *Hey, Wait a Minute! I Wrote a Book!*, Madden recounted the story of landing his first paying coaching job: San Luis Obispo's athletic director, Phil Prijitel, had a son on the team in which Al Baldock, the visiting coach, was interested. While Baldock was there, he asked Prijitel if he knew of anyone who was qualified to be his line coach at Hancock Junior College, in Santa Maria, California. "I've got just the guy for you," Phil said. "He's running our spring practice."

Madden's coaching career had officially begun. For the next six years—part of which were spent earning his master's degree—Madden taught and coached at both Hancock and later at San Diego State University, where he took a position on Don Coryell's staff as a defensive coordinator in 1964. He learned important lessons about football while teaching in college classrooms. "Coaching *is* teaching," he said. "Some coaches try to make what they do sound mysterious and complicated when it's not. It's just football. But to be a good coach, you have to be a good teacher.

"In preparing for a class, a teacher has to be organized. Once in the classroom, a teacher has to get the students to settle down, to pay attention, to understand. After you teach, you discuss and then you test. Coaching football is basically the same thing. You teach in the meetings. You discuss on the practice field. You test in the game."

In 1967, John Madden took a position in professional football as linebackers coach on John Rauch's staff with the AFL's Oakland Raiders. Rauch had taken over the Raiders' head coaching responsibilities in 1966 when Oakland's managing general partner, Al Davis, relinquished the reins. During Madden's initial season, the Raiders earned a 13–1 record and advanced all the way to Super Bowl II before being beaten by Vince Lombardi's Green Bay Packers 33–14. Madden, who by now possessed a keen football intellect as well as a fanatical passion for the game, quickly impressed the Raiders, particularly Al Davis.

After another successful year in 1968, John Rauch left Oakland to take the head coaching position in Buffalo with the AFL's Bills. Rauch's departure shocked everyone. The Raiders were coming off a 12–2 season, and though they had been beaten by Joe Namath and the New York Jets for the AFC title 27–23, they were blossoming just in time for the AFL–NFL merger, which was to take effect for the 1970 season. Rauch and Davis were not getting along, though, and Rauch even accused the Raiders' boss of micromanaging and infringing on his coaching responsibilities.

Most people close to the situation assumed that Davis would hire either Ollie Spencer, longtime Raiders' assistant, or Chuck Noll, whom Davis had known since they were both assistant coaches under Sid Gillman with the San Diego Chargers in the early 1960s, as the new Raiders coach. Madden received an interview for the position, but he really didn't think he had a legitimate shot at the job given the credentials and experience of the other candidates. When Noll was hired by the Pittsburgh Steelers in late January, however, Madden's slim chances were enhanced. On February 4, 1969, in a somewhat surprising move—due to his youth and lack of seasoning—John Madden was named head coach of the Oakland Raiders. Al Davis chose a thirty-two-year-old man with an eighteen-year-old's fervor for the game of football. "The word is 'passion,'" Davis said years later. "What I saw in John is what you still see in John. It's his love of football, his love of friendship, his loyalty, and goal-oriented things."

Madden's nature was gregarious, colorful, and animated. He was also very forthright, never pulled punches, and always believed that if you let the other person know where you stand that relationships would be easier in the end. These characteristics afforded him the ability to communicate better than most people, and they were especially helpful with his new boss. While John Rauch apparently had great difficulty mastering the art of dealing with Al Davis, John Madden never had a problem. "Al knows football," Madden said. "But he never interfered with me like some people assumed. In my ten years as the Raiders' head coach, Al and I had a great relationship."

One of Madden's first rules when he took over the operation of the Oakland Raiders was that there weren't going to be many rules. "The more rules you have," he theorized, "the more rules there are to be broken." Madden implemented three basic regulations for the Raiders—be on time, pay attention, and play like hell when it's time. There were no dress codes, no mandates as to shaving or beard length, and no restrictive measures other than the three stated above. Madden believed that players should have fun playing football and that they should be allowed to express themselves and retain their individualism as long as that freedom caused no detriment to the team. Too many trivial instructions, he thought, could discourage his players' spirit and inhibit their enthusiasm.

In conjunction with his liberal team regulations and somewhat relaxed style of leadership, Madden was also one of the few coaches who believed that it was okay, even desirable, to become close with his players, to become their friend. "I never thought it was bad to let my players know I really liked them," he said. "Once they knew that, it was easier to communicate with them." And for Madden, that also meant that it was easier for him to yell at a player who made a foolish mistake or reprimand someone for being late to a meeting. "If they know that you care and that you like them as a person, it makes it much easier for them to accept a tirade when they deserve it," he said. Every day, Madden made a special effort to speak with each player, even if it was just a brief hello. "I never wanted to have the lines of communication broken," he said.

Since Oakland was coming off an excellent 1968 season, Madden didn't have to start from scratch and overhaul his entire roster. What he did have to do, however, was keep a good football team good—a task that some believe is even more difficult than rebuilding. Pittsburgh Steelers' Hall of Fame coach Chuck Noll (who won four Super Bowls in six years and was a close friend of Madden's while John was at San Diego State) had some interesting observations about sustaining success. "Being the best and staying the best are different challenges," he said. "I never believed that one was easier than the other." During Noll's years in Pittsburgh, he succeeded at both ends of the spectrum, resurrecting a floundering team and then prolonging their supremacy once they reached prominence. Relative to the latter, Noll said, "I tried to emulate Paul Brown's Cleveland team [of which he was a member] that stayed good for so long in the 1940s and '50s. We had to strive to stay focused. I told our players [with the Steelers in the 1970s] that winning a Super Bowl was much like walking a tightrope. If you look down and see how high you are, you may get dizzy and fall. But if you keep your eyes straight ahead and focus on the next game, you will keep going."

Although Madden didn't have a Super Bowl–winning team to keep focused, he did have a club that had been to the AFL title game in each of the last two years and one that had lost in Super Bowl II. As a result, he needed to devise a strategy to keep his club at peak production, resolutely motivated and passionate in their quest for a championship trophy. "Raiders' pride, a commitment to excellence"—that became Oakland's organizational motto, born of Al Davis's zest for perfection and John Madden's devotion to victory. "People with pride make a commitment to be the best, to win all their games, to lead the league," Madden said. "For those people, fear of failure is the greatest motivator. Their pride pushes against their fear."

In what turned out to be a most interesting year, Madden and the Raiders got off to a rousing start in 1969. The team was unbeaten (6–0–1) in their first seven games before succumbing to the Cincinnati Bengals in week eight. That loss represented the only setback the club sustained all season. Oakland finished the year with a 12–1–1 record (the AFL's best), led the league in scoring, finished second in points allowed, and won the Western Division by a game and a half over the Kansas City Chiefs. Strangely, though, while the Raiders led the AFL with 377 points (almost twenty-seven per game), their offensive accomplishments were the product of an extremely unbalanced attack, which, as a consequence of its highly successful yet one-dimensional nature, created some of the most bizarre statistical results imaginable. Utilizing Charlie Smith, Hewritt Dixon, Pete Banaszak, and Marv Hubbard as their primary ballcarriers, the Raiders averaged just 3.8 yards per carry (eighth out of ten teams) and finished last in the league with only four rushing touchdowns (table 7-1). In fact, the lowly Buffalo Bills—who finished next to last in the AFL with seven rushing scores—almost doubled Oakland's total.

Believe it or not, the Raiders' meager production of four rushing touchdowns in 1969 represents the lowest figure of any conference or division winner in the history of professional football, dating back to 1932 when the statistic was first recorded.

To compensate for Oakland's deficient ground attack, Madden relied on an extremely effective passing game that led the AFL in yardage (3,375), was second in yards per attempt (7.7), and accounted for the sensational total of thirty-six touchdowns. In 1969, only two teams had ever thrown for more scores in a season—the NFL's 1963 New York Giants (thirty-nine), and the AFL's 1961 Houston Oilers (forty-eight).

Oakland's dynamic aerial attack was spearheaded by a tall, rifle-armed quarterback from Notre Dame named Daryle Lamonica. Under John Rauch, from 1966 to 1968, Lamonica and the Raiders had developed a penchant for the long pass, a tactic John Madden was also a proponent of. Madden believed that if you made the defense cover the entire field, as opposed to only the first twenty yards beyond the line of scrimmage, you would automatically increase your passing efficiency. "By throwing deep [thirty to forty yards or more downfield], you loosen up the cornerbacks and safeties," he said.

Table 7-1. Rushing Touchdowns, 1969 AFL

Team	Record	Rushing TDs
Kansas City	11–3	19
San Diego	8–6	18
New York Jets	10–4	14
Denver	5–8–1	12
Houston	6–6–2	12
Miami	3–10–1	12
Boston	4–10	11
Cincinnati	4–9–1	10
Buffalo	4–10	7
Oakland	12–1–1	4

"Even a long incomplete pass keeps the defense guessing. The next time your wide receiver takes off [acts as if he's going deep] the cornerback has no choice but to turn and run with him. That's when your wide receiver can cut over the middle."

Exasperated with Oakland's inconsistent rushing attack in 1969 and cognizant of the fact that Lamonica's deep passing abilities were perfectly suited to exploit the most prevalent defensive schemes of that era, Madden wholeheartedly approved of a Raiders' strategy that emphasized the long ball. "In those years, most teams used man-to-man defenses against the pass, not the zone defenses they went to later," Madden said. "With his strong arm, Daryle could throw against a man-to-man as well as anyone. Against a man-to-man, a quarterback can usually predetermine his receiver. Daryle loved to zoom in on one receiver, either Fred Biletnikoff short, or Warren Wells deep. 'The Mad Bomber,' they called him. In six seasons he threw thirty-two touchdown passes of forty or more yards."

Nevertheless, as proficient as Oakland's passing game was in 1969, without a viable ground game to support it, the Raiders' offense could be stymied by a capable defense featuring a skilled secondary and an accomplished pass rush. This caught up to the Raiders in the playoffs when they faced the Kansas City Chiefs, a gifted defensive club that excelled in both areas.

After crushing the overmatched Houston Oilers 56–7 in the 1969 divisional playoff round, the Raiders hosted the Chiefs in the AFL championship game. Coached by the wily Hank Stram, the Chiefs had assembled some of the finest talent in professional football, including future Hall of Fame quarterback Len Dawson and several other future Hall of Fame defenders. Kansas City's entire defensive unit was spectacular, perhaps one of the all-time best, though few people ever recognize them as such. The Chiefs started eight all-stars on defense—Aaron Brown, defensive end; "Buck" Buchanan, defensive tackle (HOF); Curley Culp, defensive tackle; Bobby Bell, linebacker (HOF); Willie Lanier, middle linebacker (HOF); Jim Marsalis, cornerback; Emmitt Thomas, cornerback; and Johnny Robinson, safety. To give you an idea of the Chiefs' defensive presence in that era, consider that the average AFL team from 1968 to 1969 gave up approximately three hundred points per year. The Chiefs, however, permitted just 170 points in 1968 and 177 in 1969—both of which were a whopping 40-plus percent better than the league average. To put that in perspective, it would be equivalent to having allowed 175 points in the NFL season of 2001, 28 fewer than the league-leading Bears and a figure surpassed only once (Baltimore Ravens, 165 points in 2000) since the advent of the sixteen-game schedule (1978).

Kansas City's defense dominated the Raiders in the 1969 AFL championship contest. The Chiefs easily controlled Oakland's mediocre ground game, limiting the Raiders to just seventy-nine rushing yards and less than three yards per attempt on the afternoon. They were subsequently able to focus more of their attention on neutralizing Oakland's passing attack. As a result, the Raiders were forced to throw in the face of a fierce Kansas City pass rush. Daryle Lamonica, who missed eight minutes of the third quarter with a hand injury, was sacked four times despite the fact that Raiders' quarterbacks were sacked only twelve times the entire season. He was victimized for three interceptions as well. The Chiefs toppled Oakland 17–7 and proceeded to upset the NFL's Minnesota Vikings one week later in Super Bowl IV, 23–7.

In the 1970 NFL draft, the Raiders hoped to remedy their running-game problems by selecting Ted Koy, a halfback from Texas, in the second round. Koy, though, proved to be a bust and never even carried the ball for Oakland. He was released after just one season. The Raiders, however, had better luck in the first round of that year's draft, when they took a chance on a player that the scouts referred to as a "projection."

Raymond Chester was a multidimensional player from Morgan State, the small, black school in Maryland that had produced Cleveland's star halfback and future Hall of Famer Leroy Kelly. Chester was considered to be a risky first-round selection because he fit into one of two categories of players who were always labeled as "projections." Some players are considered to be projections because they never played their intended NFL position while they were in college. Chester, on the other hand, was regarded as a projection because he was unable to devote his complete, undivided attention to just one position while in college, which would have allowed him to develop the subtleties necessary to excel at that spot. Chester played linebacker, running back, and tight end at Morgan State. Due to his versatility, he never had sufficient time to refine his techniques at tight end, his intended NFL spot. As a result, he was, in essence, a double gamble. Not only was he a risk as a player from an obscure school who had not been exposed to big-time college competition—Kelly's success notwithstanding—but he was also a speculative selection in that he was somewhat raw and undeveloped at his projected position. Few NFL clubs would have taken a chance on drafting a player like Chester in the first round. Nevertheless, he proved to be everything Al Davis, John Madden, and Raiders' scout Ron Wolf hoped he would be, and he paid immediate dividends in his rookie season (table 7-2).

Chester was one of many talented players the Raiders drafted from black colleges in the 1960s and '70s, most of whom started and/or played key roles in Oakland's success (table 7-3)

Following the AFL–NFL merger of 1970, the Raiders were placed in the AFC's Western Division with Kansas City, San Diego, and Denver. Oakland won the division that year by compiling an 8–4–2 record. Curiously, Oakland outscored their opponents by the slim margin of just seven points (300–293), counterindicative of their first-place record. Madden, however, succeeded in getting the Raiders into the playoffs. In the first round, they hosted the upstart Miami Dolphins at the Oakland Coliseum.

Miami had been the laughingstock of the AFL. But in their first NFL season, the Dolphins—who had recently changed coaches—suddenly and inexplicably began to

Table 7-2. Raymond Chester's 1970 Performance

Year	Catches	Yards	Average	TDs
1970	42	556	13.2	7

Table 7-3. Oakland Drafts, 1967–1976

Year	Player	College	Round
Pre-Madden Years' Draftees			
1967	Gene Upshaw	Texas A & I	1
1968	Art Shell	Maryland Eastern Shore	3
1968	George Atkinson	Morris Brown	7
Madden Draftees			
1970	Raymond Chester	Morgan State	1
1970	Gerald Irons	Maryland Eastern Shore	3
1974	Henry Lawrence	Florida A & M	1
1976	Charles Philyaw	Texas Southern	2

play like champions, winning ten games and losing just four. Though no one knew it at the time, Miami would experience only two losing seasons in the next twenty-five years—thanks to a coach by the name of Don Shula. However, on the strength of two Daryle Lamonica scoring passes and an eighty-two-yard interception return for a touchdown by future Hall of Fame cornerback Willie Brown, the Raiders overcame a 7–0 Dolphins' lead to win the 1970 playoff contest 21–14.

The Raiders then traveled to Memorial Stadium in Baltimore to face the Colts. With aging quarterback Johnny Unitas at the helm, the Colts had compiled the second-best record in the NFL in 1970, 11–2–1. Baltimore held a 10–3 advantage at halftime, but Oakland rallied to tie the game early in the third quarter when George Blanda—filling in for an injured Daryle Lamonica at quarterback—hit wide receiver Fred Biletnikoff with a thirty-eight-yard touchdown pass. The Colts quickly regained the lead when kicker Jim O'Brien booted a twenty-three-yard field goal and halfback Norm Bulaich scored on an eleven-yard run. The Raiders countered with a fifteen-yard touchdown pass from Blanda to wide receiver Warren Wells to slice the lead to 20–17 early in the final quarter. But Unitas connected on a sixty-eight-yard touchdown pass to wide receiver Ray Perkins in the closing minutes of the game to seal the victory for Baltimore, 27–17.

The Raiders' loss to the Colts marked their fourth straight year of postseason disappointment. And though their 4–4 playoff record and 1968 Super Bowl appearance were none too shabby, the fact was that Oakland kept coming up short of a championship. Madden, who had been in charge for only two seasons (he was an assistant for the other two), couldn't help but wonder if he was missing some key detail that was impeding the team's progress. So, along with Al Davis, he performed a teamwide assessment to ponder the evidence.

Quarterbacking was solid. With Lamonica and Blanda, few, if any, clubs had a better one-two combination. And despite the fact that Blanda was "ancient" (forty-three years old), Madden expected no precipitous drop-off in his skills during the next year or two.

The wide receivers seemed fine as well, with sure-handed Fred Biletnikoff handling most of the shorter routes while speedster Warren Wells executed the deeper patterns.

With Raymond Chester developing into a dangerous weapon at tight end, Oakland possessed a gifted trio of pass catchers.

The offensive line had developed into a formidable group of pass blockers. While the Raiders' rushing game was certainly a sore spot, Madden and Davis had determined that the line was not the primary cause of the problem. With eventual Hall of Famers Art Shell (tackle), Gene Upshaw (guard), and Jim Otto (center) leading the way, great things were expected from this group in the immediate future.

Oakland's running-back situation, however, was a different story. While Madden was pleased with the slow but steady progress of youngster Marv Hubbard at fullback, he was well aware that the halfback position was in desperate need of an upgrade. Other than Hewritt Dixon, no halfback on the roster seemed to be of starting quality. And though Dixon had an excellent 4.4 average and had gained 861 yards in 1970, he was inconsistent and would be turning thirty-one years old during the coming season. To further demonstrate the necessity for a more productive running game, statistics indicated that the 1970 Raiders were similar to the 1969 team in two dubious areas. Oakland placed twenty-third out of twenty-six teams in rushing touchdowns in 1970 and were outscored by their opponents (ten touchdowns to seven) in that same category—the only playoff team that year with such a distinction. While the Raiders league-leading total of twenty-eight touchdown passes tended to mitigate against their low number of rushing scores—as it had in 1969—it was becoming quite obvious that the combination of numerous touchdown passes and very few rushing scores was an insufficient formula to produce postseason success. Though Madden didn't abandon the passing game or forgo his strategy of attacking opponents with deep passes down the field, both he and Al Davis knew that it was imperative for Oakland to significantly improve their ground game if they hoped to conquer the elite teams of the NFL in the near future.

On defense, Oakland had regressed badly from their outstanding performance of 1969. They slipped from second in the AFL in points allowed (permitting an average of 17.3 per game) to a tie for nineteenth in the NFL in 1970 (yielding an average of 20.9 per contest). They also declined from averages of 3.8 and 6.0 yards allowed on rushing and passing plays respectively in 1969 to 4.4 and 7.0 in 1970. Though the competition was better in the NFL, the Raiders' defensive ranking of twentieth in the NFL (total yardage allowed) out of twenty-six teams placed them well below many of the AFL teams they had easily bettered in 1969. These numbers were disturbing to Madden and the coaching staff. They knew that they had to rectify the Raiders' defensive inadequacies if Oakland was to have a chance to fulfill its championship aspirations.

In the 1971 draft (table 7-4), the Raiders selected three players who filled pivotal roles for the club over the next several seasons. Most importantly, each seemed to plug a hole in one of the team's most deficient areas.

Jack Tatum patrolled the Raiders' secondary for the next nine years (1971–1979). He was the toughest, hardest-hitting safety in the game, and his nickname, "The Assassin," was well deserved. "He was a great player for the Raiders," Madden said,

Table 7-4. Oakland Raiders' 1971 Draft

Round	Player	Position	College
1	Jack Tatum	S	Ohio State
2	Phil Villapiano	LB	Bowling Green
4	Clarence Davis	HB	UCS

"not just a good player, a great player." Tatum, who was eventually perceived as being a dirty player, made opposing receivers think twice, maybe even three times before attempting to catch a ball over the middle of the field. He also filled holes in the team's run defense, making ballcarriers pay the price each time they met. Unfortunately, one of Tatum's hits permanently paralyzed New England Patriots' wide receiver Darryl Stingley in 1978. After the incident, Tatum's character came into question, and his reputation took a bigger hit than even *he* could deliver. Madden nonetheless never wavered in his defense of Tatum. "It [the hit] didn't appear to be any harder than he hit some other receivers—maybe not even as hard," Madden said. "Darryl got caught in midair, and maybe if he was on his feet he might have been able to absorb some of the hit. After it happened, nobody felt worse about it than Jack."

Phil Villapiano was one of Madden's favorite linebackers. "To me, there are three types of people, whether they're football players or not," Madden said. "People who make things happen, people who watch things happen, and people who don't know what's happening. Phil *made* things happen. He had a linebacker's personality, he loved to hit—like Dick Butkus did. Believe me, not many guys love to hit, but Phil did."

Like Tatum and Villapiano, running back Clarence Davis was also a hard hitter—he hit the *hole* hard. Some runners dance around in the backfield, some like to follow their blockers through the line, some try to outrun the defenders, and others just hit the hole hard and fast, hoping to catch the defense out of position, before they have a chance to react. Though Davis was small and possessed excellent speed, his mentality was the latter. He loved contact and possessed a running style usually reserved for bigger backs.

Davis, who had been a guard in high school, provided Oakland with everything they desired in a halfback: speed, toughness, pass-catching ability, and blocking. Madden loved him, not only because he gave the team a breakaway threat out of the backfield, but because he played the game with a reckless abandon that typified the Raiders' mentality. "Clarence was probably the best blocking halfback I've ever known," Madden said. "I never was interested in the great runner who couldn't block, and in Clarence [though smaller than most backs], I got a good runner and a great blocker. He didn't just block, he leveled people."

Unfortunately, when you play with a fullback's mentality and you're only 5' 10", 195 pounds, you're going to take some wicked hits. Though Davis played "bigger" than his size and could take a beating, he still was not sturdy enough to endure the burden of Oakland's entire offensive load. So Madden alternated him with other halfbacks during his time with the Raiders, extending Davis's career and prolonging his effectiveness in Oakland's backfield.

Table 7-5. Oakland Raiders' Rushing Offense and Defense, 1970–72

	1970	1971	1972
Average per rush	4.2	4.5	4.6
Rushing TDs	7	19	20
Average per rush against	4.4	3.6	3.8
Rushing TDs allowed	10	14	9

In 1971 and 1972, the Raiders began to correct the deficiencies that had haunted them for the last two seasons (table 7-5). They completely reversed their rushing statistics, averaging 4.5 yards per carry in 1971 (third in the NFL) while limiting their opponents to an average of just 3.6 (good enough for eighth defensively). They almost tripled their touchdown total on the ground, increasing their rushing scores to nineteen in 1971 and twenty in 1972. The addition of Davis and the emergence of Hubbard finally gave the Raiders a running attack that could compete with the league's best.

Oakland's statistical advancement, though quite commendable, failed to increase the team's victory total in 1971. The Raiders finished with the identical 8–4–2 record they had achieved in 1970 and were beaten out of the last playoff spot by the Colts, who finished with a 10–4 record. In 1972, however, with even more improvement, the Raiders redeemed themselves, compiling a 10–3–1 mark and reclaiming the AFC's Western Division title. In the playoffs, they traveled to Pittsburgh to face a Steelers team that was making their first postseason appearance since 1947.

Pittsburgh coach Chuck Noll was one of Madden's closest friends in professional football. They first met when Madden was an assistant at San Diego State and Noll was in the NFL as a member of the San Diego Chargers' staff. In fact, Noll attempted to enlist Madden as his defensive coordinator immediately after the Steelers hired him in 1969. Madden, of course, declined the offer and was named head coach of the Raiders shortly thereafter. During Noll's first three years in Pittsburgh (1969–1971), his teams were abysmal, collecting just twelve victories in forty-two games. But after several crops of young players had a chance to mature, the Steelers turned the corner and won eleven games (including a victory over the Raiders in week one) and a division title in 1972.

Pittsburgh's strength was their defense. Led by defensive tackle Joe Greene and linebacker Jack Ham (both future Hall of Famers), the Steelers were building one of the most feared defensive units in the history of the league. In 1972, Pittsburgh allowed just 175 points (second in the NFL) while finishing fourth in the AFC against the run and leading the league with twenty-eight interceptions. Offensively, however, the Steelers were strictly a one-dimensional team. Quarterback Terry Bradshaw was young and erratic. As a result, Pittsburgh relied almost exclusively on a superior ground game which led the NFL with a remarkable 5.1 yards per carry. Rookie running back Franco Harris exploded on the scene by gaining more than one thousand yards and averaging an incredible 5.6 yards per attempt—almost 37 percent better than the league standard of 4.1.

Since Oakland's offense, equipped with a new and improved running game, had finished third in the NFL in scoring (26.1 per game), and their defense led the AFC in rushing average allowed (3.8), the playoff meeting created a classic matchup of two irresistible forces (Pittsburgh's ground game and Oakland's high-scoring attack) meeting two immovable objects (the opposing defensive units). The key to the game seemed to be Oakland's ability to stop Franco Harris. If the Raiders could stifle the Steelers' dynamic young halfback—thus forcing the inexperienced and interception-prone Bradshaw to be the focus of the Pittsburgh offense—Oakland would have a distinct advantage. Madden stacked the deck in his favor by deciding to commit more players to run support (to stop Harris), almost daring Bradshaw to beat them in the air.

The game immediately developed into a defensive struggle, and the first half ended in a scoreless tie. Pittsburgh took a 6–0 lead in the second half on the strength of two short Roy Gerela field goals, the second of which came with just 4:18 remaining in the contest. On the next possession, Oakland—led by backup quarterback Kenny Stabler, who had taken over for an injured Daryle Lamonica—moved the ball into Steelers' territory. The Raiders had reached the Pittsburgh thirty-yard line when a unusual occurrence turned the tide of the football game. Stabler, who had the mobility of a pet rock, dropped back to pass against a Steelers' blitz. Stabler deftly sidestepped the onslaught and plodded towards the end zone with the adroitness of an ox and the speed of a lame turtle. The Steelers—who must have been either laughing too hard at the sight of Stabler's gait or had a sudden case of disorientation—were nowhere to be found, and the Raiders grabbed a 7–6 lead with just 1:13 left on the clock. The outright implausibility of this play could only be appreciated many years later, when, upon his retirement from the NFL, a quick peek at the record books revealed that Kenny Stabler had amassed the grand total of 93 rushing yards in his fifteen-year career, for a 0.8 average per carry. Yet, in one illustrious instance, the lumbering signal caller gained thirty vitally important yards against one of the best defenses of the era.

Pittsburgh was doomed. Especially when the ensuing kickoff resulted in a touchback. Bradshaw, an unaccomplished and unreliable quarterback at the time, would have to negotiate a drive of approximately forty yards in just seventy seconds in order for the Steelers to attempt a field goal.

Throughout the game, Oakland's strategy in pass defense had been to keep Bradshaw in the pocket, making him earn yardage in a conventional fashion, not with his scrambling or improvisational abilities. In the final minute, that plan did not change. "Just keep him in the pocket, don't let him get outside the ends," Madden implored.

The Raiders' defense did just that, forcing Pittsburgh into a fourth-and-ten from their own forty-yard line with just twenty-two seconds remaining. But this time, Bradshaw dropped back to pass and escaped from the containment of the Raiders' three-man pass rush. He scrambled for a few seconds, then threw a "prayer" in the middle of the field to running back "Frenchy" Fuqua. The pass reached Fuqua just as Raiders' safety Jack Tatum arrived to hit him, resulting in a carom that directed the ball high in the air and back towards the line of scrimmage. Just before Raiders' fans, coaches, and players were about to begin slapping each other in a congratulatory fashion, running back Franco Harris—who had been pass blocking near the line of scrimmage—rushed towards the ball. As the gravity-induced pigskin plummeted towards the artificial turf of Three Rivers Stadium, Harris miraculously scooped the ball up just before it hit the ground and raced forty-two yards, untouched, for what would amount to a sixty-yard, game-winning touchdown pass—if it was ruled a completion.

The stadium was a madhouse, fans incredulous as to the late heroics of their upstart Steelers. The officials were frantic, one not knowing what the other saw, and all vainly attempting to ascertain what exactly *did* transpire in the last few seconds of the game. Madden chased an official, yelling, "No good, no good." Players huddled around the referee, pleading their cases. Fuqua, who was stunned that Bradshaw even threw him the ball (because he was well covered), described the play from his vantage point. "He [Bradshaw] should have hit [Preston] Pearson, he was open. But I looked directly into those blue eyes and knew he was going to throw to me. I could see Tatum heading towards me. I just wanted to get my body between him and the ball." Which is exactly what Fuqua did. The question then became whether Tatum touched the ball before Harris caught the ricochet. In those days, rules specified that two offensive players could not touch a passed ball without a defender touching it in between. If the ball never hit Tatum, then the play had to be ruled an incomplete pass. To this day, replays are inconclusive. Nevertheless, the officials determined that the "Immaculate Reception" was legal, and the rest is history: Pittsburgh 13, Oakland 7—the toughest loss of John Madden's career.

To succeed in the NFL you need a break every now and again. The Raiders did not get one in 1972. Oakland's defense held Harris in check all day (until the last twenty-two seconds, that is), limiting the Steelers' halfback to just sixty-four yards on eighteen carries, well below his 5.6 yard average. Bradshaw was ineffective, completing only ten of twenty-four passes for a total of 115 yards and one interception. But one pass is neglected on that statistical review—the Immaculate Reception, which gave Bradshaw an additional completion of sixty yards and perhaps the most celebrated, though controversial, touchdown in NFL history. Ironically, Oakland did exactly what they set out to do—stop Harris on the ground and force Bradshaw to beat them in the air—which is quite literally what happened.

As the 1973 season began, Daryle Lamonica, at age thirty-two, showed signs of wear and tear that greatly diminished his tremendous natural ability. His throws lacked the zip and crispness that had been his trademark throughout his career. And with Oakland's second-round selection from the 1968 draft, Ken Stabler, waiting in the wings and raring to go, Madden had a quarterback controversy on his hands. By this time, perennial backup George Blanda was no more than an emergency third quarterback and wasn't being considered for the starting spot. Madden had to choose between a declining Lamonica and an inexperienced Stabler.

Madden, unlike many other coaches, had no disdain for quarterback controversies that resulted in more than one signal caller receiving extended playing time. He never believed that players rebelled or even cared that much in regard to who was playing quarterback during the intensity of a game. "If an offensive tackle is trying to block a defensive end, he's not thinking about who the quarterback is behind him," Madden said. "Sure, they might express an opinion or make their feelings public during the week, but by and large, when the game was on the line, they did their jobs and didn't worry about who was playing another position." So when the Raiders were faced with their quarterback dilemma, Madden took it in stride and didn't worry much about team morale or cohesion.

Madden chose Lamonica to start the 1973 season based on his experience. He knew that Stabler would be upset with the decision. Stabler had been in the league for five years, and though some of the circumstances that resulted in his lack of playing time were related to injuries and personal problems, Stabler believed he deserved more of a chance than the 129 passes he had attempted. Rather than let the situation deteriorate into an all-out war between himself and his young quarterback, Madden— being the straightforward, honest individual that he was—confronted Stabler directly. He told Stabler that if he wanted to start he would have to earn the position and take it away from Lamonica. "If you want to be the starter, fight for it," he told Stabler. "Don't talk about wanting it, make it happen." Madden challenged his young quarterback, and Stabler responded by outplaying Lamonica in practice every day of the week. After Lamonica turned in poor performances against Miami and Kansas City (the second and third games of the season), games in which Oakland did not score a touchdown, Madden made the switch.

Kenny Stabler, the soft-spoken left-hander from Alabama, was a masterful passer, crafty and savvy, even as a young quarterback. He didn't have the flashy, rifle arm of a Sonny Jurgensen or a Ken Anderson, and he didn't have the speed or elusiveness of a Fran Tarkenton or Roger Staubach. What he did have was a winning attitude, a quick release, and as accurate an arm as any the game had ever seen.

Oakland, however, needed to be especially attentive to protecting Stabler in the pocket. With little or no mobility—his thirty-yard scamper versus the Steelers notwithstanding—Stabler was a sitting duck for opposing pass rushers. Fortuitously for the Raiders, pass blocking was somewhat of a passion for their coach. As a former offensive lineman, Madden relished the opportunity to teach the fundamentals and subtleties of the art of pass protection, and he had become quite the expert at it. Oakland stressed basic pass blocking essentials more than any other team in the league, and Madden emphasized finishing blocks in order to ensure success.

"In pass protection, you've got to use your hands on the defensive man, you've got to ride him to the outside," Madden said. "You've got to keep him away from your quarterback as long as necessary. Some coaches tell their pass blockers that their quarterback needs three seconds to get his pass off. But when I was coaching, I didn't want time to be a factor. I taught my linemen to protect the passer until a second after he threw the ball, something that saved my quarterbacks from taking some of the multitude of hits that they usually absorb after the ball had been released. You have to protect the passer until after he gets rid of the ball."

On one occasion, Madden employed a unique yet somewhat outlandish strategy in an attempt to counteract the pass rush effect of Cedrick Hardman, an exceptionally quick defensive end with the San Francisco 49ers. Madden gained the assistance of speedy wide receiver Cliff Branch to simulate the quickness of Hardman and the pressure it would place on his left tackle, Art Shell, to contain him. Madden figured that if Shell could stay even remotely close to Branch as he darted up the field at the snap, then it would more than adequately prepare him for Hardman's onslaught. Shell eventually became a Hall of Fame offensive tackle and was considered to be one of the finest pass blockers to ever play in the NFL.

Under Madden, the Raiders were also one of the first teams to analyze sacks in order to attribute the cause of an offensive breakdown. "We had three categories," Madden said. "Sometimes an offensive lineman simply got beat by the pass rusher; other times, the quarterback floated and caused the sack; and still other times, the receiver did not react as planned, causing the sack." "Floating" was a term the Raiders' used to designate instances when the quarterback, usually a youngster, would get nervous feet and move into the sack himself. Most of the time with an experienced signal caller, the problem was that a lineman got beat, or the receiver did not adjust his pattern correctly. The time and energy spent on teaching pass protection and "researching" individual sacks led to the Oakland Raiders being one of the most proficient pass blocking teams in the NFL on an annual basis—another Madden progression.

Madden's ability to effectively and comprehensively convey the nuances of pass blocking as well as other football techniques was a benefit of his education degree from Cal Poly. "I learned that one of the most important tenets of teaching is repetition," he said. "Tell the class over and over what you want it to learn. As a coach, I applied that same principle. Show the players the play on paper. Show it to them on film. And show it to them on the field."

Madden's penchant for teaching players through repetition was never more evident than it was in his technique for analyzing game films. While many teams watched the tapes, pointed out their deficiencies, and moved on, the Raiders pointed out their deficiencies *over and over*—attempting to correct the problem right there in the film room. Whether it was faulty technique, a poor angle, a bad read, a shoddy reaction, whatever the dilemma, the Raiders sat in the film room and tried to analyze how to best overcome the problem. "Those films never lied," Madden said. "Most players sat in the room and waited for their big moment—a good run, a good tackle. I always sat there with the clicker that stops the film, runs it backwards, then runs it forward again.

"With most players, as soon as they saw themselves make a good play, they always asked the coach to show them the film again and again. But if they were beaten or made a mistake, they never said a word. Except for Jim Otto, the Raiders' center and future Hall of Famer. When he made a good play, Jim never asked to see it again. But Jim was the only player to ever to want to watch his mistakes or plays where he got beat over again. 'Keep running that back and forth,' he would say. 'I want to see what happened here.'

"He would have me run the play ten or twelve times until he was satisfied that he knew what happened—so it would never happen again," Madden said. "By doing that, Jim taught me how every player should watch game films. For what he did *wrong*, not right. 'You've got to watch for what you don't want to see,' I told the players. 'You have to listen for what you don't want to hear.'"

The practice of harping on one's mistakes rather than one's conquests was echoed by another consummate professional in addition to Jim Otto. His name—Jack Nicklaus, the quintessential professional golfer. On a flight from San Francisco to New Orleans in 1975, Madden and Nicklaus were introduced. After a brief conversation regarding football, Madden asked Jack a question: "What makes the difference in golfers?" After detailing his definition of *difference* to mean the distinction between the good golfers (professionals, but also-rans in the tournaments) and the superb players (the money winners, like Jack himself), Madden anxiously awaited Nicklaus's answer.

"Practice," Nicklaus said.

Madden was stunned. He expected to hear Nicklaus explain that the better golfers have more nerve, or more powerful wrists, or better overall skills, something of that nature.

"Practice?" Madden repeated.

Nicklaus went on to explain that when he finished a round he would begin to practice and prepare for the next round. In doing so, he would always practice the shots that he hit poorly that day, as opposed to the normal routine of many golfers who insist on practicing the shots they hit well. "All golfers like to practice the shots they hit well," Nicklaus said. "Conversely, not enough practice the shots they don't hit well. As a result, they don't get any better."

Madden needed no more evidence to convince himself that practice itself does not improve an individual or a team unless they practice what they need to do in order to get better. It's a logical, rational notion, yet one that is constantly neglected in professional sports.

The Raiders stood at 1–2 when Kenny Stabler took over at quarterback in 1973. They proceeded to go 4–0–1 in their next five games and finished the season as AFC Western Division champions with a 9–4–1 record. Oakland's rejuvenated running game continued to be effective, as Clarence Davis and Marv Hubbard helped the team rack up an average of 4.6 yards per carry—good enough for third in the NFL (table 7-6).

Table 7-6. Clarence Davis and Marv Hubbard, 1973 Rushing Performance

Attempts	Yards	Average	TDs
Davis			
116	609	5.3	4
Hubbard			
193	903	4.7	6

Table 7-7. Oakland Raiders' 1973 Defensive Statistics (26 teams)

Category	Number	League Ranking
Points allowed	175	3
Yardage allowed	3465	2
Average per rush against	3.4	2
Rushing touchdowns allowed	5	T-1
Average per pass att. against	5.4	4

Defensively, the additions of defensive linemen Otis Sistrunk and Bubba Smith (1972 and 1973 respectively), as well as the continued development of Tatum and Villapiano, helped Oakland to sustain the resurgence they had begun after their mediocre 1970 performance. As a result, the Raiders' 1973 defense established itself as one of the premier units in the NFL (table 7-7).

One of the keys to the Raiders' defensive dominance during the Madden era was their ability to single out gifted cornerbacks to select high in the draft. Al Davis felt that quarterback and cornerback were the two most important positions on a football team. Madden believed that quarterback and offensive line were the two most important. But Madden discovered a technique early in his coaching career that helped him distinguish the better cornerback prospects in any given draft. "One-steppers" was the term he used to describe them.

Normally, teams projected cornerbacks based on a system that evaluated their height, weight, speed, agility, tenacity, and productivity. If a cornerback could run the forty-yard dash in 4.5 seconds or quicker, was 5' 11" or taller, weighed 175 pounds or more, was athletic, a decent tackler, and made a few interceptions, he was a candidate to be taken high in the draft. A corner's speed was of prime importance to the scouts. It gave the athlete the wherewithal to stay stride for stride with the fastest offensive players and was directly related to an individual's ability to correct coverage mistakes as the ball traveled from the quarterback to an open receiver, a talent often referred to as "catch-up" speed. Though speed and catch-up speed were related, they were a little bit different.

Catch-up speed had three fundamental properties—straight-line speed, coverage skills, and reaction time. These were considered the key components to a player's ability to read and react to the movements of the receiver and the quarterback's release of the football. A player with average straight-line corner speed—say, 4.52— could actually play "faster" than a player with 4.42 speed due to superior coverage ability and quicker reflexes. These would place him nearer to the receiver and allow him to react and close on the ball faster than someone with exceptional speed but less dexterity. So scouts developed agility drills designed to decipher a corner's "true" game speed—his catch-up speed. Cornerbacks were timed as they ran around several plastic traffic cones placed at fixed locations on the field, an exercise which supposedly simulated reaction times under game conditions. Trouble was, there was no quarterback, no moving receiver, and no ball traveling towards them as they ran what amounted to an obstacle course. Oftentimes, the eventual clocking would not adequately translate to a realistic game situation. Therefore, cornerback mistakes were among the most prevalent in the draft, a situation which prevails to this day.

John Madden simplified and improved the process of cornerback evaluation. But he felt it best to keep the information to himself and the Raiders and refused to share it with his "friends" on other NFL teams. "Watching game films, I stopped the projector as the receiver made his cut," he said. "At that frozen moment, the cornerback was usually backpedaling. But how many more steps did he take before reacting and moving towards the receiver? That's how I measured a cornerback.

"The best cornerbacks usually take one more backward step before reacting. Hence the term 'one-steppers.' Other corners take two or three more backwards steps, some even take four.

"Anybody who is a two-stepper is usually a good cornerback in the NFL. But a three- or four-stepper has trouble staying with a good receiver. You'd be surprised how many three- and four-steppers stay around for many years without much production."

The scouts' tools, particularly the way they measured catch-up speed (the obstacle course) were grossly inadequate. If a slower player had good coverage ability (i.e., he was never far behind the receiver) and quick reactions (a one-stepper), then his questionable speed—both his straight-line speed and, perhaps, his obstacle course time, neither of which adequately gauged coverage skills or in-game reactive capabilities—was of less consequence. Conversely, if a faster player had poor coverage ability and slower reactions (a four-stepper), his greater speed would be of little benefit. The Raiders' unique scouting method gave them a huge edge in determining which cornerbacks were gifted pass defenders as opposed to those who were track stars masquerading as football players.

Raiders' cornerbacks, in both the John Madden era and later, after he retired, were among the best in NFL history. And most were chosen based on Madden's selection system, most notably Mike Haynes, Lester Hayes, Neal Colzie, Terry McDaniel, and Charles Woodson—five of the absolute best in the NFL since 1975.

In addition to his ingenious player evaluation technique, Madden also developed a pass defense scheme that he believed greatly enhanced the coverage abilities of his cornerbacks as well as the team's overall defensive effectiveness. "No matter how quick a cornerback was, I never wanted him to line up more than seven yards off the wide receiver," Madden explained. "In training camp, in fact, I never let them line up more than five yards off their man. That way, it forced them to cover tight and short. When a corner was more than seven yards off his man, I always felt he tended to sit back and wait for something to happen, rather than reacting to what *was* happening." "Soft" coverage of this type permitted countless short but critical completions, something that drove Madden crazy.

Most coaches disdain tight coverage, insisting that it's too risky. Actually, it winds up being much more effective in the long run, since it enables your cornerbacks to break up numerous short, drive-saving offensive plays that would otherwise result in first downs.

Obviously, a high percentage of passes are of the short variety. On short throws, the defender is either in close proximity to the play or it usually results in a completion. If the defensive back is too far away (soft coverage), he has absolutely no chance to react and defend the play, as the ball reaches its target very quickly. There will be instances when a defensive back employing tight coverage gets beat by a receiver faking a shorter route and going long. But on those passes, the defender still has a chance to catch up to the play while the ball is in the air, which, on deep throws, can be as long as three or four seconds. Since the majority of deep passes are slightly underthrown anyway, that gives the defensive back even more of an opportunity to recover and knock down or intercept the pass. The multitude of short passes that can be broken up will more than offset the few instances where a receiver going long gets a step or two on the defensive back. It usually takes a perfect throw to complete a deep pass play, while shorter routes—especially with no defender in the vicinity—can often succeed with poor execution. Certainly, players and coaches need to be sensible in the application of a close-coverage system, as it can backfire if it is overemphasized. Nevertheless, it is clear that an aggressive pass defense scheme will work better than a conservative one. Only the most intelligent and confident coaches, however, will have the courage to engage the tactic.

As a result of Oakland's tight-coverage strategy, the Raiders' defense led the NFL by permitting the lowest completion percentage average (46.1 percent) from 1972 to 1975 (see table 7-8). Only once (1971) during Madden's tenure (1969–1978) did Oakland's defense allow a higher completion rate than the league average. Furthermore, Oakland won 103 games in ten years and finished among the top ten teams in points allowed six times during that stretch. All of which tends to validate the effectiveness of Madden's brilliant approach to pass defense.

Ironically, as accomplished as the Raiders' defense was in limiting opponents' completion percentage, Oakland's new starting quarterback, Kenny Stabler, was just as adept at accumulating a high completion rate. After taking over for Lamonica in week four of the 1973 season, Stabler proceeded to lead the league in completion percentage (62.7) and compiled quite impressive overall numbers (table 7-9).

Table 7-8. Oakland Raiders' Opponent Completion Percentage

Year	Percent	NFL Avg	+/– NFL Avg	Rank/ Teams	Points Allowed	Rank/ Teams	Team Record
1972	47.7	51.7	+7.7	4/26	248	8/26	10–3–1
1973	45.9	52.0	+11.7	3/26	175	3/26	9–4–1
1974	47.7	52.5	+9.1	5/26	228	9/26	12–2
1975	43.0	52.5	+18.1	1/26	255	7/26	11–3
4-year avg	46.1	52.2	+11.7	3.25/26	226.5	6.75/26	—

Table 7-9. Ken Stabler's 1973 Passing Performance

Year	Att	Comp	Comp%	Yards	YPA	TD	INT	Rating
1973	260	163	62.7	1997	7.68	14	10	88.3

With Stabler now entrenched as the starter; with clutch receivers in the form of Fred Biletnikoff and speed merchant Cliff Branch (drafted in 1972); with a young speed back like Clarence Davis to complement fullback Marv Hubbard; with a formidable, experienced offensive line led by Otto, Shell, and Upshaw; and with an intimidating defense headed by linebacker Phil Villapiano, cornerback Willie Brown, and safety Jack Tatum, Oakland entered the 1973 playoffs seemingly poised for a run at Super Bowl VIII.

In the opening round of the NFL's postseason extravaganza, the Raiders once more matched up with the Pittsburgh Steelers. This time, however, the game was played in the friendly confines of the Oakland–Alameda County Coliseum. Home field hadn't helped the Raiders during the regular season, as the Steelers once again had Oakland's number, 17–9. Interestingly, a heated debate raged both during and after that regular season game—a debate that fueled the fire for what was quickly becoming one of the fiercest rivalries in the NFL. It seems the Steelers accused Oakland of clock malfeasance—among other things—insinuating that the Raiders had their clock operator give them an unfair advantage on a late first-half drive that took Oakland deep into Steelers' territory.

"There were twelve seconds left in the second quarter when Lamonica threw a pass to Mike Siani, and he was tackled in the middle of the field at the sixteen-yard line," said Pittsburgh coach Chuck Noll. "We thought time had run out, but the clock was stopped with one second left on a supposed timeout. We didn't see anybody on the field call it, and if it came from the bench it was illegal." Oakland proceeded to kick a field goal just before the gun ended the half.

In addition, although Pittsburgh's vaunted front four sacked Oakland's quarterbacks five times and forced four interceptions during that game, the Steelers claimed that the Raiders' offensive linemen illegally covered their jerseys with some sort of slippery substance to prevent the Steelers' defense from grabbing them. "It seemed too slick to just be water," said Steelers' defensive end Dwight White. "I don't know what it was, but it might be worth an investigation."

Madden, of course, was furious. "In the first place, all those things they're talking about are in the officials' jurisdiction," he said. "If the Steelers claimed there was anything wrong, it was the officials' job to correct it."

In light of the fact that Madden would do almost anything it took to win, especially against the Steelers—a team quickly becoming his most hated rival—the scenario is not quite as outlandish as one might think. Also, considering that a chapter in his later book, *Hey, Wait a Minute! I Wrote a Book!*, was titled "My Fair Advantage" and spoke of a myriad of tricks and gimmicks he initiated over the years in an effort to undermine his opponents, it would not be the least bit shocking to discover that Oakland was, at the very least, guilty of wearing some sort of gel or salve to prevent the Steelers' linemen from grabbing their jerseys.

In any event, with the Raiders still seething from the indignity they suffered in the 1972 playoffs and the Steelers' accusations during the 1973 regular season contest, the 1973 playoff game was sure to be entertaining.

Oakland stormed out to a 10–0 lead in the second period. Pittsburgh countered with a Terry Bradshaw touchdown pass to Barry Pearson to cut the lead to 10–7 at the intermission. In the second half, however, the Raiders dominated. Kenny Stabler, who completed fourteen of seventeen passes for 142 yards on the day, led Oakland on several long scoring drives that produced huge amounts of yardage and demoralized the Pittsburgh defense. Marv Hubbard and Clarence Davis combined to rush for 164 yards on thirty-seven carries (a 4.4 average) against a Steelers' defense that had allowed averages of just 118 yards and a 3.4-yards-per-carry during the season. The Raiders' offensive total of 361 yards exceeded Pittsburgh's average per game yield (255) by almost 42 percent (106 yards). Meanwhile, Oakland's defense limited the Steelers to 223 total yards and completely negated the impact of halfback Franco Harris by holding him to just twenty-nine yards on nineteen attempts. In contrast to previous encounters with the Steelers, when Oakland had experienced multiple fumbles and interceptions, the Raiders suffered no turnovers en route to a 33–14 victory.

This game was a classic illustration of one of John Madden's prime coaching philosophies. "I never believed in taking what the other team gives you," he said. "If the other team gives you the short pass, it's because they *want* you to take the short pass. And that means they *don't* want you to go for the long pass. If you take what the other team gives you, chances are you're taking what you don't want."

Pittsburgh never gave anybody the running game. Their entire defensive philosophy was predicated on smothering opponents' ground attacks and forcing them to pass more frequently than desired. This enabled the Steelers to unleash their quick, physical defensive linemen who unburdened from run obligations were free to concentrate on tormenting opposing quarterbacks and forcing them into numerous mistakes. To make this tactic successful, Pittsburgh needed to be dominant at the point of attack. Since Noll and Joe Greene had joined the organization back in 1969, Pittsburgh had become one of the NFL's most accomplished run-defending teams, and their 1973 average of 3.4 yards per carry allowed ranked third in the league. It would have been easy for the Raiders to admit that they couldn't run the ball against the Steelers. That concession, though, would have forced Oakland into a passing mode, which would have enhanced Pittsburgh's pass-rush capabilities as well as the Steelers' interception opportunities. So Madden and the Raiders decided to take what *they* wanted, a running game, which disrupted the rhythm of the entire Pittsburgh defense. It forced the Steelers to become more vigilant in regard to suppressing Oakland's ground attack and, as a result, neutralized their pass rush. Had Pittsburgh not been concerned with containing the Raiders' rushing game, they could simply have teed off on Stabler and would likely have harassed him into several blunders. The end result was an easy victory for the Raiders and an AFC championship date with Don Shula and the Miami Dolphins.

In Miami, the Raiders ran into a juggernaut. The Dolphins had won the 1972 Super Bowl, finishing that year with a 17–0 record. It was the first perfect season in NFL history. In 1973, Miami did little to disprove the notion that they were one of the greatest teams of all time. The Dolphins easily defeated Oakland 27–10, and they did it in a methodical, decisive fashion that produced an awesome total of 266 rushing yards on fifty-three attempts (a 5.0 average). Although the Raiders' defense led the AFC in both rushing yardage allowed (1470) and average per carry (3.38), Miami's offensive line dominated Oakland's front four. Larry Csonka, the bruising fullback from Syracuse, led the Dolphins with 117 yards while his flashy counterpart, Mercury Morris, finished with eighty-six. Bob Griese, the Dolphins' quarterback, was arm weary after the game, having thrown the ball all of six times on the day.

In the 1974 playoffs, Oakland exacted revenge against Miami. The game is remembered as one of the most exciting in playoff history, and it began to establish the Raiders' knack for winning crucial games in the final moments. Trailing 26–21 with just 2:08 left to play and the ball at their own thirty-three, Kenny Stabler moved the Raiders down the field with masterful proficiency—staying calm, managing the clock, mixing his plays, and marching towards the goal line. The Raiders reached the Dolphins' eight-yard line with just thirty-five seconds remaining. On a first-and-goal play, Stabler dropped back to throw and was forced out of the pocket by the Miami pass rush. He started to run to his left when he was suddenly grabbed at the knees and began to go down. Just before his knee struck the field of play, he released a soft, arching pass directed in the vicinity of Clarence Davis and three Miami defenders who were grouped in the end zone. Davis miraculously outwrestled everyone for the ball and scored the winning touchdown with just twenty-six seconds left in the game on a pass attempt now commonly referred to as the "Sea of Hands Play"—a reference to the number of hands reaching for the floating football. Oakland defeated Miami 28–26 and advanced to host the Pittsburgh Steelers in the 1974 AFC championship game.

With a Super Bowl berth at stake, Oakland and Pittsburgh matched field goals to produce a 3–3 halftime tie. In the third quarter, Kenny Stabler hit wide receiver Cliff Branch with an electrifying thirty-eight-yard touchdown strike to give the Raiders a 10–3 advantage. Branch and Stabler had developed into one of the NFL's most feared combinations in 1974 (table 7-10), a result of their inherent natural abilities, exquisite timing, and impeccable coaching.

Table 7-10. Cliff Branch's 1974 Performance

Year	Receptions	Yards	Average	TDs
1974	60	1092*	18.2	13*

*Led league

Branch, a fourth-round selection in the 1972 draft, was probably the fastest player in the NFL. He was more than just a sprinter, though. Branch ran precise routes, knew how to set up defensive backs, and, with the help of teammate and fellow wide receiver Fred Biletnikoff, had developed reliable hands. During Branch's career in Oakland, both he and Biletnikoff perfected several timing patterns with quarterback Kenny Stabler that were almost impossible to defend when executed properly. One of these plays was a deep pass to the corner of the end zone that Branch, in particular, performed almost flawlessly.

When the Raiders approached their opponent's twenty-yard line and believed that the defense would be in man-for-man coverage, they sometimes called the "corner post" to score a quick touchdown. Branch would start to run what was essentially a "fly" pattern, a deep route straight down the field. But on the corner post, he would cut towards the far corner of the end zone the moment he reached the ten-yard line. Stabler would release his pass an instant before Branch changed direction, giving the defense very little time to react after the cut. With Branch's world-class speed and Stabler's deft touch, the play was often indefensible. "Figuring the quarterback's drop to near the twenty-seven-yard line and the ten yards of the end zone, that's nearly a forty-yard pass," Madden said. "But we knew if the pass was thrown when the receiver was at the ten, the timing of it was such that it would reach the far corner of the end zone when the receiver did. When the timing was perfect, we had a touchdown." In 1974, Branch led the NFL with thirteen scoring receptions.

Following Branch's touchdown catch in the third quarter of the 1974 AFC championship game, however, Pittsburgh took control of the contest. Franco Harris scored from eight yards out early in the fourth period to tie the game at ten. Then, after a Stabler pass was intercepted by linebacker Jack Ham, Terry Bradshaw hit Lynn Swann with a six-yard touchdown pass to give the Steelers a 17–10 lead. Oakland responded with a George Blanda twenty-four-yard field goal to cut the margin to four. But Harris scored again, this time on a twenty-one-yard run in the closing moments of the game to give Pittsburgh a 24–13 victory. The key to the game was the Steelers' rushing dominance. Pittsburgh accumulated 224 yards on fifty carries while limiting Oakland to just twenty-nine rushing yards on twenty-one attempts. Franco Harris led all running backs with 111 yards on twenty-nine tries. Two weeks later, in Super Bowl IX, the Steelers gained 249 more rushing yards as they dismantled the overmatched Minnesota Vikings 16–6 to earn their first NFL championship.

In 1975, Oakland compiled an 11–3 record and won their division for the sixth time in Madden's seven-year career to that point. After edging Cincinnati 31–28 in their first postseason game, the Raiders advanced to a fourth consecutive playoff encounter with the Steelers, their second straight AFC championship showdown. In a game that featured numerous turnovers, Pittsburgh took an early 10–0 lead, then held on in frigid weather conditions to secure a 16–10 victory, their third postseason conquest of the Raiders in four attempts. Once again, the Steelers' ability to control Oakland's ground attack was a crucial factor in the game's outcome. During the regular season, the Raiders' average of 184 rushing yards per game placed them third in the NFL. Yet, on this day, Oakland managed just 93 yards on the ground.

The championship game defeats of 1974 and 1975 were terribly frustrating for Madden and the Raiders. They had collected twenty-three victories in those two seasons combined and each time had advanced to the Super Bowl's doorstep only to be defeated by a team, Pittsburgh, that had become their archenemy. Though Madden's first reactions after the 1975 playoff setback were rage and anger, he knew that lambasting his club would serve no practical purpose. He was certain that the best course of action for both himself and the team was to unwind emotionally during the off-season, regroup, and attempt to develop an appropriate strategy to defeat the Steelers should the two teams meet in a future playoff encounter.

When the smoke cleared from the 1976 season, Oakland found themselves atop the NFL with a 13–1 record, having easily captured their fifth straight AFC Western Division title. The Raiders' offense, directed by the cool and composed Kenny Stabler, was simply superb that season. They led the league in both completion percentage (64.3) and touchdown passes (33), were second in yards per pass attempt (8.9), and fourth in scoring (350). However, the memory of three straight AFC championship game losses—the last two of which came against their despised rivals, the Pittsburgh Steelers—overshadowed Oakland's outstanding regular season performance. As the team headed into the 1976 playoffs, the Raiders, to a man, felt that they had to win the AFC championship, beat the Steelers in the process, and win a Super Bowl in order to truly validate their success. Though it took a miraculous fourteen-point rally in the fourth quarter to overcome the New England Patriots, 24–21, in their first postseason encounter that year, Oakland got their chance to confront Pittsburgh and avenge their previous defeats.

Pittsburgh had finished the season with a 10–4 record, winning their third straight AFC Central Division title. They subsequently blasted the Colts (in Baltimore) in the first round of the playoffs, 40–14, setting up another bitter, contentious, postseason encounter with the Raiders.

The Raiders had been preparing for this game for fifty-one weeks, dating back to the aftermath of the 1975 AFC championship contest. As a result, much of their strategy had already been determined. Defensively, Madden was confident that Oakland could rebound and contain Franco Harris and the Pittsburgh ground game. In addition, he was certain that the Raiders' defensive backs could limit the impact of the Steelers' talented young wide receiver, Lynn Swann. Offensively, however, the Raiders were still struggling to devise a suitable blocking scheme to negate the effectiveness of Pittsburgh defensive tackle Joe Greene and middle linebacker Jack Lambert. According to Madden, those two truly defined the "Steel Curtain" defense. "If you tried to block Greene, you couldn't block Lambert, and if you tried to block Lambert, then you couldn't block Greene," Madden said.

It was a vicious circle. If you attempted to double-team Greene at the point of attack with the center and a guard, then Lambert would blow up the play in the hole. If you

Table 7-11. Pittsburgh Steelers' Defensive Statistics, 1976 (28 teams)

Category	Number	NFL rank
Points allowed	138	1
Average per rush	3.2	1
Rushing TDs	5	1
Pass completion pct	42.1	2
Average per pass att	5.8	3
Rushing yards	1457	1
Total yards	3323	1

tried to single Greene, you might as well punt on first down. And Lambert was so quick and agile that it was hard to even get a man to the second level (the linebacker area) to block him in the first place. No matter what teams did, it seemed Pittsburgh's defense always had the advantage (table 7-11).

Amid all of the strategic machinations, however, Madden knew one thing for certain. If Oakland had any intention of defeating the Steelers, a modification of their offensive tactics was mandatory. In the Raiders' three playoff losses to Pittsburgh (1972, 1974, and 1975), they attempted thirty, thirty-six, and forty-two passes, respectively, while suffering the combined total of seven costly interceptions. In addition, they averaged just eighty-seven rushing yards in those three encounters, compared to their per-game standard of 174. In their only postseason victory over the Steelers (1973), they threw just seventeen passes, incurred no interceptions, and gained 232 rushing yards. Clearly, when forced to forgo their running game and engage Pittsburgh with a more risky, wide-open attack, Oakland faltered. The Steelers, inattentive to the ground game, were able to savage Raiders' quarterbacks with their relentless pass rush pressure and force Oakland into a multitude of turnovers.

In order to have the best chance for success in their upcoming encounter, the Raiders needed to reduce their passing attempts and eliminate interceptions by running the football. To accomplish this feat, Madden reinvented his conservative offensive game plan of 1973, which accentuated the ground game. Though Pittsburgh's defense was famous for destroying rushing attacks and forcing opponents to pass, Oakland was resolved to establish a running game. In essence, the Raiders were, once again, following Madden's strategy of taking what they wanted, regardless of what the defense gave them. A methodical ground attack, even a mediocre one, would be the key to Oakland's success. Not only would it automatically reduce their passing attempts, but it would also slow down Pittsburgh's pass rush by requiring them to defend a recurring ground assault. As a result, the Raiders' exposure to interceptions would be greatly diminished. The game would then hinge on Oakland's ability to produce a sufficient number of points in spite of their cautious offensive scheme. The Raiders had abandoned this approach in their last two playoff encounters with the Steelers, and it had cost them dearly. Madden was determined to not let that happen again.

In what was becoming an annual AFC championship matchup (this being the third straight between the two teams), Pittsburgh and Oakland met on December 26, 1976, in Oakland. The Raiders received a break when it was announced that both Franco Harris and Rocky Bleier, Pittsburgh's starting backfield, would miss the game due to injuries suffered versus the Colts. Buoyed by the Steelers' misfortune and a superb game plan, Oakland followed their deliberate offensive approach and took a 10–7 lead late into the second quarter. The Raiders then backed the Steelers against the proverbial wall by scoring a crucial touchdown in the last twenty seconds of the half. On a first down at the Pittsburgh four, Stabler brought Oakland out in a tight, goal-line formation, normally indicative of a running play. He faked out the Steelers' defense by tossing a play-action pass to reserve tight end Warren Bankston for a touchdown, giving the Raiders all of the momentum and a commanding 17–7 lead heading into the locker room at halftime.

In the third quarter, the Raiders put together another one of their patented "Steelers-busting" scoring drives (long and conservative), which frustrated Pittsburgh and netted Oakland a five-yard touchdown run by reserve halfback Pete Banaszak. The twelve-play, sixty-three-yard excursion ended the scoring and gave the Raiders a well-deserved 24–7 victory over Pittsburgh. Oakland was headed back to the Super Bowl for the first time since 1968, having vanquished their demons in the process.

The final statistics for the 1976 AFC championship game were quite revealing. On the ground, the Raiders gained 157 yards on fifty-one rushes for a mediocre 3.1 yards per carry. Those modest numbers, nevertheless, made it possible for Oakland to move the football—albeit, gradually—while limiting their pass attempts to sixteen. Armed with a serviceable running game, Oakland was able to avoid many obvious passing situations where Pittsburgh could deliver the full fury of its awesome pass rush. As a result, the Steelers' opportunities to induce Oakland turnovers in the passing game were greatly reduced. Kenny Stabler completed ten of Oakland's sixteen pass attempts on the day for the meager total of eighty-eight yards, but he faced a much subdued Steelers' rush and consequently suffered nary an interception. Madden's strategy worked perfectly, and the Raiders had an AFC championship trophy to prove it.

Oakland's opponents in Super Bowl XI were the Minnesota Vikings, led by head coach Bud Grant. Although any Super Bowl adversary presents a formidable challenge, the Vikings were especially worrisome to John Madden. Minnesota, a veteran team, was a three-time loser in the NFL's premier event. They had been defeated by the Kansas City Chiefs (Super Bowl IV), the Miami Dolphins (Super Bowl VIII), and the Pittsburgh Steelers (Super Bowl IX) in their prior attempts at glory, and in each instance the Vikings had been manhandled. Minnesota had never scored more than seven points in any one game and had been beaten by at least ten points in each contest. Consequently, Madden expected the Vikings' players to approach the game like wounded animals—scratching and clawing for any conceivable advantage—figuring it could very well be their last opportunity for a championship ring.

Now making his career in the announcers' booth, John Madden coached the Oakland Raiders for ten years with an amazing .750 winning percentage, earning a Super Bowl title in the process.

The Vikings' greatest asset was a quick, rugged defensive line that applied relentless pass rush pressure on opposing quarterbacks. At tackle, Minnesota featured the cat-quick, future Hall of Famer Alan Page, as well as cagey veteran Doug Sutherland. Their defensive ends were Carl Eller and Jim Marshall. Eller was known for his power and strength, while Marshall was famous for his speed and quickness off the weak side. Two factors, however, were in Oakland's favor regarding the matchup with the Vikings' defensive line. First, pass blocking was a Raiders' strength. Thanks to the techniques taught by Madden, Oakland was usually well-prepared to handle the task of protecting Kenny Stabler. Second, as talented and effective as the Minnesota linemen were, they were not as formidable as the Pittsburgh Steelers' front four, with whom the Raiders had much experience, as well as recent success.

Offensively, Oakland's game plan for the Super Bowl was relatively simple—mix plays to befuddle the Vikings' defense and mitigate against their pass-rush pressure. "We didn't want to be predictable," Madden said. "We wanted to run on passing downs, to pass on running downs, to run on running downs, and pass on passing downs. We wanted *not* to get into a regular pattern." Though few people would have described it in such an explicit, almost kindergarten-like manner, Madden delineated the precise game plan that would be necessary to properly engage his strategy.

Many times, an offense that attempts to become unpredictable takes the approach too far and succeeds in becoming exactly what they set out *not* to be—predictable. If you always do the opposite of what your opponent expects, then you eventually become predictable—you become *predictably unpredictable*—hence Madden's insistence on stressing the "running on running downs" and "passing on passing downs" part of the game plan.

Defensively, Oakland's strategy focused on containing Minnesota's aerial attack. Vikings' quarterback Fran Tarkenton was a crafty sixteen-year veteran who utilized his backs extensively in the passing game. Halfback Chuck Foreman was his favorite target. Minnesota often isolated Foreman on a linebacker to create a mismatch and exploit his speed and quickness. Oakland, however, could counter with Ted Hendricks, their future Hall of Fame linebacker. At 6′ 7″ and possessing superior instincts and veteran savvy, Hendricks excelled in pass coverage and gave the Raiders a legitimate answer to Chuck Foreman.

The game began ominously for the Raiders. In the first quarter, placekicker Errol Mann missed a twenty-nine-yard field goal attempt when the ball hit the upright. Shortly thereafter, Ray Guy had a punt blocked, and Minnesota recovered at the Oakland three-yard line. On the second play after the block, however, Vikings' running back Brent McClanahan fumbled and the Raiders recovered. An eventful first quarter ended in a scoreless tie.

In the second quarter, Oakland got rolling. After a ninety-yard drive that stalled at the Minnesota seven-yard line, Mann booted a twenty-four-yard field goal to put Oakland ahead 3–0. On the Raiders' next possession, they drove sixty-four yards in ten plays, scoring on a one-yard pass from Stabler to tight end Dave Casper that extended their advantage to 10–0. Following a Vikings' punt, Pete Banaszak scored on a one-yard run to give Oakland a commanding 16–0 lead at halftime.

Oakland increased their margin to nineteen when Mann kicked a forty-yard field goal in the third period. Minnesota tried to make a game of it when Fran Tarkenton hit wide receiver Sammy White with an eight-yard touchdown pass late in the quarter to cut the lead to 19–7. But the Raiders, who accumulated a then–Super Bowl record of 429 total yards, continued to mix their plays, which kept the Minnesota defense off balance and helped run out the clock. Oakland scored two more touchdowns on the day, the last of which came on a Willie Brown seventy-five-yard interception return, and beat the Vikings handily, 32–14. Although the final numbers indicate that Oakland outgained Minnesota by less than eighty yards (429–353), that statistic is not representative of the Raiders' dominance. Much of Minnesota's yardage came after the game had already been decided. In fact, the Vikings were limited to just eighty-six yards in the entire first half. Oakland exploited Minnesota in every aspect of the game, and their brilliant tactics worked to perfection.

Minnesota's Carl Eller summed up Madden's attack strategy. "The Raiders executed real well. We didn't put much pressure on Stabler all day. They just dictated to us pretty much what they wanted to do all day long."

Veteran Raiders' offensive lineman Art Shell put the victory in perspective. "When we beat Pittsburgh two weeks ago, we were very happy, but we felt we hadn't accomplished anything. If we lost the Super Bowl, the season wouldn't have been a success. Winning today makes our season complete. Snake [Stabler] called a super game. He was like a computer. He mixed our passes with the run so well the Vikings couldn't handle us."

"Great game," Madden told his players. "We're the champions. This is what it's all about. Nobody can say we can't win the big one."

In 1977, Oakland finished with an 11–3 record and gained entrance into the postseason as the AFC wild-card team. Defense of their Super Bowl victory began in Baltimore. Kenny Stabler and the Raiders were already famous for their last-minute victory over Miami in 1974 when they hooked up with the Colts in a celebrated overtime playoff contest on December 24, 1977. While Stabler and John Madden were always prepared to meet the tactical challenges associated with late-game strategy, the way each went about his "two-minute" routine was very different—so different that it was actually somewhat comical.

Stabler and Madden were never quite simpatico in the first place. Stabler was quiet, unassuming, and laid back. Nothing rattled him. Even in the heat of the battle, during the most trying of circumstances, he was cool as a cucumber. Madden, on the other hand, had a much more expressive personality and was demonstrative and excitable during games. He was famous for his flamboyant sideline tirades against officials and for scolding and interrogating players when they committed mental errors. Unlike Stabler, Madden was a nervous individual, restless and jittery. He had to force himself to stay out of the team's locker room prior to big games, for fear of transferring his apprehensiveness to the younger players. Madden's demeanor, though, never adversely affected his coaching abilities. In fact, it probably enhanced his effectiveness. Due to his nervous tendencies—which sometimes bordered on paranoia—Madden was obsessive with regard to preparation. Since he was fearful of overlooking a useful strategy, his game plans were among the most comprehensive in football. Consequently, during time-outs in the final moments of a close game, Madden's primary concern was to present the quarterback with all of the potential options outlined in his extensive collection of plays.

Late in the fourth quarter of their famous 1977 playoff game with Baltimore, Oakland trailed 31–28. The Raiders then began a drive in an effort to tie or win the game in regulation. All day long, Stabler had completed key third-down passes to keep Oakland drives alive. Each time the Colts thought they had the Raiders right where they wanted them, Stabler responded with a big play. There was less than a minute to go in the game when Oakland was faced with a third-and-long on their own forty-four-yard line. Stabler dropped back to throw, surveyed his receivers, and launched a pass to tight end Dave Casper in the middle of the field. Casper caught the ball and rambled all the way down to the Baltimore fourteen-yard line.

That Stabler-to-Casper completion was a microcosm of the futility of the Colts' defensive efforts the entire game. Stabler had more than four seconds to throw the ball before a Baltimore lineman got near him. The Colts' front four of John Dutton, Fred Cook, Joe Ehrmann, and Mike Barnes were one of the fiercest pass-rushing groups in the NFL, collecting almost 150 sacks from 1975–1977. On that day, however, the Raiders' offensive line completely stymied Baltimore's pressure. Despite forty Oakland pass attempts, the Colts—who averaged almost five sacks per forty opponent passes—trapped Stabler only twice. Art Shell, in particular, kept John Dutton—Baltimore's leading "stalker," with more than 40 sacks in three years—in check all game long. The beleaguered Colts' secondary—not known for their tight coverage in the first place—were no match for the superior Raiders' receivers, especially with so much time for Stabler to sit in the pocket.

After Casper's reception, Errol Mann sent the game into overtime by converting a twenty-two-yard field goal with just twenty-nine seconds remaining. Neither team scored in the first extra quarter, a rarity since the inception of overtime in 1974. But the Raiders had begun to move the ball late in that extra period, and, as time expired, they had reached the Baltimore thirteen-yard line. Stabler then meandered over to the sidelines, and, according to Madden's own account—in an excerpt from his book—the conversation was anything but inspirational and strategic.

"All right [Ken], now let's . . ." Madden waved his arms and rattled off plays he thought might work. In his usual frenzied manner, Madden was doing what he did best—planning how to win. Stabler did not seem to be very interested in his coach's strategy session. He gulped water from a paper cup and stared into the stands.

"You know what, John?" Stabler said, interrupting Madden.

"What, what?" Madden replied. "Know what?"

Stabler looked around at the crowd. "All these people are really getting their money's worth," he said. In his usual relaxed and casual manner, Stabler was doing what *he* did best—planning how to win. And though he did it in a very peculiar fashion, Stabler's demeanor was to stay calm and matter-of-factly do his job.

"Yeah, yeah, they sure are," Madden said and went back to frantically rattling off potential plays. By then, the time-out was over, and so was Madden's crash course in strategy.

As Stabler walked back into the huddle, Madden knew that he was going to score a touchdown. Deep down, Madden didn't really care that much if Stabler had seemed preoccupied during the time-out. He knew that Stabler was as well prepared as any quarterback he had ever coached. Whatever Stabler was going to do would be fine with him. Sure, Madden would have liked to discuss the strategy a little before its implementation, but that wasn't Stabler's style, and Madden knew it. Stabler called most of his own plays, and the team responded to that. And though it was Madden's job as head coach to offer input and make suggestions, in the end, he always gave Stabler the final say. "I always believed that if a quarterback is calling his plays, then they're *his* plays," Madden said, referring to plays called on the quarterback's own initiative versus ones called by the coaches on the sidelines. "I think any quarterback would rather use his plays, those he thinks will work, those he has confidence in." Stabler's teammates echoed the thoughts of their coach. "Just the way Snake called it," said Art Shell, referring to the confidence in Ken's voice, "you'd think, 'Yeah, it'll go.'" Just like it did when Dave Casper caught the game-winning touchdown pass in the left corner of the end zone to defeat the Colts in their 1977 playoff game, 37–31.

The Raiders traveled to Denver the following week to play in the 1977 AFC championship game. The Broncos, who had won the AFC's Western Division by compiling a 12–2 record, took a 14–3 lead into the fourth quarter and held on to defeat the Raiders 20–17. That loss marked the final postseason appearance of John Madden's illustrious career.

Oakland finished the 1978 campaign with a 9–7 record but failed to qualify for a playoff berth. After the season, due to a bad ulcer and the overall mental and physical stress associated with the head coaching position, John Madden retired. Whatever drive and intensity that remained within him was likely quashed by the 1978 preseason incident in which Darryl Stingley was paralyzed from his collision with Jack Tatum. Despite the fact that Madden never believed Tatum purposely intended to injure Stingley, that play seemed to finalize his decision to call it a career. Though still quite young for an NFL head coach (forty-two), his zest and enthusiasm for championships were gone forever.

After his retirement, Madden considered a career in broadcasting. His indisputable knowledge of football, combined with his dynamic personality, made him a prime candidate to be a commentator on one of the NFL's television networks. He quickly became America's favorite football broadcaster and is today recognized as one of the most entertaining, passionate, and insightful analysts ever to scrutinize the sport.

All of John Madden's distinctive qualities contributed to his triumphant career as a head coach. His background in education and his outgoing personality enabled him to excel in teaching the game of football and communicating with his athletes. His unique capacity to convey even the most complex tactics in a simple format gave his players the wherewithal to implement those strategies in a timely and proficient manner. His ingenious scouting methods afforded Oakland the opportunity to acquire the most talented players despite the fact that they selected near the bottom of the draft almost every year. And his sincere and candid relationship with his players created an atmosphere of mutual trust and respect, which produced an environment that was extremely conducive to winning. Playing football for John Madden was both a rewarding and enjoyable experience, and his players responded with an effort and intensity level that only a revered coach could elicit.

Ex-Raiders' safety George Atkinson, who played nine seasons for Madden, assessed his former mentor in this fashion. "His ability to communicate and his respect for his players made him a good coach. He also had a sense of the game, and that shows in his broadcasting. He loves football. How can you be successful and not love what you're doing?"

Al Davis, Madden's boss and lifelong friend, said, "I felt when I made John the head coach we could be friends, that he wouldn't be afraid of my assistance. He wasn't afraid to learn, and he had a quick mind. He was stubborn and proud, but we were like kids in a candy store. He had dreams. We had dreams." And those dreams were indeed realized.

Madden's accomplishments on the field included a Super Bowl victory, seven division titles, six double-digit winning seasons out of ten, eight playoff appearances, ten consecutive winning seasons, and the highest winning percentage (.750) of any coach with over sixty wins in the history of the NFL.

Few people in the history of professional football have had as extensive an impact on the game as John Madden. His superstar talents, both on and off the field, have elevated him to legendary status. He is the preeminent NFL personality of the contemporary era. His quirky style, enthusiastic voice, and animated mannerisms have become synonymous with the game itself.

John Madden is as much a part of the NFL as Bugs Bunny is a part of the Cartoon Network. And I'm not sure which one is the bigger "character"!

John Madden's Coaching Capsule

Category	Numbers
Seasons	10
Wins	103
Losses	32
Ties	7
Winning pct.	.750
Pct. >/< avg. Super Bowl–winning coach (.601)*	+24.8%
World championships[†]	1
World championship game appearances[†]	1
World championship pct. (champ/seasons)	10%
Losing seasons	0
Pct. of losing seasons	0%
Playoff record	9–7
Playoff winning percentage	.563
Average wins per 16 games (a current season)	12.0
Average losses per 16 games	4.0

NOTE: Ties count as a half-win and a half-loss in calculating percentages.
*See Epilogue
[†]Super Bowls or NFL championships 1920–1965.

3 Years Before and After Madden

City	Years	Record	Percentage	Madden's Career Pct
				.750
Before				
Oakland	1966–1968	33–8–1	.798	
After				
Oakland	1979–81	27–21	.563	

Yearly Records

Year	Team	Wins	Losses	Ties	Playoffs
1969	Oak	12	1	1	1–1
1970	Oak	8	4	2	1–1
1971	Oak	8	4	2	
1972	Oak	10	3	1	0–1
1973	Oak	9	4	1	1–1
1974	Oak	12	2	0	1–1
1975	Oak	11	3	0	1–1
1976	Oak	13	1	0	3–0*
1977	Oak	11	3	0	1–1
1978	Oak	9	7	0	
Totals		103	32	7	9–7

*Won Super Bowl

Chapter 8

CHUCK NOLL

O n January 27, 1969, Charles Henry Noll became the seventeenth head coach in the history of Pittsburgh professional football. Though most would have considered an appointment as head coach in the NFL as an occasion to celebrate, I'm not sure they would have included a position in Pittsburgh among the prime employment opportunities.

Chuck Noll was born on January 5, 1932, in Cleveland, Ohio. He attended Benedictine High School, where he excelled in academics and also played on the football team. Noll was originally a running back in high school, but when the coach asked him to move to the offensive line for the benefit of the team, he was more than willing to accommodate. The position change turned out well for Noll, as he eventually earned all-star recognition as a tackle. Most college scouts, however, were unimpressed with his talents, and Noll was bypassed by the big-time college football programs. Nevertheless—with excellent grades in addition to his football skills—he was able to earn a scholarship to the University of Dayton. With the Flyers, Noll prospered in both the classroom and on the football field. He graduated with a degree in education in 1953, and though he was overlooked coming out of high school, he was good enough to be selected by the Cleveland Browns in the twentieth round of that year's NFL draft.

During his seven-year NFL career, Noll played linebacker, guard, and center for a Browns team that claimed two championships. He was one of the original "messenger" guards for coach Paul Brown in Cleveland, as he alternated with other linemen to shuttle plays in from the Browns' bench. Early in his career, it was apparent that Noll had the attributes to become an exceptional coach. He made a lasting impression on Paul Brown. "Chuck could've called the plays without any help from me," he said, in a testament to Noll's intelligence and practical football knowledge. "That's the kind of football student he was."

In 1960, at the ripe old age of twenty-seven, Noll ended his playing days and accepted a position as defensive backfield coach on Sid Gillman's staff with the Los

Angeles (soon to become San Diego) Chargers. Six years later, he moved to Baltimore to serve in the same capacity for Don Shula and the Colts from 1966 to 1968.

Noll learned as much as he could from the highly respected head coaches for whom he worked. "You learn something from everyone," he said. "Sid was one of the game's prime researchers and offensive specialists. He loved to dissect films of other teams to see what they were doing, to determine if it was a step ahead of what we were doing. In six years there, I had more exposure to football than I normally would have received in twelve years." From Shula, Noll gained insight on organizational responsibilities and attention to detail. Placed in the unenviable position of attempting to stabilize the infamous Pittsburgh Steelers' franchise, Noll would need all the knowledge he could accumulate.

Pittsburgh's football history in the NFL started with the Pirates from 1933 to 1939. And no, Roberto Clemente never played for these football Pirates. In fact, many of the Pirates' players "never played" either, as the team managed a paltry 22–55–3 record (a .294 percentage). From 1940 to 1944, Pittsburgh's history becomes rather nebulous. The Pirates merged with the Philadelphia Eagles and the Chicago Cardinals during that time, once being known as the Steagles (Steelers–Eagles) and another year being referred to as the Carpets (Cardinals–Pitt, get it?). But the equally nebulous monikers did not help the inept franchise clear things up, as Pittsburgh finished with a combined 15–34–4 record during those five seasons.

From 1945 through 1968, the Pittsburgh franchise finally retained some stability, at least from a nickname standpoint. The Steelers, however, were far from stable on the football field. Pittsburgh produced just six winning seasons in twenty-four years and never appeared in a title game (indicating that they never won their conference crown). Even the renowned Raymond (Buddy) Parker—who had amassed a 53–28–3 record (.649) and two championships with the Chicago Cardinals and Detroit Lions from 1949 to 1956—could barely keep Pittsburgh at the .500 mark. In Parker's eight-year career with Pittsburgh (1957–1964), the Steelers went 51–47–6 and had only four winning seasons. Overall, Pittsburgh had compiled a distressing 124–165–12 (.432) record since 1945. To say that the Steelers were dreadful was akin to saying that Three Mile Island had a *slight* nuclear problem in 1979. "Steelers" had become synonymous with "losers." Changing that classification and the stigma associated with football in Pittsburgh would be no simple task.

When one recalls the exploits of the Pittsburgh Steelers in the Chuck Noll era, the words toughness, grit, determination, physicality, and intimidation come to mind. The Steelers' teams of that period—perhaps more so than any other franchise in the history of the NFL—seemed to exemplify the true essence of their fans and their city.

Pittsburgh was a steel town, and steelworkers *had* to be tough. Entire families toiled and labored exhaustively, day after day, sometimes working sixty-hour weeks in the dust and gloom of the Pennsylvania steel mills. The physical nature of the job deteriorated the mind, body, and soul, and the daily monotonous grind sapped enthusiasm and spirit. But the depressing and demanding lifestyle also made workers mentally and physically stronger, supplying them with a burning desire to achieve and advance beyond the menial existence of manual labor. That toughness and determination, which defined the people of Pittsburgh, would serve to uniquely characterize the Steelers during the Chuck Noll era.

Pittsburgh had been a losing football city for almost forty years when Noll took over in 1969. And as far as some people could see, that history would continue forever. Steelers fans were extremely skeptical as to how a neophyte head coach—who had been a below-average NFL player—could reverse the fortunes of such a monumentally moribund franchise, especially since the team was coming off a horrendous 2–11–1 season in 1968. During Noll's initial press conference in Pittsburgh upon being selected as the new "sacrificial lamb," someone posed a question as to the immediate objectives of the team: "Will you strive for respectability this year?"

"Respectability, who wants to be respectable?" Noll retorted. "That's spoken like a true loser. We're aiming for a championship—right now! We're not aiming for respectability or any other such words. The only true respectability in this game is winning a championship."

The first step towards Noll's championship goal was to bring aboard some players who actually had ability. During his career, Noll would establish himself as one of the shrewdest talent evaluators on the planet. The day before his first NFL draft as head coach of the Steelers, he made an enlightening statement when asked about his strategy for the upcoming event. "I coached against this club last year [in Baltimore], and from what I saw we need help everywhere," he said. "Tomorrow, when our turn comes, we'll just take the *best player on the board,* regardless of his position. You know he's got to be better than whoever we had there last season." Some experts scoffed at the idea of making a potentially "redundant" pick—a player at a position where the club already had a serviceable, albeit mediocre, player—when there were so many problem areas on the team. But the determined, highly educated Noll knew better.

Noll was a fundamentalist. He adhered to the belief that the only way to win consistently in the NFL was to line up opposite your competitor and blow him off the ball. And he was convinced that in order to win with such a system, he needed *premium* talent throughout his roster, not marginal athletes who filled "needs" at particular positions but in the end served only to cover up weaknesses as opposed to solving inherent problems. Noll demanded pure, athletic football prowess. He believed that talent, when properly harnessed, could devastate opponents in almost every facet of the game. He wasn't interested in drafting for need instead of ability, or in taking on players released by other NFL teams. "What we have to do is get the best players on the [draft] board and build around them," he said. "We aren't going to build this team by picking up players that can't make somebody else's roster. If you start bringing in quality athletes, you'll start winning games."

So that's exactly what Noll and the Steelers set out to do: build through the draft and select the best players available, regardless of the positions they played or the specific needs of the team.

Attitude would be a crucial measuring stick of any draft prospect the Steelers considered. "There are many impediments to winning," Noll said, "and most of them lie in the area of attitude. Nothing impedes problem solving more than a lousy attitude. And a bad attitude can spread through a locker room in a hurry." In addition, defensive players were usually ranked slightly higher than offensive players of equal ability in Noll's evaluation system. His blueprint for selecting the best available players notwithstanding, Noll was a proponent of the "defense-first" mentality. "All teams that get to the Super Bowl are good on defense," Noll said. "In order to win, you first don't lose it." Therefore—though always careful not to overly inflate a defender's rating—Noll typically chose defensive players over offensive players in situations where the prospects were evenly ranked. So when the 1969 draft presented a highly motivated defensive tackle from obscure North Texas State as the best player available at the Steelers' fourth spot in the first round, Noll was ecstatic. Joe Greene, a quick, strong, 6′ 4″, 275-pound athletic marvel was Chuck Noll's prized possession.

Greene was an instant hit for the Steelers. He was the pride of the coaching staff and a nightmare for opposing offensive linemen. "When Joe arrived at our first training camp, he changed the face of Steelers' football," Noll said. "He was so good, so relentless—even in practice—that he set a tempo which made the other players work harder." During the next decade, Greene—a future Hall of Famer—dominated the defensive line as few had ever done before.

In addition to Greene, the Steelers also chose Jon Kolb, an offensive lineman from Oklahoma State in the third round, and a defensive lineman, L.C. Greenwood, from another obscure college, Arkansas-Pine Bluff, in the tenth round. Both players eventually became all-stars, like Greene. But before the accolades began to accumulate, the Steelers and their young prodigies experienced a few growing pains.

On September 21, 1969, the Pittsburgh Steelers opened their season with a 16–13 victory over the Detroit Lions. Chuck Noll had won his first game as a head coach. Fortunately, he was not asked to hold his breath until the next conquest, as Pittsburgh failed to win another game all season. The Steelers registered a 1–13 record, were outscored by 186 points, and along with the Chicago Bears endured the worst record in the league. Though shaken by the course of events, Noll remained optimistic. "We weren't being blown off the field," he said, "we were losing because of our mistakes." But no matter how much Noll tried to downplay the appalling exhibition, the Steelers *were* being blown out, and they were far from competitive.

To declare that the Steelers "had a long way to go" would have been putting it mildly. Deep inside, though he wouldn't admit it publicly, Noll must have felt as if he had a thousand-piece jigsaw puzzle to solve and someone had just blindfolded him.

His statement to the media at his initial press conference suggested that Pittsburgh would strive for a championship in his first year, but that had been coaching rhetoric. While Noll firmly believed that his Steelers would eventually win, he also knew that building through the draft would take some time.

Rebuilding an NFL team in the 1960s and '70s was a painstaking process, much more difficult than it had been back in the 1950s. With the advent of the AFL in 1960 and the increase in the number of NFL teams to twenty-six at the time of the merger in 1970, there was much more competition for good football players than there had been in the twelve- to thirteen-team NFL of the 1950s. Available athletes (both draft eligible and recently released veterans) were divided among many more teams in the 1960s and '70s, making the reconstruction process both harder and longer. It was not uncommon for 1950s teams to add six or seven competent new players to their rosters every season, yet it was difficult to find more than three or four of these players after the AFL emerged in 1960. And since true free agency did not begin until the 1990s, the only feasible way to upgrade a club in the 1960s and '70s was by adding talented younger players over the course of several college drafts. It took time to rebuild a team. Unfortunately, time is not something with which young, inexperienced coaches are blessed. And winning just one game in your first season can shorten the time limit.

There was some good news for Chuck Noll, however. In exchange for their atrocious 1–13 record, the Steelers received the rights to the very first selection in the 1970 NFL draft. With Greene, Kolb, and Greenwood developing nicely, and the likelihood of adding a few more precocious athletes in the upcoming draft, Pittsburgh's future was not as bleak as it might have appeared to be.

His full given name was Terry Paxton Bradshaw. He was a 6' 3", 215-pound rifle-armed quarterback from Louisiana Tech who was as tough as they come. Most experts ranked him in the top five players of the 1970 draft class, though some considered Purdue's Mike Phipps to be the better quarterback prospect. Phipps had the experience of playing against top-flight competition on a weekly basis and was the more polished passer coming out of school.

Table 8-1 is a look at how the first five selections of the 1970 NFL draft actually went.

Of these players, only one would have success worthy of such high selection—Bradshaw. Mike McCoy played eleven years in the NFL and was considered a solid defensive tackle. In hindsight, however, he would not have been considered a player

Table 8-1. 1970 NFL Draft, First Five Selections

Round	Player	Position	Team
1	Terry Bradshaw	Quarterback	Pittsburgh
2	Mike McCoy	Defensive tackle	Green Bay
3	Mike Phipps	Quarterback	Cleveland Browns
4	Phil Olsen	Defensive tackle	Boston Patriots
5	Al Cowlings	Defensive end	Buffalo Bills

on whom to invest a premium draft selection. Mike Phipps's career was a total disaster, as was his selection in the third overall position by the Browns. The other two players became household names—celebrities that almost everyone seemed to know—but great football players they were not. Phil Olsen's claim to fame was that he was the brother of future Hall of Famer Merlin Olsen, a defensive tackle with the Rams at the time. Being as big and strong as Merlin, and playing at his brother's alma mater, Utah State, Phil was rated by some scouts a lot higher than he merited based on his actual abilities. Phil Olsen lasted six seasons in the league, but he was a huge disappointment. Al Cowlings played nine seasons in the NFL, but he, too, was a poor selection. Cowlings become famous, though, when a friend of his named after a breakfast drink had a run-in with the law relative to a double murder in California.

Terry Bradshaw's NFL career began inauspiciously as well. The NFL's average pass completion percentage in 1970 was 51.1; Bradshaw checked in at 38.1. Don't start screaming, yet. It gets worse. Quarterbacks that season averaged 16.4 touchdowns and 19.6 interceptions. Bradshaw accounted for six touchdowns while suffering the indignity of twenty-four "indiscretions." In Bradshaw's defense, rookie quarterbacks of that era generally experienced dismal seasons. It was commonplace for young signal callers to be inaccurate and indecisive. Nonetheless, his one-to-four touchdown-to-turnover ratio (six touchdowns and twenty-four interceptions) *was* a bit on the extreme side.

Two other Steelers' rookies drafted along with Bradshaw showed promise during the 1970 season. Ron Shanklin—a wide receiver selected in the second round out of Joe Greene's alma mater, North Texas State—emerged as a legitimate deep threat in the passing game. At 6' 1", 190 pounds, Shanklin was a big receiver who possessed the extra burst of speed necessary to rush past defensive backs and run under a long pass. While Bradshaw struggled with the complexities of an NFL passing scheme relative to the short, underneath (the coverage) throws, he excelled when asked to unleash the ball downfield. Shanklin caught thirty passes in his rookie season, which roughly equates to sixty catches in the present-day NFL. He averaged a gaudy twenty-three yards per catch in addition to collecting four touchdown receptions.

Mel Blount was drafted as a defensive back in the third round out of Southern University. At 6' 3", 205 pounds, Blount was big for a defensive back, even for a safety. As a cornerback—which is where he would earn his living with the Steelers—he was enormous. Blount had the physical ability to dominate as both a run and pass defender, a rare commodity at cornerback in the NFL. In 1970, he began a glorious career that would result in his image being cast for a bust in the NFL Hall of Fame.

The Steelers improved to a 5–9 record in 1970. They avoided a last-place finish in their division for the first time in four years. Despite the fact that the team had progressed, Noll was concerned about the club's offensive problems. Bradshaw's sporadic play at quarterback resulted in Pittsburgh scoring just 210 points in 1970, placing the Steelers twenty-first out of twenty-six teams in that category. Though Noll expected substantial progress from his inexperienced quarterback in the near future—and believed the offense would improve accordingly—he also searched for ways to make

Table 8-2. Additional Players in Pittsburgh's 1971 Draft Class

Round	Player	Position	College
2	Jack Ham	Linebacker	Penn State
4	Dwight White	Defensive end	East Texas State
5	Larry Brown	Tight end	Kansas
8	Ernie Holmes	Defensive tackle	Texas Southern
11	Mike Wagner	Defensive back	Western Illinois

Bradshaw's plight easier. As luck would have it, the Steelers assessed wide receiver Frank Lewis to be the best available player at the eighth position in the first round of the 1971 NFL draft. Lewis, like Shanklin, was a large target—6' 1", 196 pounds, with speed to burn. The addition of Lewis afforded Bradshaw the choice of two imposing speedsters on the outside, assets that Noll hoped would increase his yards-per-attempt figure and decrease his interception rate.

Table 8-2 shows some of the rest of Pittsburgh's 1971 draft class. Including Lewis, the Steelers added six future starters in this draft. Linebacker Jack Ham eventually made the Hall of Fame, while all of the others listed (except for Brown) became Pro Bowl–caliber performers. In just three seasons, Noll had put together the nucleus of a formidable football team in Pittsburgh. And he had done it his way, by obtaining superior, young talent—the best football players available, regardless of position—through the draft.

Slowly but surely, the pieces of the puzzle seemed to be finding their way into Chuck Noll's picture. As the 1971 season approached, Pittsburgh even appeared to be on the verge of entering that "respectable" category that Noll seemed to disdain.

The 1971 season was the key year in the Pittsburgh Steelers' transformation under Chuck Noll. Not because they won that season—they did not. Pittsburgh finished with a 6–8 record. However, 1971 was the year the Steelers started to learn *how* to win. Young players need time to mesh and to learn the nuances of the professional game—the tricks of the trade, as it were. In 1971, Pittsburgh's inexperienced squad began to do just that. Defensive linemen Joe Greene, L.C. Greenwood, Ernie Holmes, and Dwight White synchronized their efforts and concentrated on perfecting their pass-rushing techniques. Defensive backs Mel Blount and Mike Wagner started to develop a rapport in the secondary and worked on reducing their reaction times to pass patterns. Most importantly, by that year's end—after his second straight miserable season—quarterback Terry Bradshaw finally comprehended that success in the NFL would not come easily. He realized that in order to fully develop his talents, he needed to completely dedicate himself, mentally and physically, to the game of professional football.

Table 8-3. Terry Bradshaw's 1970–71 Passing Performance

Year	Att	Comp	Comp%	Yards	YPA	TD	INT	Rating
1970	218	83	38.1	1410	6.47	6	24	30.4
1971	373	203	54.4	2259	6.06	13	22	59.7

Table 8-4. Pittsburgh, 1971 Offensive Statistics

Category	Total	League Rank
Yards per pass attempt	5.9	23/26
Interceptions	26	20/26
Points	246	17/26

Although the Steelers had to endure many mistakes and another losing season in order to hone their skills, it was well worth the education that they received.

Due to Bradshaw's aforementioned ineffectiveness (table 8-3), the offense sputtered and was once again the team's primary concern during the off-season.

Of the twenty-six teams in the NFL, Pittsburgh ranked near the bottom of the league in the two most important passing categories—yards per attempt and interceptions, both of which contributed to the team's inferior scoring total (table 8-4). Clearly, Pittsburgh's quarterback play had to improve for the club to challenge for a playoff berth. Nevertheless, while diligently working with Bradshaw to correct the problems that had plagued his early career, the Steelers still needed to exhibit patience with their slow-developing signal caller.

The transition from college quarterback to reliable NFL passer was extremely difficult in the 1960s and '70s. In those days, college football was predominantly a running game. Many teams threw the ball less than fifteen times per contest. When they dared to put the ball in the air, it was usually a simple swing pass to a back, or a very basic route involving the tight end or wide receiver. College quarterbacks were rarely asked to decipher the weakness of the defensive alignment before throwing the football. In the NFL, however, teams employed complex passing schemes that relied heavily on the quarterback's ability to make instantaneous decisions (reads) based on the position and movement of defensive players just before and immediately after the snap of the football. As a result, college signal callers entering professional football were completely bewildered and required time to comprehend the system. The learning curve generally stretched into three seasons, and pressuring novice quarterbacks too early in their development often resulted in irreparable damage to their confidence.

Bradshaw was very talented, and Chuck Noll was convinced that he was capable of mastering the techniques necessary to prosper in the NFL. When Noll invested the number-one overall draft selection in 1970 for the raw playmaker, he figured that the learning process could stretch into three and possibly even four seasons. One of Noll's greatest strengths was that of a teacher and mentor, which he hoped would ease the transitional period for his prized student. Though Noll was often frustrated with decisions Bradshaw made during games—extremely poor judgments that often led to interceptions—and frequently engaged in heated discussions with his inconsistent young quarterback, he exhibited enormous tolerance under the circumstances and always refrained from denouncing Bradshaw in public.

"I made that mistake once," Noll admitted, referring to an incident when he publicly singled out Mel Blount for a blown coverage. Blount was subsequently lambasted in the newspapers and mercilessly booed in Three Rivers Stadium. "I made sure I never made that mistake again," Noll said.

So when Bradshaw made errors, Noll handled it privately. He was keenly aware that no quarterback could perform adequately when every mistake he made was magnified and exposed to the media—especially not a youngster. Nonetheless, though Noll displayed incredible patience with his inexperienced quarterback, he knew that Bradshaw's maturation process would have to begin soon. The natives were getting restless.

Long frustrated with the incompetent performance of the club, disillusioned Steelers fans began unleashing their angst and frustration in Bradshaw's direction. "Bradshaw-bashing" became so prevalent that Noll worried that his young quarterback might not be able to tolerate it much longer. But Terry Bradshaw was a tough, emotionally stable individual, and though it bothered him at first, he quickly learned to ignore the ridicule.

"I always wanted everyone to like me," Bradshaw said. "I wanted the city of Pittsburgh to be proud of me. But my first few seasons, I could count the number of people on my bandwagon on one finger. I had people call me a dummy and a hick. I had a lady stop me outside the stadium and tell me I stunk. I heard the people cheer when I got hurt. Rub up against enough briar patches and your hide will get pretty tough. Mine did."

Bradshaw had three main problems as a professional quarterback: poor throwing mechanics, an inability to read defenses consistently, and inadequate preparation. The mechanical deficiencies were easy to correct. Pittsburgh offensive coaches had the young quarterback repeat various drop-back procedures (foot movements) and throwing techniques over and over until the proper methods were rooted in his memory. Bradshaw's other difficulties, however, were manifestations of a more complex problem. Terry Bradshaw needed to learn how to win football games at the NFL level. Though it may sound simple, the art of teaching someone how to become a winning professional quarterback is a complex process.

Noll had been attempting to teach Bradshaw his systematic approach to winning quarterback play since the youngster's rookie season in 1970. But there were several impediments to the learning process. First, Noll's concept had to be accepted by the pupil, or it was doomed before it began. Second, as is the case with any complicated system, it had to be studied and performed repeatedly before it was mastered. Since Bradshaw didn't think he needed much help to develop into a star quarterback (believing his extraordinary talent would suffice), the young signal caller never really embraced the program and did not dedicate himself to the practice and preparatory routines necessary to successfully implement the procedures. The unfortunate axiom of human nature that states that youngsters tend to disregard advice until *after* they have experienced failure also played a role in the dilemma.

Since Bradshaw neglected to take advantage of the system during the first two years of his career, Noll decided that the best way to proceed would be to start over and get back to basics. Noll had to teach Bradshaw that winning quarterback play starts with preparation: reviewing game film and learning what to expect from certain defenses in specific situations. He then had to improve Terry's method of reading defensive keys and movement patterns before the snap. Most importantly, he had to teach his quarterback how to *not lose* a football game.

"Before you can win a game, you must first not lose it," Chuck Noll would say.

What Noll meant was that most NFL games are actually *lost,* not won. Very infrequently is a great play made that actually wins a game. More times than not, a quarterback throws an ill-advised pass that gets intercepted, or a defensive secondary blows a coverage resulting in a touchdown. And since the quarterback controls the football more than any other player on the field, it figures that he would be the one in danger of losing more games than anyone else.

In order to avoid these crucial mistakes, Bradshaw needed to learn the subtleties of offensive football. He had to know when to throw the ball away (out of bounds or into the dirt) rather than forcing it into coverage, thereby risking the interceptions that so haunted his early tenure in the NFL. He needed to understand how to read defenses and determine the "hot" receiver who would be left uncovered as the result of an impending blitz. He had to be able to instantly recognize a zone defense and exploit its weakness. Furthermore, he needed to learn the nuances of calling the precise play at the most opportune time. Back in the 1970s, many quarterbacks still called their own plays, a concept totally archaic to contemporary NFL strategists. Bradshaw had to be capable of mixing the right plays with the right formations against the most susceptible defenses. It was a lot for the young quarterback to grasp, and after two terrible years (1970–1971), it was imperative for Bradshaw to make substantial progress in a hurry.

The 1972 season was of critical importance to Noll, Bradshaw, owner Art Rooney, and the entire Pittsburgh football operation. The team needed to win that year or risk the friction and divisiveness that would surely have ensued from Noll's fourth straight losing year.

In his previous three drafts, Noll had demonstrated the willingness to gamble on players from small, lesser-known colleges. Greene, Blount, and Bradshaw were high picks from uncelebrated schools with no national reputation. But they could play, and each had the "measurables" to stack up against the premium competition that prevailed in the NFL.

This time—with the thirteenth selection in the 1972 draft—the Steelers chose a player from a school that people in Pittsburgh had actually heard of. His name was

Franco Harris, a running back from Penn State. Trouble was, Harris was not Penn State's most productive back—that distinction belonged to Lydell Mitchell (drafted by the Colts in the second round that season). Harris, however, was bigger, stronger, and faster than Mitchell. And though Joe Paterno—who as it turns out was Noll's chief competitor for the Steelers' head coaching job back in 1969—allowed Mitchell to be the Nittany Lions' prime weapon, NFL scouts made Harris the better prospect, and so did Noll.

John "Frenchy" Fuqua had been the Steelers' prime ground threat in 1970 and 1971. He had performed admirably, especially considering that he was an eleventh-round pick by the New York Giants in 1969. But even though Fuqua averaged 4.0 yards per carry in 1971 (155–625), Noll wanted a bigger back, one who could carry the team's entire workload, a player who would be more physical and durable than the 5' 11", 205-pound Fuqua.

Chuck Noll teams were never "cute." They never tried to beat their opponents with fancy plays or slick maneuvers. Noll preferred to stare his opponent in the eyes and play macho, helmet-on-helmet football and have the better team win. Former Steelers' linebacker Andy Russell recalled Noll's rudimentary football philosophy. "He always believed that if a team was trying to get fancy and utilize trick plays or decep-tive concepts, that they were all but admitting that they couldn't beat you straight up."

Enter Franco Harris. At 6' 2", 230 pounds, Harris ran the forty-yard dash in under 4.6 seconds— decent for an average-sized back, excellent for his massive size. That size-speed combination made Harris the perfect weapon in Noll's offense, and Noll wasted little time implementing him in the Steelers' lineup. In his rookie season of 1972, Harris carried the ball 188 times for 1,055 yards and a stupendous average per carry of 5.6. The Steelers as a team averaged an almost incomprehensible 5.1 yards per rushing attempt, a figure that led the league by far and was almost 25 percent greater than the NFL average of 4.1.

Pittsburgh's ground game served a dual purpose for Noll. It allowed for a fairly conservative game plan that accentuated short, elementary passing routes and empha-sized Harris's abilities to demoralize opponents with a relentless, methodical rushing attack. This took the pressure off of Bradshaw and made his reads and objectives eas-ier. The Steelers were able to keep the defense off guard and throw the ball in many second-and-four or second-and-five situations, when the defense expected a running play. Bradshaw received less pass-rush pressure and oftentimes was asked to deliver only a short completion in order to secure a first down. Since Harris could carry the ball over and over with no discernible drop-off in his play, the system seemed to have very few flaws.

Bradshaw's numbers improved. He increased his quarterback rating by paring his interception total down to twelve and equaling that figure with a like number of touch-downs. His yards per pass attempt statistic of 6.13 was still much lower than the league average (6.8), but that was acceptable, as much a result of Noll's pragmatic attack strategy as it was of Bradshaw's inaccuracy. Bradshaw was still somewhat tentative,

Table 8-5. Terry Bradshaw's 1970–72 Passing Performance

Year	Att	Comp	Comp%	Yards	YPA	TD	INT	Rating
1970	218	83	38.1	1410	6.47	6	24	30.4
1971	373	203	54.4	2259	6.06	13	22	59.7
1972	308	147	47.7	1887	6.13	12	12	64.1

still unsure of some of his keys and reads, and slightly inaccurate. But he rarely threw into coverage and made significantly fewer "losing" plays than he had in the past. As a result of Bradshaw's improvement (table 8-5), and Harris's presence in the backfield, Pittsburgh increased its scoring total to 343 points, fifth in the NFL that season.

On the defensive side of the ball, the Steelers began to exhibit the trademarks that would come to define Steelers football for the next decade. Led by veteran Andy Russell—and the contingent of eager, young talent drafted by Noll—the Steelers permitted only 175 points, placing them second in the entire league behind the Super Bowl–winning Miami Dolphins. All of the young players contributed: Blount, Greene, Greenwood, Ham, Holmes, Wagner, and White. The Steelers' staunch run defense stifled opposition ballcarriers and permitted only 3.9 yards per carry, forcing teams into many second- and third-and-long situations. Since the Steelers also possessed a superior pass rush, they would often force opponents to throw the ball well before the play developed. Consequently, Pittsburgh's pass defense permitted a stellar 5.8 yards per attempt, second in the league, and their twenty-eight interceptions led the NFL. Just before Vince Lombardi died in 1970, he made a prediction. "Noll is building a helluva team up there in Pittsburgh," he said. "They'll likely be a formidable foe in the '70s. Remember I made that prediction." It's good practice to remember a lot of things that man said.

The Steelers completed the 1972 season with eleven wins and three losses. Not only was it the Steelers' first winning season since 1963, but it catapulted them into their first postseason appearance since 1947! Pittsburgh won the AFC Central Division crown and would meet the Oakland Raiders in a playoff contest at Three Rivers Stadium in Pittsburgh.

In one of the most dramatic games in NFL history, Noll's youthful, hungry Steelers shocked the Raiders with a controversial 13–7 win. Franco Harris's "immaculate reception" snatched victory from the jaws of defeat in the waning seconds of the contest. On a broken play, Bradshaw was forced to scramble. After dodging several Raiders' pass rushers, the rocket-armed quarterback rifled a pass in the direction of Frenchy Fuqua. The ball, Fuqua, and Raiders' defensive back Jack Tatum all arrived simultaneously. The pass ricocheted off the two players and bounced several yards backwards towards the line of scrimmage. Harris, who was trailing the play by about fifteen yards, scooped up the ball just before it reached the ground and rambled, untouched, forty-two yards for the winning touchdown. Bedlam ensued. The Raiders—claiming that the ball did not actually hit Tatum, thereby rendering the play illegal in those days (two offensive players could not touch a pass without a defender touching it in between)—were furious. The Steelers—who had not seen the referee issue the touchdown signal—

were screaming for the "official ruling" of a score. Several minutes later, the referees huddled and ruled the play a touchdown.

Noll developed a motto for his Steelers' teams in the early 1970s. "Whatever it takes to win," he said, "that's what we will do." And while I'm quite sure that even Noll himself could not have imagined the extreme to which his players would take the message, Harris's incredible reactions—along with a little luck from above—probably gave Noll reason to believe that perhaps even God had become a Steelers' fan. Unfortunately, Noll did not have to wait long to witness God's proclivity for abstaining from football matters as a "perfect" performance by the soon-to-become Super Bowl champion Miami Dolphins kept the Steelers from an appearance in the NFL's spotlight event. No matter, the Steelers and Noll would become synonymous with the words "Super Bowl" in the near future.

Inspired by their stunning performance in 1972, Pittsburgh had grandiose aspirations in 1973. The Steelers possessed a superb young defense, a dynamic halfback, developing offensive and defensive lines, excellent speed at receiver, and a coach they believed in. However, though Terry Bradshaw had improved slightly in 1972, the major concern continued to be whether or not he was capable of effectively leading the Steelers' attack. Could Terry Bradshaw perform well enough to consistently create points for Pittsburgh's offense, despite his questionable track record?

The answer created a paradox of sorts and produced some interesting statistical anomalies. No, the Steelers did not get consistently effective quarterback play from Bradshaw, but they did score points. In fact, Pittsburgh wound up as one of the highest-scoring teams in 1973, while Bradshaw seemed to regress (table 8-6).

Even Franco Harris struggled that season, gaining just 698 yards on the same amount of attempts as his rookie campaign (188), for a meager 3.7 average. Given Bradshaw's and Harris's statistics, one would be led to believe that the Steelers had an appalling offensive performance in 1973. Bradshaw's quarterback rating plummeted 15 percent, and he threw more interceptions than touchdowns (10–15). Harris had a huge drop-off from his rookie year, producing about 33 percent below his yardage and average standards of the previous season. But the team scored 347 points—an average of almost twenty-five per game—good for fourth in the NFL. It didn't make much sense. In fact, the 1973 team scored more points than the 1972 club, despite the fact that Bradshaw and Harris had much better years in 1972, and the league's scoring totals were 5 percent greater that season as well. How was this possible?

Early in the 1973 season, with Bradshaw's play still erratic, Noll made two significant changes to the Steelers' offense. First, he began to utilize backup quarterback Terry Hanratty more frequently and eventually named him as the team's new starting quarterback. Hanratty, a fifth-year player from Notre Dame, had relieved Bradshaw

Table 8-6. Terry Bradshaw's 1973 Passing Performance

Year	Att	Comp	Comp%	Yards	YPA	TD	INT	Rating
1973	180	89	49.4	1183	6.57	10	15	54.5

from time to time since 1970, although he had experienced little success in his career to that point. Noll, however, believed that the Steelers needed a spark, and with Bradshaw struggling, he figured a quarterback change couldn't hurt. Second, since none of Pittsburgh's three quarterbacks (Bradshaw, Hanratty, or Joe Gilliam) were extremely accurate or consistent passers at that stage in their careers yet all three possessed the ability to throw deep, Noll modified the club's offensive philosophy. Pittsburgh still utilized a run-first approach, grinding out rushing yardage with Harris, Fuqua (457 yards in 1973), and Preston Pearson (554 yards) and passing only when necessary. However, unlike the 1972 squad, which emphasized a conservative, short passing strategy, when the 1973 Steelers did pass, they went deep—*frequently.*

"One of the worst things you can do as a head coach is to take an idea and jam it down the throats of your team," Noll said. "Ideas, even good ones, have to be sold to the team first and then objectively evaluated on the field." Though Bradshaw had improved slightly in the conservative offensive system of 1972, he began to retrogress in that same system at the start of the 1973 season. At that point, it became obvious to Noll that Pittsburgh's strength—as *objectively evaluated on the field*—was not in the short-to-intermediate passing game, at least not at the present time. So Noll adjusted the game plan to play to his team's advantage. He did something that only the best coaches would dare consider. He implemented a new, more appropriate offensive strategy to accentuate the strengths of his club. He did not force *his* system on the team. He let his team's abilities dictate his choice of systems. And in 1973, Noll's decision to attack opponents with the long pass paid off handsomely.

In 1973, Pittsburgh averaged 7.0 yards per pass attempt in conjunction with a completion percentage of just 45.3. The NFL averages that season were 6.6 and 52.0, respectively. Since average per attempt is obviously a function of completion percentage and the length of passing plays, it stands to reason that Pittsburgh's success was due more to the distance of their passes than to the frequency of their success. To aid in establishing my point, a graphic comparison of the Steelers' 1972 and 1973 passing statistics relative to the league might help (table 8-7).

In 1972, Pittsburgh averaged just 6.0 yards per pass attempt, almost 12 percent below the league average of 6.8. They accomplished this feat with a completion

Table 8-7. Steelers' 1972–73 Passing Compared to NFL Averages

	Steelers	League Average	+/– League Average
1972			
Average yards per pass attempt	6.0	6.8	−11.8%
Completion percentage	48.1	51.7	−7.0%
Average yards per completion	12.55	13.18	−4.8%
1973			
Average yards per pass attempt	7.0	6.6	+6.1%
Completion percentage	45.3	52.0	−12.9%
Average yards per completion	15.4	12.6	+22%

percentage of 48.1. In completing 156 passes that year and gaining 1,958 yards, their average per completion figured to 12.55 yards, about 5 percent below the league average (13.18).

Pittsburgh averaged 7.0 yards per pass attempt in 1973, 16.7 percent more than their 1972 average and 6.1 percent better than the league average of 6.6. They accomplished this feat with a completion percentage of just 45.3, the fourth lowest in the NFL. In completing 140 passes that year and gaining 2,157 yards, their average per completion figured to an incredible 15.4 yards—23 percent better than their own mark in 1972, a whopping 22 percent better than the league average (12.6), and almost 5.5 percent better than the next closest team, the Los Angeles Rams (14.6). Quite obviously, Noll's decision to open up the offense proved successful.

All three of Pittsburgh's quarterbacks played in 1973. Terry Hanratty was injured shortly after replacing Bradshaw and was limited to just sixty-nine passes for the year (table 8-8). However, there is no doubt that his outstanding performance (including a phenomenal 9.32 yards per attempt despite a suspect completion percentage, indicative of Noll's new passing strategy) contributed greatly to Pittsburgh's offensive success that season. Joe Gilliam's poor showing offset some of Hanratty's achievements (table 8-9). Although he did manage an extremely high yards-per-completion average of 16.6, Gilliam displayed very few positive attributes.

Terry Bradshaw's performance was certainly nothing to write home about (see table 8-6 on page 172), but it was not as dismal as it may have appeared to be. Bradshaw did suffer from the interception bug, throwing fifteen errant tosses in 180 attempts. However, quarterbacks who consistently throw long are invariably going to sustain higher interception percentages than those who throw short. Given Bradshaw's relatively high average-per-completion figure of 13.3 versus the NFL average of 12.6—a clear indication that he threw longer-than-average passes that season—he was likely to experience more interceptions than usual. Although his interception percentage of 8.3 was still too high for comfort (5.3 was the league average), the fact that his yards-per-attempt total (6.57) essentially equaled the NFL standard (6.6) indicated that he was probably much closer to an average quarterback that season than most people realized.

The Pittsburgh Steelers' offense faced many obstacles in 1973. Halfback Franco Harris had a mediocre season, and two of the team's quarterbacks, Terry Bradshaw

Table 8-8. Terry Hanratty's 1973 Passing Performance

Year	Att	Comp	Comp%	Yards	YPA	TD	INT	Rating
1973	69	31	44.9	643	9.32	8	5	86.8

Table 8-9. Joe Gilliam's 1973 Passing Performance

Year	Att	Comp	Comp%	Yards	YPA	TD	INT	Rating
1973	60	20	33.3	331	5.52	2	6	55.4

and Joe Gilliam—who between them accounted for almost 80 percent of the team's passes—combined to throw almost twice as many interceptions as touchdowns and compiled quarterback ratings in the mid-fifties. Considering all of that misfortune, it was an amazing accomplishment for the Steelers to amass 347 points and finish fourth in the NFL in scoring.

Many factors contributed to Pittsburgh's inconceivable offensive success in 1973: Noll's revised offensive philosophy, which dictated a more befitting attack strategy given the team's personnel; the decision to insert Hanratty as the team's starting quarterback, which supplied the Steelers with a badly needed boost, if only for a brief time; and last but certainly not least, the Steelers' defense, which provided outstanding field position for the offense on a regular basis. All of these elements, in addition to placekicker Roy Gerela's remarkable season (an AFC-leading 123 points, including twenty-nine field goals), combined to make the 1973 Pittsburgh Steelers a surprisingly productive though somewhat inefficient offensive unit, as well as a statistical fascination.

Chuck Noll's ability to adapt his strategy to fit his offensive personnel resulted in more points from less production in 1973. His ability to identify superior defensive personnel in the NFL draft resulted in Pittsburgh developing a progressively intimidating group of defenders as well. Although they permitted 210 points in 1973 (eighth-best in the league), their total—like the rest of the Steelers' team that season—was misleading. Pittsburgh's offense was plagued by turnovers. Bradshaw's interceptions were notorious, but even Franco Harris was smitten with the habit. In 1973, Harris fumbled eight times in 198 touches, a 4-percent turnover rate. The average NFL fumbling percentage was about 2.3 percent. Between Bradshaw's interceptions and Harris's fumbles, the Steelers' defense was often put in poor field position and, therefore, surrendered more points than their statistical performance indicated.

Pittsburgh dominated against both the run and the pass. Opposing ballcarriers managed just 3.4 yards per carry against the Steelers' front seven. Pittsburgh's pass rush was the key factor against opponent aerial attacks. Often, the Steelers would engulf rival quarterbacks and snatch lame-duck passes as they fluttered by receivers. Pittsburgh's total of thirty-seven interceptions in 1973 led the NFL by far. In fact, the Steelers' interception total was the NFL's highest since 1959. Overall, Pittsburgh's scintillating pass defense finished second in the NFL, allowing a mere 5.4 yards per attempt.

At the conclusion of this most interesting year, Pittsburgh registered a 10–4 record, tying Paul Brown's Cincinnati Bengals for first place in the AFC Central division. Unfortunately, the Steelers lost both the tiebreaker for the division title and their playoff game. The Oakland Raiders delighted their hometown fans by clobbering Pittsburgh 33–14. Though the Steelers had beaten the Raiders in the regular season 17–9, John Madden's team had revenge on their minds for the last-second playoff defeat of the previous year and ruined Pittsburgh's chances to enjoy an even more remarkable season in 1973.

Then came 1974, better known as the Year of the Steelers.

Table 8-10. Pittsburgh's First Four 1974 Draft Selections

Round	Player	Position	College
1	Lynn Swann	Wide receiver	USC
2	Jack Lambert	Linebacker	Kent State
3	*Choice to Oakland*		
4	John Stallworth	Wide receiver	Alabama A&M
5	Mike Webster	Center	Wisconsin

It started with the legendary "draft of the ages," undoubtedly the best draft in the history of the NFL. Pittsburgh's first four selections that season are shown in table 8-10. Four picks, four starters, four Pro Bowlers, four All-Pros, and four Hall of Famers with sixteen Super Bowl rings—not bad. Since the inception of the NFL draft in 1936, the Steelers are the only team to have selected more than two Hall of Famers in the same year. Without a doubt, this crop put the exclamation point on a devastatingly effective progression of drafts and set the tone for the Steelers' inordinate run to glory. Furthermore, it cemented the distinction of both Noll and his front-office personnel team as the best talent scouts in the business.

Noll concentrated on speed and skill in evaluating an athlete, not size. Even when assessing the talents of a non-skill-position player, he concentrated more on athletic attributes and strength as opposed to stature or bulk. He believed that hitting and tackling ability were not necessarily linked to the sheer mass of an individual. "It's not the size of the dog, that whole thing," he said. "It's skills, sure, but vision is very important and that's not part of being big. It's speed, ability to hit. That doesn't necessarily go with mammoth size. Paul Brown always talked about fat guys. 'They *think* fat,' he said. 'They lean on people, they don't hit.' So we weren't necessarily interested in how big a player was, but rather how tough, how quick, how fast, how smart." One pick in the 1974 draft who seemed to emphasize Noll's philosophy was Jack Lambert. At 6′ 4″, 220 pounds, Lambert was not large for an NFL middle linebacker. In fact, many believed he was somewhat frail, lacking the ballast to effectively play the inside run. Ideally, teams would have preferred him to be in the neighborhood of 240 pounds to be able to take on guards face to face. But Noll was not concerned. He knew that Lambert was a devastating hitter with the attitude and temperament of a caged lion. And he had the speed, hitting ability, instincts, and toughness that Noll coveted.

Noll's estimation of Lynn Swann's ability increased after the USC wide receiver quieted critics by running a 4.59 forty-yard dash. Up to that point, many personnel evaluators, Noll included, were wary of drafting him in the first round.

A fortuitous occurrence gave the Steelers the opportunity to acquire John Stallworth in the fourth round. "Noll really did like Stallworth, and he thought he was worthy of a first-round pick," said Tim Rooney, Pittsburgh's director of player personnel. "He was put into the Senior Bowl as a defensive back, and that was a tremendous break for us because he wasn't showcased as a receiver and he was put at a position he wasn't real comfortable with." The Steelers selected Swann and won their gamble that Stallworth would still be available later in the draft.

When undersized center Mike Webster (6' 1" 250 pounds) was still on the board at Pittsburgh's spot in the fifth round, it was an easy decision for Noll to draft the strong, tenacious lineman. "I saw him in the East-West game," Noll said. "Everybody kind of downgraded him on his size. He wasn't 6' 6", three hundred pounds or anything like that, but he was playing against a defensive tackle who had those dimensions and he handled him like nothing. I saw that and I said the heck with the size, this guy has the wherewithal to play."

Pittsburgh's wherewithal to dominate teams defensively continued in 1974. The Steelers permitted just 189 points (second in the NFL) and finished among the league's top five teams in almost every defensive category.

Offensively, the Steelers' plans were influenced by what turned out to be an abbreviated strike by many NFL veterans. In search of higher salaries and some free agency options, players held out from training camps starting in July. Consequently, both Terry Bradshaw and Terry Hanratty did not participate in any of the team's early drills in the summer of 1974, and any tactical strategies Noll planned to implement for Pittsburgh's "high maintenance" passing game were scuttled. Joe Gilliam, who was entering only his third season, did not participate in the strike and became the team's starting quarterback by default. But since Noll was not sold on Gilliam's ability to lead the Steelers offense, and since Pittsburgh had the talent to control games with a dominant rushing attack and a superior defense, Noll instituted a relatively cautious offensive game plan featuring Franco Harris and a conservative passing game.

Bradshaw and Hanratty returned to the squad when the strike ended in mid-August, but Gilliam opened the season as the starter. Despite the fact that the Steelers began the year with a 4–1–1 record, Gilliam played poorly, and Bradshaw replaced him. When he took over, Bradshaw's lack of practice time and game competition made him extremely rusty and inaccurate. He completed just 45.3 percent of his passes on the year. Even Hanratty suffered from the effects of the layoff, as he connected on just three of twenty-six passes in limited action. As a result, Pittsburgh's passing game imploded. Bradshaw and Gilliam finished the year with quarterback ratings in the mid-fifties, again, and the Steelers finished twenty-first in the league in passing yardage. The club's league-leading figure of 15.4 yards per completion in 1973 dwindled to a measly 12.9 in 1974. Nevertheless, thanks to Noll's decision to tone down the aerial attack—which enabled Pittsburgh to drastically reduce their interception percentage from 8.4 in 1973 to 5.4 in 1974—and the NFL's second-ranked rushing game and defense, Pittsburgh finished the 1974 campaign with a 10–3–1 record and won the AFC Central Division for the second time in three years.

In many ways, the Pittsburgh teams of the early- to mid-1970s, particularly 1974, mirrored another great defensive club whose players were, for the most part, not even born when Chuck Noll took over the Steelers—the 2000 Baltimore Ravens. There were amazing comparisons between the two clubs. Both dominated defensively, either leading the league or ranking in the top five in almost every defensive category. Both created a great number of turnovers with their defense. Both possessed a power rushing attack—Harris for the Steelers and Jamal Lewis for the Ravens. Both suffered from suspect quarterback play—Bradshaw, Gilliam, and Hanratty for Pittsburgh, and Tony Banks and Trent Dilfer for Baltimore. And both relied heavily on their kickers—Gerela for Pittsburgh and Matt Stover for Baltimore. Ultimately, both teams allowed their running games and defenses to determine their fate, and they advanced all the way to the Super Bowl. The debate as to which club had the better defense may continue forever. One thing, however, is certain. Both teams retained head coaches (Noll and Brian Billick) who were willing and able to adjust their game plans to best suit the personnel at their disposal.

Pittsburgh began their 1974 postseason Super Bowl advance by defeating the Buffalo Bills 32–14 at Three Rivers Stadium. The Steelers exploded for twenty-six points in the second quarter and were able to coast home from there. Bradshaw enjoyed one of the finest games of his career to that point, completing twelve of nineteen passes for 203 yards and a score. Franco Harris rushed for three touchdowns, while the Steelers' defense held the Bills' star running back, future Hall of Famer O.J. Simpson, to just forty-nine yards on fifteen carries.

A rematch with the Raiders was next. The teams' heated rivalry had now progressed to a third straight playoff confrontation. Noll and Raiders' coach John Madden, who had once been very good friends when they worked in San Diego, were now estranged. And I'll go out on a limb and say that the players—the actual combatants in this "war"—were also estranged. Pittsburgh had won the initial playoff encounter in 1972, and the Raiders had prevailed in 1973. Now it was time for the grudge match. The game was tied at three after the first half, but the Raiders were in trouble. Pittsburgh had taken Oakland completely out of their game plan by disabling the Raiders' ground attack, which had finished third in the NFL with more than twenty-three hundred yards that year. The Raiders managed just twenty-nine yards on twenty-one carries for the entire game and were forced into throwing thirty-six passes (they averaged twenty-four during the season). Meanwhile, Harris and Steelers' halfback Rocky Bleier were chewing up Oakland's defense and finished the contest with 224 yards on fifty rushing attempts. Ultimately, the Steelers won the game 24–13, and with it, the chance to go to the NFL title game for the first time in the franchise's forty-two-year history.

The Minnesota Vikings were the Steelers' opponent in Super Bowl IX. Minnesota was a similar team to the Steelers defensively. They possessed a fierce pass-rushing front four, led by Alan Page and Carl Eller, and their imposing defense had permitted just six more points than Pittsburgh's that season (195). Noll decided that the best way to handle the Minnesota defense was to lure the Vikings to Bradshaw and then utilize draw plays, traps, and screens to eventually make them hesitate, negating their quick pursuit to the ball. On defense, Noll and his coordinator Bud Carson had to deal with the scrambling of Minnesota quarterback Fran Tarkenton, who employed speed and elusiveness in order to give his receivers more time to find openings in the secondary. "We were convinced the only way the Vikings could beat us was with Tarkenton scrambling and completing those short rollout passes," Carson said after the game. "Our plan was to shut their run down early to force them to throw the football. Our front four put on too big a rush to permit Tarkenton to have success throwing the football. Our biggest problem was that regular linebackers Lambert and Russell got hurt. We didn't know how their replacements would do, but [Ed] Bradley and [Loren] Toews did good jobs."

The Steelers dominated the overmatched Vikings. Pittsburgh set a Super Bowl record by allowing Minnesota just 119 yards in total offense, including the staggering figure of seventeen yards in twenty-one rushing attempts. On offense, the Steelers gained 333 yards, 158 of which belonged to Franco Harris on those draws and trap plays. The 16–6 margin of victory belied the total and complete physical dominance exhibited by the Steelers. The game might as well have been a 40–0 rout.

Pittsburgh's incredible defense was never more effective in its storied history than it had been during the 1974 playoffs. The Steelers permitted just thirty-three points in three games and limited their opponents to the mind-boggling total of just forty-six yards on forty-two carries (a 1.1 average) in the AFC championship and Super Bowl games.

After the Super Bowl, Noll was awestruck by the team's defensive performance, especially that of "Mean" Joe Greene. "That Greene," he said, shaking his head as if to imply disbelief in his miraculous effort, "he gets off the ball so quickly. He's moving right with the ball. He doesn't go around people, he goes through people." Later, reflecting on the entire postseason run and Greene's influence on the defense, Noll said, "In these playoffs, Joe Greene was the best defensive tackle—no, best defensive lineman— I ever saw."

Chuck Noll was basking in the glory of a marvelous achievement, and deservedly so. He had quite literally brought the Pittsburgh franchise to life. His Steelers had won a total of twelve games in his first three years in Pittsburgh (1969–1971). Now, they had thirty one victories in the last three years and a Super Bowl trophy to boot. "There isn't a great deal of difference between the teams on the bottom and the teams on the top," Noll said after his first championship. "With us, I think it is desire and the mental aspects of our football team"—more to the point, the desire and mental aspects that Noll instilled in them.

In 1975 Terry Bradshaw finally got it. By every conceivable statistic that you could use to rate a quarterback, Bradshaw was better—much better (table 8-11). With an eighty-eight passer rating—which would prove to be his highest ever—Bradshaw finished fourth among AFC quarterbacks. And his 7.19 yards per pass attempt was easily the best of his career to that point. It does not take a mental giant to accurately predict the impact and significance that a highly effective quarterback would have on the fortunes of a team as talented as the 1975 Pittsburgh Steelers. With an accomplished

Table 8-11. Terry Bradshaw's 1975 Passing Performance

Year	Att	Comp	Comp%	Yards	YPA	TD	INT	Rating
1975	286	165	57.7	2055	7.19	18	9	88.0

passing game to augment Harris (who gained a career-high 1,248 yards that year), the Steelers finally possessed an offense capable of defeating opponents on its own merit. This allowed Noll to revise the playbook, implement a worthy intermediate passing scheme (to supplement the Steelers' deep game), and utilize his special, seemingly latent, receiving talents named Swann and Stallworth.

After a rookie season in which he caught just eleven passes in limited duty, the graceful, acrobatic Swann developed into an unstoppable threat in 1975. His production soared to forty-nine catches for 781 yards and eleven scores. Swann averaged almost sixteen yards per catch and finished in the top ten receivers in the AFC. Stallworth caught just twenty passes that season but for an incredible 21.2 yards per grab and four touchdowns.

As a result of their offensive exploits, the Steelers finished the 1975 season with their best record ever, 12–2, and edged Cincinnati for the AFC Central title. In the playoffs, Pittsburgh easily dispatched the Baltimore Colts 28–10, then for a second straight year defeated Oakland, 16–10, for the AFC championship. They matched up against the Dallas Cowboys in Super Bowl X.

Dallas had finished the season as a 10–4 wild-card team. They upset the Vikings in their first playoff game 17–14, as Cowboys' quarterback Roger Staubach threw a fifty-yard "Hail Mary" touchdown pass to wide receiver Drew Pearson with twenty-four seconds remaining. The play should have been ruled offensive pass interference, since Pearson nudged Vikings' cornerback Nate Wright out of the way to catch the ball. Nonetheless, the Cowboys advanced to face Los Angeles for the NFC championship the next week and justified their presence by soundly drubbing the favored Rams 37–7.

In the Super Bowl, the Steelers turned the tables on Dallas and won the game with a late touchdown pass of their own. Terry Bradshaw hit Lynn Swann on a sixty-four-yard scoring play with just over three minutes left in the contest. Pittsburgh's defense—which allowed just 162 points in the regular season—intercepted a Staubach pass in the game's waning seconds to secure a 21–17 victory and the Steelers' second consecutive championship.

The maturation of Terry Bradshaw in 1975 finally enabled Chuck Noll to unleash a legitimate, full-fledged NFL passing game to match the talents of the rest of his squad. For several seasons, Pittsburgh had relied on the combination of a fierce defense and an excellent running game to overcome their quarterbacks' inadequacies. But when Bradshaw blossomed, Noll's Steelers became one of the truly dominant teams in pro football history. "Realistically the quarterback should be $\frac{1}{22}$ of the team," Noll said, "but that's not quite the way it works. Terry is a much bigger part of us than that. He's the one that makes us go. He's the leader out there, the driving force."

In 1976—coming off of two straight Super Bowl victories—Pittsburgh finished the season with a 10–4 record, good enough to win their division for the fourth time in five years. And though the results may seem incomprehensible, a statistical analysis of the Steelers that season, table 8-12, reveals some amazing facts.

Table 8-12. Pittsburgh Steelers, 1976 Team Statistics and League Ranking

Offense		Defense	
Rushing yards:	2633 (2nd/28 teams)	Rushing yards:	1457 (1st)
Average per rush:	4.5 (3rd)	Average per rush:	3.2 (1st)
Rushing TDs:	33 (1st)	Rushing TDs:	5 (1st)
Passing yards:	1935 (23rd)	Points allowed:	138 (1st)
Total pass att:	277 (28th)	Pass completion pct:	42.1 (2nd)
*YPA: 7.0	(12th)	*YPA:	5.8 (3rd)
Total yards:	3646 (1st)		

*Yards per pass attempt

Offensively, Bradshaw struggled, due to injuries, and the Steelers passing game suffered. Pittsburgh attempted fewer passes than any team in the league in 1976 and finished with less than two thousand yards through the air. In the running game, Franco Harris averaged just 3.9 yards per carry. But Harris scored a career- and league-high fourteen rushing touchdowns as the Steelers literally manhandled their adversaries to the tune of a 33–5 rushing touchdown advantage—a statistic usually indicative of exceptional talent in both the offensive and defensive lines. Pittsburgh's thirty-three rushing scores and their twenty-eight touchdown supremacy over their opponents represented the NFL's highest totals in those categories since the 1962 Green Bay Packers' 36–4 superiority.

The Steelers' defensive statistics delineated above—including their achievement of just five rushing touchdowns allowed—were certainly remarkable. However, several other defensive accomplishments that year were positively extraordinary. In truth, Pittsburgh's defensive exploits in 1976 represent one of the most incredible performances in the history of the NFL. Consider that in the team's last nine games that season, the defense recorded five shutouts and permitted only two touchdowns. They allowed just 28 points—in total—during that span of nine games (the equivalent of forty-five points for an entire season). Guess what? They won all nine games during this stretch of defensive domination. That's right. This vaunted Steelers' team of 1976 started off the season with a record of 1–4. The team needed a superhuman effort to make the playoffs, and the defense provided just that.

"Part of Chuck Noll's philosophy was when one department [the passing game] was floundering, another had to pick up the slack," said Steelers' defensive end Dwight White. "Chuck did a great psych job on us. We were playing terrific defense, but it was never good enough. We'd hold a team to 125 yards and you'd get this attitude like, hell, they were only supposed to get seventy-five. It made you want to turn it up a bit more."

Pittsburgh's first playoff game in 1976 was in Baltimore on December 19. On the Steelers' opening drive, Bradshaw hit Frank Lewis in full stride for a seventy-six-yard touchdown pass. Pittsburgh subsequently demolished the Colts for the second straight year, 40–14. Had it not been for injuries to both Harris and Bleier in the Baltimore game,

Table 8-13. Terry Bradshaw's 1977 Passing Performance

Year	Att	Comp	Comp%	Yards	YPA	TD	INT	Rating
1977	314	162	51.6	2523	8.04	17	19	71.4

the Steelers might have won a third consecutive Super Bowl. However, forced to face the Oakland Raiders in the AFC championship game without their two best backs proved too great an obstacle. Oakland defeated Pittsburgh 24–7 and proceeded to a 32–14 blowout victory over Minnesota in Super Bowl XI.

In 1977, the Steelers won yet another division title with a 9–5 record. Terry Bradshaw, who had broken through in 1975 with a season worthy of his number-one overall draft selection only to suffer a disappointing, injury-plagued season in 1976, had somewhat mixed results (table 8-13). Though his yards per attempt figure (8.04) was outstanding (the NFL average was 6.5), interception problems again limited his effectiveness. In the team's playoff game in Denver, Bradshaw's three interceptions and a Franco Harris fumble led to disaster. The Broncos capitalized on the turnovers and pulled away from the Steelers late in the game to earn a 34–21 victory.

The following year, 1978, was one of redemption for the Steelers. Noll had grown tired of the losing, even if it was in the playoffs, and even though the Steelers had pieced together a remarkable run since 1972. The two-time champions had endured back-to-back mediocre seasons, and Bradshaw in particular had regressed since his fabulous season of 1975. It was time to get back to work, time to win another NFL crown. No team had ever won three Super Bowls, but Noll, Bradshaw, and the entire Steelers team were determined to make 1978 a very special year.

The results were spectacular (table 8-14). Injury free and confident as ever, Bradshaw enjoyed the second-best season of his career. Pittsburgh finished with a scintillating 14–2 record, easily capturing the Central Division title. In the playoffs, the Steelers were devastating. In quick succession, they demolished the Denver Broncos and Houston Oilers, 33–10, and 34–5, respectively. They outgained Denver 425–218 and forced the Oilers into nine turnovers. Pittsburgh was headed back to another Super Bowl. Only a rematch with the Dallas Cowboys, their victims of 1976, stood between them and NFL history.

Pittsburgh scored first when Bradshaw hit John Stallworth on a twenty-eight-yard pass that was the result of a tendency Noll and the coaching staff discovered when scouting the Dallas secondary. "We exploited a Cowboy weakness we spotted on film," explained Stallworth. "We saw the cornerbacks jumping around, so I took a slant, then cut back to the outside and Terry lobbed the ball to me." The Cowboys' secondary was

Table 8-14. Terry Bradshaw's 1978 Passing Performance

Year	Att	Comp	Comp%	Yards	YPA	TD	INT	Rating
1978	368	207	56.3	2915	7.92	28*	20	84.7

*Led league

too unsettled to properly cover the pattern, and Pittsburgh led 7–0. But Dallas stormed back with two quick scores to stun the Steelers and took a 14–7 lead early in the second quarter. Bradshaw, however, was not to be denied that day. He responded to the Cowboys' onslaught with a flurry of his own, the first of which came on a seventy-five-yard pass to Stallworth just after the Cowboys scored their second touchdown. He followed that up with a seven-yard toss to running back Rocky Bleier to give the Steelers a 21–14 lead at halftime. Pittsburgh eventually opened up an eighteen-point lead, then held on for a 35–31 victory, securing their third Super Bowl title in the process. True to his statistics for the season, Bradshaw was very accurate with his throws and extremely consistent on his reads in the Super Bowl. He completed seventeen of thirty passes for 318 yards and four touchdowns while suffering just one interception and was named game MVP.

Success often breeds contentment. Contentment often leads to complacency. It is, after all, human nature to seek the easy way out and work only as hard as you have to in order to get by. Since the Steelers had already made history by winning three Super Bowls, one would think that Noll might have been worried about complacency, especially in 1979. As it turns out, Noll was never too concerned with his players' emotional state. "I gave up trying to determine if players are ready emotionally a long time ago," he said at the time. "I don't worry about the mental aspect. I just prepare the players for the game and what to expect from the other team. [In the end] it will all come down to blocking and tackling, that's all." Pittsburgh blocked and tackled better than any team on earth, so even if they were at a psychological disadvantage, they were still a very powerful adversary.

Pittsburgh completed the 1979 season with a 12–4 mark. Bradshaw had a solid year, and the Steelers blitzed through their first two playoff games in their usual dominant style. They annihilated the Miami Dolphins 34–14 and slammed the Oilers again, 27–13. They advanced to meet the Los Angeles Rams in Super Bowl XIV in Pasadena, California. The lead went back and forth through the first three quarters of the game, and Los Angeles held a 19–17 advantage at the end of forty-five minutes. Three minutes into the fourth period, however, Bradshaw hit Stallworth for another of his long Super Bowl touchdown passes (seventy-three yards) to give Pittsburgh the lead for good. The Steelers went on to defeat the Rams 31–19 and won their fourth Super Bowl in the process.

In light of the incomparable achievements of Noll's 1970s Steelers teams, comparisons with some of the greatest coaches in NFL history were inevitable. In fact, one of his players had thoughts on the matter in the winner's locker room immediately following the 1980 Super Bowl. "Winning a fourth Super Bowl should put us in a special category," said cornerback Mel Blount. "I think this is the best team ever assembled. They talk about Vince Lombardi, but I think the Chuck Noll era is even greater."

Noll and the Steelers had gone where no team had before—or after. They achieved the almost unfathomable distinction of becoming four-time champions in a six-year period. If someone ever walks into the Pittsburgh trophy room and becomes

Chuck Noll led the Pittsburgh Steelers to an incredible four Super Bowl championships in just six years.

confused—thinking they might have accidentally entered the NFL Hall of Fame—no one would laugh at them. There are enough championship trophies from the Noll era to fill a few rooms in Canton.

Chuck Noll coached for twelve more seasons after his victory over the Los Angeles Rams in Super Bowl XIV. The Steelers won two more division titles and made four additional playoff appearances, but they failed to reach a fifth Super Bowl. Noll retired after his twenty-third season in 1991 with a career record of 193–148–1.

When Noll was named coach of the Steelers in 1969, he had a vision—a vision of drafting for success and building his team from the ground up. The Pittsburgh Steelers were constructed in exactly that fashion. Under Noll, Pittsburgh was consistently able to identify and select the right players at the right time with the right attitudes and the right attributes. From 1969 to 1974, Noll drafted nine Hall of Famers and fourteen Pro Bowlers—an absolutely incredible achievement and very likely the finest collection of draftees ever in such a short window of time. The list includes: Mel Blount, Terry Bradshaw, Glen Edwards, Joe Greene, L.C. Greenwood, Franco Harris, Jack Lambert, Donnie Shell, Lynn Swann, John Stallworth, Mike Webster, Dwight White, Jack Ham, and Mike Wagner. These players—all selected in the first six years of Noll's tenure—became the foundation of a system that put a city on the NFL map and a coach in the Hall of Fame.

Chuck Noll had a passion for coaching. But his passion was not related solely to winning football games. It was born of the satisfaction he received with regard to instructing and preparing players in the proper fashion. His goal was to work with players who possessed a willing attitude and then convey the appropriate methods and techniques that would allow them to maximize their talents and upgrade the team. As a tactician, he advocated flexible systems and strategies. This enabled him to structure his game plans to accentuate the capabilities of various players at different times, ultimately giving his teams the best chance for success. And if the outcomes were not winning ones, then so be it. Noll still took enormous pride in the effort and dedication that both he and his players exhibited. "A life of frustration is inevitable for any coach whose main enjoyment is winning," he said. Winning was definitely a goal for Noll's teams, it just wasn't the only goal. Chuck Noll enjoyed coaching and winning. But mainly, he enjoyed coaching "winning" individuals.

Noll's relationship with his players was greatly misunderstood. He was one of the few coaches who could be both a disciplinarian and a player's coach at the same time—often a tricky proposition. He took great pride in the fact that he was able to become both a leader and a friend to his athletes. While he often seemed unemotional and cold to the public, Noll was very close with many of his players. As Hall of Famer Jack Ham put it: "To the people on the outside looking in, Chuck was very stoic and uncaring about his players. In reality, he cared immensely about all of us."

When John Stallworth retired from football in 1987, he and Noll stood next to each other on the field for the last time. Noll leaned over to Stallworth. "John, I feel like crying. That would be appropriate, wouldn't it?" he asked.

"No, it wouldn't," Stallworth retorted.

"He was losing one of the guys he had bonded with, and I think he was emotional about it. That part of Chuck Noll I don't think a lot of people saw," Stallworth said.

Linebacker Andy Russell was drafted by the Steelers in the sixteenth round in 1963. He played twelve years in the NFL, all with the Steelers, and retired with two Super Bowl rings. His fondest memory of Noll was in relation to his demeanor and player-friendly practice habits. "He was very stern, very strict," Russell said. "On the other hand, he was realistic about what the players could or could not do. He didn't wear us out at practice; Sundays were our hard days. To that extent he was a player's coach." A player's coach who could also be a disciplinarian when necessary. When a player blew an assignment or made a foolish mistake, he would often find himself on the receiving end of the Chuck Noll glare—a sharp scowl, the wrinkled brow look of anger, disgust, and contempt. "If you were on the wrong end of the Chuck Noll glare, that was all the motivation you needed," said Pittsburgh guard Craig Wolfley.

Chuck Noll was an extremely intelligent individual who benefited from a well-rounded educational background. He graduated from Dayton, attended law school, studied medicine briefly, and even earned his pilot's license. He received two honorary Ph.D.s, one from Duquesne in humanitarian services and the other from Robert Morris College in commercial science. When he took control of the Steelers in 1969, Noll was quoted as saying, "My thing is preparation and teaching." In regard to NFL football in Pittsburgh, no one was *ever* more prepared to teach the Steelers how to win championships. When students earn a Ph.D., they typically author a dissertation detailing a new idea or concept relative to their discipline, thus making a substantive contribution to their field of study. In my opinion, Chuck Noll earned a Ph.D. from the Pittsburgh Steelers' organization for conveying the concept of winning football to a franchise that was notorious for losing.

Chuck Noll changed the perception of professional football in Pittsburgh and ultimately instilled an irrepressible will to achieve into the entire organization. He was the principal architect of one of the greatest teams of all time and led that squad to a record four Super Bowl victories in a six-year period. The Steelers compiled an aggregate regular season record of 67–20–1 (.767) during those magical years from 1974 to 1979. When Noll retired in 1991—having notched fifteen winning seasons and nine division titles in addition to his Super Bowl conquests—Steelers' fans could honestly say they had witnessed professional football at its very best.

Noll was very gracious, almost embarrassed, upon learning of his induction into the Pro Football Hall of Fame in 1993. He always believed that the players deserved the limelight, not the coach. However, Jack Ham paid a special tribute to the man and his legacy, one that contradicted Noll's estimation of his value to the Pittsburgh franchise. "I think of all the people who were involved in the Steelers' organization during our Super Bowl years that Chuck Noll is by far the most deserving to be inducted into the Pro Football Hall of Fame," he said. "I was fortunate to be around winners my whole football career. I played with people like Bradshaw, Franco, Greenwood, Webster, Blount, and a lot more. But we couldn't have won all those games, all those Super Bowls, except for one man, pure and simple—Chuck Noll."

Chuck Noll's Coaching Capsule

Category	Numbers
Seasons	23
Wins	193
Losses	148
Ties	1
Winning pct.	.566
Pct. >/< avg. Super Bowl–winning coach (.601)*	−5.8%
World championships†	4
World championship game appearances†	4
World championship pct. (champ/seasons)	17.4%
Losing seasons	7
Pct. of losing seasons	30.4%
Playoff record	16–8
Playoff winning percentage	.667
Average wins per 16 games (a current season)	9.1
Average losses per 16 games	6.9

NOTE: Ties count as a half-win and a half-loss in calculating percentages.
*See Epilogue
†Super Bowls or NFL championships 1920–1965.

3 Years Before and After Noll

City	Years	Record	Percentage	Noll's Career Pct
				.566
Before				
Pittsburgh	1966–1968	11–28–3	.298	
After				
Pittsburgh	1992–1994	32–16	.667	

(continued next page)

Chuck Noll's Coaching Capsule (continued)

Yearly Records

Year	Team	Wins	Losses	Ties	Playoffs
1969	Pit	1	13	0	
1970	Pit	5	9	0	
1971	Pit	6	8	0	
1972	Pit	11	3	0	1–1
1973	Pit	10	4	0	0–1
1974	Pit	10	3	1	3–0*
1975	Pit	12	2	0	3–0*
1976	Pit	10	4	0	1–1
1977	Pit	9	5	0	0–1
1978	Pit	14	2	0	3–0*
1979	Pit	12	4	0	3–0*
1980	Pit	9	7	0	
1981	Pit	8	8	0	
1982	Pit	6	3	0	0–1
1983	Pit	10	6	0	0–1
1984	Pit	9	7	0	1–1
1985	Pit	7	9	0	
1986	Pit	6	10	0	
1987	Pit	8	7	0	
1988	Pit	5	11	0	
1989	Pit	9	7	0	1–1
1990	Pit	9	7	0	
1991	Pit	7	9	0	
Totals		193	148	1	16–8

*Won Super Bowl

Chapter 9

BILL WALSH

I n 1979, San Francisco 49ers fans found themselves longing for the days when former Stanford quarterback John Brodie would saunter up to the line of scrimmage, call the signals, and execute a winning play the way it was drawn on the chalkboard. Since Brodie retired in 1973, the 49ers' record had been dreadful—31–55, a .360 winning percentage. During those six years, San Francisco went through coaches like McDonald's goes through hamburgers. Dick Nolan left after the 1975 season; Monte Clarke, Ken Meyer, Pete McCulley, and Fred O'Connor each lasted one year or less. Enough was enough. Six years of pitiful football, no stability, no plan, and no foreseeable end to the tumultuous trend of torture. It was obvious what the team needed—another Stanford guy. So 49ers' owner Eddie DeBartolo hired a gentleman by the name of Bill Walsh.

Bill Walsh was born on November 30, 1931, in Los Angeles, California. His father worked in an auto repair shop. As a youngster, Walsh loved sports and was a fine athlete. He excelled in both baseball and football in high school, first attending Washington High and later graduating from Hayward High. He decided to further his education and athletic pursuits at San Mateo Community College, where he again played baseball and football. Later, Walsh enrolled at San Jose State University and played wide receiver in a limited capacity for the Spartans. In 1955, Walsh graduated from San Jose State with a degree in business. Shortly thereafter, he took the first head coaching position of his career at his former school, Washington High, in Fremont, California. In 1959, after a three-year stint as a high school coach, Walsh went back to San Jose State and earned a master's degree from his alma mater in education.

Walsh's college coaching career began in 1960 when Marv Levy (future coach of the Kansas City Chiefs and Buffalo Bills) hired him as an assistant at Cal Berkeley. Three years later, Walsh accepted his first position at Stanford University. John Ralston, later head coach of the Denver Broncos, brought Walsh aboard as an assistant coach and administrative associate.

In 1966, Walsh progressed to coach at the professional level. He was hired by John Rauch, coach of the AFL's Oakland Raiders, as an offensive assistant. Oakland's attack, instituted by owner/coach Al Davis several years earlier, was based on an unusual style of offense, one that seemed to pervade the new league. The system utilized short passes to the backs and tight end as its primary method of moving the football, and it had been quite successful for the Raiders. Walsh spent just one season in Oakland, however. In 1967, he took a chance to move up the coaching ladder with another upstart professional football association, the Continental Football League, and was named head coach of the San Jose Apaches. The team went bankrupt before the 1968 season, however, and Walsh found himself unemployed. Luckily, the Cincinnati Bengals—an AFL expansion team slated to begin play in 1968—were looking for an offensive assistant. Legendary head coach Paul Brown called Walsh and offered him a position as receivers' coach. Walsh spent eight years in Cincinnati, eventually moving up to offensive coordinator.

Walsh took full advantage of the opportunity to study the techniques of the successful coaches under whom he served. "With the Raiders [under Rauch and Davis], I learned the value of a full-dimensional passing game," Walsh said, "one that forces defenses to play the whole field and thereby expose their weaknesses." In Cincinnati, under Brown, Walsh learned the intricacies of a precision passing offense, where the quarterback and receiver hooked up on exactly defined patterns based on timing. This tactic enabled the quarterback to throw the ball before the receiver had even cut, making the play extremely difficult to defend. Another Brown innovation that intrigued Walsh was his concept of "scripting" plays—a process of selecting and sequencing the team's first eight to twelve plays before the game began.

While working as offensive coordinator with the Bengals, Brown would often ask Walsh on the morning of the game, "What are your openers?" In other words, Brown was inquiring as to the plays Walsh had decided to run on the first series of downs. To be completely prepared for his coach's interrogation each Sunday morning, Walsh decided to compile a list of ten to twelve plays—usually the day before the game—and present them at breakfast the next day. "It allowed us to make critical decisions on our opening possession in a clinical atmosphere, with time to concentrate," Walsh said. "Secondly, it limited the chance of becoming predictable. Some coaches fall into a trap in which their play calling follows a pattern. They may not even realize it, but they used the same formation on eight out of ten third-down plays. By scripting plays, you can avoid being predictable and make the defense's job harder." The system also gave the Bengals' players the opportunity to concentrate on their assignments well before lining up opposite their opponent. "The players liked it," Walsh said. "They felt it eliminated some pregame anxiety, because they knew ahead of time what they would be doing on the first series. They had a chance to think about it, and most of the time they even slept better."

After the 1975 season, Paul Brown retired. Walsh believed he had an excellent opportunity to become the Bengals' new head coach. It was not to be, however, as Cincinnati named Bill Johnson for the position. Walsh, eager for another head-coaching opportunity, felt his best bet would be to move back to the West Coast, where he took a job as offensive coordinator of the San Diego Chargers in 1976. Good thing, too; otherwise, his futuristic West Coast offense might never have been invented. Everyone in the NFL would be running some weird version of a Paul Brown attack called the East Coast offense (ha, ha). Walsh worked for coach Tommy Prothro in San Diego for just one season before his wish to become a head coach was fulfilled. Stanford University named Walsh to that position in 1977. He spent two years with the Cardinals, posting a 17–7 record and winning bowl games both seasons. In 1979, the NFL's San Francisco 49ers named Walsh as their head coach, and the rest is history. But since I like history, and since this is a good story, I think it would be worthwhile to investigate the methodology and career achievements that made Bill Walsh famous.

Most coaches develop a philosophy based upon their assessment of the theories and procedures that they encountered while working their way up the coaching ladder. They mix and match what they perceive to be the best tactics and styles and mold them into a structured combination of strategies that they call their "system"—in essence, an assemblage of eclectic policies and guidelines.

Bill Walsh was different. He didn't just adopt someone else's programs and package them into an offensive system—he designed his own. Sure, he borrowed bits and pieces of different concepts that he encountered in his coaching experiences, but he then enhanced those fragments and formulated them into an innovative strategy that redefined NFL football in the latter part of the twentieth century.

Since its origination in 1920, the NFL had always been a run-first league. For many years, passing was considered taboo, even cowardly, in the macho world of the NFL. Gradually, though, beliefs began to change. In 1978, two rule changes aimed at spicing up the game for television and increasing scoring were instituted. The first revision permitted offensive linemen to fully extend their hands in pass protection, thus affording quarterbacks more time to deliver their throws. The second change eliminated the defensive players' advantage of "chucking," or impeding a receiver beyond five yards of the line scrimmage. These adaptations eventually led to a proliferation of the passing game, which began to surpass the run as the chief means of advancing the ball in the mid-1980s.

Walsh realized the benefits of an efficient passing game as well as the implications of the rule changes much before the rest of the league. So he took the elementary form of Paul Brown's progressive passing offense of the 1940s and '50s—a system that relied on precise patterns and synchronization between the quarterbacks and receivers—enhanced the concept for several different applications, and modified it for advantageous use in the contemporary NFL. The West Coast offense, as it came to be known, was instituted by Walsh with the San Francisco 49ers in 1979. The basic goal of Walsh's approach—considered radical at the time, despite the aforementioned rule changes—was to use the passing game to set up the running game, totally opposite of the conventional manner of directing an NFL offense. In fact, the passing game would be *substituted* for a running game in certain situations.

Walsh added his own special elements to the basic design Brown developed in Cleveland back in the late 1940s. First, Walsh incorporated flexible pass patterns into the system. He demanded that his quarterbacks and receivers "read" the defense and execute adjustable patterns, as needed, to precisely counter the prevailing defensive setup. Second, Walsh designed patterns that tended to accentuate the play-making abilities of the receivers after they made the catch. Therefore, he required wideouts who were elusive and had no reservations about running with the football. Third, Walsh devised a shorter drop (setup) for his quarterbacks, mitigating against the adverse effects of a superior pass rush. And last, though certainly not least, Walsh heightened the usefulness of the entire package by implementing it with a pass-first approach, whereas Paul Brown's Cleveland and Cincinnati teams used their passing attacks judiciously.

Walsh's main objectives were to give his quarterback several options on any one play and to accumulate a high completion percentage from quick-developing short passes that might then be converted into longer plays with the aid of receivers who were adept at avoiding tacklers in the open field. The entire system was based on the principle that short, flexible passing routes that attacked the seams (between defenders) of a zone defense or were implemented as crossing (across the field) patterns against a man-to-man defense could not be defended very well. The key to the strategy was that the plays had to be practiced over and over, against every type of defense the opponent could employ. Optimal conditions were realized when players flawlessly executed the proper pass patterns—performing the plays as if they were choreographed for a Broadway production—even though there were many spontaneous modifications. These modifications, when necessary, were crucial to the outcomes of the plays. Since Walsh expanded the timing pattern approach that Brown developed to include flexible pass patterns that worked better against zone defenses, the quarterback and receiver had to be able to make consistent, simultaneous conclusions as to the most favorable pattern against a particular defensive alignment. If they were not in sync, the play could be ruined, as the receiver might go one way while the ball went the other. After the catch, the receiver would be expected to finish the play by making the first defender miss the tackle, thereby adding several more yards to the completion.

Defenses were at a huge disadvantage against Walsh's brilliant scheme. The pass routes were usually too quick for the defensive linemen to get anywhere near the quarterback. And because Walsh modified the quarterback's drop—three to four steps back before delivering the ball, as opposed to the normal five to seven—many times the edge pass rushers had the wrong angle to make the sack anyway. The linebackers were usually too close to the "box" (an imaginary rectangle beginning at the line of scrimmage, spanning the width of the offensive line, and extending out approximately six to eight yards into the secondary) and often too slow in their drops (backpedal into coverage) to give much support to the defensive backs. The resultant completions placed a huge burden on the cornerbacks and safeties, as they were left to defend the passing lanes with no help from the pass rush and little or no help from their line-backers—often translating into large gains from very short passes.

The implementation of the West Coast offense proved to be a sizable task. First, Walsh needed to identify and acquire players whose offensive talents matched the tactics. Second, he had to indoctrinate them in the new approach and give them the time to comprehend the intricate details of the scheme. Third, he had to tinker with the system as he went along, revising bits and pieces of it to fully develop its potential. Looking back on his career well after he retired from coaching—and realizing the magnitude of his accomplishment with regard to installing a complex new system—Walsh felt that he was ultimately better off having to wait a little longer than he had planned in order to get his first NFL head coaching job. "I was fortunate in some ways that I had to wait so long, I was able to refine my thoughts, " he said. "I had developed an offensive system through my own devices, and having learned from other people, I could teach it in its entirety. And because of my experiences with the Raiders, and especially the Bengals, I learned to evaluate talent, going all the way with Cincinnati from locating a player, evaluating him, drafting him, and actually going out and signing him."

Walsh knew that he needed players whose talents were uniquely suited to his system in order to achieve the maximum benefits of his imaginative offensive program. He required a quick-thinking quarterback who was extremely accurate, had a good arm, and great touch—attributes that translate into the capability of throwing a "catchable" ball, time after time. A catchable ball is one that is between the belt buckle and the eyes, has enough zip on it to negate nearby defenders, yet not so much zip that the ball is difficult to snatch out of the air (in full stride) by the receiver.

The receivers had to be fairly tall, possess great hands, excellent quickness, and impeccable instincts to find and exploit the soft spots of the defense. Tall receivers were preferable because they were usually more difficult to jam at the line of scrimmage, and they offered a larger target for the quarterback. Great hands were of primary importance. When teams run, even unsuccessfully, they often gain a yard or two. Since the West Coast offense was a pass-first and run-second system, any drops (incompletions) were going to be magnified by creating far too many second- and third-and-ten situations. And the difference between third and six as opposed to third and ten is monumental. Consequently, the ability to catch most everything thrown in your direction was essential to the functionality of the offense. The attack could withstand a receiver who might not be super fast, as it was more important to have the ability to get open (not always easier just because a receiver is fast). In some cases—especially against a zone defense—a particular defender would be set up in a perfect position to foil the pattern that had been called. Other times, the defense might call for a bump-and-run scheme, which would necessitate an improvised passing route. In either case, the receiver had to possess the recognition skills and route-running capability to get open, and both he and the quarterback had to be synchronized in order to convert the play.

Table 9-1. Steve Deberg's 1978 Passing Performance

Year	Att	Comp	Comp%	Yards	YPA	TD	INT	Rating
1978	302	137	45.4	1570	5.20	8	22	40.0

If Walsh could acquire the necessary talent to adequately employ his unique strategy, he believed he would have a chance to redefine offensive football in the NFL.

When Walsh took over at San Francisco in 1979, he inherited a quarterback who was not highly regarded. Steve Deberg had been a tenth-round selection of the Dallas Cowboys in 1977 and was later released before being picked up by the 49ers in 1978.

Deberg started for the 49ers that year and experienced great difficulty (table 9-1).

After viewing film of the previous season and witnessing Deberg in practice, Walsh knew that he needed to find another quarterback. Deberg, though somewhat talented, did not appear to have the necessary tools to thrive in Walsh's offense. Despite the probability that the young quarterback would improve with experience, Walsh determined that Deberg did not fit into his future plans. A replacement had to found, and the first place to look was naturally the draft.

The year 1979 was not a great one for quarterbacks in the NFL draft, at least not from a quantitative standpoint. It didn't help that San Francisco entered the draft without picks in the first, third, and fourth rounds as payment for previous trades. Only three quarterbacks figured to go in the first two rounds: Jack Thompson, from Washington State; Phil Simms, from Morehead State; and Steve Fuller, from Clemson. The rest of the lesser-thought-of quarterback candidates would likely be mixed in from rounds three through twelve.

The draft unfolded according to plan. In the first round, Thompson was selected by the Bengals at the third overall spot, Simms was taken by the New York Giants at seven, and Fuller was chosen by the Kansas City Chiefs at twenty-three. No other quarterbacks were taken until the eighty-second selection of the entire draft, in the latter part of the third round. Luckily for the 49ers, they had managed to acquire that particular pick as part of a trade with the Seattle Seahawks, who had received the pick from its original owner, the Dallas Cowboys.

Walsh decided on a scrawny Notre Dame quarterback named Joe Montana. At 6' 2", 190 pounds, Montana looked more like a basketball player than a football player. But Walsh noticed several qualities that he liked in the young man. First of all, he was accurate. He almost never missed his target, even on the run. Second, he had a good arm and often threw a great deep ball, arching the throw high enough to allow the receiver to run under the pass. Third, despite being somewhat frail, he was tough and seemed as if he could withstand a beating, which, when being drafted as a quarterback for a 2–14 club (San Francisco's 1978 record), was a foregone conclusion. Fourth, he had excellent footwork and was extremely smooth and fluid in his mechanics. And last, though certainly not least, he was smart, and he figured to be able to handle the mental demands associated with the quarterback position in the West Coast offense.

Table 9-2. Steve Deberg's 1979 Passing Performance

Year	Att	Comp	Comp%	Yards	YPA	TD	INT	Rating
1979	578	347	60.0	3652	6.32	17	21	73.1

Bill Walsh's coaching debut took place on September 2, 1979, against the Vikings in Minnesota. The 49ers lost that contest 28–22 and continued their losing ways for the next six weeks, compiling an 0–7 mark for their rookie head coach. Walsh's agonizing first season ended with just two victories and no improvement from San Francisco's cellar-dwelling mark of the previous season.

Steve Deberg was once again the starting quarterback in 1979. Though he improved from his horrific season of 1978, he continued to experience interception problems and compiled a low yards per attempt figure (6.32) (table 9-2), two tendencies that Walsh frowned upon.

Although Deberg was still young and likely to improve even more, Walsh decided that it was time to work Joe Montana into the quarterback rotation. Montana had played sparingly in his rookie season, throwing just twenty-three passes. Nonetheless, he looked at ease in the pocket and seemed fairly comfortable with San Francisco's intricate offensive system. Deberg was to remain the starter, but Montana would get ample opportunity to display his skills during the coming season.

The 49ers began the 1980 campaign with three straight victories, the first time since 1952 that a San Francisco team had a 3–0 start. Fans started to think playoffs, and the coaching staff believed that the club was ready to meet the challenge. In retrospect, however, the printing of playoff tickets would have been quite foolish.

San Francisco had defeated the New Orleans Saints, the St. Louis Cardinals, and the New York Jets—not exactly showcase NFL teams. Take a look in table 9-3 at the final regular-season records of those teams in 1980 and you'll see what I mean.

The fact that the 49ers proceeded to lose their next eight games would have come as no shock to anyone capable of discerning the true abilities of the teams that they had beaten. The losing streak started with a 20–17 loss to the Atlanta Falcons and ended with a 17–13 setback at the hands of the Miami Dolphins. Sandwiched somewhere in between were two particularly embarrassing defeats to the Los Angeles Rams and Dallas Cowboys—48–26 and 59–14, respectively.

Table 9-3. 1980 Records for the Saints, Cardinals, and Jets

	W	L	T
New Orleans Saints	1	15	0
St. Louis Cardinals	5	11	0
New York Jets	4	12	0
Totals	10	38	0

In addition to the misery and humiliation suffered by the players as a result of the tailspin, Walsh began to doubt his ability to coach in the NFL. After the Dolphins' loss, he had an emotional breakdown that convinced him to resign. Walsh described his feelings at the time. "I felt that I had failed," he said. "I was convinced that I could not get the job done. I decided to talk to owner Eddie DeBartolo [the next day] and offer to finish the season as coach, but that was it. I would ask for a job in the front office somewhere."

Bill Walsh was an intelligent, meticulous individual who endeavored to solve his problems with an honest, objective approach. With more time to think—and emotionally unwind—Walsh calmed down and took a different perspective on his predicament. He rationalized that losing streaks, however disconcerting, were part of the growth process. "There will be times of disappointment," he said in retrospect, "but you can still be making progress, even though the results at the moment don't reflect it. As the leader, you cannot let the setbacks so overwhelm you that you lose sight of the overall progress."

Walsh had fallen into the trap of expecting instantaneous gratification from his coaching efforts. He lost sight of the fact that his team, albeit dejected by the losing streak, had indeed made some progress. Three victories in a row—even over the Little Sisters of the Poor—was quite an achievement for a club that had won just four of their previous thirty-two encounters. Walsh overestimated the abilities of his team due to their unexpected 3–0 start against what turned out to be inferior competition. He assumed that the club was well ahead of their anticipated schedule and made the mistake of expecting too much, too soon, from his young squad. He eventually resigned himself to the fact that the club would experience growing pains during the revitalization process and that they weren't going to take off and become in one fell swoop a 12–4 juggernaut from the 2–14 abomination they had been. Walsh reconsidered his resignation and decided to finish out the year before making any future plans.

Although Deberg started the first six games of the 1980 season, he encountered many of the same problems that had plagued him in the past. Consequently, Joe Montana was given the chance to start seven of the team's last ten games. It did not take Montana long to clearly establish himself as San Francisco's number one quarterback (table 9-4). The second-year player from Monongahela, Pennsylvania—with all of twenty-three passes under his belt from his rookie season—was amazingly effective.

For an inexperienced quarterback to thrive in such a complex system was almost incomprehensible. Montana led the NFL in completion percentage, and his outstanding 15–9 touchdown-to-interception ratio was highly irregular for a second-year player. With more seasoning and better athletes surrounding Montana, Walsh knew he had a quarterback worthy of his brilliant offensive tactics.

Table 9-4. Joe Montana's 1980 Passing Performance

Year	Att	Comp	Comp%	Yards	YPA	TD	INT	Rating
1980	273	176	64.5	1795	6.58	15	9	87.8

One of Montana's favorite targets during the latter half of the 1980 season was a little-known wide receiver from Clemson University named Dwight Clark. Drafted along with Montana in 1979, Clark—a lowly tenth-round selection—caught only eighteen passes as a rookie. He exploded, however, for eighty-two catches and eight touchdowns in his sophomore season. Clark finished second in the NFC in catches (to teammate, running back Earl Cooper) and showed a propensity for finding openings in the defense while catching everything thrown in his direction. Hmm—sounds like a perfect West Coast offense receiver. In addition, Clark and Montana seemed to work well together.

San Francisco won three of their last five games to finish at 6–10 in 1980. The six wins represented 50 percent more victories than the previous two seasons combined. The fact remained, however, that the 49ers had accumulated just ten wins in their last three seasons, earned just one winning record in the last eight years, endured three consecutive double-digit losing campaigns, and changed coaches five times since 1975. It couldn't get much worse. Though the club had shown slight improvement in 1980 (table 9-5), the depressing performances of the prior two seasons overshadowed any minor advancement the team had made. To casual fans, the team still seemed inept in many areas. If Walsh couldn't fix the problems soon, he might be on his way out, too. This time, however, it wouldn't be of his own volition.

Clearly, San Francisco's offense had improved utilizing Walsh's newfangled attack. The 49ers had climbed from last in the league in points scored in 1978 to twelfth in 1980 (table 9-6). Actually, San Francisco had risen from the bottom of the league into the top echelon of clubs in four statistical categories. Not bad for a 6–10 team.

The numbers were undeniable. San Francisco was quickly becoming an offensive force under Bill Walsh. Accomplishing this feat with a dearth of offensive talent and a pair of inexperienced quarterbacks made the achievement that much more impressive. Walsh began to think that the sky was the limit if they could acquire better athletes at the skill positions and gain more experience for Joe Montana.

As fabulous and invigorating as it was to finally see statistical evidence of offensive growth, it was nevertheless distressing to assess the defense and discover several fatal flaws. The 49ers surrendered 415 points in 1980, finishing twenty-sixth in the

Table 9-5. San Francisco 49ers' 1973–80 Record

	W	L	T	Pct
1973	5	9	0	.357
1974	6	8	0	.429
1975	5	9	0	.357
1976	8	6	0	.571
1977	5	9	0	.357
1978	2	14	0	.125
1979	2	14	0	.125
1980	6	10	0	.375
Totals	33	69	0	.324

Table 9-6. San Francisco 49ers' Offensive Statistics, 1978–80

Year	Points	Comp Pct	Passing Yards	TD Passes
1978	219 (28)	43.7 (27)	2,306 (25)	9 (26)
1979	308 (16)	60.0 (4)	3,760 (6)	18 (15-T)
1980	320 (12-T)	60.8 (3)	3,799 (6)	27 (7-T)

NOTE: T designates tied in ranking
*NFL Ranking in parentheses, out of 28 teams

league. They also permitted the outrageous totals of 66.1 percent opponent pass completions and 3,958 passing yards—far too much to expect to have any chance at winning consistently. With those statistics, it almost seemed as if the offense had set out
to be the trendsetters of the West Coast offense, while the defense set out to be the
roadkill in the wake of that onslaught.

Bill Walsh was an offensive specialist. Although his thesis in graduate school at
San Jose State—believe it or not—was written on "Stopping the Pro-Spread Offense,"
he was obviously more adept at running that offense. Consequently, he relied on his
assistant coaches with regard to the defensive matters in which he was less skilled. He
enlisted the help of capable defensive specialists and empowered them with comprehensive authority. Walsh believed that a football coach had to possess specific attributes and operate in a certain fashion in order to reach his ultimate potential. "It takes
some seasoning, experience; the ability to communicate; an excellent football theory
and strategy; and the ability to judge other people [assistant coaches] and delegate
authority, yet monitor their progress," he said. That was how he worked in San Francisco, entrusting his defensive assistants with authority and closely tracking their progress. Unfortunately, Walsh had determined that his defensive *assistants* in 1980 (secondary coach George Seifert, in particular) were clearly in need of *assistance*—at least to
the extent of locating quality football talent.

Though Walsh admittedly assumed a subordinate role relative to the defensive
decisions made on the field, he had one compelling virtue in the search for defensive
manpower—his unrivaled prowess at identifying and procuring capable players. "My
chief contribution to the defense was to make sure that we had the best collection of
great players possible," he said. "So I spent more time drafting defensive players than I
did offensive players. Most importantly, I brought to the team some truly great defensive
talent." The 1981 NFL draft was one of many examples of his adroitness in this regard.

San Francisco had the luxury of four picks in the first three rounds that year and
chose three defensive backs in those four slots. Ronnie Lott, a hard-hitting safety from
USC, was the 49ers' first-round selection; Eric Wright, from Missouri, and Carlton Williamson, from Pittsburgh, were second- and third-round picks, respectively. All three
players became immediate starters, and they made a huge difference in the 49ers' secondary during their rookie seasons.

The 1981 season was a crucial one for Bill Walsh. First-year coaches generally
receive a grace period in which they are absolved from any blame for the team's inconsistent play. Gradually, during the second year, the coach begins to attract more and
more of the criticism for poor results. Finally, in the third season, the gloves come off,
and the coach basically sinks or swims. As the city of San Francisco awaited Walsh's
third try at reviving the team, the coach had Joe Montana busy attempting to master
the subtleties of the West Coast offense.

Week after week in the off-season, Montana, Walsh, offensive assistant Sam
Wyche, and various backs and receivers worked through the 49ers' offensive repertoire
and made minor adjustments to their modernistic system. "There was a lot of time

spent studying," Montana said. "Sam [Wyche] helped me with the little keys, the knowledge of what a defense was or was not capable of in a certain situation—pre-reads we call it—knowing where not to go before the ball is even snapped. You'd learn to work on individuals [defenders]. We would see a film, and Sam would say, 'See, this guy can't cover that far, but he tries to.' Bill's [Walsh's] system works only if the guy running the routes is able to read. Most of our routes had a lot of options built into them, according to zone or man coverage. Everyone had to be on the same page. We never wanted to be at the point where one defense could cover a route completely." The additional practice time was instrumental in making the execution of the West Coast offense second nature for the talented young quarterback and his pass catchers.

Heading into the 1981 season, the 49ers seemed to have a quarterback in whom they believed, several new, capable, athletic defenders in the secondary, and a confident attitude, the result of a respectable finish in 1980. In combination with the extra training the offense received during the off-season, it seemed like the opportune time for the organization to emerge from its eight-year slumber and reap the rewards of its hard work. "I'm a pragmatic person when it comes to coaching," Walsh says. "I believe most games are won on preparation and execution, and certainly not on luck. Fortune is perhaps 25 percent of the game. If your standards of preparation are high, there is an excellent chance that your standard of play will be high. That is how you win football games."

San Francisco traveled to Detroit to meet the Lions in the 1981 season opener. Detroit was a notoriously tough team to defeat at home, but the Lions were coming off a 2–14 season, and the 49ers expected to win the game. Detroit lived up to its reputation and defeated the 49ers 24–17. Nevertheless, the team rebounded to win three of their next four games, bringing their record to 3–2. Then came the first big test of the season, a home game versus the fearsome Dallas Cowboys. Dallas had recorded a 12–4 record in 1980 before losing to the Philadelphia Eagles in the NFC championship game. They were also the team that almost forced Walsh into early retirement, the result of their 59–14 drubbing of the 49ers the previous season. The Cowboys entered the 1981 matchup with a 4–1 record. This time, however, the 49ers sent the 'Boys back to Dallas with a good old fashioned "whoopin'" of their own. The 45–14 thrashing of the Cowboys marked the third straight win for San Francisco and gave the team the confidence they needed to realize their full potential. The winning streak eventually reached seven, and the 49ers finished the season with a remarkable 13–3 record, winning the NFC Western Division title for the first time since 1972.

Walsh's West Coast offense once again paid huge dividends. San Francisco finished the season with 357 points, seventh in the NFL. The team's 64.3 completion percentage (the result of the system's reliance on high-probability passes) led the league by far and was almost 18 percent superior to the NFL average of 54.6. The 49ers also vindicated themselves on the defensive side of the ball. The team allowed just 250 points, taking a miraculous jump from twenty-sixth in the league in 1980 to second in 1981. In particular, pass defense proved to be the difference. The acquisition of defensive end Fred

Dean bolstered the pass rush, and despite starting three rookies in the secondary, the team intercepted twenty-seven passes (fifth in the NFL), ten more than the 1980 squad that finished tied for twenty-fourth in the league with only seventeen.

San Francisco hosted the New York Giants in the team's first playoff game in nine years. The 49ers held an early 10–7 advantage in the second quarter, when the game was decided in a matter of seconds. Ronnie Lott picked off a pass, and three plays later Montana hit wide receiver Freddie Solomon with a fifty-eight-yard touchdown strike. The ensuing kickoff was mishandled by New York, and the 49ers recovered and scored again, blowing the game wide open, 24–7. The game ended in a 38–24 San Francisco victory, and the 49ers were primed for an NFC championship game against the Cowboys the next week.

It is remembered simply as "The Catch." With 4:54 remaining in the contest, the Cowboys led 27–21. Montana and the 49ers were forced to begin their last drive at their own eleven-yard line. Ten plays, eighty-three yards, and 3:52 later, San Francisco stood at the Dallas six-yard line and attempted a third-down pass that would instantly take its place among the greatest plays in professional football history. Montana dropped back to throw. Pressured, he dashed to his right, looking for a receiver. As he neared the sideline, he lofted a high, off-balance pass towards the back of the end zone, seemingly throwing the ball away to avoid a sack. Somehow—perhaps through divine intervention (remember, Montana was from Notre Dame)—the ball appeared to stall in midair about four feet from the back line of the end zone. Though the ball seemed about twenty feet high, Dwight Clark—all six feet, four inches of him—came racing across the field, jumped as high as he possibly could, and snatched victory from the Cowboys, a Super Bowl appearance for the 49ers, and a heroic NFL moment for himself and Montana. The 49ers defeated the Cowboys 28–27 in a game for the ages.

To this day, most observers still believe that Montana was trying to throw the ball away but didn't get enough power on the pass. Walsh, however, vehemently disagrees. "We practiced what other teams wrote off as broken plays," he said, "plays on which the first option broke down and the quarterback had to run out of the pocket and either carry the ball himself or find another receiver."

The strategy called for San Francisco receivers to run specific routes when the quarterback was scrambling to one side of the field or the other. So when the play broke down and Montana was in trouble, he knew where Clark was supposed to be. "We practiced the scrambling, off-balance throw," Walsh says. "It wasn't accidental when he [Montana] did it. It was a carefully practiced thing. I'd tell him, 'Timed pattern to the first receiver. If he's covered, move, and look for the second. Then scramble and throw off-balance, and jerk it to the third. By the time you're reading the third receiver, someone's [a defensive player] got a hold of you [forcing you to throw off-balance]. That's what we'd practice.'" And Montana threw the pass high enough that if Clark did not catch it, no one else would. "Some Cowboys' players still contend that Montana was trying to throw the ball away," Walsh says. "They say he was as surprised as anyone when

Clark made the catch. That isn't true. It was a play we worked on just for that specific situation. It was not dumb luck—it was planning and superb execution.

"We developed a degree of precision that allowed us to make plays in clutch situations. The timing between our quarterbacks and receivers was so precise that the receivers knew exactly where the ball would be thrown, when to turn, and where to look."

In Super Bowl XVI, San Francisco met Walsh's former team, the Cincinnati Bengals. The 49ers surged to a 20–0 halftime lead en route to a 26–21 victory that was not as close as the game's final score would indicate. The 49ers' defense made the important plays in the third quarter. Trailing 20–7, the Bengals drove down the field and had a first down at the San Francisco three-yard line. On the first play, Pete Johnson ran to the one. On the next three plays the Bengals were stopped cold. The goal-line stand completely demoralized Cincinnati, and San Francisco was poised for its first-ever championship. Joe Montana won the game's MVP award, and kicker Ray Wersching tallied four field goals. The San Francisco 49ers had arrived. From the depths of despair to the exhilaration of a world championship, Bill Walsh had revived professional football in San Francisco, all in very short order.

Bill Walsh won more than just a game in the Super Bowl. He won the admiration and respect from his peers that he so richly deserved. His revolutionary offensive system had proven beyond a shadow of a doubt that teams could win in the NFL with a passing game first and a running game second. In 1981, the 49ers' leading ground gainer was Ricky Patton. Patton gained just 543 yards and averaged 3.6 yards per carry—mediocre numbers for a championship team. In fact, the world champion 49ers finished dead last in average per carry in the NFL in 1981 (3.4). Walsh's bold new philosophy and cutting-edge offensive system had redefined offensive football and would become firmly ensconced in NFL playbooks during the next ten years.

In 1982, a players' strike reduced the season to just nine games. The 49ers finished the year at 3–6 and missed the playoffs. During the season, Walsh noticed that defenses were slowly but surely altering their tactics to offset the advantage of his novel offense. Although San Francisco led the NFC in passing yardage and finished seventh in the NFL in points scored, Walsh knew he would have to adjust his approach to keep pace with the league.

In the 1983 off-season, Walsh made two significant acquisitions to enhance San Francisco's offense. First, he invested a second-round draft selection on a halfback from Nebraska named Roger Craig. Although the 49ers' attack was not predicated on the running game, it obviously couldn't hurt to have a back who could tote the pigskin when the situation dictated. As long as that back was also capable of catching the football—something at which Craig excelled—the services of a good running back could be extremely valuable, especially with defenses clamping down on the passing game. Craig's presence as a running threat gave Walsh a crucial edge. It limited opportunities for San Francisco's opponents to stack their defenses against the pass, helping Montana

Table 9-7. Joe Montana's 1983 Passing Performance

Year	Att	Comp	Comp%	Yards	YPA	TD	INT	Rating
1983	515	332	64.5	3910	7.59	26	12	94.6

avoid many of the blitz packages and nickel-back (five-defensive-back) situations that were being utilized against the 49ers' dominant aerial attack. In addition to Craig, Walsh also added a veteran halfback to the club. Wendell Tyler was acquired from the Rams in exchange for draft picks. Tyler added six years of experience to the backfield, and he, too, excelled as both a runner and receiver.

When the 1983 season began, the 49ers possessed a lethal offense. With the aid of a formidable ground game, Montana began to compile the statistics that would pave the way for his journey to Canton. He set new career highs in yardage, average per attempt, touchdowns, and quarterback rating (table 9-7).

San Francisco once again led the NFL in completion percentage, finished fifth in the league in passing yardage, and seventh in yards per attempt.

Craig and Tyler combined for outstanding statistics from the halfback position as well (table 9-8).

San Francisco finished the 1983 season at 10–6 and won the NFC's Western Division title for the second time under Walsh. After a first-round bye, they hosted the Detroit Lions in their first playoff game. The 49ers picked up where they left off in the 1981 playoffs, racing out to a 14–3 lead early in the second quarter. But the Lions, led by halfback Billy Sims, came roaring back and took a 23–17 lead in the final period. Montana was required to perform his magic once more. He completed six of six passes on the game-winning drive in the final three minutes, including a fourteen-yard touchdown toss to Freddie Solomon. The 49ers defeated the Lions 24–23.

San Francisco then traveled to Washington to meet the Redskins for the NFC championship. Under the direction of Joe Gibbs, Washington had finished the season with fourteen wins and set an all-time NFL record for points scored (541) in the process. For three quarters they tossed the 49ers around like rag dolls, building a seemingly insurmountable 21–0 advantage. San Francisco had two fellows named Walsh and Montana, however, and they wouldn't go down without a fight. The 49ers stormed back and tied the game on the strength of three Joe Montana touchdown passes in the final quarter. Finally, the Redskins mustered some offense of their own, and Mark Moseley kicked a game-winning twenty-five-yard field goal to secure a 24–21 victory for Washington in the waning seconds of the contest.

Playoff disappointment notwithstanding, the 1983 season was greatly satisfying for Walsh. Teams around the league had begun to refer to the 49ers as an "artful" team,

Table 9-8. Craig and Tyler, 1983 Halfback Performance

Attempts	Yards	Average	Receptions	Yards	Average	TDs
352	1581	4.5	82	712	8.7	18

a club that relied more on tactical manifestations and schemes to produce victory as opposed to old-school physicality. "Because we threw the ball so much, we were labeled a finesse team," he said. "I always felt that had a negative connotation. It reminded me of the nickel-and-dime label from my Cincinnati years.

"Often we were winning with less talent than the other teams. We had more dimension to our game plans, more options for the quarterback, and usually more precision in our play. We would defeat teams, yet they had contempt for the way we beat them. Their attitude seemed to be, 'This isn't real football. Why would you play this kind of football when you could play tough, physical football?'" But in 1983, with the running of Craig and Tyler, the 49ers began to prove they could smash the ball down your throat *or* throw it over your head; and either way, they were almost assuredly going to beat you.

Which is exactly what they did the next season.

San Francisco went 15–1 and completely annihilated almost every team they encountered in 1984. The only blemish on an otherwise perfect record occurred in week seven, when the Pittsburgh Steelers edged the 49ers 20–17. San Francisco more than doubled their opponents' point production on the year, scoring 475 points while allowing just 227. And the dynamic backfield play of Craig and Tyler (almost two thousand rushing and one thousand receiving yards between them—table 9-9) reinforced the message that the 49ers were not strictly a finesse team.

Establishing more balance in the 49ers' attack was the consequence of Walsh's fear of becoming one dimensional—and therefore easier to defend—as opposed to proving a point to the rest of the league about the physical abilities of his team. Walsh was always one step ahead of his competitors. He never rested on his laurels and never allowed himself or his teams to become complacent. San Francisco would not sit idly by while their opponents developed strategies to defeat their system. "Football teams that are slow to move ahead get left behind," Walsh said. "If a team stubbornly sticks with one style of offense and doesn't change to try and stay a step ahead, it will often find itself losing by three touchdowns in the fourth quarter."

Montana had his finest season yet in 1984 (table 9-10). When a quarterback has a high enough passer rating to keep you in bed with the flu, you can be certain it was a stellar performance.

The 1984 playoffs started with a game against Bill Parcells's New York Giants at Candlestick Park in San Francisco. Montana accounted for every touchdown in the

Table 9-9. Craig and Tyler, 1984 Halfback Performance

Attempts	Yards	Average	Receptions	Yards	Average	TDs
401	1911	4.8	99	905	9.1	19

Table 9-10. Joe Montana's 1984 Passing Performance

Year	Att	Comp	Comp%	Yards	YPA	TD	INT	Rating
1984	432	279	64.6	3630	8.40	28	10	102.9

game, including an errant pass that resulted in a Harry Carson interception returned for a Giants' score. Nevertheless, Montana's three touchdowns to the guys in cardinal and gold more than compensated for the single indiscretion. The game ended in a 21–10 San Francisco victory, launching the 49ers into another NFC championship game.

The upstart Chicago Bears, led by the indomitable Mike Ditka, invaded the Bay Area to appear in their first NFC title game ever. Chicago had defeated the Redskins 23–19 in the first round of the playoffs. They possessed an awesome defense and were sky high for the contest against the highly touted San Francisco attack. The 49ers could muster only two field goals by halftime as Montana, uncharacteristically sloppy, was intercepted twice, both times deep in Bears' territory. Fortunately, Chicago, led by backup quarterback Steve Fuller—who was subbing for starter Jim McMahon—did not come close to scoring, and the 49ers led 6–0. In the second half, San Francisco slowly and methodically wore down the Bears as Chicago's defense grew increasingly weary in light of their offense's shortcomings. San Francisco's defense, on the other hand, turned up the heat on Fuller. They sacked the overmatched quarterback nine times on the afternoon, spearheading a 23–0 victory that moved San Francisco one step closer to another Super Bowl title.

Super Bowl XIX matched two of the most prolific passers in history, Dan Marino of the Miami Dolphins and Joe Montana. It also featured two of the most productive offenses. The 49ers scored 475 points in the regular season, and the Dolphins' league-leading total of 513 points was second most in NFL history at the time.

Miami, coached by the incomparable Don Shula, had finished their season with a 14–2 record. They had easily dispatched Seattle and Pittsburgh in the playoffs to reach the Super Bowl. Dan Marino had perhaps the finest season an NFL quarterback ever posted (table 9-11).

Walsh knew that this game represented the sternest test his defense would probably ever face (other than the 150 or so practices every year against Montana). He also knew that he had to somehow neutralize Miami's offensive firepower. So he collaborated with his defensive coordinator George Seifert (who was promoted from secondary coach to coordinator in 1983) to develop a scheme to slow down Marino and the Dolphins' passing attack.

Seifert devised an ingenious pass-rush tactic that delivered a thrust up the middle of the Dolphins' line rather than at the edges, where the defense typically mounts their pressure. In conjunction with the pass-rush technique, Walsh incorporated a

Table 9-11. Dan Marino's 1984 Passing Performance

Year	Att	Comp	Comp%	Yards	YPA	TD	INT	Rating
1984	564	362	64.2	5084	9.01	48	17	108.9

strategy of deploying six defensive backs for much of the game. This enabled Miami to initiate a ground attack versus a weakened defensive front (defensive backs as opposed to linebackers versus the run) but afforded San Francisco the luxury of two additional pass defenders to counteract Marino's effectiveness.

Walsh's logic was simple. He would rather concern himself with stopping Tony Nathan and Woody Bennett—Miami's running backs—than he would with Dan Marino. During the season, the Dolphins could only equal the NFL average of 4.0 yards per rushing attempt—not a particularly threatening statistic. Nathan, the better of the two backs (4.7 average), was not big enough to withstand the entire running load for the Dolphins, and fullback Woody Bennett (4.2) was not elusive enough to be a consistent weapon. Walsh would do everything in his power to negate Marino's impact and would make *anyone* else on the Miami team beat him.

The results were impressive. Marino was sacked four times after suffering just thirteen sacks all year. He was held to just 289 yards on a whopping fifty passes, for a 5.78 yards per attempt ratio as compared to his league-leading and quite flashy 9.01 regular-season figure. The Miami ground game mustered just twenty-five yards. Joe Montana was named game MVP, as he completed twenty-four of thirty-five passes for 331 yards and three touchdowns. Roger Craig scored three touchdowns of his own and combined with Wendell Tyler to gain 123 yards on the ground. San Francisco outgained the vaunted Dolphins' offensive machine 537–314 and easily won the game, 38–16.

Bill Walsh had beaten a very worthy foe in Don Shula, and he did it by being innovative and employing unconventional schemes and strategies—even for a game as big as the Super Bowl. Whereas most coaches talk tough and espouse the old "we'll do what we do best and let them try to stop us" philosophy, Walsh was different. He didn't want to rely exclusively on his team's strengths to carry the 49ers to victory. He attempted to take advantage of every conceivable tactic at his disposal in an effort to ensure success. "He was never afraid to try things," said TV analyst and coach Dick Vermeil in a testimonial to Walsh's ability to adapt to different situations. "He wasn't afraid if it didn't work."

Walsh had taken the 49ers from consecutive 2–14 seasons to multiple Super Bowl victories, all in the span of seven years. San Francisco was considered the best team in the NFL. And they weren't finished yet.

In the 1985 draft, Walsh hoped to upgrade the 49ers' receiving corps. His wide receivers were getting up in age (Freddie Solomon turned thirty-two just before the Super Bowl), and the unit lacked the size and ability he preferred. If the opportunity presented itself, the 49ers would take a chance on a wide receiver early in the draft.

His name was Jerry Rice, and he played at a little-known school called Mississippi Valley State. Through a series of trades, the 49ers wound up with the sixteenth pick in the draft, New England's original spot. Before the April draft, speculation was that Rice would be gone by the sixth or seventh selection. He had compiled incredible numbers in college, had great size (6' 2", two hundred pounds) and excellent hands. But somewhere along the line, people began to question his speed. When timed in the forty-yard dash, Rice clocked in at 4.5 to 4.55, rather pedestrian for a wide receiver about to be taken with a top-ten pick, most thought. Bill Walsh, however, was not discouraged. "Every time I saw him on film, he was never caught from behind," Walsh said. "Sometimes a player is faster in a football uniform, in a football game, than he is in shorts on a Tuesday morning."

While many scouts and general managers often fall into the trap of drafting *athletes* instead of football players, Walsh never lost sight of the skills and tools necessary to excel on the field of play. Not that he didn't pay attention to the "measurables"— speed, height, weight, shuttle times, et cetera—but he always accounted for football skills before he became ecstatic about a player's athletic potential. "He was very adept at understanding the nuances that would be important for different positions, and what would separate the great players from the good ones," said Carmen Policy, president of the Cleveland Browns and general manager of the 49ers during Walsh's tenure.

The scuttlebutt on draft day was that either Indianapolis at five, the New York Jets at ten, or the Cincinnati Bengals at thirteen, would take a shot on Rice. Walsh, at sixteen, would be out of luck. As the drama unfolded, Indianapolis took linebacker Duane Bickett; New York took a receiver from a more recognized school, Al Toon from Wisconsin; and Cincinnati did the same, taking wide receiver Eddie Brown from Miami. San Francisco took Rice at sixteen, and the rest is history.

Jerry Rice—with the assistance of Joe Montana and, later, Steve Young—developed into the most feared receiver in the history of the NFL. Rice became *the* element of the 49ers' offense that other teams had to specifically attempt to countervail. He became the offensive equivalent to the Giants' Lawrence Taylor on defense, as both were always the focal point of the opposition's game plan.

The maneuvering to acquire the sixteenth pick on draft day, in order to select Rice, was an effective tool that Walsh utilized time and again during his tenancy with San Francisco. In his ten-year career as head coach, from 1979 to 1988, Walsh made more than forty trades involving draft selections, sometimes moving up the draft ladder to select a certain athlete before he was chosen, or down, when no players inspired his enthusiasm, thus allowing the 49ers to appropriate additional picks. At times, it seemed as if both he and Dallas coach Jimmy Johnson—who also dabbled in the "Let's Make a Deal" craze—would make trades just for the sake of spicing up their team's draft and creating media speculation, a belief that was echoed by Carmen Policy. "I think he would trade for the sake of invigorating the draft room, the organization, and himself," he said.

In Jerry Rice's rookie season, 1985, he collaborated with Montana to catch forty-nine passes for a spectacular 18.9 average and three touchdowns. And though he dropped many throws that could have gone for huge amounts of yardage—often attempting to run before he had the ball—Walsh knew that was a correctable flaw and that he possessed a diamond in the rough. Rice's deep-play potential instantly paid

Jerry Rice, *left,* and Dwight Clark, *right,* flank Bill Walsh on the sideline. The two receivers would play big roles in three San Francisco Super Bowl seasons under Walsh.

Table 9-12. Craig and Tyler, 1985 Running Back Performance

Attempts	Yards	Average	Receptions	Yards	Average	TDs
			Craig			
214	1050	4.9	92	1016	9.5	15
			Tyler			
171	867	5.1	20	154	7.7	8

dividends by freeing up other 49ers' offensive players, particularly running backs Roger Craig and Wendell Tyler. Craig and Tyler were a formidable duo before Rice entered the offensive scheme. But now—with Montana, Clark, former All-Pro tight end Russ Francis (acquired from New England), and Rice—opponents didn't have enough players to cope with the abundance of talented 49ers' personnel, and San Francisco's backfield combo exploded for an incomparable season (table 9-12). Craig became the first player in NFL history to gain more than one thousand yards rushing and receiving.

San Francisco's defense also fulfilled its role in 1985, allowing just 263 points (second best in the NFL). Curiously, however, the season ended in disappointment. The 49ers slipped to a 10–6 record and had to settle for a wild-card playoff berth in which they were defeated by the Giants in New York, 17–3. But with the nucleus of the team still firmly intact, Walsh believed San Francisco's run was far from over.

In typical Walsh style, the 49ers enjoyed an exceptional draft in 1986. The success of this harvest, however, was not evidenced in the form of superstars, but more in the overall scope of the talent (table 9-13).

Ironically, every pick except for Roberts (the highest selection) ended up starting and playing a pivotal role in the team's future. Haley in particular proved to be an integral part of the 49ers' defense. He provided a steady dose of pass-rush pressure for six seasons and finished his career with almost one hundred sacks. Taylor—another tall wide receiver from an obscure school, Delaware State—started his career slowly but ultimately established himself as a viable threat opposite Rice. Rathman, McKyer, Wallace, Fagan, and Griffin all became key contributors and enjoyed lengthy careers in the NFL.

Table 9-13. San Francisco 49ers, 1986 Draft

Round	Player	Position	College
1	*Choice to Dallas*		
2	Larry Roberts	DE	Alabama
3	Tom Rathman	RB	Nebraska
3	Tim McKyer	DB	Texas-Arlington
3	John Taylor	WR	Delaware State
4	Charles Haley	LB	James Madison
4	Steve Wallace	T	Auburn
4	Kevin Fagan	DT	Miami
6	Don Griffin	DB	Middle Tennessee State

During each of the next two seasons, San Francisco suffered the indignity of winning their division but losing their first playoff game. In 1986, Joe Montana—who turned thirty years old before the year began—missed eight games due to an injured back that would plague him until he retired. Not at his best that season, he threw more interceptions than touchdowns for the only time in his illustrious fifteen-year career. Backup quarterback Jeff Kemp filled in admirably, however, and the 49ers claimed the Western Division title for the fourth time in five years. In the playoffs, San Francisco traveled to the Meadowlands and ran into a buzz saw called the New York Giants. The Giants had finished the season with a 14–2 record and proceeded to cut the 49ers to pieces in a 49–3 rout that became a postseason springboard for their Super Bowl victory that year. Montana started the playoff debacle, but a concussion sustained just before halftime kept him on the sidelines for the remainder of the game.

In the strike season of 1987, Montana rebounded with a superb year and led the 49ers to the best record in the league, 13–2 (table 9-14). Nevertheless, San Francisco squandered their opportunity for a third Super Bowl trophy when they were upset at home in the 1986 playoffs by the Minnesota Vikings, 36–24.

One bright spot amid the disappointments of 1986 and 1987 was the emergence of Jerry Rice, who began to display the incredible skills that would eventually earn him the distinction as the NFL's all-time best receiver. In 1986, Rice snared eighty-six passes for an NFL record (at the time) 1,570 yards and sixteen touchdowns. In 1987—playing in just twelve games of the strike-shortened/replacement-player season—Rice caught sixty-five passes for 1,078 yards, accumulating the amazing total of twenty-two touchdown receptions, another league record.

In 1988, Bill Walsh, at fifty-seven years of age, was clearly growing tired—burned out from the rigors of nine-and-a-half grueling NFL seasons. San Francisco had not won a playoff game since their Super Bowl victory of 1984, and they had suffered embarrassing playoff defeats to the Giants and Vikings in 1986 and 1987, respectively. To make matters worse, they experienced a rash of injuries during the 1988 season. The results were a mediocre 6–5 record, a lethargic group of players, and seemingly little chance of a playoff berth heading into the final five games of the year. Weary and frustrated by the recent setbacks he had endured, Walsh desperately attempted to invigorate the 49ers for a run at a third Super Bowl title. He beseeched the club to circle the wagons and take the remaining five games one at a time. "I talked to the team in a very direct way," he said. " 'Here's where we are,' I told them, '6–5, but we can still make the playoffs. Look at the opposition. Are we as good as this team? How about that team? Can we beat that team?' "

Table 9-14. Joe Montana's 1987 Passing Performance

Year	Att	Comp	Comp%	Yards	YPA	TD	INT	Rating
1987	398	266	66.8	3054	7.67	31*	13	102.1*

*Led league

Walsh had evaluated the 49ers' predicament and determined that he needed to redefine the team's goals in order to have any chance to salvage the season. San Francisco was still a talent-laden club. However, due to injuries, age, and—quite frankly—quality competition, the 49ers were somewhat demoralized and had lost a little bit of their edge. Walsh decided that the team needed a basic, uncomplicated plan of progression to get them back on track. So he simplified the team's immediate goals by imploring them to focus on winning just *one game*—the next game on their schedule—hoping that two or three consecutive victories in this fashion would put them back in the playoff hunt, stimulate their appetite for success, and result in a teamwide rededication to championship-quality football.

Mike White—former Raiders' head coach, longtime friend, and one-time Walsh assistant—admired Walsh's leadership capabilities, especially those exhibited in trying circumstances. "Bill has a great ability to assess the situation," he said during Walsh's tenure in San Francisco. "And one thing people do not give him credit for is that he understands the role of head coach more than anybody." In this particular situation, Walsh determined that his primary responsibility as head coach was to supply the team with an attainable short-term goal—winning a single game—and then let the circumstances of a playoff race and the players' natural competitiveness take over from there.

The plan worked. San Francisco won four straight games to earn another division title and then annihilated the Vikings (34–9) and Bears (28–3) in their two playoff games to advance to the Super Bowl. Montana and Rice were spectacular in the two postseason encounters, connecting for a total of five touchdown passes in the two games.

In Super Bowl XXIII—again facing his old team, the Cincinnati Bengals—Walsh enjoyed perhaps his finest moment as a head coach. With San Francisco trailing 16–13 and about three minutes left in the contest, the 49ers started a drive at their own eight-yard line. The eyes of the world were watching. It was as if God had specifically fabricated the situation to afford the public one final rendition of the precision, execution, and relentlessness that had come to define 49ers' football under Bill Walsh. It was the West Coast offense at its best. Short passes, pinpoint routes, runs after the catch, check-offs to second and third receivers, even a few running plays mixed in just to confuse everybody. The drive incorporated a little Johnny Unitas guile, a little Joe Namath daring, and a lot of Joe Montana cunning and Bill Walsh genius.

On the first two plays, Montana completed passes over the middle to Roger Craig and tight end John Frank to give the 49ers a first down at their own twenty-three-yard line. On the next series, a seven-yard flat pass to Jerry Rice and a one-yard run by Craig created a critical third-and-two at the thirty-one. With Cincinnati expecting a pass, Montana crossed them up and again handed off to Craig, who bulled his way forward for four yards and another first down. San Francisco then called their first time-out.

The scoreboard clock showed 1:54 remaining in the game, and the 49ers had a first down at the thirty-five-yard line. At that point, Montana connected with Rice again, on a seventeen-yard down-and-out pattern in which Bengals' cornerback Eric Thomas was late coming out of his backpedal. The catch moved the 49ers into Bengals' territory, and Cincinnati began to sweat.

On the next play, Montana hit Craig once again, this time for thirteen yards and a first down at the Cincinnati thirty-five. Trouble ensued, however, when an incomplete pass was followed by an illegal-man-downfield penalty. The infraction moved the ball back to the Bengals' forty-five and created a second-and-twenty predicament with about a minute remaining. The 49ers' backs were against the proverbial wall. But as they say, when the going gets tough, the tough get going. Joe Montana faded back, and Jerry Rice ran a beautiful slant over the middle. The ball met Rice thirteen yards downfield, and Rice added another fourteen on his run after the reception. The result was a twenty-seven-yard gain and a first down at the Cincinnati eighteen-yard line. Another pass over the middle to Craig moved San Francisco eight yards closer.

With thirty-nine seconds remaining in the game, and facing a second-and-two at the Bengals' ten-yard line, the 49ers called for a halfback curl pass to Craig. When the offense set up at the line of scrimmage, however, fullback Tom Rathman lined up incorrectly, forcing Craig to do the same. Montana had no time to correct the mistake and ran the play as called. Craig—who was lined up on the wrong side of the field—was double-teamed on his pattern. Montana immediately looked for his second option, wide receiver John Taylor. Taylor had encountered single coverage from nickel-back Ray Horton and was able to work his way free in the back of the end zone. Montana rifled a pass in Taylor's direction. Taylor caught the historic throw with just thirty-four ticks left on the clock. As he did, a euphoric rush overcame Walsh, the city of San Francisco, the millions watching the event on television, and probably the Almighty himself.

In *Game Plans for Success*, Walsh recollects the thrilling moments of Super Bowl XXIII:

> "That final drive against Cincinnati reflected what I love most about football," he said. "The artistic aspect of the game, the orchestration of the players, is beautiful to me. One reason we were successful in that drive was that we went against the so-called book. We did the opposite of what most teams would do in that situation. When most teams are driving late in the game, they throw passes to the outside, where receivers can catch the ball and step out of bounds to stop the clock. The Bengals set their defense accordingly, with most of the coverage on the outside, to take away the sideline pass. We turned that tendency to our advantage, by running our patterns over the middle, where there was more room. Of course, having Montana (twenty-three completions on thirty-six attempts for 357 yards and two touchdowns) and Rice (game MVP with eleven catches for 215 yards—both Super Bowl records—and one touchdown) to carry out the assignments helped immensely. I don't think there has ever been a greater clutch performer at either position."

After San Francisco's victory in Super Bowl XXIII, Bill Walsh retired. In his ten seasons as coach of the 49ers, his teams won three world championships and six NFC Western Division titles. In 1993, he was inducted into the Pro Football Hall of Fame.

Bill Walsh took segments of Paul Brown's unique passing philosophy and turned them into one of the most progressive attacks in the history of the NFL. Walsh's tactics and schemes became the measuring sticks for every other offense of his era and are still predominant today. During his career with San Francisco—from 1979 to 1988—the 49ers' scored 3,714 points in 152 games for a league-leading average of 24.4 per contest. Their passing efficiency was truly something to behold. San Francisco was the only team in the decade of the 1980s to average greater than 60 percent completions (62.6). The two quarterbacks Walsh acquired and trained, Joe Montana and Steve Young, became perennial all-stars. Montana reached the Hall of Fame in 2000, while Young will almost certainly follow in the near future. And though Young emerged as a star under George Seifert (Walsh's successor), that does not diminish Walsh's extensive influence in his early development. Walsh's recommendation was instrumental in the 49ers' decision to acquire Young from Tampa Bay, and Walsh subsequently tutored the talented left-hander during his first two seasons in San Francisco (1986–1987), before Seifert assumed command of the team.

With intelligence, ingenuity, and dedication, Bill Walsh built the 49ers into a dominating, championship-quality football team, something the city of San Francisco had never before witnessed. He revitalized the struggling franchise with his refreshing new style and unrivaled leadership capabilities. "His organizational and administrative skills are what shaped this team," said John McVay, 49ers' vice president. "Walsh drove *himself* as well as everyone else."

Ron Wolf, former general manager of the Green Bay Packers, said of Walsh, "He had a Hall of Fame career. He did such a marvelous job as a coach and now has so many of his disciples still in the league spreading his system, which truly dominates the NFL right now." Wolf, who himself retired after the 2000 season, also credited Walsh for being one of the shrewdest evaluators of talent the NFL has ever seen. "He created a dynasty through his personnel decisions. It is a great credit to him and how he created his team and how he managed it." In acquiring the likes of Joe Montana and Steve Young for the paltry compensation of three (second-, third-, and fourth-round) insignificant draft picks and some cash, Walsh elevated his talent assessment legacy to that of legendary proportion. In retrospect, Montana and Young were probably worth the equivalent of a decade of high first-round picks, maybe more.

After witnessing the 49ers' third Super Bowl triumph, former 49ers' quarterback John Brodie called Walsh the greatest coach he had ever seen. "It takes three things to make a great coach," he said. "First, you have to totally understand the game. Next, you have to be able to organize people. Third, you have to be able to communicate to your people what you've learned and what you've organized. Bill is terrific at all three."

Roger Craig summed up his former coach by saying, "Bill had a great presence, great charisma. He would walk into a locker room and the whole atmosphere would change. He had a glow about him, the glow of a champion."

Perhaps it was Art Spander, writer for ANG Newspapers, who put it best when he said of Walsh's ingenious West Coast offense and detailed approach to coaching, "even more important than a play that sent a receiver short, was a plan that sank a foundation deep."

Walsh's contributions to the 49ers' organization are still being felt in the new millennium. As a consultant immediately after his retirement from coaching, and as the club's general manager from 1999 to 2001, he helped rescue the team from salary cap troubles, as well as playing a major role in their personnel department. Walsh was solely responsible for San Francisco's acquisition of former Canadian Football League quarterback Jeff Garcia in 1999. No one dared take a chance on the diminutive signal caller from, of all places, San Jose State, until he was championed by the quarterback guru of the ages, Bill Walsh. Garcia became a principal factor in the 49ers' resurgence to prominence after double-digit losing seasons in 1999 and 2000. In 2001, Garcia led the 49ers to an NFC Western Division title and was a finalist for MVP honors in the NFL.

When asked how the 49ers were able to sustain their excellence for so long during the 1980s and '90s, Walsh responded, "It's because we were well organized. We had a philosophy and a theme to what we did. We had some of the greatest players of all time, and we developed and prepared them to win." Walsh's exhaustive preparatory routines readied his teams beyond the established protocols of the past, never relying on the oft-accepted fallacy that NFL football games could be won with emotion and hustle. "I believe the emotional factor is overemphasized," he said. "You cannot pin your hopes on something as vague as effort. You win with intelligence, preparation, and talent"—three things with which Bill Walsh's San Francisco teams were always abundantly blessed.

Bill Walsh designed an ingenious method of offensive football based on an innovative passing strategy light years ahead of its time. His system permanently changed the platform of offensive football from a tedious, methodical approach to that of an exciting, aggressive style of play. He will always be remembered as the trailblazer for the contemporary passing schemes of the NFL. And his name will forever be synonymous with winning.

Bill Walsh's Coaching Capsule

Category	Numbers
Seasons	10
Wins	92
Losses	59
Ties	1
Winning pct.	.609
Pct. >/< avg. Super Bowl–winning coach (.601)*	+1.3%
World championships[†]	3
World championship game appearances[†]	3
World championship pct. (champ/seasons)	30.0%
Losing seasons	3
Pct. of losing seasons	30.0%
Playoff record	10–4
Playoff winning percentage	.714
Average wins per 16 games (a current season)	9.7
Average losses per 16 games	6.3

NOTE: Ties count as a half-win and a half-loss in calculating percentages.
* See Epilogue
[†] Super Bowls or NFL championships 1920–1965.

3 Years Before and After Walsh

City	Years	Record	Percentage	Walsh's Career Pct
				.609
Before				
San Francisco	1976–1978	15–29–0	.341	
After				
San Francisco	1989–1991	38–10	.792	

Yearly Records

Year	Team	Wins	Losses	Ties	Playoffs
1979	SF	2	14	0	
1980	SF	6	10	0	
1981	SF	13	3	0	3–0*
1982	SF	3	6	0	
1983	SF	10	6	0	1–1
1984	SF	15	1	0	3–0*
1985	SF	10	6	0	0–1
1986	SF	10	5	1	0–1
1987	SF	13	2	0	0–1
1988	SF	10	6	0	3–0*
Totals		92	59	1	10–4

*Won Super Bowl

Chapter 10

JOE GIBBS

O n January 13, 1981, the Washington Redskins hired a two-time national racquetball champion to be their new head coach. The Redskins would soon benefit from the hiring by winning a few national championships themselves.

Joe Gibbs was born on November 25, 1940, in Mocksville, North Carolina. His father was the county sheriff. Early in his life, Gibbs's mother instilled a deeply spiritual nature into her son's character, and Joe was often lectured by his grandmother on religious matters. Gibbs believed that his faith in God sustained him during adversity and humbled him in times of triumph.

The Gibbs family moved to California while Joe was still a youngster, and he would ultimately attend Santa Fe Springs High School in San Diego, where he excelled in football. In 1959, Gibbs decided to continue his football career while attending Cerritos Junior College. Upon graduating from Cerritos two years later, Gibbs took advantage of an opportunity to compete at the Division I level of college football at San Diego State University. From 1961 to 1962, he played tight end, linebacker, and guard for head coach Don Coryell.

After his college football career ended, Gibbs aspired to become a coach. He enrolled as a graduate student at San Diego State and shortly thereafter offered his services as a nonpaid assistant coach on Coryell's staff—a unit that included future Raiders' head coach John Madden. Gibbs was eventually promoted to a full-time, paid assistant and was placed in charge of the offensive line. During his three-year assignment with San Diego State (1964–1966), Gibbs helped the school earn a 27–4 record and was able to obtain a master's degree in physical education at the same time. In 1967, Gibbs left San Diego State and began a six-year tour that afforded him the opportunity to broaden his football horizons by coaching under Bill Peterson at Florida State, John McKay at Southern California, and Frank Broyles at Arkansas, two years at each institution.

The experience of working with Coryell and McKay would prove beneficial in the ensuing years, as both coaches eventually earned positions in the NFL. Coryell became head coach of the St. Louis Cardinals (1973–1977) and San Diego Chargers (1978–1986), and McKay was named head coach of the Tampa Bay Buccaneers (1976-1984). Gibbs took a position as Coryell's offensive backfield coach with the Cardinals in 1973, then became McKay's offensive coordinator in Tampa in 1978. The next season, Gibbs returned to Coryell's staff—this time with the Chargers—as offensive coordinator.

Under Coryell and Gibbs, San Diego gained notoriety as the most prolific passing team of the era. To give you an idea of the breadth and effectiveness of the Chargers' air attack under the two offensive gurus, consider that, in the years 1979 and 1980, the San Diego Chargers accounted for 4.8 percent of the aggregate passing yardage gained by the *entire* NFL (table 10-1). The average NFL team would have managed 3.57 percent of the total passing yardage league-wide each year, meaning that the Chargers were more than 34 percent superior to the average team during that time frame. The Cleveland Browns, who finished second to San Diego in passing yardage in 1980, were more than six hundred yards behind the league-leading Chargers (4,132) that year. Directed by Gibbs and Coryell and fueled by the rifle arm of quarterback Dan Fouts and the enormous talents of tight end Kellen Winslow, San Diego averaged almost twenty-six points per game while accumulating twenty-three wins and two playoff appearances during that two-year span.

Contrast those achievements with the fact that the 1981 Washington Redskins ushered in the Joe Gibbs era by being outscored 149–77 (an average of 29.8–15.4 per game) and suffering five straight defeats. Gibbs must have believed that he was having a bad dream. With the Redskins' defense permitting almost thirty points per game and his offense struggling as well, it was as if a little voice had to remind him, "Hey, you're not supposed to be *playing* the San Diego Chargers' offense each week, you're supposed to *be* that offense."

Gibbs had always desired to be a head coach in the NFL, but somehow—even in his worst nightmare—I don't believe he could have envisioned his first five games being such a disaster. "I began to think I'd be the only coach ever fired before winning a game," he later joked.

My first reaction to the circumstances surrounding the team from the nation's capital in 1981 was one of both pity and empathy. The previous year (1980), under head coach Jack Pardee, Washington finished with a 6–10 record and was one of the worst offensive teams in the league. In addition, due mainly to the methods of George

Table 10-1. San Diego Chargers' Percentage of Aggregate NFL Passing Yardage, 1979–80

Year	Passing Yardage	NFL Aggregate	Percentage of Aggregate
1979	4138	89170	4.64%
1980	4741	95935	4.94%
Totals	8879	185105	4.80%

Allen (head coach, 1971–1977)—and, to an extent, Bobby Beathard (GM, 1978–1988)—the Redskins were an older team, bereft of young talent, and lacking premium draft picks for the next two seasons. Every organization goes through a reorganization from time to time, and I had a strong suspicion that Washington Redskins' fans were in for a long, arduous decade in the 1980s. What a prognosticator I was—not!

Washington's media had ballyhooed the unveiling of a "genius" offensive specialist—a coaching marvel—as the club's new leader in 1981. Gibbs, they were told, could instantly revive the organization and invigorate the aging team with a plethora of strategic manifestations that would dazzle and bewilder their opponents.

But the Redskins' future, genius or not, seemed very much in doubt that Sunday, October 4, 1981. Washington had just been thrashed at home by the San Francisco 49ers, 30–17. They had yielded almost twice as many points as they had scored in the first five games of the Gibbs regime, and serious questions began to emerge as to the leadership capabilities of their new head coach. Perhaps Gibbs was just another one of those overrated coordinators who had no real clue as to the techniques necessary to fully cultivate the virtues of a professional football team. Or perhaps the enormous stress and numerous responsibilities associated with the head coaching position—as compared to the ancillary duties of an assistant coach—were too great for him to manage. In any event, many Redskins' fans had already begun to campaign for Gibbs's resignation.

But Joe Gibbs was no quitter. He was an intelligent, detail-oriented individual who strove to overcome adversity through hard work and systematic analysis. And though the early dilemma of the Washington Redskins would test both his perseverance and problem-solving capabilities to their fullest, Gibbs was bound and determined to correct the glitches in Washington's game plan and reverse the losing trend of the organization—even if it took hundreds of hours of tedious effort. "It's easy to be motivated on game day with sixty thousand people in the stands," he said. "But it's harder to push yourself through the bad times, or the third hour of practice, or take a film home with you at night. That takes a little extra. Yet the extra effort may decide who wins on Sundays."

True to his nature, Gibbs went back to work reviewing game films and considering changes in order to rectify the Redskins' problems. "We learned a lot about ourselves as a team in that five-game losing streak," he later said. "It opened my eyes as to some personnel changes that had to be made. Also, while looking for a way to improve our offense, we hit upon the one-back set. That became our bread-and-butter formation."

The one-back set allowed the Redskins to add an extra tight end or receiver to their offensive scheme, causing instantaneous matchup problems for conventional defenses. Blocking at the point of attack suffered somewhat without a lead back to make the hole bigger, but numerous advantages easily outweighed that drawback. In addition to situations where a linebacker wound up covering a wide receiver, Washington also benefited from superior pass blocking and a balanced front line. Utilization of a second tight end permitted the team the luxury of keeping one of the those ends in to pass block, as opposed to the inferior blocking of a running back. Furthermore, it created a balanced offensive line (the same number of players on each side of the center) and forced the Redskins' opponents to spread out their personnel in an attempt to equally defend both sides of the field—as opposed to the normal strategy of concentrating their manpower on the offense's "strong" side.

"Offensively, I want to dictate to the defense," Gibbs said. "I don't want to slow down offensively and adjust to what the defense is doing. I want an offense that is fast-paced, that is aggressive, that makes the defense keep up with us." And the one-back set—which would become a staple of NFL offenses in the future—afforded Washington an excellent opportunity to confound defenses with numerous matchup and formation problems. The Redskins averaged twenty-five points per game in their last eleven contests of 1981, as compared to the fifteen points they averaged during their first five encounters that season. The "genius" offensive mind of Joe Gibbs had finally begun to pay dividends.

When Gibbs accepted the Redskins' head coaching position, he knew his strengths and his weaknesses. More importantly, he was willing to admit his limitations. Offense, naturally, was his bailiwick. There were likely few creatures on earth who knew more about NFL offenses than Joe Gibbs. Defensive strategy, however, was a completely different animal.

"I'll lean heavily on my defensive staff," Gibbs conceded at the time of his hiring. "As an offensive coach, I know what to expect from defenses. So I'll have input into the defense. But it will be very important for me to have somebody I can lean on—heavily—somebody who has proven that he can do the job as a defensive coordinator."

Gibbs always insisted that he was only as good as the people with whom he surrounded himself, both players and coaches. "I truly believe that picking the right people is the single most important thing a coach can do," he said. "If you pick sharp, highly motivated people, you're going to be successful. Because the best game plan in the world is worthless if the coaches aren't capable of teaching it or the players aren't capable of absorbing it." And if Gibbs was going to delegate authority and put his trust and the bulk of his defensive game planning and strategies into the hands of another coach, you can rest assured that his choice would be one of the "right" people.

Ultimately, Richie Petitbon, a member of the Redskins' coaching staff under Jack Pardee, was selected by Gibbs to lead the Washington defense. Petitbon had several years of experience with NFL defensive schemes, though none as a coordinator. Nevertheless, he turned out to be the "right people," and the Redskins' defense eventually prospered. Gibbs ostensibly gave Petitbon complete autonomy to do as he pleased. "I would sit in on Tuesday meetings and that was about it," Gibbs said. This allowed Petitbon the opportunity to shape the defense to his expert specifications and gave Gibbs more time to concentrate on turning the Redskins into an offensive juggernaut.

Both sides of the ball played exceptionally well in week six of the 1981 season as Washington beat the lowly Chicago Bears 24–7 for Gibbs's initial visit to the NFL's winner's circle. And though the Redskins were defeated by a tough Dolphins team the next Sunday, 13–10, the atmosphere seemed to be changing. Gibbs appeared to have righted the ship and implemented the new schemes and methodical practice habits that he believed would guide the organization to success.

Gibbs always believed practice to be of prime importance, especially since he had designed a very complex offensive system that was predicated on the flawless execution of specific plays from a multitude of different alignments. "We'll run the same play from maybe thirty different formations," he said. "Because I believe that repetition is the key to success, and because I am convinced that defense is based on recognition of formations." And to take full advantage of their coach's complicated network of schemes, the Redskins needed to continually rehearse Gibbs's choreography.

The Redskins evidently practiced well in the latter stages of the 1981 season, winning seven of their final nine contests to secure a .500 (8–8) record. A newly found confidence, even bordering on bravado, took over the entire organization. The players actually began to believe that if they listened to their coach—and prepared properly for every contest—they could win football games consistently. One player in particular who chose to believe in Gibbs and his comprehensive philosophies was a 6' 0", 192-pound quarterback from Notre Dame named Joseph Robert Theismann.

Theismann had endured a tenuous career in the NFL since being acquired by Washington in 1974 as a refugee from the Canadian Football League. Through his first seven seasons in the league, Theismann had thrown for sixty-seven touchdowns while suffering sixty-nine interceptions. He had been the Redskins' starting quarterback since 1978. During that period, his statistics were as shown in table 10-2.

In 1981, Theismann's first year under Gibbs, the former Notre Dame star produced numbers similar to those of his previous seasons in Washington (table 10-3).

Theismann turned thirty-two years old just as the 1981 season began. He had been in the league for eight years. And even though he had sacrificed a portion of his NFL career while playing in Canada, he was still well past the point in his career when significant improvement could logically be expected. But Theismann enjoyed one luxury that most quarterbacks did not—he had a gifted coach who aspired to be a champion and who demanded the same of his athletes. He possessed the services, intellect, cunning, and innovation of the NFL's offensive guru of the 1980s—Joe Gibbs.

Table 10-2. Joe Theismann's 1978–80 Passing Performance

Year	Att	Comp	Comp%	Yards	YPA	TD	INT	Rating
1978	390	187	47.9	2593	6.65	13	18	61.6
1979	395	233	59.0	2797	7.08	20	13	83.9
1980	454	262	57.7	2962	6.52	17	16	75.2

Table 10-3. Joe Theismann's 1981 Passing Performance

Year	Att	Comp	Comp%	Yards	YPA	TD	INT	Rating
1981	496	293	59.1	3568	7.19	19	20	77.3

Most coaches and general managers will tell you that it often takes a full season for a new coach to successfully implement a complex offensive system. Deciphering the nomenclature, schemes, and nuances of such a program can be quite an undertaking. And since much of an NFL offensive game plan is predicated on precision timing, instantaneous recognition, and systematic progressions, there is usually some early turbulence on the flight path to victory—an unavoidable learning curve. So when Joe Gibbs took command of the Redskins in 1981, it was no surprise to many experts that his system was not an immediate success and that some players—his quarterback, in particular—would need a year to adjust to the new schemes.

In 1982, with a mediocre first season under his belt and the subtleties of Gibbs's sophisticated system firmly entrenched in his mind, Joe Theismann began to realize his ultimate potential. For the next three years—not coincidentally, the second, third, and fourth seasons of the Joe Gibbs era—and from the ages of thirty-three to thirty-five, Theismann would achieve the finest statistics of his professional life (table 10-4), as complete and eventful a turnaround as anyone could have imagined.

Gibbs took advantage of Theismann's strengths—his mobility and short-passing skills. He utilized Theismann on numerous rollout plays and exploited his incomparable ability to execute a medium-range aerial attack—tactics that Washington's previous coaches had failed to perfect.

Orchestrating a Gibbs system tailored to his capabilities essentially saved Theismann's career. From 1982 to 1984, instead of a relatively equal distribution of touchdowns and interceptions, Theismann threw for sixty-six touchdowns as opposed to only thirty-three interceptions—a remarkable reversal. He twice skyrocketed into the eight-plus category in the all-important statistical measurement of yards per attempt. And, as opposed to the pedestrian passer-ratings he had achieved in the past, Theismann finished well into the nineties twice under Gibbs's tutelage. "Theismann was a fiery guy," Gibbs said. "He was adept at moving around, rolling out, and throwing the ball. He was also smart, tough, and had a will to win like few other quarterbacks in the league. He executed our system perfectly." Theismann's dramatic improvement in 1982 was the impetus for Washington's ascent to the top of the NFL hierarchy.

The 1982 season began with a great degree of optimism. The Redskins' offensive had used the 1981 season to perfect the elaborate system initiated by Gibbs, and the club was buoyed by their miraculous turnaround at the end of that year. Consequently, when the team won their first two games over Philadelphia and Tampa Bay in 1982—both on the road—Washington began to think playoffs.

Table 10-4. Joe Theismann's 1982–84 Passing Performance

Year	Att	Comp	Comp%	Yards	YPA	TD	INT	Rating
1982	252	161	63.9	2033	8.07	13	9	91.3
1983	459	276	60.1	3714	8.09	29	11	97.0
1984	477	283	59.3	3391	7.11	24	13	86.6

Unfortunately, the Redskins and many other teams also began to think "strike." Seven games would be lost to the turmoil that ensued in the worst labor dispute in NFL history. The entire momentum of the season was disrupted. When the players' union and management finally reached a settlement, the league mandated a truncated season that would encompass a nine-game schedule, followed by a special, reformed playoff system.

The entire league was in a chaotic state during the first couple of weeks after the settlement was announced. Coaches who had struggled with their preconceived notions of what it took to earn a conventional playoff berth were now completely baffled as to the procedures that might lead to supremacy during this abridged campaign.

As the teams returned from their "vacations," numerous players reported back to work out of shape and unfocused. Coaches frantically searched for the most advantageous methods of restoring players to their prestrike fitness without wearing them out or risking injury in the process. The extreme circumstances that unfolded as a result of the labor dispute in 1982 would test each coach's ability to modify his tactics and strategies in an effort to overcome the outside influences that had altered the landscape.

Interestingly enough—in a season as convoluted and unsettled as any the league had ever witnessed—the coaches who finished in the first two positions in the standings for each conference (the NFL treated each conference as one large division that season) were Tom Flores (Los Angeles Raiders), Don Shula (Miami Dolphins), Joe Gibbs (Redskins), and Tom Landry (Dallas Cowboys). Together, these coaches would amass career records that included 799 wins, a .633 winning percentage, nine Super Bowl victories, and eight other Super Bowl appearances. And each of them won at least two Super Bowls of his own—another example of great coaches winning regardless of the talent or conditions that surround them.

Gibbs eventually led the Redskins to an 8–1 finish in 1982, earning Washington its first postseason appearance since 1976. Their first playoff game would match them against the Detroit Lions at home in the friendly confines of RFK Stadium. The game was a complete mismatch, as the Redskins surged to a 24–0 lead before halftime. When it was over, Joe Theismann had thrown three touchdown passes to wide receiver Alvin Garrett—each over twenty yards—and the Redskins easily dispatched the Lions 31–7.

Next up would be another home game against the Minnesota Vikings. Once again, the contest was decided quickly, as Washington scored on their first two possessions to take a commanding 14–0 lead after one quarter. In a game dominated by Washington's offensive line, future Hall of Fame running back John Riggins carried the ball thirty-seven times for 185 yards and a touchdown, and Washington cruised to a 21-7 victory.

The win over the Vikings meant that the Redskins would participate in the NFC championship game against their hated rivals, the Dallas Cowboys. The Cowboys had beaten the Redskins in Washington during the regular season, 24–10. This contest would also be played at RFK Stadium. The outcome, however, would be much different.

The game started out with Dallas gaining a 3–0 advantage on a Rafael Septien twenty-seven-yard field goal. But Washington's ensuing drive culminated in a Joe Theismann–to–Charlie Brown touchdown pass of nineteen yards to give the Redskins a 7–3 advantage. In the second quarter, Washington recovered a fumble at the Dallas eleven. Shortly thereafter, John Riggins powered in behind the Redskins' robust offensive line for a one-yard score (one of his two rushing touchdowns in the game) to increase the Redskins' margin to 14-3.

Heading into the Dallas game, Gibbs had made a subtle yet instrumental change in the Redskins' blocking schemes. Washington had lost to Dallas earlier in the year due, in part, to the inferior play of the Redskins' offensive line. And though the Cowboys possessed a ferocious defensive unit—led by future Hall of Fame defensive tackle Randy White—Gibbs believed the techniques he had used had more to do with the problem than did the Dallas personnel. "We decided to use more man-to-man blocking today," he said after the NFC championship contest. "We were zone blocking against them in the first game, and we seemed a bit sluggish." This time, the Redskins took it right to the Cowboys and challenged the Dallas defense directly.

Joe Gibbs always preferred a power brand of football. Throughout the years, two trademarks of his Redskins' teams were strong, stout offensive linemen, and big, physical running backs. Utilizing Joe Jacoby, Russ Grimm, George Starke, Mark May, and others throughout the Gibbs era, Washington consistently overpowered opponents with straight-ahead, in-your-face blocking tactics from their offensive line. A large, often overlooked ingredient to the success that Gibbs enjoyed in this fashion was directly attributable to his strength and conditioning coach, Dan Riley.

During his tenure with the Redskins, Riley was considered the best in the NFL. Every year the Redskins' linemen spent numerous hours in the weight room. Every year the Redskins' linemen got bigger. Every year the Redskins' linemen got stronger. And every year the Redskins' linemen dominated the scrimmage area with brute force, which—when followed up with powerful backs like John Riggins, Gerald Riggs, or George Rogers—made defenders cringe in fear.

The combination of the Redskins' physical offensive line in conjunction with Gibbs's decision to forgo the finesse of a zone blocking scheme against Dallas in the 1982 NFC championship paid off handsomely. John Riggins accumulated 140 yards on thirty-six carries and was the primary factor in the Redskins' 31–17 victory. Washington had earned the right to represent the NFC in Super Bowl XVII against the Miami Dolphins in Pasadena, California.

The Dolphins, under head coach Don Shula, had finished the strike-shortened season with a 7–2 slate. The strength of their squad was the defense. Since Miami was forced to depend on two unproven quarterbacks that year—youngster David Woodley and career backup Don Strock—Shula relied on his defense to carry the team to victory. And the Dolphins' defensive unit responded with a marvelous effort, permitting just 131 points on the season, second in the league to the Redskins' 128.

Though the strength of the Redskins' offense in 1982 had been quarterback Joe Theismann and his short-passing expertise, Gibbs concluded that the key to defeating Miami in the Super Bowl would be to establish John Riggins on the ground. Gibbs realized that the Dolphins' defense matched up well with the Redskins' offense (Miami led the NFL in passing yardage allowed (1281) and interceptions (nineteen). And despite the fact that running back John Riggins had not enjoyed a particularly good season that year, Gibbs believed that Washington could exploit the Dolphins' run defense more easily than they could overcome their pass defense. While Miami dominated teams that attempted to challenge them through the air, their rushing defense finished a lowly twenty-fourth in the league in yardage allowed (1285) and dead last in average per carry (4.4).

Gibbs's major concern was that Shula would concentrate his defensive forces at the line of scrimmage in an attempt to nullify Riggins's effectiveness. This could force the Redskins into a one-dimensional aerial attack and allow Miami to take full advantage of their brilliant pass defense. In order to avoid this potential scenario, Gibbs made some changes to the Redskins' offensive game plan before the Super Bowl.

In an effort to divert as much attention as possible away from Riggins—and in the process confuse the Miami pass defenders—Gibbs implemented a unique and clever strategy predicated on motion. Washington's coaches were huddled in a meeting one night when the topic of motion came up. In addition to assisting the quarterback in ascertaining the defensive coverage (man or zone) and allowing a receiver to build up some momentum before the snap—in hopes of gaining a step on his defender—player motion, or movement, can also ruffle the defense's concentration and confuse them as to their basic responsibilities on a given play. Only one player can be in motion at the snap, but as many as five—or even six if you include the quarterback—can be in motion *before* the snap. Gibbs decided to incorporate a five-player movement scheme in a grandiose attempt to camouflage his intention to feature Riggins as the Redskins' major weapon. He called the package "Explode."

"We put it in at 3:30 in the morning," offensive coordinator Joe Bugel said later. "It was at the end of our coaches' meeting. We were trying to think of something special [for the motion scheme]. All of a sudden Coach Gibbs says, 'How about moving everybody?' And one guy said, 'Now you're talking.' And the Explode package was born—five receivers, all moving in different directions. That morning at ten o'clock we presented it to the team." Ultimately, the Redskins' new scheme would involve the Explode package and several other trick plays designed to disorient the Dolphins and keep them from keying on Riggins.

Miami opened the scoring on their second possession of the game. David Woodley hit wide receiver Jimmy Cefalo on a seventy-six-yard pass to give the Dolphins an early 7–0 advantage. The teams traded field goals, then the Redskins scored on a four-yard

Theismann-to-Garrett pass with just under two minutes left in the second quarter—a touchdown that resulted from the Explode package. Unfortunately, Miami's Fulton Walker returned the ensuing kickoff ninety-eight yards for a touchdown, and Washington trailed at halftime, 17–10.

In the locker room, Gibbs told his team, "This is the way it was meant to be. If you want to be champions, you have to overcome deficits and beat the best the game has to offer. This is your chance for immortality." Evidently, the Redskins aspired for enduring fame, and they achieved their destiny in dramatic fashion.

After three quarters, Washington had inched closer, 17–13. Then, with 10:01 left in the game, facing a fourth and one at the Miami forty-three, Gibbs decided to go for the first down. He called Riggins's number—"Seventy Chip," an inside running play. Riggins—a notoriously tough player to tackle one on one—broke through the line and ran through the tackle attempt of Miami defensive back Don McNeal en route to a forty-three-yard score that keyed the Redskins' rally. Quarterback Joe Theismann then sealed the victory by tossing a six-yard touchdown pass to Charlie Brown in the game's last two minutes. Washington defeated Miami 27–17, earning the Redskins a Super Bowl trophy and the city its first NFL title since 1942.

After the game, Gibbs expounded on the change in his offensive philosophy. "It's the first time we did that all year," he said. "The idea of the reverses, the flea flickers, the Explode, was to keep them loose, to keep them from getting after John [Riggins]. We wanted a situation where John could get decent yardage on first down so we wouldn't have to throw when they were expecting it. In the second half we accomplished that. Give the offensive line credit for a lot of that." All told, Washington piled up four hundred yards of total offense against a Miami squad that had permitted just 285 yards per game all season.

In the span of four weeks, Joe Gibbs had beaten three of the winningest coaches of all time: Bud Grant (Minnesota), Tom Landry (Dallas), and Don Shula. And he had a Super Bowl ring to prove it. Not bad for a second-year coach with all of twenty-five NFL games under his belt.

Part of the reason for Gibbs's early success was that he had already discovered one of the fundamental secrets for survival in the NFL. Although Gibbs was still a relative neophyte as a head coach, he realized that victories were as much a function of the work accomplished during the week of practice as they were the result of the action that occurred on the field every Sunday. And since Gibbs's passion to succeed was only surpassed by his passion for hard work, no one would ever gain an advantage over the Redskins in regard to their preparation for game day.

Gibbs often toiled late in the evening and sometimes well into the night in order to prepare for an opponent. At times, he even slept in his office. "A winning effort begins with preparation," he said. "The game may be played on Sunday, but it's won on the practice field during the week, in the meeting rooms—where the coaches and players prepare the game plan—and in the weight room, where the best players do a few extra repetitions." And as the head coach and team leader, Gibbs felt compelled to practice what he preached. "To win at all, a team has to be obsessive about fundamentals and the little things, and that includes the coach," he said.

The 1982 NFL strike obviously had a huge impact on the season. Some historians would place an asterisk next to the records that year—as well they should. Nine games does not an NFL season make. In fact, the league never played fewer than ten games in any other season in its history. Consequently, experts agreed that the 1983 season would offer a more accurate assessment of the Redskins' abilities. No one would over-look a game versus the Super Bowl winners. Opponents would have sixteen weeks in which to debase the strike-season accomplishments of the "lucky" upstart team. A defiant Joe Gibbs, however, was anxious to prove that Washington was a worthy cham-pion, that 1982 was no fluke, and that he and the Redskins would be quite the adver-sary for years to come.

Conveniently, for Redskins' fans, Joe Gibbs finally started to listen to that little voice that spoke to him during the five-game losing streak that marked his NFL debut in 1981. In 1983, Washington would *become* the San Diego Chargers' offense that Gibbs directed from 1979 to 1980.

The Redskins began their 1983 campaign with an agonizing 31–30 loss to the Dallas Cowboys on the opening Monday night of the year. The defeat was so discon-certing that most observers believed the Redskins' psyche could not absorb another loss. Well, maybe one. Washington proceeded to win fourteen of their next fifteen games, losing only a hard-fought defensive struggle (ha, ha) to the Green Bay Packers on Monday, October 17, by the score of 48–47. At the conclusion of the season, the Redskins appeared to be the most dominant team in the league. They posted a scintil-lating 14–2 record and became the NFL's all-time single-season scoring leader by accu-mulating the stunning total of 541 points—an average of nearly thirty-four per game.

The perplexing aspect of the 1983 season was that the Redskins' offensive statistics were not indicative of a team that finished 14–2 and certainly not representative of a team that set an all-time record for points scored. Though Washington did manage to achieve an incredibly huge 30–9 edge in rushing touchdowns over opponents, the Redskins' league rankings in almost every other major category, while good, were not superlative. In fact, the "greatest offensive team of the millennium" did not finish first in the NFL in *any* of the most important offensive categories other than points scored.

Take a look in table 10-5 at the stats for the 1983 Washington Redskins.

Now take a look in table 10-6 at a comparable team, the 1984 Miami Dolphins. The Dolphins also went 14–2, scored an inordinate number of points (513), and advanced to the Super Bowl. But Miami's statistics reflect those of a vastly superior offensive force. The Dolphins finished first in five of the seven categories examined. In addition, Miami outgained the Redskins by 674 yards. To put that in its proper context, Washington would have needed to play almost two more entire games (given their average of 399 yards per contest) to equal Miami's total. And though Miami enjoyed a

Table 10-5. 1983 Redskins' Offensive Stats

	Washington	League Average	Percentage > League Avg	NFL Rank
Rushing yardage	2625	2076	26.4	3
Average per rush	4.2	4.1	2.4	12
Passing yards	3765	3604	4.5	11
Average per passing attempt	8.13	7.18	13.2	2
Passing completion percentage	60.0	56.9	5.4	5
Total yards gained	6390	5680	12.5	3
Points scored	541	349	55.0	1

Table 10-6. 1984 Dolphins' Offensive Stats

	Miami	League Average	Percentage > League Avg	NFL Rank
Rushing yardage	1918	1982	(3.2)	16
Average per rush	4.0	4.0	—	15
Passing yards	5146	3651	40.9	1
Average per passing attempt	9.00	7.14	26.1	1
Passing completion percentage	64.2	56.4	13.8	1
Total yards gained	7064	5633	25.4	1
Points scored	513	339	51.3	1

rare offensive explosion in 1984—one that in comparison with the Redskins of 1983 should certainly merit competitive recognition—no one would expect to find such a lopsided dominance in favor of the Dolphins upon inspection of this data.

Granted, a team that runs the football, like Washington, is usually not going to dominate statistical yardage wars with pass-happy teams, but this was a record-setting season, and Washington didn't finish first in rushing yardage or average per rushing attempt. To add fuel to the fire, while the 1984 Dolphins threw the ball more than the 1983 Redskins (572–463), five teams in the NFL threw more passes than Miami did in 1984, so it's not like Miami went crazy and passed on every play.

The Redskins' 1983 record of 14–2 was the league's best mark. The next best clubs—the Cowboys, Raiders, and Dolphins—could muster no more than twelve wins apiece. Given that superiority, along with the knowledge that Washington set the all-time record for points scored, one would likely imagine offensive firepower that completely overwhelmed the opposition. As you can see, however, that was not the case. And while every NFL statistician worth his salt will tell you that numbers can be misleading, they will also tell you that they can—in many instances—be quite enlightening.

The 1983 Washington Redskins—a club that set the record for points scored in a season—did not finish first in *any* relevant statistical offensive category that was examined in this research other than points scored. And when compared to a worthy offensive match (1984 Miami) they were vastly inferior. What happened? Were the

Redskins just lucky? Were the Redskins unworthy of their extraordinary achievement? No.

The 1983 Redskins were efficient. Quite efficient. And they had a coach, Joe Gibbs, who got the absolute most out of the talent allotted to him. His schemes, tactics, and strategic manifestations frequently surmounted his club's deficiencies, often generating a teamwide performance that was greater than the sum of its parts.

Many Redskins players (including the aforementioned Joe Theismann) enjoyed noteworthy seasons that year, in which they epitomized the team's efficiency under Gibbs. Wide receiver Art Monk made the most of his modest forty-seven catches by averaging 15.9 yards per grab, almost 18 percent greater than his lifetime mark of 13.5. And his 5:47 (10.6 percent) touchdown-per-catch ratio amounted to a 47 percent increase over his lifetime average of 7.2 percent (68:940). The team's other wideout, Charlie Brown, caught seventy-eight passes and tied his career best mark of eight touchdowns.

John Riggins had a very interesting 1983 campaign. While he gained 1,347 yards rushing—the highest total of his career—he averaged only 3.6 yards per attempt. Of the sixteen top ground gainers that year, Riggins finished fifth in yardage but dead last, by far, in average per carry. Nonetheless, Riggins (with great assistance from his offensive line, the Pigs, I mean, the Hogs) erupted for twenty-four touchdowns, almost double his career best to that point. The next closest league competitor in the rushing touchdown category was future Hall of Famer Eric Dickerson, who finished with a modest (by comparison) eighteen scores.

There were two keys to the Redskins' success in 1983: Joe Gibbs and turnovers—or the lack thereof. Washington's turnover ratio of +43 was phenomenal. The Redskins recovered twenty-seven of their opponents' fumbles and picked off thirty-four passes, while losing but seven fumbles and throwing just eleven interceptions of their own. Turnovers are a major key to winning games in the NFL, and Gibbs knew this better than anyone. By instituting an offensive scheme that emphasized Joe Theismann's assets, by utilizing cutting-edge formations such as the one-back set, and by mixing plays to keep opponents off balance, Gibbs was able to limit the "exposure" of his quarterback and reduce Theismann's interception percentage all the way down to 2.4 percent (see table 10-4, page 220). There were very few instances where the opponent's defense held the upper hand during the season. In most cases, as Gibbs preferred, his offense "dictated" to the defense. And this enabled the Redskins to institute a nearly flawless attack.

To open the 1983 NFL playoffs, the Los Angeles Rams traveled to RFK Stadium to play the Redskins. The Rams had upset the favored Cowboys in the first round of the playoffs a week earlier. Los Angeles capitalized on three Dallas turnovers and defeated the Cowboys 24–17. They would not receive the help of turnovers from Washington. In fact, the only thing they received was a whipping, to the tune of 51–7. The Redskins scored on their first five possessions and led at the half, 38–7. Eric Dickerson was held to just sixteen yards on ten carries, and Richie Petitbon's defense intercepted Rams' quarterback Vince Feragamo three times.

Next, Washington would take on Bill Walsh's San Francisco 49ers. In step with a fabulous regular season and an overpowering demonstration of superiority at the expense of the Rams, the Redskins followed what seemed to be a Super Bowl–winning destiny by taking a commanding 21–0 lead on the 49ers heading into the last quarter of play. However, San Francisco had a budding superstar by the name of Joe Montana at quarterback. Led by Montana's passing, the 49ers staggered the defending Super Bowl champs with three quick touchdowns in the fourth period to tie the game at twenty-one.

But Washington's own "Joe," quarterback Joe Theismann, led the Redskins on a methodical thirteen-play drive that culminated in a Mark Moseley twenty-five-yard field goal with forty seconds remaining on the clock. Washington survived, 24–21, and was headed back to the "big dance."

Tom Flores and the Los Angeles Raiders were the opponent in Super Bowl XVIII. The Raiders finished the season at 12–4 and had easily defeated both Pittsburgh and Seattle in the playoffs to reach the title game. The Super Bowl would actually be the second meeting of the two titans that year. The teams played in the season's fifth week in Washington, engaging in an offensive slugfest with the Redskins prevailing 37–35.

This time, though, it would be different—much different. The Raiders scored in the thirties again, but the Redskins never showed up. Los Angeles destroyed Washington 38–9. Running back Marcus Allen decimated the Redskins' defense for 191 yards on just twenty attempts and was named game MVP. The contest was probably decided as early as the first quarter, when Los Angeles blocked a Redskins' punt and recovered in the end zone for a touchdown.

Although Washington had lost the Super Bowl, they gained much respect around the NFL in 1983. They had proven their worthiness in a sixteen-game season and set records in the process. No longer would the Redskins be characterized as "upstarts " or "lucky." The Redskins finished short of their goal for a second championship, but they had demonstrated their abilities as a formidable football team, and Joe Gibbs was quickly maturing into a coach for the ages.

In 1984, the Redskins finished the season with an 11–5 slate, winning the NFC's Eastern Division by two games over the Giants. Disappointment would follow in the playoffs, however, as the Chicago Bears traveled to RFK and upset the favored Redskins 23–19. Chicago sacked Joe Theismann seven times and held John Riggins to but fifty yards rushing.

The next season, the Redskins suffered a terrible blow. Joe Theismann was injured as the result of a hit delivered by New York Giants' linebacker Lawrence Taylor in a Monday night contest in November. The hit would end Theismann's career, as his leg was broken in several places. Though Washington went on to win the game 23–21, the Redskins never recovered from the devastating play. The team finished with a respectable 10–6 record in 1985 (though, curiously, they were outscored on the year 297–312), but missed the playoffs. In an ironic ending to a forgettable season,

Washington lost out in the wild-card tiebreakers to the 49ers and, of all teams, the Giants.

The Redskins needed a new quarterback for the 1986 season, and Jay Schroeder—the team's third-round choice from 1984—would have to be the man. There was no one else. Schroeder possessed one of the strongest arms in the history of the NFL, which was a characteristic that Gibbs in particular loved in a quarterback. During Gibbs's tenure in Washington he employed the following starting quarterbacks: Joe Theismann, Doug Williams, Jay Schroeder, Mark Rypien, and Stan Humphries. All five had above-average arm strength, with the latter four possessing exceptionally powerful arms.

If a quarterback lacked a strong arm, Gibbs had little interest in his services. It had been his experience that quarterbacks with insufficient arm strength had great difficulty in the NFL. Not that an occasional signal caller couldn't be successful with average velocity, but Gibbs knew it was extremely rare for a quarterback to prosper under those circumstances. With the amazing physical attributes of NFL defensive backs and the enormous amount of time spent on both film study and coverage techniques, professional football was loaded with defensive players who could capitalize on any small advantage, especially that of a quarterback who could not deliver the ball quickly. If a quarterback lacked zip, it permitted defenders more time to react to the ball as it traveled towards the receiver. This fault usually resulted in too many interceptions, so Gibbs preferred to employ quarterbacks who maintained above-average arm strength.

With Schroeder at the helm, the Redskins managed to win twelve games in 1986. They finished second to the Giants in the division and began the playoffs at home, in the wild-card game against the Los Angeles Rams. The Rams outgained the Redskins 324–228, but Washington capitalized on six Los Angeles turnovers and defeated the Rams 19–7. That set up a grudge match with the Chicago Bears, who had upset Washington in the 1984 playoffs.

The Bears were the defending NFL champions, having blasted the New England Patriots in Super Bowl XX, 46–10. In 1986, Chicago finished the year with a 14–2 mark, allowing what was at the time (in a sixteen-game season) an NFL-record low of 187 points.

The Bears led the game 13–7 at the half. But the Redskins' Art Monk hauled in a twenty-three-yard strike from Schroeder to put Washington ahead 14–13 heading into the last quarter. Chicago responded with a long drive that ended when future Hall of Famer Walter Payton fumbled at the Redskins' seventeen-yard line. Washington then drove the length of the field on the vaunted Bears' defense, and George Rogers scored on a one-yard run to increase Washington's advantage. The Redskins ultimately won, 27-13, and headed to the NFC championship game to face their hated rival, the New York Giants.

The game was ugly. The Giants' defense smothered Schroeder and the Redskins with the aid of a gusting thirty-five-mile-an-hour wind. Trailing 17–0 at halftime, Gibbs decided he had to pull out all the stops in an effort to turn the tide. Washington ran the

Table 10-7. Jay Schroeder's 1986 Passing Performance

Year	Att	Comp	Comp%	Yards	YPA	TD	INT	Rating
1986	541	276	51.0	4109	7.60	22	22	72.9

ball just once in the entire second half, as Schroeder threw thirty-four times during those two quarters. Despite fifty Washington passing attempts overall, New York's defense limited the Redskins to only 150 yards through the air and held them to an incredible 0–18 on combined third- and fourth-down conversions. The Giants defeated Washington by the same 17–0 margin that was evident at halftime. New York proceeded to defeat the Denver Broncos in the Super Bowl, 39–20.

Jay Schroeder completed many a long pass in 1986 (table 10-7), but his inability to connect on short, drive-saving plays drove the coaching staff crazy. Washington finished the season twenty-fourth out of twenty-eight teams in completion percentage.

Schroeder, it seemed, couldn't hit an open receiver consistently if his life depended on it. And in Washington, under Gibbs, his NFL life *did* depend on it. Though Schroeder gave it everything he had and did have some moments of glory, Gibbs was not convinced that he would be a long-term asset as the team's starting quarterback. Consequently—though Schroeder would be given every opportunity to progress in the near future—Gibbs had to make contingency plans in the event that Schroeder did not improve sufficiently.

After Joe Theismann's injury-induced retirement at the conclusion of the 1985 season, Washington was forced to scramble in order to replenish its roster with a competent replacement. Schroeder was to be given his shot at the starting job the next season, but the club still needed another quarterback, preferably a veteran, to act as insurance in the event that Schroeder encountered problems in 1986.

Thanks to a rival league going under and the foresight of Joe Gibbs, the Redskins signed a capable signal caller who would be ready, willing, and able to perform if and when Gibbs decided it was time to apply his talents.

Doug Williams was selected by the Tampa Bay Buccaneers in the first round of the 1978 draft. His offensive coordinator at the time was none other than Joe Gibbs. Gibbs loved Williams's athletic ability and arm strength. "He was probably one of the most talented people I've ever seen," Gibbs later admitted. "Even when he was young [in Tampa], he was a natural leader." Williams, however, was never the quarterback that the Buccaneers envisioned him to be, and though Gibbs believed he had promise, the team decided to release him after the 1982 season.

Gibbs thought that Williams received too much of the blame for the Buccaneers' misfortunes in Tampa. And despite the fact that Williams never lived up to his potential, Gibbs had no doubt that he could be a useful NFL signal caller. One particular asset that made Williams especially appealing to Gibbs was his ability to avoid costly turnovers. Though he was always under pass-rush pressure in his early years with Tampa and was always the point man to blame for an ineffective offense, he rarely gave in to the pressures by throwing ill-advised passes that could be intercepted. For these reasons, Gibbs coveted Williams as a backup quarterback, and when he was available during the 1986 season—having been released from his USFL contract after the league folded—Gibbs took the opportunity to sign him. With the additional experience and maturation he had gained since his days in Tampa, and with much less pressure to perform in Washington, Williams could, Gibbs believed, be effective in the Redskins' system.

During the 1987 season, Joe Gibbs faced two major dilemmas: another NFL players' strike, and Washington's inevitable quarterback controversy, the outcomes of which offered further proof of his uncanny ability to modify his strategies to meet the requirements of the situation.

After two weeks of the 1987 season, NFL players went on strike. The league quickly decided to play the scheduled games with "replacement players," who would substitute for the actual players until an agreement was reached. Many franchises, disgusted with the entire labor situation, did not invest the proper time and effort necessary to field an adequate team of replacement athletes to compete during the strike. Others, like the Redskins (with Gibbs and general manager Beathard), realized the far-reaching implications of the impasse and the potential significance of the replacement games. Consequently, they took advantage of the situation by signing some of the best available players before many teams even began to look. As a result, Washington's replacement players went 3–0, a feat that made winning the division much easier when the time came for the regular players to take the field again.

One of those regular players, Jay Schroeder, received his chance to improve as the Redskins' starting quarterback in 1987. But when his completion percentage had dipped to a pitiful 48 percent by November, he was replaced by Doug Williams in the eleventh game of the season. Williams immediately flourished, leading the Redskins to a 4–1 finish in the last five games of another strike-shortened season. In the process, he compiled a passer rating of 94.0 (table 10-8)—the highest of his career, by far.

Williams completed a much higher percentage of passes than Schroeder—as his yards-per-attempt statistic of over eight will attest—and he had an outstanding touchdown-to-interception ratio as well. With Williams, the Redskins became a truer version of a Joe Gibbs team—capable, efficient, and worrisome to defensive coordinators around the league.

Meanwhile, Richie Petitbon, the Redskins' defensive coordinator, was maximizing Washington's talent to stifle opposing offenses. After leading the league in points allowed during the 1982 season, the Redskins—though never a defensive juggernaut—were almost always ranked in the upper third of the NFL in scoring defense from 1983 to 1987. In typical Redskins' fashion, the defensive unit was mainly comprised of

Table 10-8. Doug Williams's 1987 Passing Performance

Year	Att	Comp	Comp%	Yards	YPA	TD	INT	Rating
1987	143	81	56.6	1156	8.08	11	5	94.0

lower-round draft picks who blossomed in Washington's system. Of the primary contributors—Dexter Manley, Charles Mann, Darryl Grant, Dave Butz (originally drafted by the Cardinals), Neil Olkewicz, Monte Coleman, and Darrell Green—only Green (taken last in 1983's first round) had been drafted by the Redskins in the first or second rounds. Manley and Mann, the team's defensive ends, combined to form the most prolific pass-rushing twosome in the NFL during that era. Petitbon's dynamic duo accounted for the staggering total of 110 sacks in five seasons.

Washington won the NFC's Eastern Division with an 11–4 mark in 1987. In the playoffs, under Doug Williams's direction, the team overcame an early 14–0 deficit to defeat the Chicago Bears 21–17. Williams threw a touchdown pass to tight end Clint Didier to tie the game just before the half and give the Redskins momentum for the win.

In the NFC championship game, Washington toppled the Minnesota Vikings 17–10 as Williams completed scoring passes to Gary Clark and Kelvin Bryant. The Redskins were going back to the Super Bowl again in a strike-altered season.

Joe Gibbs has a Darwinian motto. "Adapt or die," he often says. "You have to stay on top of what's going on, or the game is over for you." In 1987, Gibbs adapted well enough to straighten out the Redskins' quarterback problems and to play *another* "strike-interruption card" to the best of his advantage.

Gibbs had become the king of strike seasons, adapting to the conditions of the league mandate and capitalizing on his applied strategies. In return for his intelligent planning and impeccable judgment, he would now have another opportunity to win his second Super Bowl. Once more, though, his adapt-or-die strategy would have a significant impact on the outcome of the game.

After a team meeting during the 1987 season, Redskins' assistant coach Don Breaux approached Gibbs. He had seen the Nebraska Cornhuskers (a college team) run a play that devastated their competition, and he thought it might be worthwhile for the Redskins to consider using it. Basically, the play involved misdirection, only an entire side of the line was used for the subterfuge. The right guard and tackle would pull, as if the play were designed to be a sweep, then the guard and tackle from the opposite side would surge up the middle, followed by the ballcarrier. The running back would show sweep motion on his first step—this, along with the pulling linemen, would get the defensive linemen and linebackers moving outside, to cover the end run. Then the running back would cut underneath, behind the pulling offensive linemen, and follow the left side of the line up the middle. It was a counter play with the entire offensive line involved. Gibbs, who was anxious to improve the Redskins' rushing attack and was always open to creative ideas, decided to give it a try. The effect was quite impressive. Washington's rushing attack progressed from the bottom of the NFC to near the top of the conference almost overnight (table 10-9).

In Super Bowl XXII on January 31, 1988, George Rogers, Washington's starting running back, was hurt. The Redskins were forced to use rookie running back Timmy Smith as their starting halfback against the Denver Broncos. But as long as the Redskins had a back with some speed, it almost didn't matter who they started. Since

Table 10-9. Washington Redskins' Rushing Statistics, 1986–87

	Conference Ranking out of 14 Teams	
	1986	1987
Total yards gained	13	3
Average per attempt	14	2

Washington's offensive line was huge and capable of moving well, and since Denver's defensive line and linebackers were relatively small, Breaux's "counter gap," as it was called, was impossible for the Broncos to stop. Smith gained 204 yards that day, and the Redskins easily won the game, 42–10. The Redskins had now been to the Super Bowl in three of the past six seasons and collected two Lombardi trophies (presented to the NFL champions) in the process. The Washington Redskins were now considered one of the NFL's elite franchises, and they owed it all to their elite head coach.

In 1988, teams eventually caught up with the counter gap, so Gibbs needed a new strategy to overcome adapting NFL defenses. He installed a pass play off the counter gap, initiating the most convincing run-action (play-action) on a passing play that the league had seen in some time. The maneuver froze linebackers and defensive linemen long enough for the Redskins to take advantage of several long passing plays. Gibbs was always one step ahead of the competition.

The 1988 season, however, would represent the only blemish on Joe Gibbs's coaching résumé. Washington finished the season with a disappointing 7–9 mark. The main culprit was that the running game had again lapsed into mediocrity. Timmy Smith was much more a product of the Gibbs system than he was a great back. Smith gained just 477 yards that year and averaged a meager 3.0 yards per carry. His backups, Kelvin Bryant and Jamie Morris, were not full-time backs either. Bryant was better than Smith and Morris, rushing for 498 yards on 108 attempts (4.6). But Bryant was better suited for duty as a third-down back and pass receiver. Subjecting him to the wear and tear of an every-down player would have been counterproductive. As a team, Washington averaged just 3.5 yards per rushing attempt that season—twenty-sixth in the league. They scored only eight rushing touchdowns—a far cry from their 1983 total of thirty— and finished in a tie for twenty-sixth in the twenty-eight-team league in that category.

Quarterback Doug Williams was adequate in 1988. He played in eleven games and helped lead the Redskins to more than forty-three hundred passing yards, good for second in the NFL. He attained a passer rating of 77.4 for the season. A strong-armed youngster named Mark Rypien—drafted in the sixth round in 1986—began to advance his skills as Williams's backup, tossing the impressive total of eighteen touchdown passes in limited action.

In 1989, the Redskins' primary concern was to develop a legitimate rushing attack to take the pressure off their passing game. As a result of John Riggins (1985) and George Rogers (1987) retiring within two years of one another, and Timmy Smith's inability to produce as a starter, Washington was in desperate need of a quality running back. They eventually acquired Gerald Riggs from the Falcons and Earnest Byner from the Browns to share the load. Both were solid—especially Riggs, who gained 834 yards while maintaining a 4.1 average.

Mark Rypien emerged as the team's starting quarterback that year. He passed for more than thirty-seven hundred yards while accounting for twenty-two touchdowns. The Redskins climbed back to a 10–6 record but again missed the playoffs, as the NFC had a rare occurrence where seven teams garnered ten or more victories.

In 1990, Earnest Byner took over as the primary running back and had a terrific season, gaining more than twelve hundred yards and averaging over 4.1 yards per attempt. Due to an injury, Rypien appeared in only ten games, but Washington made the playoffs as a 10–6 wild-card team. They beat division foe Philadelphia in the first round of the postseason, 20–6, but were soundly defeated by the 49ers the following week, 28–10.

After the 1990 season ended, numerous NFL followers—particularly those in the nation's capital—were perplexed. Joe Gibbs and the Redskins had not been to the Super Bowl for three straight years. Although his teams had a very respectable 27–21 record during that period, people had come to expect more from the "Wizard of Washington." In fact, many Redskins fans had come to believe that it was their divine right to play in the Super Bowl every season. And considering that Joe Gibbs was a devoutly religious man, combined with the incredible success his teams had achieved, who could argue with them? In any event, Washington fans would not have to wait much longer for appeasement.

In 1991, everything clicked again. In fact, if one sought to convey the essence of Joe Gibbs's offensive philosophy, the 1991 season would represent a perfect example of his ideal approach. Washington emphasized power running and vertical passing, utilizing a dominant offensive line, sure-handed wide receivers, and a strong-armed quarterback who could stretch the field.

Earnest Byner initiated the power running attack by gaining 1,048 yards behind the Redskins' mammoth offensive line. Washington led the NFL with twenty-one rushing touchdowns and totaled well over two thousand yards on the ground for the season.

In the passing game, Mark Rypien had the big, powerful arm that his coach coveted, and he enjoyed an absolutely superb season under Gibbs's leadership in 1991 (table 10-10).

Gibbs knew that Rypien's strength was throwing the deep ball and that he would likely struggle if forced to implement a conventional attack predicated on short passing. Gibbs's game plan was to aggressively attack down the field. As a result, Washington led the NFL in points scored with 485, while Rypien led the league with fourteen passing plays of twenty-five yards or more. The Washington receivers hauling in

Table 10-10. Mark Rypien's 1991 Passing Performance

Year	Att	Comp	Comp%	Yards	YPA	TD	INT	Rating
1991	421	249	59.1	3564	8.47	28	11	97.9

Joe Gibbs brought three Super Bowl trophies to Washington with three different starting quarterbacks. All three had one thing in common—playing behind the powerful offensive line known as "The Hogs."

those bombs were Art Monk (seventy-one catches), Gary Clark (seventy), and Ricky Sanders (forty-five), as reliable and talented a trio as there was in football.

The catalyst for the Redskins' offensive explosion in 1991 was the impressive play of their offensive line. Washington's burly front wall demonstrated awesome versatility by opening huge holes for the running game while simultaneously excelling in pass blocking. "The Hogs" set an NFL record by permitting the unfathomable number of only nine sacks in 447 passing attempts (one for every 49.7 passes).

Joe Gibbs's philosophy in choosing offensive linemen was similar to that of Paul Brown. Both men preferred to start with physical, dominating power blockers who immediately excelled in the running game, as opposed to beginning with slender, more nimble finesse blockers who were more proficient in pass protection during the initial stages of their careers. Gibbs and Brown preferred to teach the stronger athletes the fundamentals of foot movement in order to excel in pass blocking, rather than beefing up the leaner, more agile pass protectors in an effort to turn them into useful power blockers. The strategy worked about as well as anyone could have expected for Gibbs in his tenure in Washington. And in 1991, Joe Jacoby, Russ Grimm, Mark Schlereth, and Ed Simmons represented prime examples of the benefits of the system.

The Washington Redskins were a team of superlatives in 1991. They recorded the NFL's best winning percentage (.875, 14–2), they scored the most points (485), they more than doubled their opponents in scoring (485–224), they totaled the most rushing touchdowns (twenty-one), they achieved the highest average per pass attempt (8.4), and they possessed the NFL's second-best defense in both points allowed (224) and interceptions (twenty-seven). The team proceeded to ride this wave of domination all the way to and through Super Bowl XXVI.

Washington annihilated every opponent they encountered during their postseason run. They easily swept past Atlanta, 24–7, limiting the Falcons to under twenty-four minutes of possession. Next, they manhandled the Detroit Lions 41–10, the same team they had massacred by a 45–0 score during the regular season.

In the Super Bowl, Washington overwhelmed the Buffalo Bills and their famous "Red Gun" offense 37–24. Gibbs and Richie Petitbon concocted the perfect defensive game plan to neutralize Bills' quarterback Jim Kelly, who had led the AFC in passer rating. They agreed that the best way to stop the future Hall of Fame signal caller was to use a number of different looks and blitzes—to confuse his reads and shorten his pocket time. In addition, they noticed a flaw in Kelly's mechanics that enabled the Redskins' pass rushers to get a jump on Buffalo's offensive linemen. "We noticed that when Kelly put his hands out in the shotgun, he would then dip them and the ball would be snapped," said Redskins' linebacker Andre Collins. "We watched for that dip and went on that movement. It gave us an extra step. He couldn't stop it."

Kelly was completely flustered, completing just twenty-eight of fifty-eight passes for 275 yards and an average per attempt of but 4.74. His two touchdowns were more than overshadowed by the four interceptions he threw. "We wanted an early pass rush to get our hands on him and tell him we were around," said Redskins' safety Brad

Edwards. "We wanted to mix up coverages so he couldn't lock in [on one receiver]. If he is pressured, he doesn't have time to read. That's when you make mistakes."

Washington physically abused the Bills, outgaining them 417–283. And in addition to stopping Kelly, they also engulfed Buffalo running back Thurman Thomas, limiting the AFC's leading rusher to thirteen yards on ten carries. Joe Gibbs had finally won a "real" Super Bowl, one where there was no work stoppage and no replacement players.

Washington finished the 1992 season with a respectable 9–7 record. They entered the postseason and defeated the Vikings in the wild-card game, 24–7, before suffering a season-ending defeat at the hands of the San Francisco 49ers in the divisional playoffs, 20–13. Shortly thereafter, Joe Gibbs retired from coaching. The Washington Redskins franchise would never be the same.

Norv Turner was hired to take over for Gibbs in 1993. Turner was the "hot," precocious assistant from the Dallas Cowboys who most people thought would be the next great head coach. Turner was quite disappointing, however. The Redskins made the playoffs but once in his seven-year reign, earning a 49–59–1 record in the 109 games he coached.

Mark Rypien's career also went south after Gibbs retired. The Super Bowl–winning quarterback was relegated to mop-up duty as early as 1993, and he was released from the Redskins at the conclusion of that season. Like Joe Theismann and Doug Williams before him, Rypien was much more effective under the auspices of Joe Gibbs than he was for any other coach (table 10-11).

Joe Gibbs possessed a unique gift that enabled him to extract the absolute best from every player he coached. Whether it was Mark Rypien, Joe Theismann, or any other player during his tenure, Gibbs would discover an individual's abilities, then find

Table 10-11. Mark Rypien's Passing Performance with Gibbs and After

Team	Year	Att	Comp	Comp %	Yards	YPA	TD	INT	Rating
				With Gibbs					
Wash	1988	208	114	54.8	1730	8.32	18	13	85.2
Wash	1989	476	280	59.8	3768	7.92	22	13	88.1
Wash	1990	304	166	54.6	2070	6.81	16	11	78.4
Wash	1991	421	249	59.1	3564	8.47	28	11	97.9
Wash	1992	479	269	56.2	3282	6.85	13	17	71.7
				After Gibbs					
Wash	1993	319	166	52.07	1514	4.75	4	10	56.3
St. Louis	1994	128	59	46.1	694	5.42	4	3	63.7
Cleve	1995	217	129	59.4	1448	6.67	9	8	77.9
Phila	1996	13	10	76.9	76	5.85	1	0	116.2
	1997	39	19	48.7	270	6.92	0	2	50.2
	1998	Out of NFL							
	1999	Out of NFL							
	2000	Out of NFL							
Ind	2001	9	5	55.6	57	6.30	0	0	74.8

the most advantageous way to exploit the player's talents. In many cases, Gibbs was able to evoke quality performances from supposedly mediocre athletes. Jeff Bostic, Clint Didier, Kurt Gouveia, Darryl Grant, Joe Jacoby, Dexter Manley, Neal Olkewicz, Mark Rypien, Ricky Sanders, Mark Schlereth, and Doug Williams are just a few of the lower-round picks or reclamation projects who were properly energized under Joe Gibbs.

In the introduction to this book and in the summary chapter as well, I discuss a coach's ability to convey his systems and methods—the *manner* in which he operates. The nature of this dynamic between coach and player, relative to the transference of information and execution of techniques, was thought to be a crucial element in the formula that determines the ultimate effectiveness of a head coach. Joe Gibbs believed this interaction to be the decisive factor relative to the eventual success or failure of a head coach. "To be a good coach, you have to be a good teacher," Gibbs said. "You not only have to possess the knowledge, but you must also be able to get it across. You give it to the players visually, on film, written, on the board, and on the field. With the Redskins, we started [on the game plan] with all the players in one room and went over the whole plan. Then we would break into groups with the various coaches taking their units and reviewing their responsibilities.

"After meetings, we went out on the field and reversed the process. We did individual drills first, then unit work. Finally, the whole team worked in unison." Gibbs felt very strongly about following this repetitive system each and every week. He felt it would lessen the chance for a player to misinterpret critical information that could then undermine the team's strategy.

"As a head coach, you must always keep in mind that not everyone learns in the same way," Gibbs said. "What may reach one player may not reach another. So you can't teach just one way and expect everybody to learn at the same rate. It won't happen. Some players can learn by just listening. Others learn a play by seeing it on the blackboard or film. Still others need to get on the field and run through it. We taught our game plan in a three-step process—the players heard it, saw it, and then performed it."

When the time came to motivate his athletes, Gibbs applied a simple yet highly effective two-tiered approach. First, he felt that being honest with his players was of crucial importance. He always informed the team—well in advance—of difficult practice schedules or late-night meetings that would be forthcoming, so that the team was prepared to meet the challenge. The aftermath of Monday night games was particularly rough on players and coaches. The next week's schedule would be one full day shorter, yet the same amount of energy and preparation needed to go into the game plan and practice time. Gibbs would never candy coat the situation. "This week's going to be rough," he would say. But then if the players responded with a gutsy performance, he would lighten up the following week and give the team a breather.

Second, Gibbs believed in the age-old method of positive reinforcement, in a group setting, to promote maximum effort from his athletes. He insisted that when players or even coaches performed exceedingly well, they be identified in front of the team and rewarded, in whatever small way. This public gratification was a vital element in Gibbs's motivational routine. After victories, NFL tradition is to award game balls and ceremoniously acknowledge the personal achievements of team members. With the Redskins, under Gibbs, this practice was taken a step further. Selected individuals would receive mundane prizes such as choice parking privileges or worthless paper trophies created by teammates and coaches.

"Those things were important because players want to be recognized in front of their peers," Gibbs stated. "Many coaches motivate out of fear—the players are afraid of the head coach. Others, like Coryell, did it with intensity. There are a lot of different ways of doing this [motivating players]. Tom Landry didn't get close to his players; he was a technical guy with a lot of creative offensive things—creative defense as well. His approach was more, 'If you do this, we're going to win. Do your job.' You see other guys who were more emotional in dealing with players on a one-to-one basis. There was Bill Parcells playing his little con games, getting them up. He'd tell Lawrence Taylor, 'Hey, those guys are making fun of you.' There are all kinds of games. Chuck Noll was very standoffish: 'Hey, do your job, or I'll fire you.'" Gibbs, though, refused to play mind games and preferred a more sincere approach to motivating his athletes. And his players responded by sincerely directing their attentions toward victory.

Gibbs's attentiveness to victory started every morning at 7:30. Few, if any, coaches were ever as well prepared for a game as Gibbs, who was a notorious workaholic. "If you're going to attack this job," he would say, "there is no shortcut for hours. You have to be there. Hard workers win in the end." Redskins' offensive assistants were also required to work long hours. The coaching brigade would usually meet in a small, windowless room that came to be known as "the Submarine." The men often held strategy sessions in the Submarine until two or three in the morning, with little or no contact with the outside world for hours on end. In fact, the Redskins' "Explode" package for the Super Bowl against Miami was conceived there.

Each and every play, formation, and strategy was discussed and dissected by the staff during these late-night meetings. Decisions on whether to attack an opponent's weakness or to rely on the Redskins' strengths were contemplated. Often, an individual coach would suggest a play or tactic, and every assistant coach in the room would be asked his opinion. Gibbs loved this back-and-forth routine for implementing the perfect scheme. In *Game Plans for Success,* he offered an assessment of this unique interaction between coaches: "If I suggested a play that our line coach Jim Hanifan didn't like, he would say, 'Wait a minute, that won't work,' and explain why. The thought process was that if a play or a formation was approved by the group, it had to be a sound idea."

Washington utilized one of these masterful strategies in an important game against Buddy Ryan and the Philadelphia Eagles. Ryan's trademark was a blitzing defense that sent seven or eight men after the quarterback, forcing opponents into numerous turnovers. Gibbs and his staff decided that Washington's offensive line—a formidable group of pass blockers—was up to the challenge and could afford Mark Rypien the extra time he needed to hit Redskins' receivers who would attempt to get open behind their defenders, deep in the Eagles' secondary. "The key was pass protection," Gibbs said. "If we gave our quarterback time to deliver the ball, we knew our receivers would be open for big plays."

In a 1990 playoff contest, the Redskins beat the Eagles 20–6. Washington's offensive line protected Rypien long enough to allow him to toss two touchdown passes that helped the Redskins win the game. Jeff Rutledge, Washington's backup quarterback from 1990 to 1992, said, "It's amazing the things Joe comes up with. He puts things in, they always work. It seems like he's always calling the right plays at the right time. He's a genius when it comes to offense."

"Genius?" Gibbs would say. "Jack Kent Cooke said there are no geniuses in the game, and I think he's right. This business is getting along with people. That doesn't fall under the category of guys being really bright or scholarly. You just need to be good with people."

Unfortunately, there was a negative aspect to Gibbs's lengthy strategy sessions and the exhaustive effort he and his coaches expended in the Submarine. It was incredibly time-consuming, forcing the entire staff to work seventy to eighty hours per week. Eventually, Gibbs succumbed to the rigors of his own demanding standards. When he left the coaching profession after the 1992 season, Gibbs was only fifty-two years old, completely worn out from his twelve-year ordeal.

Bobby Beathard, the Redskins' GM from 1978 to 1988—the one who hired Gibbs for owner Jack Kent Cooke—admired Gibbs's career as both an associate and an adversary. Ironically, Beathard left Washington to take the general manager's position in Gibbs's former NFL city, San Diego, in 1990. Upon his departure, he and Gibbs seemed to be at odds. But after Gibbs's retirement in 1992, and reflecting on Gibbs's tenure in Washington and contemplating his future endeavors, Beathard said, "I can't imagine him not being successful. He could go into any area and have the same results. He's a driven guy. He has a great way with his players. He knows what players want. He's a guy I call a player's coach. There's a good kind of player's coach and a bad kind. A bad one is loved by his players because he allows them to get away with anything—they don't last long. Joe, on the other hand, is very demanding and very organized. He wouldn't put up with mistakes. At the same time, he has a real sense of when players need a pat on the back as opposed to a swift kick in the butt. Once we started winning [in Washington], the players bought into the system and that pretty much carried through the entire time we were together."

Gibbs's players respected him to such an extent that they probably would have volunteered for a suicide mission if he were leading the charge. "Joe was a shining star," said defensive tackle Eric Williams. "He was honest. He was tough but honest. He was brilliant at what he did. You couldn't ask for more of a coach or a human being." Former Redskins' tight end Don Warren said, "Coach Gibbs is not a good man, he's a great man. He's a player's coach. He's not a dictator who believes there is only one way to do things."

Former Redskins' general manager Charley Casserly (now with the Houston Texans), who succeeded Beathard in 1989, was one of Gibbs's staunchest supporters. "He was an innovative coach, and he never stopped trying to improve on what he was doing," Casserly said. "His work habits were legendary." Habits that included revamping Washington's playbook by about 25 percent each year. "You have to stay on top of what's going on," Gibbs said. "If you don't update and revise your game plans and strategies, you'll likely fall *behind* by 25 percent as opposed to keeping with the pace."

George Allen, Redskins' coach from 1971 to 1977, created a victorious atmosphere in Washington by leading the franchise to seven straight winning seasons. His style was to trade away young players and future draft selections to accumulate veterans who could win immediately. Ultimately, though, he failed to gain a championship. Under head coach Jack Pardee (1978–1980), the Redskins slipped to a .500 record in three seasons and appeared to be on a downward spiral subsequent to a 6–10 finish in 1980. As a result, Gibbs inherited a spiritless team in 1981, a club wallowing in mediocrity, with few good young players and even fewer premium draft picks. He persevered, however, and eventually invigorated the squad with his upbeat style and cutting-edge offensive tactics. Ultimately, he created better football players and a superior team out of far less talent than that of his predecessors. With well-conceived strategies, brilliant schemes, and inspirational techniques fueled by his love for the game, Gibbs was able to instill a pride and confidence in his players that transformed their lackadaisical attitudes. He infused the entire city of Washington with a football passion that had never before been witnessed, not even in the Allen era. And he took the team that extra step that Allen could not, by winning three NFL championships.

The circumstances under which Gibbs was able to secure his titles in Washington notwithstanding, Gibbs's greatest accomplishment may have been that the Redskins collected their three Super Bowl victories under his direction with three different starting quarterbacks.

NFL history is replete with examples of coaches who have won multiple titles with the same quarterback. Vince Lombardi and the Packers won five titles with Bart Starr in the 1960s. Chuck Noll and the Steelers won four Super Bowls with Terry Bradshaw in the 1970s. Paul Brown won three titles in Cleveland with Otto Graham in the 1950s. Bill Walsh won three Super Bowls for the 49ers with Joe Montana in the 1980s. Many other coaches have won two championships with the same signal caller.

Offensive proficiency in the NFL is usually attained as a result of continual practice with the same players while utilizing the same schemes, year after year. To augment this advantage, good coaches will tailor their offensive strategies to fit the strengths of their personnel, especially the team's most important player, the quarterback. Consequently, the entire offensive unit becomes accustomed to certain formations, specific techniques, tendencies of their teammates, and, of course, the quarterback's personal style.

Problems ensue when the starting quarterback changes. The new signal caller may not be familiar with the system or the personnel and will undoubtedly have unique talents and a different style than the previous quarterback—any or all of which could undermine the previously established symmetry of the offense. The team will inevitably begin to lose some of its chemistry, making each transitional process (each subsequent quarterback change) that much more difficult to overcome. Hence, many NFL dynasties last only as long as the star quarterback's career. There have been only two coaches other than Joe Gibbs in the thirty-six-year history of the Super Bowl who have won championships with more than one starting quarterback—Bill Parcells with the Giants in 1986 (Phil Simms) and 1990 (Jeff Hostetler), and George Seifert with the 49ers in 1989 (Joe Montana) and 1994 (Steve Young). And Parcells's achievement is somewhat tainted in that Jeff Hostetler—his starting quarterback in Super Bowl XXV— did not begin the year as the starter. He replaced an injured Phil Simms in the Giants' fourteenth game of the season.

Joe Gibbs was able to win the Super Bowl three times with three different starting quarterbacks (Joe Theismann, Doug Williams, Mark Rypien). He is the only coach in NFL history to achieve such a distinction. And as opposed to the recurring championship scenarios listed above—where highly accomplished, Hall of Fame–caliber quarterbacks directed the offenses—Gibbs realized each of his successes with far less talent at the most important position. Williams and Rypien were considered mediocre quarterbacks at best, and Theismann, though skillful, was far from extraordinary.

Considering both the state of the Redskins' organization upon his arrival in Washington and the quarterback changes he encountered throughout his career, Gibbs's lifetime achievements of three Super Bowl victories in four appearances, the equivalent of five division titles, sixteen postseason wins against only five losses, a .674 lifetime winning percentage, and a Hall of Fame induction—all in a brief twelve-year time period—are simply amazing.

Joe Gibbs was a demanding, authoritative head coach. When circumstances called for him to back up his commanding style with toughness and intimidation— like the time he threw a tray of oranges across the locker room at the 1983 Super Bowl, or when he smashed a projector to pieces in Philadelphia during the 1989 season— Gibbs did not disappoint. And though emotional tirades were a necessary element of his coaching method, he preferred, whenever possible, to treat his players in a more dignified fashion, without resorting to drastic methods of persuasion. This honorable approach—in addition to his superior knowledge of the game—earned Gibbs the total dedication and unwavering admiration of his athletes. Joe Gibbs was indeed a player's coach—the *good* kind.

Gibbs retired from the NFL because he was physically and mentally exhausted from his gridiron escapades, and he wanted to spend more time with his family and friends and indulge in other hedonistic pursuits. Being an extremely religious man with a passion for loyalty and commitment, Gibbs was deeply devoted to God, football, his family, and his players during his career. And though one could argue the particular order he would have ranked those priorities during the pinnacle of his vocational endeavors, it is now clear, some ten years after his retirement, that football, as it should, grew to be the least important of the four.

Gibbs's achievements with the Washington Redskins' organization were genuinely magnificent. Though he was ably supported with the money, guile, and passion of one Jack Kent Cooke, the Redskins' owner during Gibbs's career in Washington, the records and accomplishments of his teams were light years beyond expectations. Gibbs's coaching record ranks with the cream of the crop in NFL history. His teams were always one step ahead of their competition. His players trusted and respected him, and in return for their sustained devotion, they gained a championship legacy that only a coach like Joe Gibbs—one who was totally and comprehensively dedicated to the zenith of football achievement—could afford them.

Joe Gibbs was, perhaps, the finest coach of his time. And he has the championships to prove it.

Joe Gibbs's Coaching Capsule

Category	Numbers
Seasons	12
Wins	124
Losses	60
Ties	0
Winning pct.	.674
Pct. >/< avg. Super Bowl–winning coach (.601)*	+12.1%
World championships[†]	3
World championship game appearances[†]	4
World championship pct. (champ/seasons)	25%
Losing seasons	1
Pct. of losing seasons	8.3%
Playoff record	16–5
Playoff winning percentage	.762
Average wins per 16 games (a current season)	10.8
Average losses per 16 games	5.2

NOTE: Ties count as a half-win and a half-loss in calculating percentages.
*See Epilogue
[†]Super Bowls or NFL championships 1920–1965.

(continued next page)

3 Years Before and After Gibbs

City	Years	Record	Percentage	Gibbs's Career Pct
				.674
	Before			
Washington	1978–1980	24–24	.500	
	After			
Washington	1993–1995	13–35	.271	

Yearly Records

Year	Team	Wins	Losses	Ties	Playoffs
1981	Was	8	8	0	
1982	Was	8	1	0	4–0*
1983	Was	14	2	0	2–1†
1984	Was	11	5	0	0–1
1985	Was	10	6	0	
1986	Was	12	4	0	2–1
1987	Was	11	4	0	3–0*
1988	Was	7	9	0	
1989	Was	10	6	0	
1990	Was	10	6	0	1–1
1991	Was	14	2	0	3–0*
1992	Was	9	7	0	1–1
Totals		124	60	0	16–5

*Won Super Bowl
†NFC champions

Chapter 11

BILL PARCELLS

If you're committed to win, you're going to like it. If you're committed to playing football, you're going to like it. If you're here just to pick up a paycheck, you're not going to like it." That was Duane Charles Parcells's assessment of what it was like to play under his regime.

Duane Parcells was born on August 22, 1941, in Englewood, New Jersey. As a child, Parcells adopted the nickname "Bill" after everyone in the neighborhood began confusing him with another youngster named Bill who looked just like him. Parcells became a three-sport star at River Dell High School, excelling in baseball, basketball, and football. It was at River Dell that Parcells first learned the strategies and philosophies of coaching, and, ironically, it was his *basketball* coach, Mickey Corcoran, who most influenced him. "It was always defense with Mickey," Parcells said. "He said that, by playing defense, you wouldn't win every game, but you'd be in every game with a chance to win." This philosophy would later define Bill Parcells the football coach and would become his first priority with every organization for which he worked.

Bill's father, Charles, was very intelligent as well as athletic. He attended prestigious Georgetown University as an undergrad and starred in both track and football. After graduating from Georgetown's law school, Charles Parcells took a position with the FBI. Later—due in part to the fact that his wife, Ida, was a chronic worrier and was concerned for his safety—the elder Parcells left government work for a position with U.S. Rubber.

From his father, Parcells inherited his athletic prowess and his intelligence— enough intelligence that he was a candidate to enter an Ivy League college. Instead, he chose Colgate University in New York. Parcells would attend Colgate for just one year, however, before transferring to Wichita State in 1961. He earned All-Missouri Valley Conference honors while playing offensive and defensive tackle for the Shockers from 1961 to 1963 and graduated with a degree in physical education.

In 1964, Parcells was selected by the Detroit Lions in the seventh round of the NFL draft. Unfortunately, Bill's professional career was over before it even started, as he was cut by the Lions during training camp in August.

Parcells, though, had no great aspirations to become a professional football player. He had a coach's mind-set from the start, and just three weeks after being released by Detroit, he accepted his first coaching job at a small school called Hastings College in Nebraska.

During the next fifteen years, Parcells honed his coaching skills at the NCAA level. After just one season at Hastings, Parcells took a position as defensive line coach for his alma mater, Wichita State, in 1965. He then teamed up with his old high school football coach, Tom Cahill, as an assistant with Army from 1966 to 1969. That four-year stint was followed by assistant coaching positions at Florida State, Vanderbilt, and Texas Tech. In 1978, Bill received his first head coaching job at the Air Force Academy in Colorado, where he compiled a 3–8 record. Then, in 1979, Parcells got a break. Ray Perkins, new coach of the NFL's New York Giants, unexpectedly called and asked Parcells to become his linebackers' coach. For Bill, the NFL was a dream come true, especially since the team that he would coach would be his hometown franchise.

Unfortunately, Parcells's wife, Judy, and their three daughters, were not enthusiastic about moving again. So Bill left for New York and planned to live in a motel until some time had passed, assuming that Judy and the kids would follow after they had a chance to get their affairs in order. After two months in New York, though, Bill realized that his family had a genuine aversion to relocating back east. So he reluctantly informed Perkins that he needed to resign and head back to Colorado.

Parcells spent several months as a real-estate salesman until Judy *also* realized something: Bill would not be happy in any profession but football. She subsequently implored him to seek another coaching position—hopefully in the NFL—and informed him that she would move wherever they had to go. Parcells immediately called Perkins, who recommended that he speak to Ron Erhardt, the new coach in New England. Shortly thereafter, Bill was named the Patriots' linebackers' coach in 1980. New England was where Bill Parcells's image was permanently changed. It was after one of his players had attempted to "put one over on him" that Parcells blurted out these immortal words: "Who do you think I am, Charlie the Tuna?" From that day on, the nickname stuck and the legend grew. Bill Parcells would forever become known as the "Big Tuna."

After the 1980 season, Ray Perkins—believe it or not—called and asked Bill to become his defensive coordinator with the Giants for the 1981 season. Parcells quickly seized the opportunity to move up the NFL coaching ladder, and he returned to New York as the leader of the Giants' defense. Under Parcells's tutelage, the Giants defense improved from an average of 26.6 points per game allowed in 1980 to 16.1 and 17.8 points per game in 1981 and 1982, respectively. New York finished at 9–7 in 1981 but disappointed with a 4–5 record in the strike-shortened season of 1982. After the frustration of the 1982 season, Ray Perkins resigned to take a position with the University of Alabama, and Parcells was named the thirteenth head coach in the history of the New York Giants.

When Parcells was promoted, he knew the transition from a losing mentality to a winning one would not occur overnight. Though the Giants had managed a winning season just two years before, they were still—by almost any definition—losers. They had reached the playoffs but once since 1963, and 1981 represented their only winning campaign in the last ten years. New York, once a proud organization in the 1950s and early '60s, had become a poor excuse for an NFL franchise. But Bill Parcells was a motivator. He believed that motivation and a desire to be the best played a large part in winning a physical game like football. With the right mix of talent, tactics, and leadership, he was certain that he could motivate the Giants and lead New York to the promised land.

Bill Parcells thought that he knew more about what it took to win football games than almost anybody else on the planet. Therefore, he insisted that both his players and assistant coaches perform their requisite duties using *his* techniques and *his* methods. And if they did not perform to *his* satisfaction, both mentally and physically, they would be cut from the team in a heartbeat. He was convinced that an effective combination of motivational and tactical strategies would revitalize almost any team and launch them on a journey to success. "Coaching is giving your players a good design and getting 'em to play hard," he often said. Right or wrong, the New York Giants would be *his* team. And win or lose, he would have nobody to blame but himself.

Parcells believed in power football and great special-teams play. His basic coaching philosophy was to establish a conservative offensive game plan predicated on running the ball, and to play tough, in-your-face defense that would hopefully stifle and intimidate the opponent, forcing them into mistakes. He theorized that these two factors, along with outstanding special-teams play, would keep his teams in most games and allow them to achieve superiority in the battle for field position, thus producing victory.

Like his childhood mentor Mickey Corcoran, Parcells believed in defense first. "Defense always keeps you in the game," he said. "There are going to be some days when the offense doesn't play that well. If the defense plays well, that gives you a chance." In conjunction with his belief in power football, Parcells demanded size in his defenders. "I want size on my entire defense, not only from my front seven, but from the secondary as well," he said. "The defensive backs have to be physical on receivers, jam them. Sure they'll get their share of catches, but they're going to pay for them." Under Parcells, New York would play a ferocious, punishing, intimidating style of defense, the kind that demoralizes opponents mentally as well as physically. And though the Giants' defense had improved tremendously since Parcells took over in 1981, each year they were faced with the monumental burden of supporting a sputtering offense that could never produce points consistently.

Despite the fact that Parcells's conservative offensive approach tended to lighten the load on their quarterback, the Giants still had huge problems on that side of the ball. They had no running game, had finished near the bottom of the league in almost every major offensive category in both 1981 and 1982, and had experienced very inconsistent play from their signal callers for several years. Scott Brunner, a sixth-round draft pick in 1980, was the starter. Jeff Rutledge, another young, journeyman type, was one of the backups. And a fair-haired youngster by the name of Phil Simms was also in the mix. Simms, New York's first-round pick in 1979, was coming off of an injury that forced him to miss the end of the 1981 season and all of 1982.

New York's offensive ineptitude and the franchise's dismal history of losing combined to make Parcells's initial season as head coach of the Giants a disaster. The team completed the year with a scant three victories in sixteen attempts. Parcells—the brash, bold, confident leader—even began to doubt himself. "My first year was a difficult one," he later recalled. "It created some uncertainty." To make matters worse, in the span of four months, Parcells and the Giants were dealt the following emotional blows:

- October 1983: Giants' backfield coach Bob Ledbetter died from a stroke. Also, Bill's father, Charles, had open-heart surgery.

- November 1983: Bill's mother, Ida, was diagnosed with cancer.

- December 1983: Doug Kotar, a former Giants' player, died from a brain tumor.

- January 1984: Ida passed away.

- February 1984: Charles passed away.

Parcells had experienced team and family tragedies of epic proportions. No one knew how he would deal with the unrelenting adversity. "Looking back now," said George Martin, ex-Giants' defensive end, "I wonder how he stood up to the pressure."

After the season, Parcells knew that if the Giants were to have any legitimate chance to improve to a playoff level, Simms would have to be the quarterback to take them there. Both Brunner and Rutledge were late-round draft picks who lacked the requisite arm strength to really challenge an NFL defense. Each had been in the league for four years and enjoyed little, if any, success. Simms, on the other hand, seemed to have all of the necessary tools to excel in the NFL, as long as he could stay healthy.

Training camp for the 1984 season began with a statement from the second-year head coach that changed the complexion of the entire team. It created a sense of urgency on a club that Parcells believed might be content with a losing mentality—a team that would begin to accept defeat and just look forward to "collecting their paychecks at the end of the week." "Everyone should watch out," Parcells said. "My back is to the wall, and everything will be different. It's no secret this is a crucial year for the Giants. You come off a 3–12–1 year and you know changes have to happen, beginning with me, or else many of us won't be here next year, including me." Linebacker Harry Carson immediately noticed a difference in his coach. "He was now making the hard decisions that resulted in a lot of people being let go," he said.

In 1984, the Giants began to do what any future Parcells's team would ultimately do—win. In week two, after a 28–27 victory over the Eagles in their opener—which saw quarterback Phil Simms throw for 409 yards—New York faced a "litmus test" against the Dallas Cowboys. Dallas was coming off a 12–4 campaign in 1983, losing to the Rams in the playoffs. In their opener that season, Dallas returned the favor to Los Angeles and beat the Rams 20-13 on *Monday Night Football.* The Cowboys had pasted the Giants and Parcells in both of their 1983 meetings (38–20 and 28–13). If the Giants were going to propel themselves forward and take the next step towards respectability, they would have to beat the Cowboys to do it.

Dallas took the pasting this time. The Giants, guided by Simms, blew the Cowboys back to Big "D," taking a 21–0 halftime lead and eventually winning the game 28–7. These two early season victories marked the "coming out" party for New York quarterback Phil Simms. Simms's career to that point had been almost as disappointing as the fans who booed the Giants for drafting him in 1979 could have envisioned. Simms, who turned twenty-five the year he came into the NFL, was now almost thirty years old. He had started the season with fewer than one thousand career passing attempts. Usually, by the time a starting quarterback hits the age of thirty, he has attempted somewhere in the neighborhood of three thousand passes. But injuries had plagued Simms early in his career, and if he did not perform in 1984—injuries or not—chances were that Parcells would have plagued Simms even more and released or traded him.

Simms had proven that he could lead the Giants to victory against a talented opponent and a hated division rival. Now came an even bigger test—the "Parcells" test. Could Simms handle the unyielding pressure of professional football at the paramount level of competition, where every play becomes magnified, and every mistake predominates the critics' minds? Could this amiable signal caller from a small college in Kentucky (Morehead State) continue to improve to the point where he could deliver the crucial pass at the precise moment to the optimal target? Could Phil Simms harness the compulsory abilities that are mandated of a playoff-caliber quarterback—leading the team to victory in dire circumstances—thereby instilling confidence and spirit in both his teammates and his head coach? And last, but certainly not least, could he do it consistently?

Consistency was always of premium concern to Parcells. "Not very many people understand what consistency is all about," Parcells said. "Consistency in sports goes to every area. It doesn't just manifest itself on the field. It's in the preparation, the practice, the classroom. You must be consistent in your preparation, your conditioning, your strategy, your motivation. If you're not consistent on the field, it's because you're not consistent in those areas."

Phil Simms became the poster boy of consistency for Parcells. And though they often engaged in heated sideline arguments, both Simms and Parcells had a genuine respect and admiration for each other. To this day Simms claims that they never really "argued" as much as they "discussed" matters on the sidelines. "He's very down to earth, and he can communicate with players so well," Simms said of Parcells. "No question, that is what separates him from a lot of the coaches in the league."

Simms finished the 1984 campaign with 4,044 passing yards—an average of more than 250 yards per contest. And considering that he did this for "Mr. Conservative," Bill Parcells, it was quite the accomplishment. Also remarkable was the fact that he averaged 7.59 yards per pass attempt that season (7.1 being the NFL average that year). This figure that would belie his somewhat suspect 53.7-percent completion rate and would seem to contradict what Parcells now says was always, at least to some degree, an exaggeration—his supposedly conservative offensive game planning.

In actuality, the game plan *was* rather conservative. But when Parcells did decide to throw the ball, there were seldom if ever restrictions on the length of Simms's attempts. Simms's high yards-per-attempt figure relative to his low completion percentage seems to prove the fact that the Giants did indeed throw the ball downfield when the opportunity presented itself.

Parcells was always content to play a running style of offense, but now, even *he* had become a believer in Simms's ability to make prudent decisions and to win football games. Not that Parcells would ever allow Simms to consistently throw thirty-five or forty times per game, mind you, but he *would* allow Simms the flexibility to throw in situations where he would have denied that same option to a less-talented quarterback.

The 1984 Giants finished at 9–7, though they were outscored 299–301. They made the playoffs for only the second time since 1963. Parcells and the gang even won a playoff game that season, beating the Rams in Los Angeles, 16–13. They eventually fell victim to three Joe Montana touchdown passes and succumbed to the eventual Super Bowl champion 49ers in the divisional playoffs, 21–10. It was not, however, a bitter defeat for the Giants. They had not been expected to go as far as they did that season, and the benefit of playoff experience, as well as the confidence that they could play on equal terms with almost any team in the NFL, would serve them well in the coming years.

In 1985, the Giants victory total hit double digits (10–6). They tied Dallas for the division championship, but two heartbreaking losses to the Cowboys resulted in their having to settle for a second straight wild-card playoff berth. Unfortunately, the luck of the draw presented the San Francisco 49ers, again, as the Giants' opponent. The Super Bowl champs from 1984 had slipped to 10–6 in 1985, but they were still a formidable foe.

The 49ers ripped the Giants' defense for more than 360 yards that day, but unlike the previous year, they could not seem to finish their drives with touchdowns or even points in most cases. And, unlike 1984, Simms would be the quarterback to throw the touchdown passes (two), and Montana would struggle. In the end, the Giants were victorious, 17–3, rewarding their hometown fans with their first home playoff victory since 1956. New York lost to the Chicago Bears the next week, 21–0, but they had proven with their victory over the 49ers that they could defeat the "big boys," and in 1986 they would strive for the Super Bowl.

Parcells, Simms, and the Giants were rolling. They were still a few pieces away from the truly talented and dominant team that they would need in order to reach

Table 11-1. New York Giants, 1986 Draft

Round	Player	Position	College
1	Eric Dorsey	Defensive end	Notre Dame
2	Mark Collins	Cornerback	Cal State Fullerton
2	Eric Howard	Defensive tackle	Washington State
2	Pepper Johnson	Linebacker	Ohio State

their goal, but they were inching closer to that point. In the 1986 draft, New York loaded up on some of that talent. Armed with several extra draft picks, the club selected four players who would play key roles in the upcoming years (table 11-1).

Parcells was very particular with draft selections. He always interviewed potential picks and would ask them a series of questions to determine their commitment to football. Often, the answer made the difference as to whether or not the Giants would select the individual. "One of the things I ask them is what the three most important things are in their life," Parcells said. "If football isn't one of them, I worry. If a guy says 'getting my degree, job opportunities, and my car,' we may have a problem." Needless to say, each of the four players listed above answered appropriately.

In 1986, the Giants played like, well, *giants*. The offense managed 371 points to finish eighth in the league, despite twenty-two interceptions thrown by Simms. The defense, led by Lawrence Taylor's linebacker record of 20.5 sacks, allowed just 236 points. New York's record swelled to 14–2. They won their first division title ever and received a first-round bye in the playoffs. The Giants then proceeded to devour the San Francisco 49ers 49–3 at the Meadowlands. Simms threw four touchdown passes, and the Giants' defense—led by Taylor—held the 49ers to just twenty-nine rushing yards. "Shattered, we were simply shattered," said 49ers' coach Bill Walsh. "They played a perfect game. They destroyed our offense, shattered our blocking angles. We were dealt with."

The Washington Redskins were the next victims. New York surged to a 17–0 advantage at halftime (which was to be the final score) and cruised home on the strength of the defense the rest of the game. Washington had scored 368 points that season, good enough for ninth in the NFL. On this day, the Giants defense—which finished second in the league in points allowed—held the Redskins' attack to a zero-for-fourteen performance on third-down conversions and zero-for-four on fourth-down attempts. "Our defense didn't play a perfect game, except in that department," Parcells said, in an attempt to downplay the incredible accomplishment of his defensive stalwarts, for fear of overconfidence. "When you hold a team to zero for eighteen, it's not perfect, it's a miracle." The Giants and their physical, miraculous defense were the talk of the NFL, and they were on their way to the Super Bowl.

In their first championship game since 1963, New York would meet John Elway and the Denver Broncos in Pasadena, California. Going into the game, Parcells was concerned more about Elway's scrambling than he was his passing ability. Elway was finishing just his fourth year in the NFL, and though he had enjoyed some success—contrary to popular belief—he did not strike tremendous fear into the opposition because of his passing prowess. Hell, he had never even managed an 80 passer rating at that point in his career. What he did have was the capacity to make winning plays out of bad situations, mostly with his running ability. Elway averaged close to five yards per carry that season, and the Giants' strategy was to keep him in the pocket and force him to beat New York through the air.

At the end of the first half, Denver led the game 10–9. Unfortunately for New York, Elway had been quite effective in both the running *and* passing departments. He had thrown for 187 yards and scored the Broncos' touchdown with a four-yard scamper. Part of the Giants' problem in defending Elway was probably the coaching staff's fault. The coaches were upset due to the lack of pressure they had generated on the Broncos' quarterback. In creating the urgency to keep him in the pocket, the Giants' coaches had made their pass rushers a bit tentative in their pursuit of Elway.

Parcells was upset with the team's effort, but he was far from the raving lunatic that one might have expected during his halftime speech to the troops. He pointed out that the pass rush deficiency and the club's overall lack of focus—causing needless penalties and an absence of concentration—were the chief culprits contributing to the deficit. He and defensive coordinator Bill Belichick made a few key adjustments to the team's pass rush schemes, and Parcells simply told the team, "You're lucky you're in the game. Now go ahead and take advantage of it—win this damn thing." After the intermission, there was no lack of focus, no lack of concentration, and no lack of pass-rush pressure. The only thing lacking in the second half was the Broncos' offense and defense.

Early in the third quarter, the Giants seized a 16–10 lead on the second of what would ultimately be three Phil Simms touchdown passes—a thirteen-yard toss to tight end Mark Bavaro. During the regular season, New York had beaten the Broncos 19–16. In that contest, Denver's secondary played basically man-to-man all game long, daring the Giants to beat them through the air, especially deep. "They hadn't shown us any respect [with their pass coverages] in the first game," said Phil Simms. "We talked all week about how people were always running down [criticizing] our wide receivers. We wanted to show them they were wrong."

With New York leading 19–10 late in the third quarter, the Giants further capitalized on their game plan to exploit the Denver secondary. New York was at the Broncos' forty-five-yard line when Simms handed off to halfback Joe Morris. Morris waited a split second, faked a running play, and then lateraled back to Simms. Simms then lofted a perfect strike to wide receiver Phil McConkey, who was finally wrestled down at the one-yard line. A Morris run secured the touchdown, and the Giants had blown the game wide open on a flea-flicker—against a disrespecting Denver defense. "We run those flea-flickers in practice, and we've never run the damn things in games," Simms said after the contest. "When I hit McConkey, I thought, 'That's it, we've won it.'" At that point, New York forced the Broncos to change their defensive strategy and commit more help to the secondary, which assisted the Giants in chewing up the clock with a methodical ground game. "In the second half, Denver started to play some two-deep zone, which is contrary to everything they believe in on defense," Simms said. "I said to myself, 'They finally respect us.'"

The Giants thoroughly dominated the second half of the game en route to a 39–20 victory over the outmanned Broncos. Phil Simms was named Super Bowl MVP, culminating a scintillating performance that produced a statistical line of twenty-two completions in twenty-five attempts for 268 yards and three touchdowns. He was so accurate that day that he completed ten straight pass attempts (a Super Bowl record) at one point. After the victory Simms would say, "I felt so good warming up that I was telling the guys, 'I've got it today.'"

Surprisingly, Mr. Conventional—Bill Parcells—had opened up his offense and even resorted to a trick play to cement his first Super Bowl victory. What was the world coming to? Parcells trusted Simms and believed in his ability. And when the Giants noticed that the Broncos would be susceptible to the passing game, Parcells didn't hesitate to alter his game plan and smash-mouth style just enough to take advantage of the mismatch. That's what great coaches do.

Simms and Lawrence Taylor both won MVP honors after the 1986 season, and Parcells garnered some Coach of the Year awards as well. But the really amazing feat, in retrospect, was the fact that *statistically* the Giants were not as superior to their opponents as their record would seem to indicate. They outscored their opposition in the regular season 371–236 (23.2–14.8 per game, or +57 percent); outrushed them 2255–1284 (+76 percent); outgained them rushing, on average, 4.0–3.7 (+8 percent); outpassed them, on average per attempt, 7.4–6.6 (+12 percent); were surpassed in both passing yards 3500–3887 (–10 percent); and completion percentage figures 55.1–56.9 (–3 percent); and collected a plus-eleven in turnover margin—all of which amounted to rather pedestrian statistics, especially when matched against those of teams with similar records.

For comparative purposes, one need look no further than the Chicago Bears and San Francisco 49ers of that same season, 1986. In addition, we can look at the 1984 San Francisco 49ers, who also finished with a similar record (fifteen wins) and won the Super Bowl (table 11-2). If you compute all of the above percentages for each of the four teams and total them, the numbers are quite lopsidedly in favor of the 49ers and Bears.

This is not to say that these particular numbers constitute the end all and be all of relevant football statistics. However, no expert could deny that these figures do seem quite disproportionate in consideration of the similar achievements of the teams in question.

But, as Parcells liked to say, they don't play the games on paper.

To me, it seems a glowing tribute to Parcells and his coaching staff that the 1986 New York Giants were able to perform at such a premium level despite rather ordinary statistics. The team was able to make the most of their talent and won with smart, conservative football—just the way Parcells liked it. They were able to defeat opponents

Table 11-2. 1986 New York Giants' Team Statistics As Compared to Three Other Dominant Teams of the Era

	New York Giants (1986)	San Francisco 49ers (1984)
Record	14–2	15–1
Scoring	+57%	+109%
Rushing yards	+76%	+37%
Rushing average	+8%	+10%
Passing yards	−10%	+9%
Passing avg/att	+12%	+19%
Completion pct.	−3%	+14%
Turnovers > < +10*	+10%	+60%
Total	+150%	+258%

	San Francisco 49ers (1986)	Chicago Bears (1986)
Record	10–5–1	14–2
Scoring	+51%	+88%
Rushing yards	+28%	+85%
Rushing average	+3%	+32%
Passing yards	+14 %	−8%
Passing avg/att	+18%	+15%
Completion pct.	+13%	+6%
Turnovers > < +10*	+100%	even
Total	+227%	+218%

*Turnover figures based on percentage above or below the +10 figure, considered to be an average figure on superior teams.

who were very likely more talented than they, and that accomplishment is always attributable to outstanding coaching. In addition, the decisiveness with which they dismantled their opponents in the playoffs further demonstrated the Giants' dominance. New York outscored their playoff adversaries by the staggering margin of 105–23, the largest such amount for any Super Bowl winner ever.

In 1987 a strike interrupted the NFL season. Replacement players performed in three contests, and a full week's worth of games were canceled. The Giants finished that year at 6–9, last in the NFC East.

The 1988 season would promise the return of labor peace, the "real" New York Giants, and the real Bill Parcells (the "replacement" Parcells did not fair too well, and it should be noted that he hated tuna fish. Please excuse me, I jest). New York enjoyed a fine season, finishing at 10–6, but in a rare occurrence, they lost out in the league's tiebreaking procedures and failed to earn a playoff berth.

The next season, New York rode the wave of a thrilling victory over the Washington Redskins on the opening Monday night game of the year (27–24) and ultimately checked in with a 12–4 mark and their second division title. The 1989 season would eventually become a bitter remembrance for the Giants, however, as they failed to defeat the Rams in the divisional playoffs, losing 19–13 at home in overtime. The Rams were able to tie the game late in the fourth quarter on a field goal by Mike Lansford. And just 1:06 into the overtime period, Jim Everett delivered a thirty-yard touchdown strike to Willie (Flipper) Anderson to deal the Giants a somewhat humiliating home playoff defeat.

In 1987 and 1988, Phil Simms had brought his game up to the next level. Exuding the confidence of a battle-tested, Super Bowl–winning quarterback, Simms escalated his game to the point where he was considered to be one of the best in the NFL. But for some reason, 1989 was a disappointing campaign for the "Blonde Bomber." His statistics reflected this downslide as he fell short of an 80 passer rating (the mark that usually differentiates the good from the not-so-good quarterbacks), and he threw the same number of interceptions as he did touchdowns, fourteen. In the prior two seasons (1987 and 1988), Simms had thrown for aggregate totals of thirty-eight touchdowns and only twenty interceptions.

The Giants, and most importantly, Bill Parcells, expected more—in fact, they *demanded* more. Guess what?

They got it.

In 1990, Simms was in the midst of an absolutely scintillating season, one in which he had completed over 59 percent of his passes and thrown for fifteen touchdowns while suffering only four interceptions. His quarterback rating of 92.7 led the NFC. The Giants were cruising along with a record of 11–3 and were primed for another run at glory. Then it happened. Simms fell victim to a severely sprained arch, an injury that would force him to miss the rest of the season and the postseason. Parcells and the Giants were forced to turn to their backup quarterback, Jeff Hostetler.

Hostetler had been drafted by the Giants in 1984. Heading into 1990 (his fifth year on the active roster) he had thrown just sixty-eight passes. Now he would be asked to guide the New York Giants into the playoffs against some of the best defenses in the NFL. First, though, he had to finish the regular season.

Parcells's first thought was that he needed to revamp his playbook, to become even more conservative (if that was possible), and to make use of Hostetler's strengths as opposed to those of Simms. Rodney Hampton and Ottis Anderson—the Giants' running backs—would be asked to shoulder even more of the load than they had during the Simms edition of the Giants' offense. Trouble was, Hampton was just a rookie, and Anderson was on the wrong side of thirty.

As the Giants prepared for the Phoenix Cardinals (week fifteen of their season), Parcells's main concern was that Hostetler might feel a subconscious need to justify his status as a worthy NFL quarterback, thereby risking costly turnovers and potentially undermining the Giants' conservative offensive strategy. On the other hand, Parcells also contemplated the possibility that his young signal caller might feel greatly inhibited—thus becoming ineffective—if he were put under the microscope and confronted on every mistake he might make. So before the start of the contest, Parcells went over to Hostetler and said, "Just play the game. Don't worry about making mistakes. Just go out and play within the structure of the offense, and we'll [the coaches] help you out as much as we can. Just don't worry about it."

The Giants ultimately defeated both the Cardinals and the New England Patriots to finish the year at 13–3. Hostetler performed more than adequately in the final two contests, compiling an aggregate total of twenty-five completions in forty-six attempts for 313 yards with two touchdowns and no interceptions. But the Cardinals and Patriots had combined for only six wins that year. In the postseason, Hostetler, the twenty-nine-year-old former West Virginia University star, would have to prove his mettle against premium defensive units.

In the Giants' first playoff game, against the Bears, Parcells decided to stray somewhat from his customary 3–4 defensive alignment in favor a 4–3 setup. The game plan was designed to negate Chicago's chief weapon, running back Neal Anderson, and to force their quarterback, Mike Tomczak, to throw the ball more than usual. The Bears had finished second in the league in rushing yardage, averaging a healthy 4.4 yards per carry. Conversely, they were an ineffective passing club, finishing with just 2,827 yards in the air, next to last in the NFL. And it was known league wide that if you pressured Tomczak (who was subbing for injured starter Jim Harbaugh), he would become prone to interceptions—much more so than the average quarterback.

New York slaughtered the Bears that day, 31–3. The game was almost never in doubt, and Hostetler would have to throw only seventeen passes to seal the Giants' victory. Parcells's defensive ploy worked to perfection. Anderson was held to just nineteen yards on twelve carries, and Tomczak was completely ineffective.

The second game of the playoffs would almost certainly be a different story. The defending Super Bowl champion 49ers were the opponent. And though the Giants possessed the most feared defense in the NFL, the 49ers possessed one of the most feared quarterbacks in Joe Montana. Production would surely be needed from Hostetler and the New York offense if the Giants wanted to advance to the Super Bowl in 1990.

As fate would have it, Montana suffered an injury midway through the fourth period. And though he was ineffective against the vaunted Giants' defense, the 49ers still led the game, 13–12. Both teams were now at the mercy of their inexperienced, second-string quarterbacks, and San Francisco had the ball with less than three minutes remaining. Luck, however, was on New York's side. Forty-niners' running back Roger Craig fumbled after a handoff from quarterback Steve Young, and the Giants' Erik Howard recovered.

With Hostetler at the helm—in a frantic two-minute mode of offense—the Giants drove thirty-three yards in six plays to set up a game-winning forty-two-yard field goal as time ran out. Parcells, Hostetler, and the New York Giants were on their way back to the Super Bowl.

Jeff Hostetler finished the game by completing fifteen of twenty-seven passes for 176 yards, but the Giants offense could muster only five field goals on the day. Parcells's "extra" conservative offense—one put in especially for Hostetler—had survived another game, but Parcells knew that they had been fortunate to beat the 49ers. He also knew that he would need to give Hostetler more latitude and take a few more chances in order to create points and win the Super Bowl.

As the Giants prepared for their second Super Bowl adventure, Parcells encountered a problem that caught him totally off guard. Superstitious by nature, Parcells tried to follow the same routines that had previously resulted in victory whenever he had the opportunity. Unfortunately, the airline pilot who chartered the squad to Super Bowl XXI had retired from active service, and New York would be forced to accept another pilot for their trip to Tampa in 1991. Or would they? Believe it or not, Parcells contacted the pilot, convinced him to get recertified, and had *him* fly the team to the Super Bowl.

The Buffalo Bills would be the Giants' opponents in Super Bowl XXV. The Bills, led by head coach Marv Levy, were famous for their "Red Gun," no-huddle offense, a powerhouse unit that led the NFL in scoring with 428 points. They featured the AFC's leading passer in Jim Kelly, the AFC's leading rusher in Thurman Thomas, and the AFC's fourth-leading receiver in Andre Reed. Parcells and defensive coordinator Bill Belichick designed a defensive strategy that would include basic sets of nickel (five defensive backs) and dime (six defensive backs) packages on almost every down—a tactic usually reserved for second- and third-and-long situations only. In addition—to confuse Kelly with different coverages at the risk of a lesser pass rush—the Giants would often drop eight men into the secondary.

Buffalo was favored in the contest, and Parcells decided to use that fact to motivate his club. "On paper, Buffalo is the far superior team," he told his squad. "If you go by a paper, there are a lot of teams superior to us. You know what. That's paper! You still have to play the game. Who's in the Big Dance? You are. So that tells you that the paper means nothing. Forget about the paper, forget about the statistics. You can make the difference. You can make things change."

Parcells's game plan was relatively simple—on "paper," that is: use a ball control offense, but let the reins loose on Hostetler just enough to confuse the Buffalo defense and keep them off balance. In addition, give Jumbo Elliott, the Giants' left tackle, all the help he needed to contain Bruce Smith, the Bills' superb pass-rushing defensive end. This strategy would keep the Bills' offensive weapons off the field as long as possible and take away their primary advantage. In regard to his tactics, Parcells was quoted just before the game: "I don't think we could win a shootout with Buffalo. I really don't. I don't think our team has proven that it can win any kind of a shootout game this year. But I think it has proved that it can win a lot of methodical games. If we play our style and keep them from playing theirs, we'll have a better chance of beating them."

The game plan worked beautifully. The superbly choreographed offensive scheme dictated the game to Buffalo, allowed Hostetler the flexibility he needed to produce points, and kept the Bills' vaunted Red Gun offense off the field. New York occupied the clock with long drives punctuated by Ottis Anderson runs and a precision passing attack initiated by Hostetler, who finished with twenty completions in thirty-two attempts for

222 yards and one touchdown. And the Giants' incredibly stingy defense—led by Lawrence Taylor and "Pepper" Johnson—permitted the Bills a scant eight minutes of offense in the entire second half, and under twenty minutes the entire game. To the Bills' credit, they played as well as a team could despite the statistical dominance of the Giants. New York was forced to withstand a last-second field goal attempt by Scott Norwood that sailed wide of the goal posts, as they held on to beat Buffalo 20–19. As Parcells indicated, the Giants would probably *not* have won a shootout game, even if they had a healthy Simms, let alone the inexperienced Hostetler. As it was, they dominated the game and *still* needed the missed field goal at the end to clinch the victory. But Parcells did what he had to do. He put his team in position to win and let the chips fall where they may.

Looking back on that Super Bowl and the late-season fate bestowed upon his club by Simms's injury, Parcells offers this recollection of the event and his subsequent strategy. "It was simply a case of an opportunity presenting itself," he said of Hostetler's performance. "Fortunately [by the time the Super Bowl game was played], we had a month or so to experiment [fine-tune the offense]. We were just trying to pick and choose, and let him execute some things in the game. And then talking to him about it and finding out what he felt comfortable with."

New York and Parcells had persevered through adversity and won the Super Bowl for the second time in five years.

Obviously, strength of schedule, blowout games, and many other objective and subjective variables can figure into the ultimate equation to accurately compare teams and their abilities. But this time New York's stats *did* seem to substantiate the excellence they ultimately displayed. The 1990 Giants even seemed superior to the 1986 team, something Parcells had constantly reminded them they were *not*—for motivational purposes. Furthermore, the overall numbers of the 1990 club seem quite competitive with those of each of the dominant teams documented earlier in this chapter, though their superiority was due more to their fabulous turnover margin as opposed to gaudy yardage totals. New York managed just a plus-eleven turnover figure in 1986, while the 1990 team almost doubled that with a plus-twenty—Phil Simms's magnificent achievement of just five interceptions in 311 attempts, the offense's ability to limit their fumbles to nine, and the relentless pass pressure exerted by the defense being the primary factors.

In some instances, a great turnover ratio is attributable to luck and not truly indicative of a team that forced turnovers defensively and/or protected the ball well on offense. The 1990 Giants, however, were not one of the "lucky" teams. They *earned* their turnover dominance by forcing their opponents into mishaps—with ferocious hitting and a fierce pass rush—and limiting their own exposure on fumbles and interceptions by way of sound fundamentals and intelligent play. Luck has little to do with a proficient offensive player carrying the ball properly and limiting fumbles. Luck also has little to do with the better quarterbacks consistently finding a way to get rid of the

Table 11-3. 1990 New York Giants' Team Statistics As Compared to 1990 Buffalo Bills

	New York Giants	Buffalo Bills
Record	13–3	13–3
Scoring	+59%	+63%
Rushing yards	+40%	+15%
Rushing average	even	+16%
Passing yards	−1%	+9%
Passing avg/att	+24%	+16%
Completion pct.	+4%	+11%
Turnovers > < +10*	+100%	+40%
Total	+226%	+170%

*Turnover figures based on percentage above or below the +10 figure, considered to be an average figure on superior teams.

ball well before the rush results in a sack or a pickoff. Those are skills and are due more to mental discipline, precise techniques, and talent. The 1990 Giants *created* their turnover dominance, and luck had little to do with it (table 11-3).

At the beginning of this chapter, I stated that Bill Parcells liked to employ a conservative offense with great defense and superb special teams. And it seems that is exactly how and why the Giants won Super Bowls. His program allowed New York to vanquish adversaries with efficient, workmanlike precision applied to each and every phase of the football team. As the stats have shown, while the Giants were quite obviously a talent-laden, athletic group of football players, they did not win games by overwhelming their opposition with massive firepower, extravagant passing exploits, and/or hazardous play calling. In fact, though New York retained the services of one of the premier quarterbacks in the NFL, they finished *both* Super Bowl seasons with *less* passing yardage than their opponents. "They call us predictable and conservative," Parcells often said, "but I know one thing, and I've coached this game for a long time: power wins football games. It's not always the fanciest way, but it can win games."

Bill Parcells had accomplished his ultimate goal—twice. He had resurrected the New York Giants' franchise from being an NFL "doormat" and turned them into the league's most powerful team. Parcells was considered one of the top coaches in the game. But the rigors of eight grueling NFL campaigns had taken its toll on his body and mind, so he made the decision to retire from the game he loved. Not by choice, but because his health and well-being demanded it. He desperately needed a break and some time to sort out his physical issues.

In 1991, Parcells contemplated a career as an analyst for one of the league's television networks. He followed through with his plan, and for two years added superb insight and colorful anecdotes to NBC's production of NFL football. In the early months of 1992—in the middle of his two-year stint with NBC—Parcells had heart bypass surgery, a procedure that made a huge difference in his physical well-being. Soon after the operation—and feeling chipper as a chipmunk—Parcells got the itch to

Bill Parcells took the New York Giants from perennial doormats to Super Bowl champions and would go on to make the New England Patriots and New York Jets contenders.

return to the sidelines. The itch had actually started as early as December of 1991, when Tampa Bay showed great interest in his services. But at that time it was too soon, and, more importantly, just *before* the all-important surgery.

By late 1992, many months after his operation and feeling ten years younger, Parcells knew that it was time to scratch the itch. The desire to return to the trenches and immerse himself in the minutiae that would be necessary to dominate the football world again completely took over his psyche.

Parcells had left the NFL on top of the world. His New York Giants had just beaten the Buffalo Bills to capture their second Super Bowl trophy in five years. Now, on January 21, 1993, he took command of a franchise that was in dire need of his unparalleled football savvy, the New England Patriots.

When Parcells took over the Giants in 1983, they were a second-rate football team. The Patriots, on the other hand, were completely inept. From 1991 to 1993, the organization had mustered a grand total of nine victories against thirty-nine losses. Their winning percentage was an abysmal .188. Rod Rust and Dick McPherson (the two coaches during that period) had molded the Patriots into a sad collection of feeble footballers that required an overhaul of incomprehensible proportions. "It was the most down-and-out, despondent, negative atmosphere you could ever imagine," Parcells said.

When asked how long it might take to build the Patriots back into a winning organization, Parcells retorted, "No one passed a rule saying you can't win in '93 if you were 2–14 in '92. If there is a rule like that, I'm certainly not aware of it."

The Parcells-coached Patriots of 1993 had, at one time or another during the season, the staggering total of thirty-six players on their roster who had not been with the team the year before. This represented a personnel turnover rate of an unprecedented 61 percent. For comparative purposes, it should be noted that in 1991 the Patriots finished with a 6–10 record, and for the 1992 season Coach McPherson decided to bring aboard nineteen new players on the fifty-three-man roster, representing a turnover rate of just 35.8 percent.

As is the case with many a great coach, Parcells sought out the best players he could scrounge up to help him rejuvenate an organization in total disarray. And it didn't matter if he had to scuttle the whole Patriots' team in the process. Within seven weeks of being named head coach, Parcells had substantially reorganized New England's depth chart. He traded former number-one draft choice and nine-year veteran wide receiver Irving Fryar to the Miami Dolphins for two draft picks. He then parted with another first-round pick, John Stephens, by trading him to the Packers for another upcoming draft selection. Then he put last year's starting quarterback, Hugh Millen, on the trading block as well.

Hart Lee Dykes was also a first-round draft choice of the Patriots, in 1989. He had played only one full season, his rookie campaign, as injuries prevented his participation in the latter part of 1990 and all of 1991 and 1992. Dykes's usual routine was to rehabilitate his injured knee at his home in Bay City, Texas. One week prior to the beginning of Parcells's initial off-season workouts with the Patriots in 1993, Dykes informed his new coach of his *own* itinerary for off-season "conditioning." As Dykes turned to walk out the door of the coach's office, Parcells offered some advice. "Before you go home, make sure you stop by and clean out your locker," he said. "If you're going home to work out, you may as well take everything with you to save a trip. You go home, you're not on this team anymore, so I wouldn't want you flying back here just to get your stuff."

Dykes was shocked. He had never encountered a coach who reacted in such a forceful and dictatorial fashion as Parcells. Dykes didn't know what he was going to do. But the very next week he showed up in the training room to begin *Parcells's* version of rehab work. Parcells regretted the fact that this story became public and admitted his own blunder in allowing that to occur. However, it was a clear warning sign to any and all New England Patriots that there was a new sheriff in town.

Parcells made an example of Dykes, and though he indicated that he made a mistake in allowing the story to leak to the media, he made it very clear that any deviation from his strict regimen would not be tolerated. "It's been my experience that those who don't want to make that kind of commitment to an off-season program are the players you wind up having problems with somewhere down the line," he said. "Frankly, I don't know what the players' attitude is on off-season workouts here [in New England]. If it's not too good, then we'll just have to get some players whose attitude is that they want to participate. I don't know anything about what transpired here in the past, but whatever it was, all those things were contributing factors to a result that was not very good."

It all harkened back to Parcells's desire for and commitment to consistency. He required it in every aspect of the game. You had to practice consistently, play consistently, and even rehab consistently. Indeed, as coach of the team, Parcells believed that even *he* had to be consistent, at least with most aspects of his leadership routine. "The only thing you don't have to be consistent in is your discipline," he said of his coaching methods. "I know that sounds crazy, but what's important with discipline is to be right. I don't want to be consistent there, I want to be right." And Parcells *was* right in regard to the Dykes situation. Human beings are hedonistic by nature. We all would rather soak up sun on a white sandy beach as the waves rush in and out rather than pump iron and run wind sprints. And when secluded and left to your own will and volition, it is inevitable for most people to seek the easy way out. Parcells did not know what Dykes actually did in past off-season programs, and he really didn't care. What he did care about, and what he would never permit, was nonparticipation in *his* conditioning agenda. Players either accepted the terms of Parcells's training philosophies, or they quickly hit the road before the coach slammed the door behind them. As former Giants' defensive lineman George Martin said, "He [Parcells] is a great communicator. He leaves very little room for misunderstanding. He's the finest motivator I had in all my years in the league. He knows what he is doing."

Most people believe that Parcells instilled fear in his players and motivated them by physical intimidation and/or the fear of being cut for any conduct deemed detrimental to the team. And though this is the Parcells that I witnessed as well, at least one of his former players seems to disagree with that assessment. "He's not a big fear guy," said Bryan Cox, who played for Parcells with the Jets. "He's a realist. If he gives you a couple of warnings about your play, you're gonna be on the waiver wire. Players respect that. He's hard, but he's fair, that's how I would sum it up. But when he's mad, stay away from him. If he don't talk to you, don't talk to him." Sounds to me like the fear factor played more of a role than Bryan likes to admit.

Parcells was a very calculating coach. He always did things for a reason, including some rather unconventional ways of challenging his players and their practice habits. In addition to the Dykes incident, Parcells actually instigated another conflict—this time in 1996—by referring to the status of the injury rehab of Patriots' first-round draft pick Terry Glenn by saying, "*She's* coming along fine." Parcells was infuriated with the amount of missed practice time that Glenn had accumulated in training camp. And his assessment of the situation—as reflected in his statement to the media regarding Glenn's recovery—was that Terry needed a resounding wake-up call in order to get him back in camp as soon as possible.

Nothing Parcells ever says or does is inadvertent. Every statement or action has a distinct purpose. He finds a person's hot buttons and engages them in order to bring out their intensity and emotion. "See, whatever I give as a coach, I took as a player," Parcells justifies. "It happened to me, and if it happened to me and I turned out all right, then my players can take it, too. The only players I hurt with my words are the ones who have an inflated opinion of their ability. I can't worry about that. I'll call somebody 'dumb' or 'stupid' if they make a dumb or stupid play. I don't know any other word for it, and if they don't like the word, that's too bad." "Coach Parcells plays all kinds of mind games," said Patriots' safety Willie Clay when Parcells was in New England, "but they are all with the purpose of making you a better player and making the team a better team."

Damn straight they are.

But while Parcells was a stickler for discipline and demanded consistent effort in practice and conditioning routines, it is important to note that he was never inflexible to the point of absolute intolerance for any deviation in his basic format. If you were a veteran who had proven your value and sacrificed your body on numerous occasions, Parcells might overlook a few minor glitches in your preparatory routine. Parcells's goal on the football field was victory, and if he knew you were a winner, there was always some latitude in his regimen for your services. "[Brad] Van Pelt [former Giants' linebacker] was never the most dedicated practice player of all time, but he never came up a quart short on Sunday that I knew about," Parcells once said.

The Patriots did not instantaneously transform themselves into winners in 1993 (Parcells's first season), but they did manage to accumulate five times as many victories as they had the year before. And it should be pointed out that they achieved this modicum of success with a rookie quarterback, Drew Bledsoe, who could muster but a 65.0 passer rating in 429 attempts.

In 1994—with the inexperienced Bledsoe still at the helm—Parcells's organizational prowess and assertive style began to pay dividends. The combination of his hand-selected talent blended symbiotically with the energetic atmosphere created by his mere presence. Though Drew Bledsoe was anything but stellar—throwing a league high 691 passes, twenty-five of which went for touchdowns, and twenty-seven of which went to guys in the other uniforms—the Patriots finished the season at 10–6 before losing an intense playoff game to the Cleveland Browns, 20–13.

Great expectations abounded as the Patriots prepared for the 1995 campaign. Bledsoe would be in his third year (traditionally a season marked by vast improvement for quarterbacks), Parcells's imprint was now firmly implanted on the team, and a newfound confidence resulted from the unexpected turnaround in 1994.

Unfortunately, the best-laid plans of mice and men often go awry. Bledsoe struggled mightily in 1995. The Patriots finished twenty-eighth out of thirty teams in average gain per pass play, twenty-sixth in average gain per offensive play, and twenty-first in third-down efficiency. The defense was even worse, finishing twenty-eighth in the league and giving up 377 points—by far the most points a Parcells-coached team had ever allowed. It was true that Bledsoe played hurt in many of that season's contests (he suffered a third-degree separation of his nonthrowing shoulder in week three at San Francisco), but still, no one—not the least of whom Parcells—expected such an ineffective performance.

Parcells cited several reasons for Bledsoe's regression that season. "He's had more snaps than a lot of guys that have been in the league quite a while," Parcells said at the time, referring to his youthful quarterback being thrown to the wolves right from the start of his career. "Basically, he had some mechanical problems, he had some read problems, and he had some accuracy problems. We need to work on all of those things. I'm not saying they were all major problems, but we do need to work on those things." The most glaring deficiency was Bledsoe's inability to consistently read the defense, often resulting in the wrong pass being thrown, and/or forcing the ball into coverage. "I don't know why it is, but I think there are times when Drew doesn't see everything the way he's supposed to," said Parcells. In addition, Bledsoe had developed a bad habit of throwing off his back foot, which manifested itself in poor accuracy—an abysmal 50.8 completion percentage in 1995. So Parcells, Bledsoe, offensive coordinator Ray Perkins, and quarterbacks' coach Chris Palmer all worked overtime during the off-season to correct the deficiencies.

The pressure mounted for 1996. Patriots' fans—who lamented the fact that they had now endured six losing seasons in the past seven years—were clamoring for results. So much tension developed that Patriots' owner Robert Kraft made a monumental decision that would ultimately cause much more grief than glory. He empowered his director of player personnel, Bobby Grier, to have final say on all player personnel decisions, a move that outraged Parcells to no end. In his own memorable, offbeat analogy, Parcells said, "If I'm the one preparing the meal, then I should be the one to buy the groceries," meaning that, as coach of the team, he should be the person to draft and sign players.

In retrospect, Parcells was right—not necessarily because of what he said, but because Kraft overreacted to the apparent lack of production the Patriots had received from several of their draft selections. From 1993 through 1995, when Parcells was in charge of New England's drafts, the club selected, among others, the following players: Drew Bledsoe, Chris Slade, Todd Rucci, Vincent Brisby, Corwin Brown, Willie McGinest, Max Lane, Ty Law, Curtis Martin, Jimmy Hitchcock, and Dave Wohlabaugh—eleven players who were at one time or are still today starters and contributors in the National Football League. And in Bledsoe, Martin, McGinest, Slade, and Law, you can also throw in the fact that they were Pro Bowl–caliber players at one time or another in their careers. I don't know about you, but I, for one, would stack those three drafts against the best of that era and feel confident that they would more than hold their own. You normally are lucky to get two, maybe three starters from any particular draft, and if you land a Pro Bowler every other year, you are doing well. Kraft would later come to regret his decision, even if he never admitted it.

The schedule makers were not kind to Bill Parcells that 1996 season. The first two games of the year were against Miami and Buffalo, both of whom had winning records in 1995, and both contests were on the road.

New England started off 0–2. The "heat" was blazing; the rumors were rampant.

"Fire the bum!"

"Genius coach—*not!*"

It seemed as though everyone wanted Parcells's head. But Bill Parcells reached deep down within his essence, figured out what he had to do, and just told his club to play the games and let the results stand for themselves. He believed wholeheartedly in his team and his approach to victory.

The Patriots proceeded to go 10–2 over the next twelve contests and finished the year at 11–5, champions of the AFC's Eastern Division. Drew Bledsoe was like a new quarterback, concluding the season with excellent numbers (table 11-4).

The Patriots ultimately won the AFC championship, beating the Jacksonville Jaguars 20–6 before succumbing to the powerful Green Bay Packers 35–21 in the Super Bowl. In just the fourth year of his coaching regime in New England, Parcells had succeeded in revitalizing *another* pathetic team that was totally bereft of talent upon his arrival. He quickly restored the Patriots' direction and purpose and systematically led New England to the promised land.

It's especially interesting to note that the 1996 New England Patriots—under the auspices of the ordinarily conservative Bill Parcells—threw the ball 628 times (second most in the NFL) while attempting just 427 rushes (almost 6 percent below the league average). The Patriots gained but 1,468 yards on the ground that season (twenty-sixth

Table 11-4. Drew Bledsoe's 1996 Passing Performance

Year	Att	Comp	Comp%	Yards	YPA	TD	INT	Rating
1996	623	373	59.9	4086	6.56	27	15	83.7

of thirty teams) while averaging just 3.4 yards per attempt—significantly below the NFL average of 3.8. Parcells realized that if this version of the Patriots was to have any chance for success, he would have to alter his conservative offensive approach and allow Drew Bledsoe to carry the offensive load. New England's offensive line was not an especially gifted run-blocking group, and Curtis Martin, though talented, did not have the ability to overcome the inadequacies of his front line. Though this strategy was totally contradictory to his fundamental coaching philosophy, Parcells did what any great coach would have done—he adapted to the situation and developed a plan to maximize his team's assets in order to win football games.

Parcells had proven his point with the Patriots. This was *his* team. The fact that Kraft had placed Grier in a position to make the personnel decisions just before the 1996 draft did not in any way mean it was Grier's team that took the field in Super Bowl XXXI. And even though it was accurately publicized that Parcells did not agree with the decision to select wide receiver Terry Glenn (a player who performed well that season) with New England's first pick in that year's draft, Parcells's indelible mark was all over the club's roster. He built the team and took them to the Super Bowl in a year when many believed the Patriots were on the verge of disaster, with several experts picking them to win no more than five games.

Parcells knew his time was up in New England. He could no longer endure the mettlesome, intrusive owner Bob Kraft and decided he would leave the Patriots and seek employment elsewhere in the NFL.

It was widely speculated that the New York Jets were very interested in the services of Coach Parcells. The Jets had just finished a horrendous season that saw them win one game while losing fifteen. Under Rich Kotite, the New Yorkers were a combined 4–28 in two frustrating years from 1995 to 1996. The Jets were in desperate need of a proven coach, and an agreement was soon reached in which the Patriots received four draft picks in exchange for waiving their rights to retain Parcells.

Parcells strolled back into the Big Apple in 1997 as the conquering hero. He had achieved paramount success with the Giants, then turned a vagabond group of pathetic athletes (the preseason Patriots of 1993) into a spirited group of football warriors in one fell swoop. Would it be possible for him to resurrect the Jets—another miserable team that had lost its will to win and was a joke to the New York fans and media?

The "New York Football Jets" had won a meager forty games during the eight-year span from 1989 through 1996. Their last winning season was in 1988, and that barely qualified for the distinction, as the Jets eked out an 8–7–1 campaign. In their home state of New York, Jets' football was considered to be as exciting as watching reruns of the Weather Channel.

But Bill Parcells never cared about a team's reputation—what it did before he got there. In fact, he often took it as a personal challenge to see if he could turn a no-win scenario into a bonanza. In an interview with the *Sporting News*, just before taking over the Jets, Parcells conveyed a fictitious analogy: "Two guys are sent to Australia to sell shoes to the Aborigines. One calls his boss and says, 'There's no opportunities here. The natives don't wear shoes.' The other guy says, 'There are a lot of opportunities here. These people don't have any shoes.' I think there's a lot of opportunity here [in New York]."

Again, Parcells put his stamp on the club from the outset. The Jets' roster for the 1997 season included twenty-five new players who had not been part of the 1996 juggernaut. And though no single individual made a huge difference that season, the aggregate effect on the team's performance was formidable.

The Jets received greatly improved production from their linebackers under the tutelage of Parcells and his newly appointed defensive coordinator, Bill Belichick (Belichick had been the Giants' defensive coordinator during Parcells's reign). After a rigorous off-season conditioning program *suggested* by Parcells—a facet of the game that had been conspicuously absent in the normal routine of former first-round pick Marvin Jones—the Jets' middle linebacker finally began to realize his vast potential. Jones also was able to stay injury free for the entire season and started all sixteen games for the first time in his career. And Mo Lewis—a former Pro Bowler whose play had slipped dramatically when his weight ballooned into the upper 260s—regained his play-making abilities under Parcells, collecting eight sacks and making several noteworthy plays in key games.

The addition of a new head coach, a new attitude, a new game plan, and a proven philosophy added up to a hugely satisfying 9–7 record for the Jets in Parcells's first year. Fully aware of Parcells's penchant for totally reversing the fortunes of inept teams—and eventually taking them deep into the playoffs—some fans actually held championship aspirations for New York in 1998.

Quarterback Vinny Testaverde was known throughout the league as a "coach killer." The definition can be confusing, so let me explain. Coach-killer quarterbacks actually have talent; the problem is they usually never reach their *potential*, which as we all know is what Charlie Brown referred to as "man's biggest burden."

Testaverde's skills were unmistakable. He possessed a strong, accurate arm, great size, a fluid passing motion, and the ability to take a hit. But he was also easily confused by coverages, fumbled often, threw too many interceptions, and was terribly inconsistent. In other words, he was good enough to routinely convince coaches that they might be able to reverse his negative tendencies and mold him into a top-flight quarterback, but never good enough to actually produce on a regular basis. Testaverde had almost single-handedly ruined the coaching careers of Ray Perkins and Richard Williamson in Tampa, Bill Belichick in Cleveland, and Ted Marchibroda in Baltimore. The aggregate record of the teams that Testaverde led up to that point in his career—just before the 1998 season—totaled 61–113–1, for a .351 winning percentage. In fact, the only winning year that Testaverde had *ever* enjoyed was with Cleveland in 1994, when the Browns' suffocating defense allowed the fewest points (204) the league had seen since the 1986 Chicago Bears, and Cleveland won despite Vinny's terrible season (a 70.7 passer rating).

Sometimes, Testaverde achieved very good passing statistics (see table 11-5). He actually made the Pro Bowl with Baltimore in 1996. But Testaverde quickly became the great enigma of the NFL. In every instance, when Testaverde enjoyed a good passer

Table 11-5. Vinny Testaverde's 1987–2002 Passing Performance

Year	Att	Comp	Comp%	Yards	YPA	TD	INT	Rating	Team Record
Tampa Bay									
1987	165	71	43.0	1081	6.55	5	6	60.2	4–11
1988	466	222	47.6	3240	6.95	13	35	48.8	5–11
1989	480	258	53.8	3133	6.53	20	22	68.9	5–11
1990	365	203	55.6	2818	7.72	17	18	75.6	6–10
1991	326	166	50.9	1994	6.12	8	15	59.0	3–13
1992	358	206	57.51	2554	7.13	14	16	74.2	5–11
Cleveland									
1993	230	130	56.5	1797	7.81	14	9	85.7	7–9
1994	376	207	55.1	2575	6.85	16	18	70.7	11–5
1995	392	241	61.5	2883	7.35	17	10	87.8	5–11
Baltimore									
1996	549	325	59.2	4177	7.61	33	19	88.7	4–12
1997	470	271	57.7	2971	6.32	18	15	75.9	6–9–1
New York Jets									
1998	421	259	61.5	3256	7.73	29	7	101.6	12–4
1999	15	10	66.7	96	6.40	1	1	78.8	8–8
2000	590	328	55.6	3732	6.33	21	25	69.0	9–7
2001	441	260	59.0	2752	6.24	15	14	75.3	10–6
2002	83	54	65.1	499	6.01	3	3	78.3	9-7
Totals	5727	3211	56.1	39558	6.91	244	233	74.8	109–145–1

rating, his teams were chronic losers. As a result, many people held to the belief that he accumulated the majority of his dominant statistics when his teams were hopelessly behind in the game, and the defense had eased up.

Testaverde's first six years in Tampa were miserable, and so were the Buccaneers. Then, in 1993—his first year in Cleveland, under Belichick—Testaverde produced to the tune of an 85.7 passer rating. The Browns, however, struggled and finished at 7–9. In 1995, Vinny delivered another fine passer rating, 87.8, the highest of his career to that point. Nevertheless, the Browns finished poorly once again (5–11), and Bill Belichick was fired. Ted Marchibroda was the next sacrificial lamb, with the Baltimore Ravens in 1996. True to form, Testaverde flourished—an 88.7 passer rating and a Pro Bowl appearance—while the Ravens finished with a dreadful 4–12 record. And since Baltimore's defense was horrific in 1996, Testaverde was able to exploit several instances in which the Ravens were behind by ten or more points (i.e., the game had already been decided), using those situations to accumulate almost 20 percent of his touchdown passes. After the 1997 season, when Testaverde's numbers matched the futility of Baltimore's record (a 75.9 passer rating and a 6–9–1 finish), the Ravens had seen enough, and Vinny was cut.

Enter Bill Parcells.

"Is the 'old man' crazy, or what?" said New York Jets' fans, who learned of the move to add Testaverde to the Jets' roster in the spring of 1998.

Even I, one of Parcells's biggest fans, questioned the strategy. But Parcells knew he had to add a veteran signal caller to the Jets' roster. It was close to training camp (June), and there were few names available. Going into the 1998 season, the Jets had

Neil O'Donnell, Glenn Foley, and Ray Lucas at quarterback. Only O'Donnell had any real experience, and he was considered a stopgap by almost every team in the league, including New York. So Parcells took a chance with Testaverde, a chance that he—the great motivator, leader, and teacher—could actually cure Vinny of his "interceptionitis" and poor decision making.

Parcells rationalized that if he could simplify Vinny's reads and decisions into a more "workable" progression, Testaverde might prosper. Parcells knew he would have to change his game plan to include more short passes and dump-offs to the running backs, and he might even have to limit Testaverde's keys to just one side of the field, but the fact was that Testaverde had all the physical attributes to excel in the NFL, he just couldn't seem to grasp the mental subtleties of the position. Good luck, Bill.

But luck had nothing to do with it. Coaching prowess did. In 1998, Testaverde achieved the numbers in table 11-6.

To this day, after sixteen years in the league under eight different head coaches (Perkins, Williamson, Sam Wyche, Belichick, Marchibroda, Parcells, Al Groh, and Herman Edwards), only *once* has Vinny Testaverde earned both a quarterback rating over eighty and a winning record for his team: in 1998 for Bill Parcells and the New York Jets. Throughout his career, when the games were important and the outcomes in doubt, Testaverde floundered—essentially proving the aforementioned theory that his quality quarterback ratings were the product of efficient play in meaningless situations. The 1998 Jets, however, were different. They finished at 12–4, won a playoff game, and came within a whisker of upsetting the Broncos in the AFC championship game—all under the guidance of Bill Parcells and a quarterback named Vinny Testaverde. If I hadn't see it with my own eyes . . .

While it is true that an elite quarterback can, at times, significantly raise the level of his team's play, it seems obvious that the head coach is the more vital factor in the equation that determines team achievement. As I document in the summary chapter of this book, in concert with poor or average coaching, even elite quarterbacks often encounter trouble winning football games. But, as proven here with Parcells and Testaverde—and by other situations such as that of Joe Gibbs with Mark Rypien and Doug Williams in Washington—many times an elite *coach* can mix and match strategies to elevate even an average quarterback to levels of unprecedented brilliance.

What Bill Parcells did with Vinny Testaverde is almost incomprehensible. NFL syndicated columnist Norman Chad once saluted Parcells as follows: "It is a wonder of nature that caterpillars turn into butterflies. It is a wonder of Parcells that Vinny Testaverde has turned into Joe Namath." A wonder of Parcells, indeed.

In 1999, after an extremely disappointing 1–6 start, Parcells and the Jets rebounded to finish the year with a respectable 8–8 record. Following the season, an exhausted

Table 11-6. Vinny Testaverde's 1998 Passing Performance

Year	Att	Comp	Comp%	Yards	YPA	TD	INT	Rating
1998	421	259	61.5	3256	7.73	29	7	101.6

Parcells decided to step away from the sidelines to take a position in the Jets' front office as director of player personnel. Defensive assistant Al Groh was eventually named as the Jets' new head coach.

Bill Parcells's career record of 138–100–1 (.579 winning percentage), while very good, is not in and of itself a scintillating mark. However, when you factor in that, during his fifteen-year career, his teams played in three Super Bowls, won two of them, and that Parcells took over and completely rejuvenated three franchises (the Giants, Patriots, and Jets) that were in disarray for years before he arrived, only then can you truly begin to appreciate the breadth of his accomplishments.

Bill Parcells was known as a stubborn, arrogant, egotistical, pigheaded coach. And those were his good qualities. Just kidding. But there, indeed, lies some truth in that last statement, for every coach must adhere to the principles, philosophies, and attitudes that he believes are necessary to perform the task at hand—to win football games. Bill Parcells did things his way. He didn't care if he offended people along the way—it wasn't his job to make them feel good. "Everyone who ever coached me was on me, coaching me hard," he once said. "But see, if you respect a player and he respects you, then you have a relationship, and in a relationship, all commentary is allowed. I can say anything to Pepper Johnson, and he will understand where I'm coming from." Though some people may have been put off by his antics, it's impossible to argue with his accomplishments as a football coach.

"Success is never final, but failure can be," is a quote Parcells often repeats, one that he learned from his father. When Parcells accepted his first NFL head coaching job with the Giants in 1983, he had nothing to lose, no reputation to uphold. But when he took the job of resurrecting the New England Patriots, he knew that his critics would be chomping at the bit to highlight every detail of the impending disaster. The Patriots had a horrible recent history, were devoid of premium talent, and had begun to accept losing. Everyone knew that Parcells faced a rigid test in his quest to turn the Patriots into a "football machine." Nevertheless, Parcells was always willing to take on the tough assignment, even though other successful coaches would never have considered such a monumental task. And though he knew that the fans and the media would likely dwell on his disappointments much more than his Super Bowl achievements—if and when he did fail—he could never seem to back down from a challenge. The opportunity to prove the critics wrong, and at the same time return to the vocation and lifestyle he loved so much, was too great a temptation. In fact, when asked why he came back to coach after winning two Super Bowls with the Giants and then surviving a heart bypass operation that had forced him into early retirement, Parcells responded emphatically, "Because Bill Parcells is a football coach." And that, as they say, was that.

Bill Parcells's career achievements seem to perfectly define the essence of this book. If I dared to fabricate a coach and his career so that it would justify the basic declaration put forth at the beginning of this manuscript, I would have encountered much difficulty in attempting to manufacture a better, more cogent example of coaching ability and its decisive influence on teams' records.

When teams consistently perform at or near their maximum capability, the head coach and, to a lesser degree, his staff merit recognition. When teams occasionally achieve beyond their talents, the head coach deserves substantial credit and regard. But when teams *regularly* perform well in excess of their abilities, the head coach should be considered a genius. Bill Parcells is such a man.

"I've always coached the same way," Parcells says. "I really believe that players do what you *make* them do, and they *don't* do what you *don't* make them do." And though Bill Parcells has ceaselessly maintained this simplistic credo in regard to his basic coaching philosophy, his results are anything but ordinary.

Of his players, Parcells may have had the most tangible influence on two Martins, George and Curtis. In *Parcells: A Biography*, George Martin reflected on his relationship with his coach and mentor:

> Bill Parcells had the greatest impact on George Martin not on the field of play, but in the field of life, he said. We always had a great deal in common, and I thought of him more as a peer than perhaps many of my teammates did. We talked about career transitions, life after football, our own mortality. In other words, we talked about a higher level of athletics and life together, more so than he did with other players.
>
> Because of that, he helped me prepare for life after football. I learned about making decisions, tough decisions, and about dedication and commitment. The funny part is, we had many of these talks during practice. He was great about pulling a guy aside and having little conversations with him. That made you feel special.

Parcells was instrumental in bringing Curtis Martin to the Jets from New England in 1998. The very next year, Martin led New York with more than fourteen hundred rushing yards. He was named the team's most valuable player. When the season ended, Martin—who grew up with no father figure—received his MVP trophy. Shortly thereafter, when Parcells decided to retire, Martin left his trophy on Bill's desk with a note expressing his appreciation of Parcells's influence on his life and career. The note was signed with Martin's pet moniker: "Love, Boy Wonder."

In an interview with *Esquire* magazine in 1995, Parcells was asked his idea of perfect contentment: "One more point than they have," he said—a comment that seems to accurately and succinctly define the man, his lifestyle, and his achievements.

Bill Parcells completely reversed the ineptitudes of three different organizations, bringing each of them to, or near to, the pinnacle of success. And he did it—quite amazingly—in a quick, decisive, definitive manner. He molded each team after his own image and his own character. In the end, Bill Parcells's epitaph should read: "Here lies Bill Parcells, whose job in life it was *to make winners out of losers.* Here lies a football coach, one of the greatest ever to walk the sidelines."

Note: In January of 2003, at the age of 61, Parcells was named head coach of the Dallas Cowboys. After obtaining a contractual guarantee from Cowboys' owner Jerry Jones ensuring him complete control over all coaching matters and extensive input regarding personnel decisions, Parcells decided to return to the NFL.

Bill Parcells's Coaching Capsule

Category	Numbers
Seasons	15
Wins	138
Losses	100
Ties	1
Winning pct.	.579
Pct. >/< avg. Super Bowl–winning coach (.601)*	−3.7%
World championships†	2
World championship game appearances†	3
World championship pct. (champ/seasons)	16.7%
Losing seasons	4
Pct. of losing seasons	33.3%
Playoff record	11–6
Playoff winning percentage	.647
Average wins per 16 games (a current season)	9.3
Average losses per 16 games	6.7

NOTE: Ties count as a half-win and a half-loss in calculating percentages.
*See Epilogue
†Super Bowls or NFL championships 1920–1965.

3 Years Before and After Parcells

City	Years	Record	Percentage	Parcells's Career Pct
				.579
Before				
NY Giants	1980–82	17–24	.415	
New England	1990–92	9–39	.188	
NY Jets	1994–96	10–38	.208	
After				
NY Giants	1991–93	25–23	.521	
New England	1997–99	27–21	.563	
NY Jets	2000–02	18–14	.563	

Yearly Records

Year	Team	Wins	Losses	Ties	Playoffs
1983	NYG	3	12	1	
1984	NYG	9	7	0	1–1
1985	NYG	10	6	0	1–1
1986	NYG	14	2	0	3–0*
1987	NYG	6	9	0	
1988	NYG	10	6	0	
1989	NYG	12	4	0	0–1
1990	NYG	13	3	0	3–0*
1993	NE	5	11	0	
1994	NE	10	6	0	0–1
1995	NE	6	10	0	
1996	NE	11	5	0	2–1†
1997	NYJ	9	7	0	
1998	NYJ	12	4	0	1–1
1999	NYJ	8	8	0	
Totals		138	100	1	11–6

*Won Super Bowl
†AFC champion

Chapter 12

MIKE HOLMGREN

At a press conference on January 11, 1992, Green Bay Packers' general manager Ron Wolf stepped up to the microphone to announce the hiring of the Packers' new head coach—the eleventh in their history. The franchise was in desperate need of help. Since 1968, the Green Bay Packers, once an icon of professional football prosperity, had suffered through five head coaches and twenty-four years of unmitigated adversity. Green Bay's aggregate record during that time was 147–203–9, for a .422 winning percentage. The club had made only two postseason appearances since 1972 and had not been to the playoffs in nine years. Former head coaches "Curly" Lambeau and Vince Lombardi—winners of eleven Packers championships and 320 games between them—had probably turned over in their graves, twice. The entire Packers organization had become flustered. It seemed they needed a refresher course in winning. So Wolf proceeded to enlist a teacher: Mike Holmgren.

Michael George Holmgren was born on June 15, 1948, in San Francisco, California. His father, Linc, a man of Swedish-Norwegian descent, was a baker and a real estate broker. Mike was a fine athlete as a youngster. He had the ability to hit a baseball a country mile and could throw a football as long and as hard as anyone. He attended Lincoln High School in San Francisco, where he starred as a quarterback and was named the city's Prep Athlete of the Year in 1965. Hall of Fame quarterback Dan Fouts, also a San Francisco native and a few years younger than Holmgren, remembers watching him in high school. "He was the best high school quarterback I ever saw," Fouts recalled.

Holmgren's gridiron prowess earned him a scholarship to the University of Southern California, one of the most prestigious football programs in the country. Luckily, Holmgren—a very intelligent athlete—took full advantage of the academic pursuits available to him at USC. Due to bad timing, injuries, and most significantly a style of play that was somewhat in contrast to the conservative approach that head coach John McKay preferred, Holmgren's college football career was a major disappointment. He played sparingly from 1966 to 1969 and was injured for his entire senior year. He did, however, graduate with a degree in business finance.

Though he had played little in college and missed his entire senior season, Holmgren was selected by the St. Louis Cardinals in the eighth round of the 1970 NFL draft in deference to his mammoth size (6' 5", 230 pounds) and outstanding arm. Holmgren made a gallant effort to stick with the Cardinals but was ultimately cut in the latter stages of training camp. He had a subsequent tryout with the New York Jets that same season but was released there as well.

After his pro football dream was shattered, Holmgren took a job in the finance sector of the construction industry. But it quickly became evident that he would never be happy or satisfied outside of football. Holmgren had a passion for the sport; he couldn't get it out of his system. So he decided that the best way to get back into the game was as a high school coach.

Holmgren's first high school job was to coach and teach history for his former school (Lincoln) in 1971. The next year, he moved on to become an assistant coach and teacher at another San Francisco high school, Sacred Heart. During Holmgren's tenure at Sacred Heart (1972–1974), the school encountered monumental problems on the football field. They had no practice facilities and very few good athletes. As a result, they struggled to a 4–24 three-year record.

In 1975, Holmgren accepted a position as offensive coordinator and quarterbacks coach for nearby Oak Grove High School. Holmgren's prized athlete at Oak Grove was a teenager by the name of Marty Mornhinweg, who would later become an assistant coach for Holmgren in Green Bay (1995–1996) and head coach of the Detroit Lions in 2001 and 2002. Under Holmgren's tutelage in the mid- to late-1970s, Mornhinweg became an outstanding high school quarterback, eventually earning a scholarship to the University of Montana. Holmgren made a lasting impression on Mornhinweg, teaching him the rudimentary elements of both quarterback play and leadership. "Mike can make anybody—whether it be a staff member, a player, or an assistant—feel wanted and important," said Mornhinweg. "He can get the most out of you. That's a special quality he has. When he talks to you one on one, or even as a group, he gets his point across." Holmgren's move to Oak Grove proved successful. The school won a regional championship during his five-year stay, which ended in 1979.

In 1980, Holmgren entered the college ranks. He assumed the position of quarterbacks coach and offensive coordinator with San Francisco State University under head coach Vic Rowen. Then, in 1982, Holmgren got a big break. Brigham Young University—a powerhouse football program that had actually recruited Holmgren out of high school—was in need of a quarterbacks coach. On Rowan's recommendation, LaVelle Edwards—Brigham Young's head coach—offered Holmgren an interview. "He didn't have a lot of experience," Edwards recalled. "But he was very personable, came highly recommended, and had good knowledge of the game." Edwards was sufficiently impressed and offered Holmgren the job.

Holmgren stayed at BYU for four years, during which time he coached a signal caller by the name of Steve Young. Young was an incredibly gifted athlete who required some assistance with his fundamentals and timing. Under Holmgren's supervision, Young developed into a more complete, technically sound quarterback—as opposed to an awesome athlete who just took the snap from the center and made plays based on pure athleticism. "Steve had great talent and ability, but he needed refinement," Edwards remembers. "Mike taught him the value of patience and waiting for things to unfold." In 1984, Young and Holmgren meshed in perfect harmony, and Brigham Young won a national championship. Several years later, coach and pupil would be reunited in the NFL.

In 1986, Holmgren caught the eye of San Francisco 49ers' head coach Bill Walsh. Though Holmgren had relatively little experience as a college coach, he enticed Walsh enough to gain an interview with the two-time Super Bowl winner. "What impressed me most about Mike when I interviewed him was how detailed he was about BYU's offense," Walsh said. "When I noted that, I thought that he was someone I could hire. He had an attention to detail and a football mind. I was really impressed with his administrative and leadership qualities." Holmgren accepted a position on the most celebrated staff in the NFL—as quarterbacks coach for the San Francisco 49ers.

From 1981 to 1985, the 49ers had been the NFL's most successful franchise. In those five years, San Francisco accumulated a 51–22 record (.699) and two Super Bowl conquests (1981 and 1984). Walsh had developed an atmosphere of football superiority in the Bay Area, and he expected nothing less than perfection from both his players and coaches. The unmerciful pressure of professional football had now fully engulfed Mike Holmgren. He was thirty-eight years old, and his chances of becoming a head coach in the NFL would largely depend on the methods and procedures he employed to advance San Francisco's quarterbacks.

Though the club did not win a playoff game in Holmgren's first two years (1986–1987), he quickly established himself as a valuable member of the 49ers' elite coaching staff. In his second season, San Francisco's offense led the league with 459 points—the seventh-highest total in NFL history at that time. Quarterbacks Joe Montana (the starter) and Steve Young (Holmgren's former pupil and the 49ers' backup signal caller) were both brilliant (table 12-1).

In 1988, San Francisco won its third Super Bowl of the decade by defeating the Cincinnati Bengals 20–16. After the season—having accomplished everything that a coach could conceive of in his short ten-year career—Bill Walsh decided to retire.

Table 12-1. Joe Montana's and Steve Young's 1987 Passing Performance

Year	Att	Comp	Comp%	Yards	YPA	TD	INT	Rating
				Joe Montana				
1987	398	266	66.8	3054	7.67	31	13	102.1
				Steve Young				
1987	69	37	53.6	570	8.26	10	0	120.8

Defensive coordinator George Seifert was chosen to replace him. Seifert had been with the club since 1980, Walsh's second season. In one of Seifert's first moves, he named Mike Holmgren as his offensive coordinator. The promotion brought Holmgren to a pivotal point in his career. If he could thrive as the offensive leader of pro football's most admired franchise, it would likely pave the way for his first head coaching position.

Over the next three years (1989–1991) under Seifert's command—with Holmgren running a modified form of Bill Walsh's trendy West Coast offense—San Francisco did not miss a beat. The club went 38–10, collected another Lombardi trophy as a result of their Super Bowl triumph in the 1989 season, and never finished worse than 10–6. During that three-year stretch, the 49ers won games with a trio of starting quarterbacks—a tribute to the systems and schemes devised by one Mike Holmgren. Joe Montana, Steve Bono, and Steve Young all took their place, at one time or another, under center for San Francisco.

Young in particular—having played for Holmgren in college and being a raw, unpolished talent at the time—was extremely appreciative of the opportunity to learn the nuances of quarterback play and offensive strategy from such an astute instructor. From both an interpersonal and tactical standpoint, Young lauded Holmgren's approach. "Mike is one of the best coaches ever, because he understands people," he said. "He can sit down and have a conversation with somebody and know what kind of a football player they are. A lot of people measure it by speed and how far you can jump—things that are just objective. He's the kind of guy that can get subjective with his personalities. He can put a team together that's going to play hard. And he can put a game plan together and attack and adjust accordingly. He's phenomenal."

Young also admired Holmgren's emotional perspective as a coach and leader. If things were going poorly, and a player was having problems, Holmgren would often seek out the individual and attempt to revitalize his spirit. "He never wanted the mood to be somber or down. No matter what, he always wanted you upbeat," Young said. But when mistakes were made and Holmgren become angered, Young recalls, you didn't want to bear his wrath. "He doesn't scream," Young said. "He'll hold it in. It builds in his neck, so that his neck actually bulges out."

As well as the San Francisco 49ers were playing, there was usually no need for screaming. In fact, the team was so successful that Holmgren had become a hot commodity by the end of the 1991 season. Several clubs were interested in his services as a head coach, and Holmgren had a bona fide interest in two of those teams—Indianapolis and Green Bay.

Part of Holmgren's intrigue with Indianapolis was related to the fact that the Colts had selected a strong-armed quarterback from Illinois, Jeff George, with the first pick back in the 1990 draft. With two years under his belt, George's learning curve was almost over, Holmgren concluded, and the young quarterback would be ready to exhibit his best performance. Holmgren quickly set up a meeting with Colts' executive Jim Irsay, son of owner Bob Irsay. After intensive discussions, however, Holmgren came away with the distinct, uneasy feeling that "total devotion towards winning"—a key sticking point with him relative to the direction of the franchise for which he would ultimately work—was not an organizational mandate in Indianapolis. While Holmgren did not demand complete authority to run the Colts as he pleased, he did want to be certain that the team he chose was dedicated to success. He did not come away with that sense from Jimmy Irsay and the Colts, who had a long history of inept performances from both their teams and their front office. So Holmgren took a trip to "cheese country."

The Green Bay Packers were in complete turmoil. The once proud franchise had not witnessed NFL glory for more than two decades. Their previous coach, Lindy Infante, had seemingly turned the corner in 1989 with a 10–6 record. But Infante made a crucial miscalculation by investing heavily in a quarterback, Don Majkowski, who did not have the skills to consistently lead the Packers to victory. Majkowski enjoyed a career year in 1989. He compiled an 82.3 quarterback rating and led the NFL with more than forty-three hundred passing yards. But Majkowski lacked the arm strength to stretch the field, and when defensive coordinators tightened their coverages and forced him to throw deep, his effectiveness was abated. As a result, Green Bay suffered through 6–10 and 4–12 seasons in 1990 and 1991, and Infante was fired.

The thought of leaving San Francisco, California, for the frozen tundra of Green Bay, Wisconsin, would be unsettling for even the most intrepid of souls. But Holmgren at least had Scandinavian ancestry and could ease the transition by bringing some of San Francisco and the 49ers with him—in the form of his own unique version of Bill Walsh's West Coast offense. After exhaustive meetings with front office officials, Holmgren decided that the Packers and their new GM, Ron Wolf, were dedicated to restoring the team to championship form. Holmgren accepted an offer to coach Green Bay and was suddenly thrust into the historic, almost surreal atmosphere of Packers' football.

Legend has it that many unsuccessful Green Bay coaches have been driven to the brink of madness by the ghosts of Lambeau and Lombardi, who were determined not to rest until the Packers' franchise was restored to prominence. But Holmgren was assured by management that the spirits are not released until after the second consecutive losing year and that, if he were interested, they now had an insurance policy that would cover a third, as well. All joking aside, the Packers were not a very good football club, and Holmgren knew that as a novice head coach, he wouldn't be given much time to sort out Green Bay's problems and reestablish a successful program.

One of Holmgren's greatest assets in his quest to revitalize the Packers was his background in teaching. Since the inception of his coaching career, he had discerned that coaching and teaching went hand in hand. "Football coaches *are* teachers," Holmgren often asserts. "In the development of young people, you realize communicating is different. But what you find is, dealing with older athletes—very gifted, very skilled athletes—the transfer of knowledge doesn't change all that much. They're like big little kids." Holmgren was certain that if he could acquire capable players with the desire to succeed, he could convey the strategies and techniques necessary to develop their talents and mold them into a formidable unit.

Holmgren's experience as a student also aided his coaching pursuits in Green Bay. "I was a student of coaches," he said, "and [Lombardi] was the one I studied." In addition to the tactical lessons he learned from his investigation of Lombardi's career, the research helped prepare him for the Lombardi comparisons that all Packers' coaches inevitably encounter. "Living up to Lombardi, I'm not sure anyone will be able to do that, so it [being measured against a legend] doesn't bother me too much," he said. "My main concern is getting better every week, coaching a young quarterback, and fielding a good team."

In his first speech to his new club, Holmgren—in typical Lombardi style—stressed the necessity for the club to start thinking like winners. "We have to establish the fact that good things are going to happen in the second half of games, not bad things," he said. "And that's a mind-set." Based on his experiences in San Francisco, Holmgren knew that confidence was a key component for success in the NFL. Timid players make mistakes and often fail to seize the opportunities that can produce victory. Holmgren desperately needed to instill an optimistic attitude in his players in order for the Packers to be victorious.

Holmgren had a blueprint for success. From the very beginning, he knew exactly what he wanted from his players. "I have a vision for this organization and what this football team should be and needs to be," he said. "And I think you develop that, you get a picture in your mind, by working with players like Joe Montana, Jerry Rice, and Tom Rathman. Players who won Super Bowls, players who know how to win."

Vince Lombardi was once asked what separates a good coach from a bad coach. "Knowing what the end result looks like," Lombardi replied. "The best coaches know what the end result looks like, whether it's an offensive play, or just some area of the organization. If you don't know what the end result is supposed to look like, you cannot possibly get there. All teams basically do the same things. We all draft. We all have a training camp, we all practice. But the inferior coaches don't know what the hell they want. They don't know what to look for, even if it's staring them right in the face. The good coaches do."

It's a simple explanation to a complex question, but it hits the nail right on the head. A good coach has to know exactly what he wants, how to convey it to his players, and how it's supposed to look when it's properly executed. Holmgren studied Lombardi, so he knew precisely what he meant. He also knew what the end result was supposed to look like—just like it did in San Francisco.

Holmgren's first order of business was to assemble a coaching staff with proven personnel. He quickly moved to establish a winning atmosphere by adding two former 49ers' assistants, Sherman Lewis and Ray Rhodes, to lead the Packers' offensive and defensive units, respectively. Then Holmgren and Ron Wolf got to work on assessing and strengthening their roster.

They determined that an upgrade at the quarterback position was mandatory, as Don Majkowski did not have the tools to get the job done. Identifying and acquiring a solid quarterback prospect in the NFL is not unlike searching for a new house—there usually aren't many that suit your needs, and those that do aren't on the market for long. As luck would have it, Wolf discovered that the Atlanta Falcons were unhappy with their second-round draft choice from the past season, a quarterback named Brett Favre. A rocket-armed Cajun from Mississippi, Favre seemed more concerned with partying and having a good time than he did with learning the subtleties of professional quarterback play. Atlanta Coach Jerry Glanville and Vice President of Player Personnel Ken Herock had apparently had enough of Favre's childish antics and lackadaisical attitude after just one season. When the Packers offered a first-round pick for the recalcitrant Favre, the Falcons quickly moved to strike a deal.

Holmgren was thrilled. Not only did he have the young quarterback that he so desperately wanted, but he had an extremely talented individual whom he believed could be molded into a tremendous competitor and outstanding player. As a teacher and a former quarterback, Holmgren was not overly concerned with Favre's youthful exuberance and questionable character. Holmgren believed that everyone, including Favre, had the ability to learn and grow, both as an individual and an athlete. He theorized that gifted young players, especially quarterbacks, just needed proper guidance, a tolerant coaching staff, and a legitimate opportunity to display their talents in order to be successful.

"We tried to acquire a young quarterback every year," Holmgren later said of his time in Green Bay. "A lot of teams don't do that. A lot of teams will wait to sign a veteran free agent and wouldn't have the patience to develop a young guy." But Holmgren, who drafted Mark Brunell, Ty Detmer, and Matt Hasselbeck and brought unknown free agent Kurt Warner into Green Bay for a tryout—all the while still loyal to Brett Favre—repeatedly invested in young signal callers regardless of the personnel already on hand.

After acquiring Favre and stabilizing the club's quarterback situation, Holmgren and Wolf began to scrutinize the rest of the Packers' roster. They wound up dismissing almost half of the 1991 team. Green Bay had finished 6–10 and 4–12 the last two years (1991–1992), and Holmgren had no desire to waste time with athletes he believed were incapable of thriving in professional football. Though the Packers couldn't release all of their inferior players in just one off-season, they could certainly begin to eliminate some of the more unproductive and/or complacent members of the group. "You can have good players on a bad team or average team, and they think—they really believe—that they are playing at a high level, but they're not," Holmgren said. "They're playing much lower. So you either have to get these players to raise the bar [if they're talented enough], or get rid of them."

What Holmgren meant was that many times players on mediocre NFL teams have no real measuring stick for success. They may have been great in college and may have enjoyed some prosperity in the professional ranks, but if there are no true superstars on their club, and if the team has never ventured deep into the playoffs, then their frames of reference are completely distorted relative to understanding what it takes to excel. Players need to compare their talents and practice habits to those of the Jerry Rices, Joe Montanas, and Dan Marinos of the NFL world—not to those of the guy across the locker room just because he happens to be a ten-year veteran. Upon his arrival in Green Bay in early 1993, all-star defensive tackle Reggie White found that many players had accepted the team's lack of success because they believed they had given a decent effort to achieve victory.

"When I got to Green Bay I told some of our guys, 'You make more excuses than anyone I've ever seen,'" he said. "We had some guys who walked around like they didn't care if we lost." As Mike Holmgren's tenure progressed and he was able to add more of his own handpicked players while simultaneously ridding the organization of slackers, that mentality changed.

Holmgren's NFL head coaching career had an inauspicious start. In his first game in 1992, the Packers suffered a frustrating overtime defeat against their division rivals, the Minnesota Vikings, 23–20. Next came a 31–3 blowout at the hands of the lowly Tampa Bay Buccaneers, who had won all of twenty-seven games in the previous seven years. The Packers then rebounded to defeat the Cincinnati Bengals and Pittsburgh Steelers, evening their record at 2–2. But their success was short-lived. Three straight losses to Atlanta, Cleveland, and Chicago created an extremely disappointing 2–5 record after the team's first seven games.

The Green Bay faithful were distraught. Facing a brutal schedule that included games against Detroit, Philadelphia, and Chicago (all playoff teams in 1991) in the ensuing four weeks, it didn't take long for both fans and media to begin berating management for another head-coaching blunder. Packers' followers resigned themselves to the prospect of several more seasons of repulsive football.

It's simply amazing at times. Just when you think the worst is upon you, and there's no way to avoid impending doom, things suddenly get better. In 1981, the Washington Redskins started the season at 0–5. Their first-year head coach, Joe Gibbs, began to think he would be fired before his initial taste of victory. As a winless team with a rookie head coach and no future draft picks, the Washington Redskins appeared to be headed for a long stay in the NFL's dungeon. But that was not to be. You see, Joe Gibbs was actually a hell of a coach. Though things had started a little rough, he wasn't about to give up and cry for his mommy. Instead, he persevered. Gibbs cracked down on his coaching staff, added a few new strategies, reinvigorated himself and his team, and bellied up to the bar for another round of the best the NFL could throw his way. The next thing you know, the Redskins finished at 8–8. The next season (1982), they won the Super Bowl.

In 2001, those same Redskins—under the guidance of Marty Schottenheimer—again started off the season at 0–5 and had been outscored by well over one hundred points along the way. With his firing imminent, his players on the verge of mutiny, and the Washington media clutching at his throat for immediate answers to every problem, Schottenheimer responded. He adjusted his personnel, regrouped his reeling defense, and proceeded to win the next five games to get back into the playoff picture.

Gibbs and Schottenheimer were both very good coaches; just look at their career records if you don't believe me. But you know what? Mike Holmgren was a pretty fair

Table 12-2. Brett Favre's 1992 Passing Performance

Year	Att	Comp	Comp%	Yards	YPA	TD	INT	Rating
1992	471	302	64.1	3227	6.85	18	13	85.3

coach in his own right. Despite their 2–5 start in 1992, the Packers were undaunted. They kept to their program and played the games one at a time. They beat Detroit 27–13, lost to the Giants 27–7, then upset both Philadelphia (27–24) and Chicago (17–3) en route to six straight victories. Only a final-game defeat at the hands of the Vikings kept Green Bay from the playoffs, and the team finished Holmgren's first season with a respectable 9–7 record.

For a second-year player who had never completed an NFL pass, quarterback Brett Favre had a tremendous season. He connected on over 64 percent of his tosses and earned an 85.3 rating—good for sixth in the league (table 12-2).

With Favre progressing nicely, young complements like all-star wide receiver Sterling Sharpe (a league-leading 108 catches in 1992), promising tight end Jackie Harris, and a solid if unspectacular offensive line, Holmgren was pleased with Green Bay's attack. In fact, the Packers' offense had compiled a statistic that is usually a portent of great success. Led by the flamboyant, charismatic Favre, Green Bay finished the season ranked among the top five NFL teams in third-down efficiency (table 12-3).

Teams that convert a high percentage of third downs historically win a lot of games in the NFL. In 1992, every team on this list—except for the Packers—made the playoffs and had legitimate Super Bowl aspirations. Given that Green Bay achieved their third-down success with an inexperienced quarterback who could be expected to improve dramatically as he matured and his pass attempts increased, the Packers had grandiose ambitions for the future.

But while the Green Bay offense had made significant progress during the 1992 campaign, the defense was another story. The Packers finished the season permitting an average of 4.5 yards per carry—poor enough to finish twenty-sixth in the twenty-eight-team league. In fact, the Packers ranked in the twenties in several important defensive categories. For the club to take the next step and advance to the playoffs, help was desperately needed on the defensive side of the ball.

Table 12-3. 1992 NFL Third-Down Efficiency

Team	Att	First Downs	Pct	Starting Qbck Career Att Before 1992	
San Francisco	187	87	46.5	Steve Young	1,104
Minnesota	212	94	44.3	Rich Gannon	724
Washington	226	98	43.4	Mark Rypien	1,409
Green Bay	214	91	42.5	Brett Favre	5
Houston	170	72	42.4	Warren Moon	3,680
Dallas	208	87	41.8	Troy Aikman	1,055
Buffalo	202	80	39.6	Jim Kelly	2,562
Miami	201	78	38.8	Dan Marino	4,730

Luckily, the Packers struck gold in the 1993 free-agent market when they signed defensive end Reggie White, formerly of the Philadelphia Eagles. Even with the advent of free agency and the salary cap, opportunities to enlist veteran superstars like Reggie White are few and far between in the NFL. White, a first-round selection of the Eagles in the supplemental draft of 1984, had collected the staggering total of 110 sacks in his first seven seasons in the league. The 6' 5", 285-pound defensive end was also adept as a run stopper. In reality, he was perhaps one of the five best defensive linemen in the history of the NFL. And he was only thirty-one years old when the Philadelphia Eagles let him go. It was widely speculated that owner Norman Braman refused to pay White a salary commensurate with his abilities, and if that was the case, it was a grave miscalculation. The addition of White instantly upgraded Green Bay's defense.

Take a look in table 12-4 at the Packers' defensive stats both before and after White's acquisition.

Though Green Bay had added several rookie defenders in the 1993 NFL draft (linebacker Wayne Simmons and defensive backs George Teague and Doug Evans), none of those players had a significant impact that season. It was obvious that Green Bay's dramatic defensive improvement was directly attributable to the exploits of Reginald Howard White. The relentless defensive end collected thirteen sacks and completely dominated the line of scrimmage. "He made us a better football team, no question about it," Holmgren said. "We went from twenty-third in total defense (yardage) to second in just one season—with no noticeable personnel changes, except for one man." White became the Packers' equivalent to New York Giants' Hall of Fame linebacker Lawrence Taylor. Opposing teams had to account for him on every play. They needed to double-team him on passing downs and stop his penetration on running plays. Though

Table 12-4. Green Bay Packers' 1992–93 Defensive Statistics

Category	Number	League Ranking
1992, Before White		
Yardage	5317	23
Average per rush	4.5	26
Average per pass att	7.2	23
Touchdowns rushing	12	T-14*
Touchdowns passing	16	T-8*
Points	296	15
1993, With White		
Yardage	4783	2
Average per rush	3.7	9
Average per pass att	6.1	2
Touchdowns rushing	6	T-1*
Touchdowns passing	16	T-7*
Points	282	9

*T indicates a tie in ranking

Table 12-5. Brett Favre's 1993 Passing Performance

Year	Att	Comp	Comp%	Yards	YPA	TD	INT	Rating
1993	522	318	60.9	3303	6.33	19	24	72.2

Holmgren was an offensive specialist, he knew that a dominant force like White brought offenses to their knees and altered the complexion of the game. "Reggie changed everything—the way we play, the other team's offensive scheme, everything," he said.

Holmgren's effusive praise of Reggie White was matched only by the all-star defensive end's high regard for his new coach. "Mike is honest, and he sets a tone that lets players know he cares about winning and he cares about you," White said at the time. "He can dictate the flow of a game with his play calling. He gets people prepared. We have a lot of respect for him around here."

Unfortunately, while Green Bay's defense thrived in 1993, their offense regressed. Brett Favre struggled (table 12-5). He was inconsistent reading defenses, ad-libbed on far too many plays, and—perhaps most troublesome—had developed a propensity to force passes into tight coverage.

Favre had awesome arm strength, an asset that would sometimes get him in trouble. He often forced passes into close coverage, relying on the ball's velocity to overcome well-defended pass patterns. If he got away with a few ill-advised throws early in the game, the young quarterback would begin to think that he was impervious to turnovers and would continue to unleash risky passes throughout the contest. This type of attack became a double-edged sword for the Packers. They scored 340 points but at the same time afforded their opposition excellent field position on numerous occasions as a result of interceptions.

Favre's problems contributed to another poor start for the Packers in 1993. Green Bay earned just one victory against three losses in the NFL's opening month. Nevertheless, by virtue of their stingy new defense, the Packers were able to win six of their next seven contests and eventually salvaged another 9–7 record. This time, however, nine wins was sufficient to make the playoffs. In their first postseason game in eleven years, Green Bay faced their division rivals, the Detroit Lions, in an NFC wild-card contest.

Favre's inconsistency was very much on display that January day in Michigan. Detroit led the game 10–7 at halftime. Then, early in the third quarter, Favre attempted a pass that was intercepted by Lion's defensive back Melvin Jenkins and returned for a touchdown. Even though the Packers beat the Lions on a last-minute Favre touchdown pass to Sterling Sharpe, the Green Bay quarterback was beginning to gain a reputation as a player who could keep *both* teams in the game at the same time.

The next week—in a game that was not as close as the score may have indicated—the Dallas Cowboys ended the Packers' playoff run, 27–17. Afterwards, both Favre and Holmgren went home knowing they had to address some problems before the club could take the next step towards the Super Bowl.

Though it was still early in both of their careers, quarterback and coach had seemingly reached a crossroads. Favre was a free sprit, and it was reflected in his style of play. He loved to shoot from the hip and make extemporaneous decisions as the game developed. Holmgren was meticulous, a stickler for detail; he needed to know that his instructions were going to be followed. He didn't care for the ultra-quick improvisations of his quarterback—not when there was ample opportunity to carry out the original play. Holmgren's frustration was so great at times that he chose to communicate with Favre through the assistant coaches rather than risk a heated exchange. Something had to give in order for these diametrically opposed personalities to coexist and prosper with the Packers.

"He [Holmgren] would insist that something be done a particular way, exactly that way, and I guess I would sort of rebel," Favre admitted later in his career. "I mean, I would listen, I would try, but some things, I really thought, for me, would be better if I did them my way. He didn't buy that—at first."

Holmgren knew there would be times in his coaching career when his authority would be challenged and he would have to reestablish his control. He also understood that there would be times when someone had a valid criticism or reasonable request that warranted consideration. Holmgren had to determine if this was one of those times. He had to decide whether he should acquiesce and allow Favre more freedom to spontaneously alter plays, or if he should insist that things be done his way—allowing Favre very little room to maneuver. Since Favre was a gifted quarterback who seemed to thrive in impromptu situations, Holmgren agreed to a compromise with his star pupil. Favre received the coach's permission to deviate from the original play at his discretion—as long as he did not abuse the privilege.

"It got to the point where I was on him so much that he was not getting any room to grow," Holmgren said. "I was so tough on him that I was squeezing the spark out of him, that special trait he has that makes him a special quarterback. I saw that I had to give. After a while, I told Brett that he was my quarterback and that together we were either going to sink or swim. But the one thing was, either way, we were going to do it together."

The key to the understanding was the way that Holmgren expressed his views to Favre. It was done with such deftness and sincerity that Favre couldn't help but realize that if he failed by being overzealous with his improvisations, he was going to take his coach with him—possibly ruining two careers at once. Holmgren made it crystal clear that the new system would be a joint effort, and both quarterback and coach would be accountable for the outcome. This tactic helped ensure that Favre would be judicious in his approach and would not attempt to dominate the compromise by taking unnecessary risks with the offense. Ultimately, Holmgren was able to give Favre more freedom yet still remain in control.

Holmgren's decision with Favre reinforced the team's confidence in their young head coach. It wasn't often that Holmgren allowed an individual to take matters into his own hands and change the coaching staff's formula for success. Everyone on the

Packers knew that Holmgren was a methodical coach, one who stressed the importance of doing things the same way each and every time his club took the field. He had no tolerance for individuals who weren't compliant with the system or took advantage of a situation in an effort to further their own cause. But Favre was a special athlete, and the players realized this as well as the coach. For Holmgren to adjust his philosophy and allow Favre more freedom with the offense was a monumental gesture—one that was offered in the spirit of unity and achievement. It gained Holmgren an even higher level of respect within the organization.

Clearly, though, the Favre case was a unique situation, reserved for special athletes with exceptional abilities. Mike Holmgren might bend his rules to accommodate a budding superstar every now and again, but it was obvious that incidents of this nature would be few and far between—the proof of which was witnessed two years later, when another signal caller decided to alter the coach's strategy.

In a 1995 game against the Vikings, quarterback T.J. Rubley—a second-year player from Tulsa—was forced into action due to injuries to Favre and backup Ty Detmer. With the score tied at twenty-four late in the game and the ball on the Minnesota twenty-nine-yard line, Holmgren called a quarterback sneak to set up a field goal attempt to win the game. Rubley, however, called an audible. The play ended up with Rubley running to one side of the field and attempting to throw back across his body to the other side. The resulting interception led to a Vikings' game-winning field goal. Shortly thereafter, Rubley was cut.

Mike Holmgren is a large man with a commanding presence. He runs his team in an authoritative and disciplined fashion and expects his instructions to be followed. While he might capitulate in order to develop the extraordinary talents of a Brett Favre, it is rare that a player is permitted to make his own decisions on Holmgren's clubs. "I want players to know that when I say something—that's it," he says. "It's not part of a negotiating process. We're not wheeling and dealing." Holmgren is quick to point out that he would never want to discourage a player from thinking or asking questions. Nevertheless, he makes it quite clear that he is not operating a democracy.

Holmgren has a credo that he often relates to young players as they enter his organization: "Listen to what I tell you and do it. If you do, three things can happen. One, it will work and you'll get the credit. Two, it won't work and I'll get the blame. Three, you'll do it wrong and you'll be gone."

If you rationalize Holmgren's beliefs, you can clearly ascertain his logic. Do whatever he asks, and you'll be insulated from the scrutiny that will ensue if the venture is unsuccessful. If you follow the recommended procedure and it works, you'll likely get credit for the accomplishment. But if you disobey his directions, you'll leave him with little choice other than to cut you—even if the result is successful. As the person who is hired by the owner to direct the team, it is the head coach who is ultimately held responsible for winning football games. In order to perform his job, he needs to be able to trust the players to execute his tactics in the designed fashion. Otherwise, his strategies become worthless and the team loses respect for his leadership capability. If

Table 12-6. Brett Favre's 1994 Passing Performance

Year	Att	Comp	Comp%	Yards	YPA	TD	INT	Rating
1994	582	363	62.4	3882	6.67	33	14	90.7

a player cannot comply with the wishes of his coach, then it makes no sense to retain that athlete's services. The T.J. Rubley incident served as a shocking reminder to all Packers' players of their coach's policy.

With a new and more practical understanding between himself and Brett Favre, Holmgren had high hopes for his quarterback in 1994. Favre did not disappoint. The fourth-year signal caller finished second in the NFC in both touchdowns and passer rating and led Green Bay to 382 points (fourth in the league) (table 12-6).

The Green Bay defense also had an excellent season in 1994, finishing fifth in the NFL in points allowed and ranking high in most other categories. Once again, though, the Packers had to finish fast to secure a playoff spot. Green Bay ended the year with three straight wins and another 9–7 record.

Given that the Packers possessed the league's fourth-most prolific offense and fifth-best defense—enabling them to outscore their opponents by the margin of 382–287—it would have been reasonable to expect an eleven- or twelve-win season for the team. However, the offense was not as efficient as it may have appeared to be (table 12-7). Though Favre had a very good year, and the club scored plenty of points, three offensive statistics revealed specific problem areas that ultimately prevented the Packers from realizing their maximum potential.

Green Bay's halfback, Edgar Bennett, had been a fourth-round selection out of Florida State in 1992. Though he had performed to the best of his abilities as a starter in 1993 and 1994, he was, in reality, a journeyman runner with pedestrian speed and power. Consequently, the Packers' ground game was deficient.

The club's mediocre yards per pass attempt was somewhat shocking. Favre had the talent to engage defenses with both a short, precision passing attack and the long ball. And Sterling Sharpe (ninety-four catches in 1994) was one of the most dangerous receivers in the NFL. Yet Green Bay did not aggressively attack their opponents with a downfield passing game, as indicated by the team's below-average yards-per-pass-attempt figure of 6.5 despite their very high completion percentage of 61.6 (see table 12-8). Yards per attempt is dependent on completion percentage and length of passes. If the Packers were well above the NFL average in the first of those categories, and if their YPA figure was still well below average, they had to be operating an extremely

Table 12-7. Green Bay Packers' Offense, 1994

Category	Number	League Ranking out of 28 Teams
Rushing yards	1543	20
Average per carry	3.7	12
Yards per pass att	6.5	21

Table 12-8. 1994 NFL Passing Statistics (teams listed in order of completion percentage)

Team	Completion Pct	YPA	YPA League Rank	Average per Completion
San Francisco	70.3	8.5	1	12.2
New Orleans	64.3	7.1	5	11.0
Buffalo	63.1	6.9	11	10.9
Dallas	62.9	7.7	2	12.3
Miami	62.5	7.2	4	11.6
Denver	62.0	7.0	8	11.3
Green Bay	61.6	6.5	21	10.6
NFL averages	58.0	6.8	—	11.7

conservative passing scheme. One look at Green Bay's modest average of 10.6 yards per completion, as compared to the league norm of 11.7, confirms that fact.

With both a subpar running game and a conservative, inefficient passing attack, the Packers still scored 382 points. How was this possible? And how could an offense that ranked fourth in the NFL—mediocre statistical performances notwithstanding—have been the primary cause of the team's lower-than-expected victory total?

The answer is, the team's offensive shortcomings led to a highly inconsistent Packers' attack that exploded to produce incredible point totals in some games but struggled mightily in others, causing several losses. Oddly enough, the quality of the defenses that Green Bay encountered in 1994 seemed to have little to do with their offensive fortunes. At times, the team scored points in bunches against premium defenses, then floundered against mediocre opponents.

The Packers erupted for thirty or more points seven times during the 1994 season. They earned a 5–2 record in those games and scored an aggregate total of 237 points (almost thirty-four a game). Included in those offensive outbursts were one game against Dallas (a 42–31 loss) and two against Chicago (40–3 and 33–6 victories). The Cowboys' defense finished third in the league that year by permitting an average of 15.5 points per game. The Bears finished ninth by allowing 19.2 points per contest. Against the teams listed in table 12-9, however—each of whom finished near the middle of the league in points allowed—the Packers managed a grand total of 63 points in five games (an average of 12.6) and lost all but one of the contests.

It seems it was feast or famine for Green Bay's offense in 1994, the result of which was a far less effective unit than one would have expected given the total number of points they produced. An offensive explosion consummating in a 40–3 blowout win (such as they enjoyed over the Bears) was still worth only one victory in the standings. Those extra points were useless in a week when Green Bay struggled to score. Had the Packers' attack more consistently approached their twenty-four-point average—as opposed to the wildly fluctuating performances they delivered—Green Bay would almost certainly have won a couple of the games they lost when their defense held opponents in the ten- to fourteen-point range (see table 12-9). In reality, however, that

Table 12-9. Green Bay Packers, 1994 Offensive Outputs of 16 Points or Fewer

Date	Opponent	Final Score (Packers' total listed first)	Result
9/4	Minnesota	16–10	Win
9/11	Miami	14–24	Loss
9/18	Philadelphia	7–13	Loss
10/2	New England	16–17	Loss
10/20	Minnesota	10–13	Loss

was not the case. Hence, the Packers' somewhat disappointing 9–7 finish, as opposed to the more appropriate 11–5 record one might have expected in light of their superior point differential.

Unfortunately, Green Bay's erratic offense was unproductive in the 1994 playoffs. The Packers managed a mere two touchdowns and twenty-five points in two games. Only a remarkable performance by the defense saved the team from ouster in their opening-round tussle with the Detroit Lions. Green Bay held Lions star running back Barry Sanders—who had gained 1,883 yards and averaged 5.7 yards per carry during the regular season—to the mind-boggling total of minus-one yard on thirteen attempts. In a defensive struggle punctuated by field goals, Green Bay slipped by Detroit 16–12. In Texas the next week, however, Troy Aikman and the Dallas Cowboys ended the Packers' season by trouncing the Green and Gold 35–9.

Green Bay's disappointing offensive performance in the postseason proved extremely disconcerting to Holmgren. He immediately began to reevaluate both the team's personnel and his own offensive scheme. The supposedly potent Packers had far too many breakdowns for their troubles to have been just coincidental. The problems had to be addressed.

Finding a more talented halfback was a priority. But since Green Bay had only one selection (the thirty-second slot) in the first sixty-four picks of the NFL draft—the result of previous trades—and since prime backs are rarely available in free agency, that prospect appeared to be unlikely.

Correcting the systemic deficiencies in the passing game, however, certainly seemed feasible. Part of the problem, Holmgren believed, was that Favre was not distributing the ball in a proportionate fashion. Favre appeared to prefer certain receivers and particular patterns, making the Packers' passing game somewhat predictable. That, in addition to the team's apparent aversion to deeper passing routes, kept Green Bay's aerial attack from reaching its full potential. After working with Favre and quarterbacks coach Steve Mariucci to remedy these flaws, Holmgren believed the offense would be much more consistent and harder to defense in 1995.

It was.

The Packers totaled 404 points in 1995 and had far fewer games where the offense disappeared. Green Bay (which averaged twenty-five points a game that year) scored

Table 12-10. Brett Favre's 1995 Passing Performance

Year	Att	Comp	Comp%	Yards	YPA	TD	INT	Rating
1995	570	359	63.0	4413*	7.74	38*	13	99.5

*Led league

fewer than twenty-four points on only four occasions, as opposed to the eight times they did it in 1994. This newfound consistency helped the Packers break through the nine-win barrier that had defined the team for the past three seasons. Green Bay finished 11–5 and captured the NFC's Central Division title for the first time since 1972!

Brett Favre had the finest season of his career to that point (table 12-10). The twenty-six-year-old quarterback led the league in touchdowns and passing yardage and won the NFL's Most Valuable Player award.

Amazingly, Favre, Holmgren, and the Packers were able to produce their gaudy offensive numbers despite two major impediments—one new and one old. First, Sterling Sharpe—Favre's favorite receiver—was forced into early retirement with a neck injury. Sharpe did not play at all in 1995. Second, the ground game was every bit as inept as it had been for the past several years, accounting for the paltry total of 1,428 yards (twenty-sixth in the thirty-team league) and averaging only 3.5 yards per carry.

Significant contributions from two former backups, however, mitigated against the negative effects of Green Bay's troubled running game and the loss of their star receiver. First, Mark Chmura, a lowly sixth-round selection out of Boston College in 1992, emerged as a legitimate threat at the tight end position. Ever since Jackie Harris had been lost to the Tampa Bay Buccaneers after the 1993 season, the Packers had lacked a quality tight end who could both block and catch. Chmura was originally drafted for the purpose of being the team's long snapper. He was not considered a candidate for a starting position. But Chmura's size (6′5″, 245 pounds) created a large presence in the secondary, essential for a tight end, and he had a keen sense of the opponents' defensive schemes. This awareness allowed him to regularly penetrate the seams of a zone defense and to get open much more frequently than anticipated. Favre was able to hit Chmura with numerous "check-off" passes and delay routes (see table 12-11). These completions made Green Bay more productive on third-down plays and, as a result, kept many drives alive.

Another pleasant surprise for the Packers that year was the play of wide receiver Robert Brooks, a 1992 third-round draft choice from the University of South Carolina, who had a tremendous season as Sterling Sharpe's replacement. Brooks had played well as Green Bay's third receiver in 1994, but no one expected the awesome performance he delivered in 1995. Not only did Brooks eclipse Sharpe's reception numbers

Table 12-11. Mark Chmura's 1995 Tight End Performance

Year	Catches	Yards	Average	TDs
1995	54	679	12.6	7

Table 12-12. Robert Brooks's 1995 Wide Receiver Performance

Year	Catches	Yards	Average	TDs
1995	102	1497	14.7	13

from the previous season (ninety-four), but his average per catch was almost three yards greater (14.7–11.9) as well (table 12-12).

As a team, the Packers soared from twenty-first in the league with a 6.5 yards-per-pass-attempt figure in 1994 to second with a 7.7 mark in 1995. Green Bay's average per completion also increased dramatically. The club gained 12.2 yards per catch (as compared to the 10.6 they managed in 1994) and finished well above the NFL average of 11.6.

Though many Packers players and coaches collaborated in an effort to advance the team's passing game, Holmgren, Favre, and Steve Mariucci were clearly the most consequential individuals. Their dedicated off-season commitment was instrumental in producing a more effective and consistent Green Bay aerial attack. Favre—whose yards per attempt climbed from 6.67 in 1994 to 7.74 (second in the NFL) in 1995—genuinely blossomed as a quarterback that season, due to both his diligence and, curiously, the circumstances created by Sterling Sharpe's injury.

"In some ways, it was a blessing that he [Favre] had to use all of his players," Steve Mariucci said, "spread the ball around and really become efficient in the system rather than try and get the ball to Sterling so much. Even though Robert Brooks caught a lot of passes, the other players chipped in more so than the previous three years. Brett became a more complete player in this system because of it and truly became the leader of this offensive team."

Green Bay opened the 1995 playoffs against the Atlanta Falcons. The game began ominously for the Packers, as halfback Eric Metcalf took a Jeff George pass and streaked sixty-five yards for an Atlanta touchdown in the game's first three minutes. But Green Bay's defense, which had finished fourth in the league that season (314 points allowed), stiffened, and the Falcons' offense soon wilted in the presence of a daunting pass rush. Despite the fact that defensive end Reggie White missed the game with an injury, the Packers still managed to apply great pressure on George and finished the game with three sacks. Holmgren and defensive coordinator Fritz Shurmur engaged a strategy that the Packers had utilized against the Falcons in 1994—a 3–3–5 alignment predicated on numerous blitz packages that were designed to confuse Atlanta's blocking schemes. "We were a little short of speed rushers with Reggie out," Shurmur said. "And it kind of disrupted their rhythm a little." Green Bay also held Falcons running back Craig "Ironhead" Heyward to twenty-one yards on nine carries. This forced George into many second-and-long and third-and-long predicaments that afforded the Packers the luxury of ignoring the run to concentrate on harassing the Atlanta signal caller.

Meanwhile, Favre enjoyed an efficient, workmanlike day against the Atlanta defense. The MVP quarterback completed twenty-four of thirty-five passes for 199 yards and two touchdowns. Running back Edgar Bennett chipped in with one of the best games of his career. He was able to produce 108 yards on twenty-four carries against a Falcons' run defense that had finished ninth in the league. Green Bay won the game 37–20 and advanced to face Holmgren's old team, the San Francisco 49ers.

The San Francisco game marked the return of Mike Holmgren to the Bay Area for the first time since he had left to become head coach of the Packers back in 1992. The 49ers were the defending Super Bowl champions, and a victory by the Packers would do much to bolster Green Bay's confidence in their quest to become legitimate title contenders, not to mention the fact that it would also propel them into the NFC championship game.

Heading into the contest, the media was having a field day with the "Holmgren coming home" angle. In the process of one interview, Holmgren made a slightly controversial comment. When queried as to Green Bay's chances on Saturday (game day), he simply said, "We're going to win it all. Why not."

Needless to say, the quote was posted in the 49ers' locker room about six minutes later. San Francisco—by far the most dominant team of the last two decades, and the defending Super Bowl champions—now had bulletin board material to inspire them. To add fuel to the fire, quarterback Brett Favre—never known to be timid—publicly supported his coach's comments. "I'm glad he said it," Favre remarked, "because I think he believes it. He wouldn't have said it last year, and in the back of his mind I bet George Seifert [the 49ers' coach] is a little worried." The gamesmanship was on, and the contest figured to be an all-out war.

Holmgren and Fritz Shurmur had one concern foremost on their minds when planning to defend the Super Bowl champs: "Cover number eighty"—a reference to 49ers' all-world wide receiver Jerry Rice. During the season, Rice set an all-time NFL record by accumulating 1,848 receiving yards. He and San Francisco quarterback Steve Young formed the most lethal offensive combination in the league. Holmgren, being very familiar with the San Francisco attack, decided that the best strategy to contain Rice was to be physical—to deny him the freedom to come off the line unabated.

Offensively, Holmgren and coordinator Sherm Lewis had plenty to worry about. The 49ers possessed the league's finest defensive unit. Take a peek in table 12-13 at a few of San Francisco's exceptional defensive accomplishments that season.

Table 12-13. San Francisco 49ers, 1995 Defensive Statistics

Category	Number	NFL Rank out of 30 Teams
Points allowed	258	2
Rushing yards allowed	1061	1
Rushing average against	3.0	1
Passing yards per att. against	5.9	1
Interceptions	26	1

The Packers had their work cut out for them. But they also had Mike Holmgren and Brett Favre, two of the fiercest competitors in the game. And Holmgren knew the 49ers better than anyone.

Just as it had the week before, the game started out precariously for the Packers. Green Bay took the opening kickoff and embarked on a seven-minute, forty-eight-yard drive that stalled at the San Francisco twenty-seven-yard line. On fourth down, Chris Jacke's forty-four-yard field goal attempt was blocked, and the 49ers had collected the first big break of the game.

But San Francisco's luck didn't last long. On the 49ers' first play, running back Adam Walker fumbled a swing pass. Packers' cornerback Craig Newsome picked up the loose football and scampered thirty-one yards for a touchdown. Shortly thereafter, Green Bay advanced sixty-two yards in four plays, the last of which was a three-yard Favre touchdown pass to reserve tight end Keith Jackson that gave the Packers a 14–0 lead.

While Green Bay was marching up and down the field on San Francisco's vaunted defense, the 49ers' offense was having little if any success against the Packers' defensive unit. Green Bay was easily able to subdue the 49ers' ground game, which, in combination with the sizable advantage the Packers had built in the first quarter, forced San Francisco quarterback Steve Young into a one-dimensional aerial attack. This effectively enhanced Green Bay's already formidable pass rush and made Young's task that much more difficult.

Early in the second period, after thwarting another San Francisco drive, Green Bay blew the game wide open. Mark Chmura's thirteen-yard touchdown reception from Brett Favre culminated a seven-play, seventy-two-yard effort that gave the Packers an insurmountable 21–0 advantage. Green Bay proceeded to defeat the 49ers 27–17.

The ten-point advantage at game's end was not indicative of the ease with which Green Bay handled San Francisco. Although San Francisco outgained the Packers 395–368, they needed twenty-eight more plays to achieve their scant twenty-seven-yard edge. As a result, the 49ers averaged only 4.6 yards per offensive play as compared to Green Bay's 6.4. Steve Young—who unleashed a playoff-record sixty-five passes but accumulated only 328 yards—averaged just 5.05 yards per pass attempt. That figure was almost 30 percent below his regular season mark of 7.16. He was also sacked three times, hurried repeatedly, and fumbled once. Jerry Rice caught eleven passes for 117 yards, but four of his catches came in the last three minutes, when Green Bay—comfortably ahead 27–10—was conceding short completions. And considering that San Francisco had attempted sixty-five passes, eleven receptions was not the phenomenal feat it may have appeared to be. Rice's 10.6 average per catch was—like Young's average per pass—30 percent below his seasonal norm (15.1). One final embarrassment for the 49ers was the production of starting halfback Derek Loville, who was held to five yards on eight carries. Brett Favre, on the other hand, was magnificent for the Packers. He completed twenty-one of twenty-eight passes (to seven different receivers) for 299 yards (a 10.7 average per attempt) and two touchdowns. He dominated San

Francisco's highly ranked pass defense and, along with Green Bay's defense, was clearly the difference in the game.

"Their coach guaranteed victory and made good on it," said 49ers' defensive tackle Dana Stubblefield. "We busted our [butts] and they came into our backyard and beat us. It's tough to explain."

The Packers' victory celebration was short-lived, however. The following week, in the NFC championship game in Dallas, the Cowboys ruined Green Bay's hopes for a Super Bowl berth by defeating the Packers, 38–27. As well as Green Bay's defense had played against the 49ers, no one expected the mediocre performance they delivered against Dallas. The Packers applied very little pressure on Cowboys' quarterback Troy Aikman and allowed running back Emmitt Smith to ramble for 150 yards on the ground. Brett Favre threw for more than three hundred yards and two touchdowns, but he also suffered two costly interceptions. Green Bay's lack of confidence in the ground game (twelve attempts for forty-eight yards) gave Dallas's defenders little reason to worry about the run. This made Favre's job that much more difficult, and the burden eventually took its toll in the form of turnovers.

The loss to the Cowboys marked the third straight year that Dallas had defeated Green Bay in the playoffs (1993–1995). But as disheartening as the defeat was for the young Packers, the fact that they were competitive with the Cowboys and had vanquished the 49ers gave the club hope for the future. Green Bay had shown the world that they were a force to be reckoned with and that they were likely on the verge of greatness. "This team *will* win a championship," said an undiscouraged Reggie White.

During the Packers' postseason evaluations—performed annually by Holmgren and his coaching staff just after each season—it was obvious, for the second straight year, that the team required more talent in the backfield. If Green Bay was to become a serious threat for the Super Bowl, they desperately needed to take some of the pressure off Favre by developing a more reliable ground attack. "It's important," Holmgren said. "You're not going to go as far as you would like without a running game. I know that. You need balance. The passing game helps set up the run here [a reference to the West Coast offense]; I believe that. But people play a little softer against us, taking away some of our passing effectiveness at times."

The problem for the Packers was how to acquire the back(s) they needed to upgrade their offense. Skilled running backs were not on sale at Sears—two for $9.99—and they were not standing on street corners, just waiting for NFL scouts to sign them.

In the 1996 draft, two highly touted running backs were available—Lawrence Phillips, from Nebraska, and Heisman Trophy–winner Eddie George, from Ohio State. It was doubtful, however, that either would last until the Packers' selection at the twenty-seventh spot in the first round. They didn't. Phillips was taken sixth by St. Louis, and George went fourteenth to Houston. Green Bay opted for tackle John Michels, from USC, with their selection in round one, and later chose running back Chris Darkins, from Minnesota, in the fourth round. Darkins, though, at 5' 11", 208 pounds, was slightly built and was more suited for duty as a third-down, pass-catching back. The Packers would have to look elsewhere to try and remedy their running game woes.

Holmgren decided to search the existing Green Bay roster for possible solutions to the dilemma. Perhaps there was a player with indistinct talent that had been overlooked by the coaching staff. It was a long shot, but since there was little else to do at the time, Holmgren felt it was worth investigating. He began to scrutinize all of his younger backs to see if there were any potential answers to his problem.

A third-year player by the name of Dorsey Levens appeared to be the only conceivable option at the halfback position. Levens had been Green Bay's fifth-round selection out of Georgia Tech in the 1994 draft. He had been quite productive in college. Fast and strong for his size (6′ 1″, 235 pounds), Levens often devastated the Yellow Jackets' ACC opponents. Unfortunately, he was also injury prone, which was one of the reasons why he had lasted so long in the draft. Upon his arrival in Green Bay, Levens had been placed at fullback. But he had only borderline size to play that position, and he lacked the necessary mind-set to function in a power-blocking role. Consequently, his development was slowed. In 1995, however, Levens had been given some reps in a reserve capacity at halfback. There, he began to show glimpses of the ability he had displayed in college—running by linebackers and plowing over defensive backs.

Fullback William Henderson, from North Carolina, was Green Bay's third-round pick in 1995. Massive and physical, at 6′ 2″, 248 pounds, Henderson *was* a true fullback. He had a lead blocker's mentality and could find the hole and make it bigger. He was also an adequate pass receiver. Henderson seemed to be a reasonable candidate to become the team's full-time blocking back in the near future.

After running a scenario through in his head, Holmgren got excited. If these two backs could compete—even if it was just at an average level—Holmgren believed Green Bay's rushing attack would be enhanced in two significant ways. Levens's move to halfback would add the missing speed and power to that position and, at the same time, would clear the way for Henderson to take over Levens's old fullback spot— effectively strengthening Green Bay's blocking. The key to the inspired plan was Levens. Holmgren was almost positive that Henderson could handle the fullback responsibilities. Levens's chances for success, however, were much tougher to gauge. Although Holmgren had confidence in the young running back, he was far from certain that Levens could pull it off.

Fortunately, both Henderson *and* Levens succeeded.

Green Bay gained 1,838 yards rushing in 1996—a 29-percent increase from their 1,428 yard total in 1995—and averaged 4.0 yards per carry for the first time in seven seasons (table 12-14).

Levens, playing mostly at halfback, carried the ball 121 times for 566 yards—averaging 4.7 yards per attempt. With Levens's speed to stretch the defense sideline to sideline, the middle of the field was opened up for Edgar Bennett, who enjoyed the best season of his career by carrying 222 times for 899 yards (a 4.0 average). Henderson

Table 12-14. Green Bay's 1990–96 Rushing Statistics

Year	Average	Year	Average
1996	4.0	1992	3.7
1995	3.5	1991	3.6
1994	3.7	1990	3.9
1993	3.6		

was every bit the pulverizing blocker Holmgren anticipated. He also caught twenty-seven passes out of the backfield. Holmgren's resourcefulness had paid off. He finally had a backfield worthy of comparison to the ones he enjoyed with the 49ers, where he employed bruising fullback Tom Rathman and multitalented halfback Roger Craig.

The Packers' improved rushing attack had a ripple effect on the rest of the team. As expected, Brett Favre's job was made easier. Opponents had to be more vigilant in their defense of the running game and could no longer concentrate solely on stopping the pass. As a result, Green Bay led the NFL in touchdown passes and scoring (see below). The Packers' defense also benefited. The invigorated ground game produced more first downs and longer drives for Green Bay's offense. The team jumped from ninth in the league in first downs in 1995 to second in 1996. This kept Green Bay's defenders fresher and contributed to the achievements of their league-leading defense.

With an effective rushing game, a lethal passing attack, and a ferocious defense, the Packers dominated the NFL in 1996. They finished in the top five of the league in almost every major statistical category (table 12-15), more than doubled their opponents' point production (456–210), and won the Central Division with a 13–3 record that tied Denver for the best mark in the NFL.

Table 12-15. Green Bay Packers' 1996 Statistics (30 teams)

Category	Number	Rank
Offense		
Points scored	456	1
Passing yards	3938	5
Passing yards per attempt	7.2	7
Touchdown passes	39	1
Interception percentage	2.37	4
Defense		
Points allowed	210	1
Rushing yards allowed	1460	4
Average per carry	3.5	4
Passing yards allowed	2740	1
Passing yards per attempt	5.4*	1
Total yards allowed	4156	1
Touchdown passes allowed	12	3
Interceptions	26	T-2[†]

*19.4 percent better than league average, and 10 percent better than next closest team.
[†]T indicates tie in ranking

In deference to their regular season superiority, the Packers' received a first-round bye in the 1996 playoffs. In the second round, they again met the San Francisco 49ers. This time, however, the game was played at the "frozen tundra."

Aided by the stunning punt-return exploits of Desmond Howard (who set an NFL record for single-season punt-return yardage that year with 875 yards), Green Bay dismantled the once-fearsome 49ers 35–14. In the opening quarter, Howard took the first 49ers' punt and sped seventy-one yards for a touchdown, giving the Packers a 7–0 lead. Later that same quarter, his forty-six-yard return set up a four-yard Brett Favre–to–Andre Rison touchdown pass that increased the advantage to 14–0.

Favre attempted only fifteen passes on the day, connecting on eleven of them. For the first time since he had been with Green Bay, he felt relaxed in a playoff game. Armed with a capable running attack, he did not feel compelled to force the issue with risky passes in order to move the club. "I'm doing what I'm coached to do, and I'm doing it well," he said. "If I heard Mike [Holmgren] say it once, I've heard him say it a million times: 'Let the system work for you.' If I would do that, I would complete every pass."

In the NFC championship game at Lambeau Field, the Carolina Panthers were the Packers' opponent. An expansion team from 1995, Carolina had quickly ascended to prominence by taking advantage of the league's lenient spending policies relative to free-agent acquisitions and by making astute use of the extra draft selections allocated to new teams. They engineered a 12–4 record in 1996, and their defense finished a close second to the Packers in points allowed (218).

Carolina's defensive strategy was predicated on a deceptive new blitz package—invented by their head coach, Dom Capers—that relied heavily on zone pass coverage. The Panthers employed a sneaky yet ingenious system, applied from their base 3–4 defense, that frequently engaged a linebacker or defensive back to rush the quarterback while a lineman dropped into zone coverage. Generally, teams that blitzed utilized man-coverage in the secondary, and it was unheard of to make use of a lineman in the defensive backfield. Opponents were befuddled. Quarterbacks had great difficulty identifying the "hot" receivers who would be left unguarded as a consequence of the impending blitz. Often, a defensive lineman would seemingly appear out of nowhere to defense a quick check-off pass. Offensive linemen were also confused. They could never seem to anticipate which defenders would be blitzing. As a result, opponents' pass-blocking schemes were completely disrupted, and Carolina recorded sixty sacks in 1996. The Panthers' defense was susceptible to the run at times, but their proficiency against the pass more than compensated. The star of Carolina's defense was linebacker Kevin Greene, who led the NFL with 14.5 sacks.

Holmgren had a bold yet somewhat conflicting offensive strategy to use against the Panthers. First, he wanted to mix plays to keep Carolina's defense guessing and off balance. This would substantially diminish the capability of any blitzing defense. At the same time, however, he hoped to be able to use the Panthers' aggressiveness to the Packers' advantage. As with any attacking defense, Holmgren knew that their greatest asset could also be their Achilles' heel. When the time was right, he wanted to lure the Panthers into traps and expose the inherent weaknesses of their daring scheme.

The temperature at game time was three degrees. The wind chill was seventeen below zero. The frigid conditions, though, didn't stop the warm-weather Panthers from striking first. Carolina quarterback Kerry Collins hit fullback Howard Griffith with a three-yard touchdown pass late in the first quarter to give the Panthers a 7–0 lead.

But the Packers owned the second period. A spectacular twenty-nine-yard reception by Dorsey Levens in the corner of the end zone capped an explosive, four-play, seventy-three-yard drive that evened the score at seven. After a twenty-two-yard field goal by John Kasay put Carolina back ahead, 10–7, Green Bay drove seventy-two yards and took the lead on a six-yard Favre touchdown pass to wide receiver Antonio Freeman. An interception by Packers' cornerback Tyrone Williams on the ensuing Panthers' possession led to a thirty-one-yard Chris Jacke field goal. Green Bay led 17–10 at the intermission.

In the second half, Green Bay finished the Panthers, and Holmgren's game plan was the key to the victory. Holmgren found the perfect opportunity to use Carolina's overzealousness to the Packers' benefit.

Leading 20–13 late in the third quarter, Green Bay anticipated a fierce Panthers' blitz on a second-and-seven play from their own thirty-yard line. At that moment, Holmgren called for one of the trap plays he had hoped to utilize during the game, to exploit Carolina's aggressive tendencies. Green Bay would run a screen pass, attempting to draw the six or seven pass rushers close enough to Favre to give the receiver plenty of room to maneuver after the catch. If everything went as planned, the Packers could have a big play. As Favre dropped back, the Panthers swarmed after him. Just before the pass rush reached him, he lofted the ball to halfback Dorsey Levens in the flat. Escorted by several Green Bay linemen, Levens raced into the emptied Panthers' secondary en route to a sixty-six-yard gain that took him to the Carolina four-yard line.

"Once I cut back and the linemen cut those guys out, it was just open field," Levens said after the game. "They [Carolina] just called the wrong play at the wrong time."

Left guard Aaron Taylor added, "We practiced this week running screens against the blitz and that's pretty much how we picked it up. And it's amazing what happens when you do things right."

On first and goal from the four, Edgar Bennett's touchdown run consummated a three-play, seventy-three-yard drive that put the Packers comfortably ahead, 27–13. A twenty-eight-yard field goal by Chris Jacke in the fourth quarter made the final score 30–13. The Packers had crushed the Panthers and ravaged their revered defense in the process. Clearly instrumental in the triumph was Holmgren's impeccable game plan. Carolina's defense was perplexed for much of the contest, never sure what type of play was coming next. Green Bay's offense accumulated the staggering total of 479 yards— 201 of which came on the ground. Edgar Bennett finished with twenty-five carries for ninety-nine yards while Dorsey Levens added eighty-eight on only ten tries. Brett Favre, who threw for 292 yards and two scores, was sacked only once in twenty-nine pass attempts by the discombobulated Panthers' pass rush. Green Bay's defense, meanwhile, held Carolina to 251 total yards, limiting Panthers' running backs to only forty-five yards on fourteen carries. After a powerful performance, the Packers were NFC champions, and they headed to the Super Bowl for the first time since the 1967 season.

The New England Patriots, another upstart club that had climbed the ladder of success under the auspices of Bill Parcells, were the Packers' opponents in Super Bowl XXXI in New Orleans, Louisiana. The Patriots had finished the 1996 season with an 11–5 slate and, ironically, had defeated the other 1995 expansion franchise, the Jacksonville Jaguars, for the right to play for the Lombardi trophy. Just four years prior, the Patriots were the NFL's worst team, sporting a 2–14 record. But Parcells had lifted them from the dark side, and infused the demoralized organization with confidence and tenacity.

New England led the AFC in scoring with 419 points in 1996, and their chief weapons were halfback Curtis Martin and quarterback Drew Bledsoe. Martin rushed for well over eleven hundred yards, while Bledsoe accounted for twenty-seven touchdown passes and 4,086 yards. Mike Holmgren decided that Green Bay's defensive strategy would be to try and contain Martin early, forcing Bledsoe to beat them while the Packers mounted a furious pass rush. Martin was a fine back, but he had averaged only 3.6 yards per carry during the season. That fact, combined with the knowledge that Green Bay's fourth-ranked run defense had been playing so well in the playoffs, gave Holmgren supreme confidence that the Packers could handle New England's ground game. Bledsoe was a talented fourth-year quarterback who had enjoyed the finest season of his young career to that point in 1996. He had two glaring weaknesses, however—a lack of mobility and poor decision making under pass-rush pressure. Since Bledsoe did not have the agility or speed to escape the pocket when harassed— a tactic that creates more time for receivers to get open—he tended to force the ball into coverage at times. As a result, he was prone to interceptions, of which Holmgren and the Packers hoped to benefit.

Offensively, Holmgren simply wanted his club to keep doing what they had done all season—establish the ground game (specifically targeting the middle of New England's smallish defense) and give Favre the chance to create big plays with his magical right arm.

The two-week layoff between the championship game and Super Bowl was a hot topic with the media in New Orleans, everyone clamoring to know how the teams would handle the different schedule. "We put the bulk of our game plan in at home [in Green Bay], and we came down here knowing there are other things for the team to do and it would be disruptive," Holmgren said. "We polished up what we had. We added a few new wrinkles, and then we backed off a little with them physically. It's something you have to think about [easy days in practice]. I think our pace has been good, and hopefully the players will be real fresh on Sunday. That's my goal." For the Packers, there was little change from their normal program. Obviously, there were seven extra days between games, but the club was somewhat accustomed to the more relaxed preparatory routine mandated by the off week. Holmgren's squads rarely practiced that long or that hard, especially during the season. "I don't need to bang all the time to see how tough the guys are," Holmgren said. And now—with the biggest game of his life quickly approaching—he saw no need to deviate from his philosophy.

Green Bay struck first in the Super Bowl. After forcing a New England punt on the opening possession of the game, Brett Favre hit a streaking Andre Rison for a fifty-four-yard score on the Packers' second play from scrimmage. For Mike Holmgren, the touchdown was a much-deserved dividend from his commitment—several years earlier—to allow Favre the play-calling freedom he needed to prosper in the NFL. As the teams lined up for the play, Favre noticed that the Patriots' safeties, Willie Clay and Lawyer Milloy, were closer to the line of scrimmage than usual—indicating a potential blitz. Favre checked off from the original down-and-out pass to Mark Chmura. Believing that Rison could easily get deep on New England cornerback Otis Smith—who would have little or no help from his safeties—Favre called for a "home-run" post pattern by his speedy receiver. "It wasn't the smoothest [audible]," Favre said after the game, "but it worked beautifully."

After a Chris Jacke field goal increased the Packers' lead to 10–0, the Patriots countered with two Drew Bledsoe touchdown passes in the next four minutes. The first came on a one-yard toss to H-back Keith Byars that was set up by an interference call on Green Bay cornerback Craig Newsome. On the following New England possession, a forty-four-yard reception by wide receiver Terry Glenn led to a four-yard touchdown pass from Bledsoe to tight end Ben Coates. After a thrilling and eventful first quarter, the Patriots led 14–10.

Green Bay was stunned, but the Packers reacted like a champion fighter who suddenly has his nose bloodied, scoring seventeen unanswered second-quarter points to quell the Patriots' spirit and reclaim the lead. The highlight of the resurgence was an eighty-one-yard touchdown pass to Antonio Freeman that was partially attributable to another Favre audible. Green Bay lined up in their three-wide-receiver formation. The Patriots, however, apparently unaware that the extra wide-out had entered the game, did not deploy a nickel cornerback to counter the Packers' alignment. In an obvious mismatch, rookie safety Lawyer Milloy was left to cover Freeman in the slot. Favre, fully aware of the golden opportunity and sensing another Patriots' blitz, audiblized to maximum pass protection and then hit a wide-open Freeman for an easy touchdown pass down the right sideline to give Green Bay a 27–14 halftime lead. "A safety on me, playing bump-and-run?" said a disbelieving Freeman following the game. "I liked my chances."

Midway through the third quarter, Curtis Martin—who had been stymied up to that point in the game—broke through for an eighteen-yard touchdown run that cut the Packers' advantage to 27–21. Seventeen seconds later, however—with Patriots' fans still rejoicing in the stands—the celebration was curtailed.

Desmond Howard (who won game MVP honors and set a Super Bowl record with 244 return yards) brought the ensuing kickoff back ninety-nine yards for a touchdown. Green Bay's coaching staff had noticed that the Patriots often kicked off to their opponents' right side. So they stationed Howard on that side to return the kick. It was a minor adaptation to a somewhat insignificant tendency, but it paid off in a major way. After a two-point conversion, the Packers led 35–21.

With a fourteen-point lead and just about eighteen minutes remaining in the contest, Green Bay released Reggie White and their vaunted pass rush. In the first half, New England had done a commendable job of restraining the Packers' pressure, despite the fact that their running game was almost useless. Curtis Martin (eleven carries for forty-two yards on the day) had very little success against Green Bay other than his eighteen-yard touchdown jaunt in the third quarter. Now, however, New England faced double trouble in their attempt to protect Drew Bledsoe. In addition to a feeble ground game, the Patriots trailed by two touchdowns with little over a quarter left to play. They would be forced to throw on almost every down—and the Packers knew it. These were the perfect conditions for Green Bay's defense to prosecute Holmgren's game plan and pressure Bledsoe. They were determined to take full advantage of the situation.

In the final period, a tormented Bledsoe threw two of his four interceptions, was caught for two of the five Packers' sacks on the day (Reggie White finished with a Super Bowl–record three), and never crossed midfield in four possessions. The score remained unchanged as the Packers worked the clock by pounding away at the undersized New England front seven with Bennett and Levens. When the stadium timer reached zero, the Green Bay Packers and Mike Holmgren had claimed the Lombardi trophy as Super Bowl champions.

In the biggest game of his career to that point, Brett Favre completed fourteen of twenty-seven passes for 245 yards and two touchdowns. He incurred no interceptions and averaged more than nine yards per pass attempt. Now a polished passer and a world champion, it was obvious that the twenty-seven-year-old Favre had come a long way since the rebellious, impatient days of his youth. When a player works to improve his game and advance his team as energetically as Favre had, his coach cannot help but feel proud. As Holmgren speaks about the characteristics and development of his prized signal caller, he seems to talk with an emotional bent, as if describing the merits of his own son.

"Brett is as fiery and competitive an athlete as I've ever been associated with," Holmgren says. "He's excitable. He rejoices, obviously, when something good happens. He gets mad when something bad happens. Yet, during the course of a game, particularly in the last few seasons, he has shown the ability to maintain his composure and continue to play at a very high level. He can beat you as a drop-back, conventional passer, or he can beat you as a more unorthodox, break-from-the-pocket passer. Either way, he has the physical tools to win."

Mike Holmgren's constant tinkering with the Packers' offense fine-tuned them into the offensive machine that tore through the NFL in 1996.

Holmgren, as a pass-first, West Coast-offense coach, expected a great deal of his quarterbacks. He regularly tested his signal callers—in writing—on the details of the game plan and their knowledge of the opponent. Of the touchdown audibles that Favre had called in the Super Bowl, Holmgren commented, "There are some formations that we use, that if the other team stays in certain coverages, we can create mismatches. That's one of the goals of any offensive team. Then it's up to the quarterback to take advantage of it. Just creating the situation isn't enough." Favre orchestrated the audibles and the game plan perfectly and passed his field test with flying colors.

Before the Packers' plane even left New Orleans, the celebration in Wisconsin was well under way. Hordes of fans and media were camped at the Green Bay airport, waiting for the team to arrive. When the airliner finally landed and the squad departed into the jubilant throng, Holmgren—ever the coach—already had concerns for the next season. Amid the hoopla and celebrations that were sure to follow, he thought, it would be quite easy for people to shirk their responsibilities and rest on their laurels. Complacency, however, was not in Holmgren's vocabulary. The Green Bay Packers were not going to be a one-year wonder. As leader of the organization, Holmgren took it upon himself to set an example for the team. He immediately canceled several of his radio and television commitments for the next year in order to properly prepare the club for defense of their NFL title and to spend more time with his family.

The players apparently took their coach's cue. Green Bay compiled a 13–3 record in 1997 and played a repeat performance in the Super Bowl. Quarterback John Elway and the Denver Broncos were the Packers' opponents in San Diego, California. In a game where neither all-star quarterback played particularly well, Terrell Davis's one-yard touchdown run in the waning moments gave Denver a 31–24 championship victory.

The last two minutes of Super Bowl XXXII were chaotic and controversial. With the game tied at twenty-four and 1:47 left on the clock, Green Bay had two time-outs remaining. Denver, on the strength of a seventeen-yard Terrell Davis run, had a second-and-goal play from the Green Bay one-yard line. Mike Holmgren, though, was under the impression that it was first and goal. Apparently, there was confusion on the Green Bay sideline as to what down it was because a penalty on the first-and-goal play preceding Davis's run had moved the ball back to the eighteen-yard line. When Davis's run gained seventeen yards (bringing the ball to the one), Green Bay's coaches mistakenly thought it was a first down. Believing it to be first and goal, Holmgren instructed his defense to let Denver score. Thinking Denver could run three plays before scoring a touchdown or attempting an easy field goal, Holmgren was concerned that Green Bay—which could stop the clock only twice—would be left with very little time when they got the ball back. Quickly conceding the seven points appeared to be the only way to give the Packers enough time to mount a game-tying drive. On their final possession, Green Bay advanced the ball to the Broncos' thirty-one-yard line before linebacker John Mobley secured the Denver win by batting away a fourth-down pass intended for tight end Mark Chmura.

Holmgren later admitted that his strategy would have been different had he known it was second down. At that point, the Packers only had to stop the Broncos twice before forcing a likely field-goal try on fourth down, and their two time-outs would have been sufficient to keep the clock from dwindling before they got the ball back. There would have been about 1:20 left for Brett Favre to attempt a comeback. And if Green Bay had been able to hold Denver to three points, it would have been much easier—even with no time-outs—to negotiate a last-minute field goal drive as opposed to having to reach the end zone.

In any event, Holmgren made a mistake. He was, after all, human. Maybe the ghost of Vince Lombardi really was there, as Lombardi, too, made a questionable decision—even though the Packers still won—when he called for a quarterback sneak in the closing moments of the 1967 NFL championship game.

After an 11–5 season in 1998—and a heartbreaking 30–27 wild-card game playoff loss to the San Francisco 49ers—the Mike Holmgren era in Green Bay came to a sad conclusion. Due to player-personnel disagreements with GM Ron Wolf, which had apparently been ongoing, Holmgren no longer believed that he could operate effectively in Green Bay. In order to accomplish his goals, Holmgren felt he needed total control over all football matters.

Green Bay President and CEO Bob Harlan was then thrust into the unenviable position of trying to play peacemaker or choosing between his talented administrators. Holmgren, as coach, had molded the Packers into a dominating force in the NFL; Wolf, as GM, had been a key figure in acquiring the talent required for the club's rise to distinction. Inevitably, there were irreconcilable differences between Wolf and Holmgren, and Harlan refused to grant Holmgren the unilateral authority he demanded. On January 8, 1999, Holmgren ended his dramatic seven-year tenure in Green Bay to take the position of executive vice president of football operations/head coach/general manager of the Seattle Seahawks.

Holmgren had what he so desperately wanted—complete command of his organization and absolute power to make any and all football-related decisions. "As a coach, I think you would always like to have as much control of your personnel as possible," he said at the time of his hiring in Seattle. "I think all of us in this business as coaches would like, if possible, to make all of the decisions to formulate your team. There are guys in the league that are doing it [coach and GM] and doing it well. Obviously, they have a formula, and I have to develop my own formula."

Unfortunately, Holmgren's formula did not prove successful in Seattle. In his four years as the club's head coach/GM (1999–2002), the Seahawks appeared in only one playoff game (a 20–17 loss to Miami in 1999) and had two losing seasons. Their overall record during that time was 31–33. Seattle's disappointing 7–9 finish in 2002 prompted numerous Seahawks' fans to question the wisdom of entrusting two difficult and time-consuming jobs to one individual. Many became convinced that the enormity of the task was detracting from Holmgren's abilities as a head coach. Seattle owner Paul Allen was apparently one of those people. In January of 2003, Holmgren, at the behest of Allen, relinquished his duties as Seahawks' GM to concentrate his efforts in a coaching capacity.

In an ironic twist of fate, the current Packers' head coach, Mike Sherman—a Holmgren disciple who was hired to replace Ray Rhodes (Holmgren's successor) in 2000—now has the full control that Holmgren dreamed of in Green Bay. Ron Wolf retired after the 2000 season, and, due to the timing of his decision, Sherman was essentially forced into assuming the GM responsibilities.

During Mike Holmgren's term as head coach in Green Bay (1992–1998), Packers' football was reinvigorated. His scintillating seven-year record (75–37, .670) and two Super Bowl appearances instilled pride and dignity back into a moribund organization. Though many Packers' fans still bristle over his decision to leave, Holmgren will always be remembered as the audacious young head coach who aspired to greatness in the face of overwhelming adversity. Holmgren's unique talents as a communicator and teacher, along with his tactical expertise, enabled him to consistently develop players to their maximum potential. His attention to detail and devotion to victory earned him the unmitigated respect and commitment of his athletes. All of these qualities combined to produce a phenomenal head coach who could extract superior performances from proficient players on a regular basis.

Hall of Fame coach Bill Walsh concurs with that appraisal of his former assistant. Of Holmgren, Walsh said, "He's very intelligent, an excellent teacher, a great technician, he has command, and he's very well organized.

"He has a way to communicate . . . a way people respond to, and yet, he's strong and firm. He's one of the great coaches in the game."

In the latter part of the twentieth century, before Mike Holmgren arrived in Green Bay, kids in Wisconsin were told that the Super Bowl was "something they used to play when your father was a boy." Under Holmgren, young Packers' fans got a chance to experience, and older fans a chance to relive, the glory and ecstasy of the 1960s—when another great coach transformed the Green and Gold from losers into champions. The ghosts of Lambeau and Lombardi can rest peacefully. Mike Holmgren brought the Green Bay Packers back from the dead.

Mike Holmgren's Coaching Capsule

Category	Numbers
Seasons	11
Wins	106
Losses	70
Ties	0
Winning pct.	.602
Pct. >/< avg. Super Bowl–winning coach (.601)*	+0.2%
World championships[†]	1
World championship game appearances[†]	2
World championship pct. (champ/seasons)	9.1%
Losing seasons	2
Pct. of losing seasons	18.2%
Playoff record	9-6
Playoff winning percentage	.600
Average wins per 16 games (a current season)	9.6
Average losses per 16 games	6.4

NOTE: Ties count as a half-win and a half-loss in calculating percentages.
*See Epilogue
[†]Super Bowls or NFL championships 1920–1965.

3 Years Before and After Holmgren

City	Years	Record	Percentage	Holmgren's Career Pct
				.602
Before				
Green Bay	1989–1991	20–28	.417	
Seattle	1996–1998	23–25	.479	
After				
Green Bay	1999–2001	29–19	.604	

Yearly Records

Year	Team	Wins	Losses	Ties	Playoffs
1992	GB	9	7	0	
1993	GB	9	7	0	1–1
1994	GB	9	7	0	1–1
1995	GB	11	5	0	2–1
1996	GB	13	3	0	3–0*
1997	GB	13	3	0	2–1[†]
1998	GB	11	5	0	0–1
1999	Sea	9	7	0	0–1
2000	Sea	6	10	0	
2001	Sea	9	7	0	
2002	Sea	7	9	0	
Totals		106	70	0	9–6

*Won Super Bowl
[†]NFC champions

Chapter 13

SUMMARY

At the beginning of this book, I made the assertion that great coaches will ultimately win regardless of the talent or conditions that surround them. Though many of the coaches whose careers we have examined assumed command of habitually inept franchises where no one expected them to succeed, each of them eventually produced winning seasons and championship-quality football on a consistent basis.

Vince Lombardi transformed the Green Bay Packers from an NFL also-ran into the most powerful dynasty the league had ever witnessed. And he performed this majestic feat in just three short years. The Packers' organization went from a catatonic state of slumber (37–93–2, .288, with eleven straight nonwinning seasons prior to his arrival) to the penthouse of achievement (89–29–4, .746, with no losing seasons and five championships) under Lombardi's direction. He then resurrected a Washington Redskins' franchise that had labored in misery while recording thirteen straight nonwinning seasons. Boom! Lombardi appears on the scene and the Redskins finish at 7–5 in his first year.

Chuck Noll took as pathetic an organization as there was in sports, the 1969 Pittsburgh Steelers, and turned them into one of the most successful teams in NFL history. Pittsburgh had an 18–49–3 (.279) record in the five years preceding Noll's arrival and had never won so much as a division title. Under Noll, they won nine divisions in twenty-three years, not to mention four Super Bowls from 1974 to 1979.

In 1979, Bill Walsh took over a San Francisco 49ers' franchise that had finished 2–14 in 1978, had a 31–55 (.360) aggregate record in the six years preceding his arrival, and had earned just two playoff victories in its twenty-eight-year existence. Walsh turned it all around and dominated the NFL for an entire decade—winning the Super Bowl in just his third season and a total of three world championships in just ten years.

In 1970, Don Shula took control of a Miami Dolphins' club that had been a doormat AFL franchise since its inception in 1966. Miami had a four-year record of futility in the AFL (15–39–2, .286) and had never won more than five games in any season. Shula inherited the additional burden of coaching the team in the more powerful NFL, after the AFL-NFL merger of 1970; yet he proceeded to go 10–4 in his first season, advanced to the Super Bowl in his second season of 1971, and won Super Bowls VII and VIII in 1972 and 1973, respectively.

Bill Parcells inherited three of the worst clubs anyone could imagine. The New York Giants were a team that could have more aptly been named the Lilliputians, given the monotonous losing tendencies that defined their existence from the mid-1960s through the early 1980s. The organization had made but one playoff appearance in twenty years and had recorded only one winning season in the ten years prior to Parcells's appointment in 1983. New York's aggregate record during their decade-long snooze from 1973 to 1982 was 46–96–1 (.325). During the next eight seasons under Parcells (1983–1990), the Giants' record improved to 77–49–1 (.610), while the team made five playoff appearances and earned two Super Bowl victories.

The New England Patriots' organization might have been better off making clam chowder from 1990 to 1992 instead of playing football. They achieved a 9–39 record (for the ungodly winning percentage of .188) in that three-year period prior to Parcells's arrival in 1993. "Parcells won't be able to help these misfits," the doubters concluded. "He's really got his work cut out for him now." In the next four seasons under Parcells, the Patriots appeared in two playoffs and participated in Super Bowl XXXI.

The next stop on Bill Parcells's "charity drive" for the underprivileged franchises of the NFL was in New York, again, in 1997. This time, however, he came to the aid of the Giants' crosstown rivals, the Jets. Under the direction of owner Leon Hess and his coach at the time, Rich Kotite, the Jets had enjoyed a brand of football that tended to bring tears to the eyes of grown men. Only it was the Jets' players who were crying—for help. Their scintillating two-year record (1995–1996) prior to Parcells's hiring was 4–28, for the quaint winning percentage of .125. Their eight-year record was *much* better, 40–88, for a .313 winning percentage, and not a winning season in the bunch.

"Well, the 'old man' [Parcells] has finally bitten off more than he can chew," they said. "Even Houdini couldn't make these Jets fly."

"Fly, fly, Miss American Pie, drove Parcells to the Meadow, and the Jets were just fine." I think that's how the song goes.

Impossible. It simply couldn't be done—not that fast, anyway.

The 1997 edition of the New York Jets—directed and choreographed by the master himself, Duane Charles Parcells—finished the season at 9–7 and outscored their opponents by a whopping sixty-one points (348–287). It only took Parcells one year to resurrect a franchise that was at rock bottom and sinking to China, fast. Through Joe Walton, Bruce Coslet, Pete Carroll, and Rich Kotite, the Jets could not muster one winning season from 1989 to 1996. Yet Parcells created a winner in his very first year, and he did it coming off a 1–15 season.

Of course, all the above scenarios could have been a strange group of coincidental occurrences over the past fifty years and not necessarily the result of superior coaching and unrivaled leadership. Couldn't they? Instead of five of the greatest coaches of all time having reversed the fortunes of those eight pathetic organizations, I'm quite certain that history would have been exactly the same for each franchise had they enlisted the services of just about any coach they might have come across at the time.

Yeah, right. And the Arizona Cardinals and Cincinnati Bengals are going to play in the Super Bowl soon, too.

Great coaches ultimately win regardless of the talent or conditions that surround them. And they seem to be able to perform their task under even the most adverse circumstances, where countless others may have failed. Otherwise, quite honestly, they wouldn't be great coaches. The fundamental reasons for their success are simple, and they have everything and nothing to do with the stereotypical explanations that the best coaches always seem to play the easiest schedules, have the most luck, and benefit from superior players.

The best coaches do seem to have favorable schedules quite often. However, when their teams are always among the best—and the vast majority of the league is inferior—any schedule will appear to be loaded with "soft" competition.

Elite coaches may also seem to be luckier than most of their counterparts. But the reality is that they create their own luck by calling the perfect plays and engaging the ideal strategies at the most favorable times.

Luck is a frequently misunderstood and commonly misapplied word. It is often defined in dictionaries as gaining success by chance. In sports, we use it to explain major upsets, like the two-hundredth-ranked player at Wimbledon defeating the top seed, or a baseball player who averages ten home runs over the course of a twelve-year career suddenly exploding for thirty-five in one season. And for many of these instances, categorizing the result as "lucky" would be an accurate assessment of the event. However, when the same football coaches achieve the same winning outcomes with the same amazing regularity, their successes cannot possibly be attributed to luck, chance, or any other form of random good fortune. On the contrary, their incredible accomplishments are the consequence of superior intelligence, tactical football knowledge, excellent preparation, outstanding communication, supreme confidence, and a whole host of other skills that combine to produce an effective, football-savvy leader.

Was Joe Gibbs just lucky to have halfback Timmy Smith on his roster when he ran for 204 yards as the replacement for injured starter George Rogers in Super Bowl XXII? Or did Gibbs adequately prepare his team to function at peak efficiency with or without Rogers? Most pundits at the time claimed Gibbs was lucky, stating that if the Redskins had not been fortunate enough to have the ace running back hidden away in the bowels of RFK Stadium all season, Washington would have been squashed by the powerful Denver Broncos in the Super Bowl. Evidently, it wasn't Gibbs's and assistant Don Breaux's innovative strategy of installing the counter-gap that made the difference in

Washington's running game—rendering the talent of the ballcarrier secondary to the scheme itself—but rather it was that the Redskins were *lucky* and had a gifted back like Smith to rely on in the Super Bowl. Right?

Wrong.

Timmy Smith was "so good" that he played only fifteen more games in his NFL career, gaining a grand total of 476 yards on 161 carries for a 2.9 yard average in those contests. At best, Smith was a mediocre running back, and his performance in the Super Bowl was a product of Joe Gibbs's incomparable system. Joe Gibbs was not lucky to have Smith; Smith was lucky to have Gibbs.

The only instance where one could possibly associate luck with the extraordinary achievements of the greatest coaches in NFL history would be to apply an informal, alternative interpretation of the word. Some people define luck as the result of preparation meeting opportunity. The best coaches prepare their teams to be in a position to take advantage of opportunistic circumstances that develop during a season. These situations, when properly exploited, can often mean the difference between victory and defeat. In this vein, the elite coaches *are* "luckier" than most. Yet, the obscure nature of the tactics employed in many of these occurrences—most of which are unrecognizable to the average fan—often yields the false impression that luck was the primary factor in the success, as opposed to the proficiency of the coach.

Was Paul Brown the beneficiary of accidental good fortune in the opening week of the 1950 season when his scheme to expose the soft middle of the Eagles' 5–2–4 defense resulted in a 35–10 Cleveland triumph? Or was this an example of a brilliant coach who engaged an inspired strategy to produce victory?

Finally, let's not forget the sarcastic yet insightful response that Don Shula had for the reporter who asked him how much of a role luck played in the NFL: "Sure, luck means a lot in football," he said. " Not having a good quarterback is bad luck." Shula always made damn sure that he was "lucky" enough to retain the most capable players.

Which brings us to the third and last of our stereotypical explanations for the success of the NFL's premier head coaches—the only one that actually has some truth to it. In many cases, these coaches do indeed have the best players. What most people fail to realize, however, is that the head coaches themselves are frequently responsible for obtaining these talented athletes and that their acquisitions are not unplanned.

All successful head coaches eventually gain considerable authority with regard to their team's personnel decisions. Most of the coaches in this book had the dominant opinion within their organization on player transactions. The other coaches shared that responsibility with their club's general manager but still retained substantial power to sign athletes they deemed essential for success. Since outstanding coaches have the capacity to conceive of and implement superior plans and game strategies *vis-à-vis* their counterparts, it should come as no surprise to anyone that they usually possess better talent-evaluation skills as well. Just as they always seem to create their own luck at a crucial juncture in a game, they also seem to acquire the most productive players on a regular basis. However, one of the keys to their mastery of player personnel matters is often overlooked.

Everyone notices the major, high-profile acquisitions that occur each year. Drafting a potential superstar in the first round, securing an impact free agent, or pulling off a major trade often creates a media circus that is followed by countless newspaper articles and television and radio interviews. For instance, when the New York Jets acquired star running back Curtis Martin from the New England Patriots in a 1998 trade, it was obviously front page news. Bill Parcells had decided that an investment of $28 million, as well as first- and third-round draft picks, were warranted for the services of Martin (whom he had selected in the third round of the 1995 draft while head coach of the Patriots). The New York media pounced on the story and inundated the city with reports on the implications of the deal and the anticipated benefits for the Jets' offense.

Few people, though, pay attention to the seemingly insignificant player moves that also contribute to success in the NFL. And except for the astute coaches who initiate the transactions, almost no one celebrates when a team adds a backup linebacker or reserve running back to their roster.

When the Jets added aging, over-the-hill veterans Pepper Johnson (LB) and Keith Byars (RB) to their team in 1997 and 1998, respectively, their acquisitions were considered to be minor personnel moves. The fans and the media acknowledged the transactions but never gave them a second thought. Nobody believed that Johnson or Byars would have a significant impact on the Jets' season. Parcells, however, knew differently. He had coached both players in the past (Johnson with the Giants, Byars with the Patriots), and he was positive that their unique talents would help the Jets win football games.

Pepper Johnson's principal function on the Jets' squad was to be a leader. His prime playing days had ostensibly ended after the 1995 season he spent in Cleveland. When Parcells brought him in for the 1997 season with the Jets, Johnson, at thirty-three years old, was relegated to limited duty as a run-stopping linebacker. Johnson, though, personified Bill Parcells–style football. He was a tough, intense leader who inspired teammates, practiced hard, and set an example for the younger players. His job in the locker room was to assist in setting the standards of commitment and essentially become a conduit for the assimilation of Parcells's system.

Keith Byars was also past his prime when he joined the Jets in 1998. As a running back/tight end during his glory days, Byars had excelled as a clutch third-down receiver. Although very few teams were interested in the thirty-four-year-old player at that late stage of his career, Parcells eagerly enlisted him to help the Jets convert crucial, drive-saving plays for their offense.

After the Jets finished the 1998 campaign with a 12–4 record and came excruciatingly close to advancing to the Super Bowl, everyone lauded Parcells's brilliant move of acquiring Curtis Martin. That recognition was well deserved, as Martin lived up to his billing by gaining almost thirteen hundred rushing yards and scoring eight touchdowns for the Jets. No one, however, mentioned the contributions of Pepper Johnson and Keith Byars. Johnson fulfilled his role-model position and was the veteran leader of New York's clubhouse. In addition, he contributed sixty-three tackles to a Jets' defensive unit that finished second in the NFL in points allowed (266). Byars caught twenty-six passes, scored three touchdowns, and converted several critical third-down plays during the season. Johnson and Byars were far from superstars, but without them, the Jets would have been hard-pressed to achieve the success that they did. Just ask Bill Parcells.

When Don Shula and the Miami Dolphins acquired tight end Keith Jackson from the Philadelphia Eagles in 1992 and selected cornerback Troy Vincent and defensive end Marco Coleman high in the first round of that year's draft, those transactions too were worthy of the front page sports news. And when Miami surged to an 11–5 record and an AFC Eastern Division title that year, all three contributed. Jackson caught forty-eight passes and scored five touchdowns, while Vincent (two interceptions) and Coleman (six sacks) enjoyed solid though unspectacular rookie seasons on the Dolphins' defense.

Another player who produced for that outstanding Miami team was starting running back Mark Higgs (whose career was discussed earlier). When Higgs signed with the Dolphins as a free agent in 1990, though, no one batted an eye. In fact, the signing probably received nothing more than the obligatory one-sentence acknowledgment in the "notes" section of the football column that day. Nevertheless, his impact on the Miami offense in 1992 was substantial. He accounted for 60 percent of Miami's rushing yardage that season and scored seven touchdowns. Had Don Shula not discerned Higgs's seemingly hidden talents two years earlier—when he signed the journeyman running back who had been cut by both the Eagles and Cowboys—it is a foregone conclusion that the 1992 Dolphins would not have won eleven games and advanced to the AFC championship contest. Higgs, the lowly free agent whose signing was considered to be of no consequence, was perhaps Miami's most valuable player other than future Hall of Fame quarterback Dan Marino in 1992. And I'm certain that Don Shula would wholeheartedly agree.

Certainly, the identification and procurement of star athletes is a very important element of the player acquisition process, and the best coaches regularly outperform their competitors in this regard. However, since it is generally easier to recognize all-star players (a fact that tends to disperse the superstars equally among teams), that edge is not nearly as consequential as the capacity to determine the functionality of the numerous backups and specialists who make up more than 50 percent of NFL rosters. It is in these instances that the ability to distinguish between the talents of many different prospects of seemingly similar capability can often make the difference between a winning and losing season. But whereas coaches and general managers usually collaborate to assess the team's major personnel moves, many of the league's head coaches are given carte blanche to pick and choose their nonmarquee players. In these situations, a coach's talent evaluation abilities, as well as his estimation of the importance of a player's particular skills as they relate to winning in his system, are of crucial significance. And just like Bill Parcells and Don Shula, the premier coaches of the NFL make the right decisions far more often than their opponents, giving their teams the most talented rosters on a consistent basis.

Since coaches and general managers each have substantial influence on their teams' personnel moves and frequently share decision-making responsibilities for significant player transactions, it is often a point of heated debate as to which individual is more important to the club's success. Franchise owners commonly have opposing viewpoints on the subject. But a couple of facts seem to categorically establish the head coach as the more consequential of the two executives and as the person most directly accountable for the team's performance.

First, the GM (in theory) never sets foot on the field, not in games and not in practice. So while the head coach has, at the very least, some involvement in the GM's realm (personnel decisions), the GM has no influence whatsoever on the team once the players sign the contracts, put on the uniforms, and hit the field. The head coach commands the players from that point forward. He becomes responsible for the daily preparatory routines of the athletes and is the one charged with developing and conveying the strategies and techniques that will produce winning football. In addition, when the competition begins, the head coach is empowered to make every strategic game-time decision. As a result, the head coach—by default—has the far more substantial impact of the two relative to victory and defeat.

Second, the fact that numerous head coaches have achieved consistent winning results with two or more franchises during their careers also tends to support the theory that the coach is the principal factor in a team's destiny. The list includes (in no particular order) Bill Parcells, Don Shula, Paul Brown, George Allen, Jimmy Johnson, Marty Schottenheimer, Chuck Knox, Jimmy Conzelman, Don Coryell, and Hank Stram, among others. Each of these coaches enjoyed notable success with multiple organizations, prospering with different general managers at each venue. Given that the coaches' presence was the only common element in each of these settings, it seems fair to assume that their influence was the decisive factor in victory—as opposed to the contributions of the different general managers. Unless, of course, some people again want to believe that these coaches just got "lucky" and by chance hooked up with extraordinary general managers in each and every situation.

The head coach's influence on the organization easily transcends that of the team's GM. A talented GM can assist the club in acquiring better players and can greatly benefit contemporary NFL franchises relative to salary cap management and contract negotiation. However, in terms of wins and losses, the head coach's impact is clearly of greater import.

Another consideration in regard to the overall effectiveness of a head coach is the significance of his assistants on the team's fortunes. Several coaches in this book concluded that the most beneficial course of action during their tenure was to delegate authority for one side of the ball to a coordinator who possessed more practical experience in that realm than they did. Joe Gibbs, basically an offensive theorist, allowed

Richie Petitbon to control the Redskins' defense. Bill Parcells, a defensive expert, gave Ray Handley autonomy relative to offensive matters with the New York Giants. In both of these scenarios—and in countless others, past and present—the head coach empowers his coordinator to design, implement, and manage the team's tactics associated with their specialty. But before some people begin to insist that the coordinators on these highly successful teams should, therefore, be given as much or more credit than the head coach in relation to their club's accomplishments, I would like to expose certain aspects of the head coach/coordinator relationship that overwhelmingly distinguish the former as the more significant factor in the team's success.

First, in almost every circumstance, the head coach chooses his assistants. Therefore, any benefit to the club as a result of the coordinator's presence is foremost attributable to the head coach. In addition, since the most successful teams generally employ the best head coaches, and since the best head coaches consistently acquire the most productive players, then it would logically follow that the coordinators for those teams are supplied with the finest athletes on a regular basis—making their jobs much easier. Given this information, it is foolhardy—no matter how brilliant and effective the tactics and strategies of the coordinators appear to be—to consider their contributions as greater than those of the head coach.

Second, though many of our subject coaches admitted granting their coordinators much freedom relative to the units they led, each coach made it abundantly clear that he closely monitored their progress. If the team began to experience problems in a certain area, the head coach instantly intervened and attempted to determine a suitable solution for the dilemma. Just like the President of the United States—who may appoint a cabinet member or an ambassador to deal with a certain problem or a certain country—you can rest assured that the final decision on all crucial topics is made at the head of the table.

Finally, if these coordinators were primarily responsible for the successes of their teams, then why do so many of them flop as head coaches when their time comes to accede to the "throne"? The list of "genius" coordinators who were unable to thrive as head coaches is endless: Norv Turner, Ray Rhodes, Ray Handley, Ted Marchibroda, Kevin Gilbride, Rod Dowhower, Rich Kotite, Chris Palmer, Joe Bugel, Bruce Coslet, Vince Tobin, Bill Arnsparger, June Jones, et cetera. Success as a coordinator does not guarantee success as a head coach. There is a huge difference between supervising one unit (offense or defense) and commanding an entire football team. The assistant coaches and coordinators are comparable to corporate managers, while the head coach is equivalent to the chief executive. And it is obvious that only a select few individuals have the capability to flourish in the latter of those two roles.

Clearly, the head coach's influence on the team is paramount to that of the GM and the assistant coaches. In fact, other than the owner, the head coach (as chief executive) is the predominant member of the franchise. His comprehensive authority penetrates almost every aspect of the organization. And though different head coaches possess varying levels of power, even the least potent individuals have substantial input with regard to their club's policies. The fate of an NFL team is directly attributable to the head coach, and the impact of all other administrators is secondary. Great coaches win anywhere, with any general manager, and with any assistants—just look at their records.

Here's an interesting research project that you can do on a rainy day, perhaps in late February, as you ponder your team's free agency options while patiently waiting for the April draft. Microwave a bag of fresh popcorn and then take out your football encyclopedia, a pen, a calculator, and an ice-cold soft drink. (All right, take out a beer if you're over twenty-one.) Go to the coaches' records section of the encyclopedia and calculate the aggregate win-loss totals of every coach included in this book. In addition, calculate the aggregate number of losing seasons they encountered during their careers. Then go right to the phone and call me—you'll save me a lot of time and effort.

Okay, okay—I'll do it myself. Geez, the next thing you know you'll want me to interpret the results, as well. Take a gander at the data in table 13-1.

The ten individuals examined in this book coached an aggregate total of 174 football seasons while experiencing only thirty-one (17.8 percent) losing records. During that extended time period, it is reasonable to assume that they encountered many instances where their general managers and/or assistant coaches were either mediocre or ineffective. But those impediments were of minor consequence. As evidenced by their remarkable records, these coaches won anyway. Their superior football intellects and consummate leadership skills, in combination with the extensive authority they maintained within their organizations, gave them the wherewithal to overcome almost any impediments to victory. In short, they were the decisive factor in their franchise's prosperity.

Table 13-1. NFL Coaching Records

Coach	Seasons	Losing Seasons	Record	Winning Percentage
Paul Brown	21	4	166–100–6	.621
Bill Parcells	15	4	138–100–1	.579
Joe Gibbs	12	1	124–60–0	.674
Mike Holmgren	11	2	106–70–0	.602
Tom Landry	29	8	250–162–6	.605
Vince Lombardi	10	0	96–34–6	.728
John Madden	10	0	103–32–7*	.750
Chuck Noll	23	7	193–148–1	.566
Bill Walsh	10	3	92–59–1	.609
Don Shula	33	2	328–156–6	.676
Totals	174	31	1596–921–34	.632

Notes:
Aggregate number of games: 2,551
Aggregate average record for a 16-game season: 10.01–5.78–.21
Aggregate average record for a 10-year/160-game career: 100–58–2
* Includes one season in AFL.

Since the best coaches seem to create their own good fortune, continually acquire the most talented players, and can often overcome the inadequacies of their general managers and assistant coaches, one might wonder: are there *any* conceivable circumstances that might inhibit the winning process for these coaching immortals?

Absolutely.

The Arizona Cardinals and Cincinnati Bengals (currently owned by Bill Bidwill and Mike Brown, respectively) and the previous regimes of the Baltimore/Indianapolis Colts (Robert Irsay), Atlanta Falcons (Rankin Smith), and Tampa Bay Buccaneers (Hugh Culverhouse) are examples of franchises that have experienced extended losing periods in the last twenty years. Why? Because a fish stinks from the head. In each of these instances—and in a majority of cases involving protracted failure in the NFL—the losing scenario is directly attributable to the owner's greed and/or ignorance.

In the contemporary NFL, owners can essentially guarantee themselves a hefty profit by keeping their organization's purse strings tight. Rather than risk a portion of their proceeds by investing in victory, some owners choose to consolidate and make do with low payrolls, inferior front office help, subpar scouting budgets, and inadequate facilities. Consequently, with limited resources and no commitment to success from the owner, the win-loss records of these particular clubs suffer.

In other situations, meddlesome owners—who usually have no clue relative to football matters—clash with the people they hire to direct their organizations. These owners consider the operation of a sports franchise to be a simple task—unlike a "real" business—and believe that anyone could realistically supervise a team. So they interfere with their general managers, coaches, and scouting staffs, or they become de facto general managers, coaches, and scouting staffs, ruining their teams in the process. Under these circumstances, it is extremely difficult, if not impossible, to win football games consistently.

How dare I, then, make the assertion that great coaches will ultimately win *regardless* of outside influences? Am I saying that these coaches are so talented that they could even overcome the Bill Bidwills, Mike Browns, Robert Irsays, Rankin Smiths, and Hugh Culverhouses of this earth?

Maybe. Maybe not.

What I am unequivocally declaring, though, is the belief that these coaches would almost never put themselves in that position in the first place. Not unless the money enticement was so great as to overwhelm them, and/or they secured a written agreement stipulating the conditions (full control) under which they would operate—something that in most cases owners of this type would be unwilling to sign.

So the scenario becomes a moot point. Superior coaches would not place themselves in untenable situations that could jeopardize their abilities to win. As a result, they would almost never encounter the obstacle of an indifferent and/or disruptive owner who was not totally dedicated to success. When Mike Holmgren decided that Indianapolis (owned by Robert Irsay at the time) was not the place for him to begin his coaching career in 1992, it wasn't because he didn't like the weather. Could someone actually imagine Holmgren, Vince Lombardi, Bill Parcells, Joe Gibbs, Don Shula, or any of the other outstanding coaches in history working for misers and incompetents like Irsay, Bill Bidwill, or Mike Brown? I sincerely believe that an owner might be assaulted in such a scenario. It would be like Jack Benny marrying Imelda Marcos. Something would have to give—both sooner *and* later.

One of the goals of this book is to identify the methods, tactics, and principles most often associated with coaching excellence—in hopes of providing a clearer understanding of the leadership elements necessary to produce consistent victory in the NFL. Throughout the preceding pages, I believe I have succeeded in revealing the policies and strategies most frequently employed by the premier coaches whose careers have been documented. But for prospective coaches who aspire to greatness, the secret to success is not as simple as copying every scheme and procedure utilized by their accomplished predecessors. Every person is different, and techniques that work for some individuals may not work for others. Therefore, it is imperative for each coach to develop a system based on methods and programs that will be most effective in conjunction with his particular football philosophy and leadership style. This customized routine will afford him the best chance for prosperity.

After each coach has devised a system, he must then sell his players on the viability of that program and the significance of their labor. For a team to function effectively as a unit, each member of the group must be sold on the belief that the coach's philosophy is sound and that a favorable outcome is likely.

In all businesses, there is a monumental difference between the ability to sell—convincing workers and/or customers of the value and advantages of your systems and products—and the ability to simply "manage" (supervising employees and handling logistical matters). As we have just discussed, assistant coaches—coordinators in particular—basically assume the job of managing the players. The head coach, on the other hand—similar to the CEO of a major company—is charged with responsibility for all aspects of the organization, which includes "managing the managers" (his assistants) and selling his philosophies and procedures to the team. And like the CEO, who is answerable for the performance of the entire company and is ultimately liable for the prosperity of the business, the head coach—the most important member of a professional football organization other than the owner—is solely accountable for the success or failure of the team. If he cannot convince his players of the validity of his system and the meaningfulness of their efforts, it will be impossible for him to elicit a strong performance from his club. If the players don't buy into the program, then the coach has not sold his system, and the team is destined to fail.

Upon selling his team on the credibility of his methods, a coach's next task is to master the subtleties of implementing his system in a sensible fashion. Never will one set of implacable rules, methods, and techniques satisfy every situation. There will always be instances when a coach is forced to alter his established blueprint—from both tactical and procedural standpoints—to account for unique circumstances. For example, an experienced head coach may have recently achieved success with a group of placid, veteran players whose talents were best utilized in combination with a complex passing offense and a conventional defense. Due to salary cap problems—which can quickly change the complexion of a club—that same coach may be presented with the assignment of leading an emotional bunch of younger, more athletic players whose abilities seem more suited for an aggressive, blitzing style of defense and a conservative offensive scheme. Different players respond to different strategies and routines; therefore, a coach's ability to adapt relative to each scenario is of crucial significance.

Don Shula's history abounds with instances where he adjusted his tactics to fit his team's circumstances. Due to injuries, Shula was forced to insert halfback Tom Matte at quarterback for the Baltimore Colts late in the 1965 season. The move required a complete restructuring of the Colts' offense in order to simplify the game plan and accentuate Matte's running skills. Nevertheless, Shula made the necessary modifications, and Baltimore—under Matte's direction—won their final game of the year to catapult them into a tie for the division title. Although Matte and the Colts succumbed the next week in a playoff game against Green Bay, Shula's ability to adapt to the situation afforded the Colts their best chance at victory.

In 1972, the Dolphins' perfect season, Shula faced another predicament when starting quarterback Bob Griese was injured early in the year. Once more, however, Shula persevered, inserting aging veteran Earl Morrall at quarterback, slightly altering his offensive strategies, and preserving the integrity of Miami's historic accomplishment.

During the Pittsburgh Steelers' rise to prosperity in the 1970s, Chuck Noll was forced to abort his attempts to institute a conventional aerial attack based on high-percentage passes. Due to quarterback Terry Bradshaw's inability to thrive in that system, Noll was compelled to restructure his offense and implement a downfield passing game that was much more compatible with the skills of his signal caller.

Mike Holmgren faced a similar dilemma in Green Bay when he was obliged to acquiesce to the idiosyncrasies of his undisciplined quarterback, Brett Favre, and permit him the freedom to alter plays and improvise much more than Holmgren preferred.

Once a coach learns to be flexible with the application of a system his players have accepted, that knowledge, along with his tactical football aptitude, creates the technical foundation for his venture into the realm of professional football. But perhaps equally as important in a coach's repertoire—and most often neglected—is the *manner* in which he operates. One of these operational functions is the process by which a coach communicates his ideas. As I conjectured earlier in this book, the true essence of coaching may exist as much in the way a coach conveys his methods and strategies as it does in the true merits of those tactics. This is not to say that a great teacher could achieve success based on unrealistic, ill-advised schemes and procedures, but rather that many otherwise viable coaches may face a difficult task imparting their knowledge to players due in large part to the ineffectual fashion in which they communicate and/or demonstrate their methods.

Former New York Giants' head coach Ray Handley comes to mind as a prime example of this postulation. Handley was, quite literally, a genius. He had an IQ of about 140, an amazing mind for numbers, and a photographic memory. After serving as an assistant coach for New York from 1984 to 1990, he was handpicked by then head coach Bill Parcells and owner Wellington Mara to lead the Giants when Parcells departed in 1991. Yet, with all of his intelligence and experience, Handley was a flop as head coach. His two-year record was 14–18 (8–8 and 6–10), and his teams had been expected to advance to the playoffs in each of those seasons.

What was the problem? Handley was a brilliant assistant coach who, by all accounts, was as sharp a football mind as there was in the business. In fact, he developed many of the successful offensive schemes and strategies utilized by Parcells. Handley, though, had no conception whatsoever of the process by which to successfully communicate strategies and techniques to his players. As Tom Landry explained in his autobiography, *Tom Landry*, "The ability to *convey knowledge* to my team earned me the respect required to lead them effectively. A leader doesn't have to be the smartest member of a group, but he does need to demonstrate a mastery of his field. Mastery means more than just knowing information and facts, it requires an understanding of the information and the ability to apply that information."

Handley encountered two major problems with regard to his ability to convey information. First, he believed that if he successfully detailed and itemized a system or method, its implementation would be a foregone conclusion. He never considered the possibility that players might not be able to fully comprehend the intricacies of those procedures (something that he, as a genius, took for granted) without further instruction or explanation. Then, when called upon to provide that additional assistance with the learning process, he lacked the ability to competently tutor his athletes. He could never seem to grasp the fact that not everyone responds to a single teaching process and that he might have to engage different educational techniques in order to ensure that everybody understood each concept. The manner in which he operated was seriously flawed.

Handley wasn't the only coach who encountered difficulty in this respect. There have been numerous coaches and managers in every sport who could not successfully impart their tactics and wisdom to their players. In many instances, the situation involves a former superstar who turns to coaching. Due to their innate abilities, every aspect of the game comes easily to natural stars. They seldom if ever struggle to succeed at their given sport and almost never require extra assistance or practice in order to excel. Consequently, these individuals are rarely exposed to the clinical atmosphere prevalent in teaching situations—a fact that tends to diminish their capacity to adequately explain and/or demonstrate techniques that could enhance a player's skills. They wind up experiencing the same communication and teaching problems that Handley encountered. Like Handley, they possess a seriously flawed manner of operation. Otto Graham, Bart Starr, Forrest Gregg, Norm Van Brocklin, Mike McCormack,

Mac Speedie, and Jim Ringo are examples of football superstars who failed as head coaches.

To prosper, a head coach must possess a combination of abilities that includes the knowledge and expertise to devise and employ a worthy system, the capacity to sell his team on the usefulness of that program, the wherewithal to adequately manage the team's infrastructure, and the teaching and communication skills to convey his concepts in a viable fashion. These are the basic elements required for success. But there are other behavioral and supervisorial components related to the manner in which a coach operates that are essential to the implementation of an effective leadership "package." Foremost among them is the ability to motivate and discipline players.

Not all athletes produce at levels consistent with their talents each and every time they take the field. Though some players seem to disappoint more than others in this regard, it is a fact of human nature that every athlete experiences incidents of underachievement from time to time in his career. There can be many different reasons for inadequate performance. By and large, however, the chief causes of failure are attributable to motivational and/or disciplinary deficiencies. Consequently, NFL coaches utilize strategies designed to counteract these emotional and behavioral shortcomings. In a sport as violent and forceful as football, the most beneficial methods of motivating and disciplining athletes are commonly based on intimidation.

Coaches employ intimidation tactics (threats) in an attempt to force their players to adhere to the appropriate standards of effort and conduct. There are two types of intimidation—physical and psychological. Occasionally, coaches combine elements of both in order to promote their agendas. Generally speaking, however, the two methods are employed separately. Each form of coercion requires that the head coach maintain a significant level of authority within the organization. If the players know that the coach does not have the requisite clout to inflict severe punishment for deviant behavior—such as dismissal from the team—then the coach's efforts will likely be futile. Once it is clear, though, that the coach does indeed have the authority to enforce a strict code of conduct, then motivational and disciplinary programs based on intimidation can be instituted.

Some coaches have the ability to control their players through physical intimidation. Since most coaches played the game, and many are large enough to use their size in a menacing manner, it almost becomes a natural progression for them to attempt to motivate and discipline their athletes in this fashion. The physical intimidation scenario is initiated when coaches immediately confront and reprimand uninspired and/or defiant players. The ensuing tongue-lashing is administered in a boisterous, threatening manner, often in front of the entire team, in order to publicly demonstrate the coach's intolerance for detrimental behavior. The essence of the communication is accentuated by a nonverbal message (threat) implying that a violent clash may occur if the desires of the coach are not fulfilled. The physical altercation aspect of the routine is generally understood by both parties to be an extremely unlikely occurrence. But, like the potential for nuclear war, which is also improbable and almost incomprehensible, in the back of the player's mind is the notion that the crazy bastard (his coach) might actually be demented enough to physically attack him one day. Therefore, in the vast majority of cases—many of which include athletes who have experienced only momentary lapses in concentration and wish to follow the program—the player acquiesces and satisfies the coach's mandates.

Some instances, however, may involve disrespectful players who refuse to conform to the coach's orders. At this point, the coach becomes much more agitated and edges closer to the physical violence threshold. When tensions reach the critical stage, though, the coach usually backs down from his demands in order to avoid further escalation of the conflict. He will continue to castigate the obstinate individual in front of the squad in order to save face and then cut or trade the rebellious player shortly thereafter.

Bill Parcells, a massive individual at 6' 2", 260 pounds, was notorious for his physically intimidating style of coaching. In 1993, former first-round pick Hart Lee Dykes, who was recovering from an injury, informed Parcells of his intention to skip the coach's off-season conditioning program in New England and work out on his own in Texas. Parcells used his threatening presence and aggressive nature to convince Dykes to reconsider his decision. Realizing that Dykes's future contributions to the team would be directly related to the level of rehabilitation he achieved over the winter— and insistent on getting the most from each player's ability—Parcells was determined to have Dykes train with the club, where he could be certain that Dykes would exert himself to the fullest. Parcells, who had recently taken over the Patriots' coaching duties, used this opportunity to send one of his first messages to the team. He confronted Dykes in an extremely contentious fashion and threatened to release him from the club if he did not agree to work out in Massachusetts. He then made certain that the entire team learned of the event by informing the press of the incident. Parcells made an example out of Dykes, but he was ultimately able to coerce the talented wide receiver into compliance without resorting to the drastic measure of cutting him from the squad. In the process, Parcells delivered a stern warning to his team that deviations from his routine would not be permitted.

Mike Holmgren, a frightening presence at 6' 5", 230 pounds, also employed a physically intimidating style of coaching. In 1993, Holmgren had modified his offense and compromised, somewhat, with superstar quarterback Brett Favre with regard to changing plays at the line of scrimmage. He did not, however, empower unproven signal caller T.J. Rubley with that same authority in 1995. After one of Rubley's altered plays backfired and cost Green Bay a victory, Holmgren lambasted the young quarterback in a heated sideline tirade that was witnessed by the entire team. This incident sent a clear message to the squad that Holmgren was making the decisions and that things would be done his way or not at all. Two weeks later, Rubley was cut. Holmgren was rarely challenged thereafter.

But while size may greatly enhance the threatening image of a coach who utilizes a physical style of intimidation, it is not a mandatory ingredient in the "formula" to physically coerce players. As the saying goes, "It's not the size of the dog in the fight, it's the size of the fight in the dog." Intestinal fortitude plays a major role in physical intimidation. Though he was only 5' 9", 185 pounds, Vince Lombardi was a master at this form of "encouragement." Lombardi possessed an aura of strength, power, and invincibility that "suggested" compliance with his dictums. When asked about Lombardi's ability to motivate players, Howard Cosell, nationally renowned sportscaster and historian said, "Men would actually believe that they had more to give than they ever really had to give in the football sense. Of course, that was his great quality of leadership."

Don Shula was just 5' 11", 190 pounds, but that never stopped him from staring down 275-pound linemen and forcing them to acknowledge his authority. Nor did it stop him from challenging free-spirit tight end Jim Mandich (6' 2", 225 pounds) in 1970 and convincing him to totally dedicate himself to football—a ploy that resulted in Mandich becoming a key member of Miami's 1973 Super Bowl team. Lombardi and Shula both possessed gutsy, indomitable, highly confrontational personalities. These qualities—which instilled genuine fear in their players' minds with regard to the consequences of insubordination and lackluster effort—enabled them to successfully engage a physically intimidating mode of leadership despite their relatively small stature.

Other coaches, though they are in the vast minority, engage in a more subtle form of intimidation. Coaches like Paul Brown and Bill Walsh—who may have lacked the imposing presence and/or aggressive demeanor to physically threaten people— enacted more of a mental approach to the persuasion process. They possessed a knack for *indirectly* threatening players, using psychological intimidation to implant a powerful fear of failure in their players' minds. They could heighten that mental anxiety to such a degree as to convince players that they were disgracing themselves as well as disappointing the team, organization, and city by not heeding the coach's advice and/or performing up to standard.

Mike McCormack was one of the finest offensive linemen ever to play professional football. His Hall of Fame career started with the New York Yankees in 1951, then took him to Cleveland, where he played nine seasons under Paul Brown. Following a Browns' game against Baltimore—in which McCormack was outplayed by Colts' future Hall of Fame defensive end Gino Marchetti—Paul Brown was unhappy with McCormack's performance. During Cleveland's film session a few days after the game—in a mild and calm fashion—Brown revealed his discontent with the star tackle. "Michael, you are our team captain, and we expect more from you than you showed on Sunday," he said. "We always felt confident, if the opposition had a tough man and he was opposite you, that you were going to do your job, that you could handle him. We relied on you, but you let us down; you hurt the team."

"I kept wishing [he'd] gotten up there and screamed at me," McCormack later said. "But [he] didn't. [He] didn't even raise his voice, and nothing [he] said was vicious. But every little barb dug deeper and deeper until I wanted to get out of that room right then, find Marchetti, and take him apart."

Paul Brown had engaged his own "delicate" form of intimidation on Mike McCormack, and he succeeded in eliciting the desired response.

Psychological intimidation in the sport of football is extremely difficult to achieve, and only the most intelligent and well-respected leaders are capable of motivating and disciplining players in this fashion. As contemporary athletes continue to gain power and prestige, due to larger salaries and longer contracts, it becomes harder to employ a successful system of psychological persuasion in the modern-day NFL. Subconscious threats and psychological ploys enacted on millionaire athletes don't seem to have as great an impact as a good, old-fashioned physical threat. A coach attempting to control players through the process of mental intimidation must possess gifted insight into the human psyche and have the genuine regard and approval of their players, or the approach could backfire and completely destroy the orderliness of the team.

While physical intimidation is based on the threat of an altercation to induce conformity whereas psychological intimidation relies on a mental "attack," both forms of coercion must instill fear and uncertainty into the hearts and minds of the players in order to be effective. Athletes must believe that unproductive deviations from the standard requirements of effort, performance, and procedure will be met with an extreme response—and ultimately dismissal from the team if the behavior is not corrected. As stated earlier, the possibility of such radical action is usually sufficient to compel most players to adhere to the conventional routines, and the intimidation program functions adequately.

Not every coach, however, will have the attributes or resources to adopt a behavioral modification system based on intimidation. Many coaches lack the dispositional characteristics and/or threatening presence to apply a physical intimidation method, while others lack the intelligence, esteem, and/or psychological expertise to engage a system based on mental intimidation. Still others fall short in the authority area, as they are limited in their power to mete out punishment—a necessary prerequisite for successful persuasion. But whatever the reason, the absence of a workable plan of intimidation designed to create beneficial levels of apprehension within the ranks—to combat undesirable conduct and energize the team—usually results in the failure of the head coach.

In 1994, the Washington Redskins hired an offensive prodigy named Norv Turner to be their new head coach. Turner was the "wizard" coordinator who created the ingenious offensive strategies that enabled the Dallas Cowboys to finish second in the NFL in points scored during each of their Super Bowl–winning seasons of 1992 and 1993. He was also responsible for the development of signal caller Troy Aikman, who blossomed into a franchise quarterback during that period. As a result of Dallas's success, Turner was the hot assistant coveted by every organization seeking a new coach during the winter of 1994. He was smart, articulate, had ample experience, and had just helped his team win back-to-back championships. How much more could an organization want?

Plenty.

While Turner's procedural football knowledge was impeccable, and though he was an accomplished teacher who could flawlessly convey concepts and techniques, his ability to inspire and control players was deficient. Turner lacked the menacing presence and/or domineering personality to successfully engage a physical style of intimidation, nor did he possess the psychological abilities and esteem necessary to employ a program of mental intimidation. With no satisfactory motivational and disciplinary system by which to instill fear and trepidation into his athletes—the result of which diminished his chances to evoke commendable performances—the players' mediocre execution of his schemes ruined the inherent brilliance of his tactics.

Turner lasted almost seven years with the Redskins, amassing a record of 49–59–1 (.454). In several of those seasons, Washington was expected to advance to the playoffs, but they made it only once, in 1999. Hiring Turner was a mistake, one that could easily have been avoided had the Redskins' front office—which included Houston's present GM Charley Casserly as its principal executive—been more diligent in their background investigations and interview processes. Although very few people did not like Turner as an assistant, many suspected that he would encounter difficulties motivating and disciplining players when assuming a preeminent leadership role. Turner was more of an engineer as opposed to a principal executive. He was more of a COO (chief operating officer) than a CEO. Fundamentally, he was a very good assistant rather than a head coach. Turner was the person to charge with the task of *developing* offensive tactics and strategy as opposed to *implementing* those plans. While the former of these two responsibilities is certainly important, the bottom line is that a lesser plan that is well executed is better than an exquisite plan that is performed inadequately. As Harvard-educated Marv Levy once said, "Systems don't win, people and execution do."

Chris Palmer was the Jacksonville Jaguars' offensive coordinator under Tom Coughlin when the team earned twenty-two victories from 1997 to 1998. Palmer was an intelligent, hardworking, offensive mastermind who engineered all aspects of the Jaguars' attack. He was credited for the ascension of quarterback Mark Brunell—who led the AFC in passer rating in 1997—and was responsible for the development of Jaguar receivers Jimmy Smith and Keenan McCardell, both of whom earned all-star recognition during that period. Palmer made the Jacksonville offense the envy of the NFL. But, like Handley and Turner, Palmer was overmatched as a head coach.

In 1999, Palmer was hired to be the head coach of the "new" Cleveland Browns. The city of Cleveland had lost its team when owner Art Modell moved the franchise to Baltimore in 1996. Shortly thereafter, the NFL promised Cleveland an expansion team that would take the field three years later. As coach of that first-year club, not much was expected of Palmer in his initial season, although in the backs of their minds both fans and management anticipated that free agency would greatly reduce the time it would take for the Browns to gain a competitive edge. Reality, however, quickly set in, as Cleveland finished with a dismal 2–14 record in 1999. They were rarely competitive and were outscored 217–437. Nevertheless, quarterback Tim Couch—the Browns' first pick in the college draft—had a decent rookie season, giving everyone optimism for a bright future.

In 2000, the Browns began the season with a 2–1 record. They even defeated their arch rivals, the Pittsburgh Steelers, 23–20. Then the roof caved in. Cleveland lost seven games in a row. Injuries mounted (Couch was among the casualties). Fans grew impatient, management was displeased with the lack of progress, and the team was in disarray. The Browns finished the season with a 3–13 record and were outscored by the almost incomprehensible margin of 161–419. During a four-game losing streak that ended the year—in which Cleveland was defeated by the aggregate total of 151–31—it was obvious that the players had quit on Palmer. After the season, Browns' management quit on Palmer, too. He was dismissed as head coach and replaced with Butch Davis.

Palmer was an easygoing, reserved individual. He lacked flair, charisma, and vigor, and there was almost no emotion or intensity in his demeanor or personality. Due to his relaxed nature, Palmer failed to convey a sense of urgency to his players in regard to their efforts. Coaches like Tom Landry and Bud Grant also lacked charisma and emotional qualities, but they compensated for those shortcomings by virtue of their commanding presence and aggressive dispositions, which enabled them to implement their own unique versions of physical intimidation. Palmer, who possessed neither of those qualities, was unable to motivate and discipline players in a similar fashion. And in contrast to Paul Brown or Bill Walsh, who maintained remarkable capacities to understand psychological processes, Palmer was unable to initiate a form of mental intimidation. Consequently, Palmer had no threatening attributes with which to work. As a result, Browns' players had no reason to fear him. It should have come as no surprise that Palmer was unsuccessful in his coaching endeavors.

When Butch Davis took control of the Browns in 2001, the team improved considerably, finishing with a 7–9 record and a much more competitive 285–319 scoring differential. The Browns seemed like a different club under Davis's direction, as if they were transformed into a *real* football team almost overnight. The squad exhibited great effort and intensity and defeated several teams of superior talent and experience. It did not take a genius to determine that a turnaround as dramatic and eventful as Cleveland's in 2001 was probably connected to the different *manner* in which the team was led. Davis was a more demanding, inspirational, and aggressive leader than Palmer, and his intolerance for mediocrity created an imperative to win. Ultimately, Davis's style, methods, and disposition were much more conducive to success. In 2002, he led the Browns to a 9–7 record and their first ever playoff appearance.

When the nonfootball fan contemplates the personality and physical makeup of an accomplished professional football coach, they envision a large, Neanderthal, caveman-type individual. They imagine a person with limited intelligence, a surly disposition, and contempt for anyone who opposes him—a professional wrestler, as it were. Obviously, this type of individual is not completely in tune with the times relative to the contemporary NFL. But as ridiculous as this stereotype is, part of the typecasting is true.

Certainly, no one would ever compare Paul Brown or Bill Walsh to Hulk Hogan, yet almost all other successful coaches in NFL history had personalities similar to that of a professional wrestler. How many outstanding coaches maintained placid dispositions? How many were thought of as considerate, tender people? And finally, how many were considered to be brusque, dominant, confrontational SOBs—the kind of men you would want on your side in a street fight? The answers—almost none, almost none, and almost *all* of them. Not that good coaches don't exhibit some polite, compassionate qualities on occasion, but by and large, civility and thoughtfulness are usually not two of their most evidentiary attributes. In fact, other than Brown or Walsh—who were generally regarded as tactful, temperate individuals who almost never shouted or verbally assaulted people—it is difficult to come up with the name of another highly successful NFL head coach who was a "gentleman's gentleman." And while this contention is unquestionably a tribute to these two coaching icons and their incredible achievements contradictory to this theory, it is also an invaluable tool that can and should be used by team owners who seek to employ an extraordinary head coach.

It is nearly impossible to identify even one other calm, discreet, noncombative head coach who had noteworthy success in the NFL. Coaches like Joe Gibbs, Hank Stram, and Marv Levy may have been rational, dignified individuals in general, but just ask one of their former players what they were like when someone made repeated mistakes in practice. They would scream and yell, often in contemptuous fashion. And unlike Brown or Walsh—who were rarely if ever witnessed in the midst of an uninhibited sideline tirade during a game—Gibbs, Stram, and Levy would all, at least sporadically, exhibit extreme emotional outbursts in the heat of battle, ranting and raving at referees and assistant coaches, as well as at players. While Brown and Walsh possessed the same intensity, desire, and competitiveness as their contemporaries and hated to lose and wouldn't tolerate detrimental behavior or insufficient effort, they were able to suppress the outward manifestations of their emotions in unfavorable situations, or they never felt the urge to display their feelings in such a conspicuously antagonistic fashion. Though I would never characterize either as easygoing or laid back, Paul Brown and Bill Walsh are perhaps the only two genuinely mild-mannered, nonconfrontational coaches to achieve significant success in the modern age of the NFL.

Brown and Walsh notwithstanding, it seems clear—based on the research and analysis performed for this book—that in addition to the myriad technical skills and executive attributes that are necessary to succeed as an NFL head coach, an overtly threatening, intimidating demeanor, as well as a hostile disposition and gruff nature, are critical—perhaps mandatory—qualities for any coach who hopes to achieve greatness at the NFL level. Great coaches like Paul Brown and Bill Walsh, whose temperament and behavior were decidedly inconsistent with these personality traits, are few and far between and should be considered as exceptions to the rule.

Charisma, while indeed a virtuous characteristic—and one that should not be disregarded—does not seem to be as essential to the coaching process as the other qualities I have documented. Bud Grant, Tom Landry, Chuck Noll, Steve Owen, and George Seifert would never have been considered charismatic individuals. In fact, many believe they were just the opposite—stoic. Yet, they and many other impassive individuals achieved unprecedented prosperity with the organizations they led. They were resolute in their desire to succeed, passionate in regard to preparation, and demanding when it came to training and behavior. All five, however, were anything but charismatic.

In a vocation where achievement is measured solely by championships, only a few select individuals can truly excel. Ray Handley, Norv Turner, Chris Palmer, and many other unsuccessful head coaches did not possess the essential attributes to thrive as the leader of a professional football team. To attain superior performance and Super Bowl conquests, everything has to be perfect. The correct *recipe*—that precise mix of tactical competency, motivational expertise, communication abilities, management capability, player-evaluation talents, administrative proficiency, disciplinary skills, and a whole host of other strategic, methodological, and philosophical variables—must mesh in synchronous efficiency to produce a winning formula that leads to victories on the playing field. Coaches without that special combination of traits, skills, and principles will forever be subjected to mediocrity.

As I indicated earlier, many accomplished coaches—those who *do* possess the special qualities necessary for success—demand the authority to control their own destiny. They feel the need to do things their way and to expand their influence well beyond X's and O's. Some even desire to make every football-related decision in the organization, including salary and personnel determinations. As a result, there has been much debate concerning the feasibility of employing a coach to perform in the dual capacity of head coach/general manager. Though the obligations are daunting, and the time constraints overwhelming—which would dissuade most coaches from even considering such a monumental task—a few individuals have thrived in this double-duty role.

Jimmy Johnson flourished as head coach of the Dallas Cowboys while he simultaneously orchestrated the team's personnel moves from 1989 to 1993. He has two Super Bowl rings to prove it. Johnson later assumed that same role for the Miami Dolphins and garnered thirty-six victories versus twenty-eight defeats while earning three playoff appearances from 1996 to 1999.

Bill Parcells led the New England Patriots to two playoff berths (including a Super Bowl appearance) from 1993 to 1996 while acting in the dual capacity of head coach/GM for much of that time period. Though many people at the time, including team owner Robert Kraft, applauded Parcells's coaching abilities but denounced him as a GM—citing his below-average draft record—the fact was (as determined several years later) that Parcells had actually been a very astute judge of talent. No draft can truly be evaluated until three or four years have passed. Since few fans or analysts have the patience or intelligence to allow for the proper amount of time in order to accurately assess a series of drafts, it is no mystery as to why the imprudent masses in New England baselessly denigrated Parcells's ability to select and develop collegiate football players. Like most rookies and second-year players, most of Parcells's selections struggled during their first two or three seasons. However, after acclimating themselves to the professional game, many of those players began to succeed in their third and fourth years. The simple retrospective analysis of Parcells's selections while in New England—chronicled earlier in this book—clearly validates his drafting prowess. Parcells was both an effective coach and GM with the Patriots. And the fact that he transformed a comatose New England franchise (1–15 in 1992) into a playoff team (1994) and Super Bowl participant (1996) in such short order goes a long way towards proving his abilities in both capacities.

But for every Johnson or Parcells, there are many more Mike Ditkas, Buddy Ryans, George Seiferts, and Mike Holmgrens—individuals who prospered in their previous coaching assignments but were unsuccessful when they aspired to the position of head coach/GM (see table 13-2).

Each of these men assumed too much control for their own good and experienced significant problems in their dual-capacity posts. Coaching in the contemporary NFL is an almost overwhelming task. The league is more competitive than it has ever been. Franchise values and salaries have skyrocketed. Owners who have made huge investments require instant results. Municipalities that have contributed large sums of money to stadiums that allow teams to earn tremendous profits put pressure on owners to win. As a result, the demands on coaches have increased tenfold. Many toil well into the evening each day during the season. They constantly review films of upcoming opponents, modify their game plans, meet to discuss strategy, and tutor their players—seeking any advantage that could earn them another victory. When a coach chooses to take on the additional duties associated with the GM's position (contract negotiation, player evaluation, coordination of scouting, salary cap issues, administrative duties, etc.), his already formidable workload becomes enormous. There is usually not enough time in the day for one person to efficiently execute the tasks required

Table 13-2. Those Who Were Successful As Head Coach but Not As Head Coach/GM

Coach	Head Coach for: (team/record)	Head Coach/GM for: (team/record)
Mike Ditka	Chicago 106–62	New Orleans 15–33
Buddy Ryan	Philadelphia 43–35–1	Arizona 12–20
George Seifert	San Francisco 98–30	Carolina 16–32
Mike Holmgren	Green Bay 75–37	Seattle 31–33

by both positions. In most cases, the monstrous obligations fatigue the individual and result in a reduction of his effectiveness as both a front-office executive and a coach on the field.

Bill Parcells and Jimmy Johnson, who realized success in the latter part of the twentieth century while bearing the burden of a "double major," are the exceptions. Both were outstanding coaches who also possessed the requisite skills to handle the organizational duties connected with the GM's job. However, the ability to perform their GM obligations in an exemplary fashion without a detrimental impact on their coaching functions is what set them apart from the rest.

Mike Ditka, Buddy Ryan, George Seifert, and Mike Holmgren—enterprising coaches who also believed that they were capable of operating in a dual capacity but failed—are the norm. Each lacked the player-evaluation skills and administrative abilities to manage their GM obligations in an efficient manner, and they were forced to spend more time in the front office in an attempt to overcome those shortcomings. As a result, they were unable to devote the same amount of time to on-the-field activities as they had in their previous positions, and the proficiency of their coaching diminished.

Very few individuals are capable of balancing their schedules to adequately attend to each and every obligation of the head coach/GM position. A prospective head coach/GM may be the finest judge of talent in the organization. He may also be the best salary cap administrator, contract negotiator, and scouting coordinator. Nevertheless, if he is unable to invest the proper amount of time and energy into those endeavors, he may execute the tasks in an inferior manner. Conversely, if the coach does expend the time and effort necessary to perform those functions in a superior fashion, then it is almost a certainty that his coaching duties will be neglected. It develops into a catch-22, because even in the rare instances where everything goes as planned and the head coach/GM is successful, the immense responsibilities placed upon the individual will probably result in his deteriorating health.

John Madden was forced into early retirement due to medical problems brought on by the rigorous schedule and pressures associated with coaching. Joe Gibbs slept in his office several nights a week in order to adequately prepare his team for victory. He wisely decided to retire before the toll on his health became too troublesome. Due to intense anxiety and overexertion, Mike Ditka suffered a heart attack as coach of the Chicago Bears. He was forced to significantly alter both his demeanor and lifestyle thereafter. Dan Reeves almost missed the Super Bowl for heart-bypass surgery while he coached the Atlanta Falcons. And none of these men were burdened with the obligations of the GM's position at the time of their infirmities.

Coaches like Johnson and Parcells, who have clearly demonstrated their capabilities as talent evaluators, deserve the final say on all personnel matters within their organizations. However, the most prudent course of action for any present-day team—given the magnitude of the burden placed upon a combination head coach/GM—is to have one coach and one general manager. The dual-capacity assignment is too great and time-consuming for one person to accomplish satisfactorily. In these situations, the head coach would still make the final decision on all player transactions, but the GM would relieve him of a myriad of other time-consuming technicalities and details that could be handled by a competent front-office executive. The GM would handle all salary negotiations and supervise the club's scouting operation. He would also regulate administrative duties within the front office. If the coach exhibits the wherewithal to make intelligent salary-cap determinations, then he should have equal input with the GM in that area. Otherwise, the GM should manage the team's salary cap and maintain the power to restructure contracts as well.

Coaches who feel that they cannot operate effectively without the exclusive, all-encompassing power authorized to them as head coach/GM must still devise a system similar to the setup just delineated. Sooner or later, the demands of performing both jobs will take their toll and result in an untenable situation. It is imperative to delegate authority to a qualified individual who can act as an executive assistant in order to relieve the head coach of some of the burdens associated with the dual-capacity role. At the very least, the assistant can supervise the less critical front-office duties associated with the day-to-day management of the club and free up the head coach to concentrate on the team's more crucial needs.

Throughout league history, franchises have generally maintained separate titles for their "field manager" (head coach) and "operations manager" (GM). There is good reason for the distinction. Each job requires a full-time employee to handle the numerous duties connected with the position. In the complex world of the modern-day NFL, with free agency, the salary cap, and larger roster sizes, there are more responsibilities than ever for both the head coach and GM. One man is incapable of effectively managing both positions for an extended period of time. Even Jimmy Johnson experienced burnout when he assumed the double-duty role in Miami. Though the Dolphins still won, they did not prosper in the playoffs. Johnson eventually succumbed to the grueling existence and retired after a four-year stint. Coaches who choose to burden themselves with the gargantuan task of the dual-capacity assignment often come to regret their decisions.

In Mike Holmgren's tenure as head coach/GM of the Seattle Seahawks (1999–2002), he experienced significant problems in his attempt to transform Seattle into consistent winners. The Seahawks made only one playoff appearance under Holmgren's guidance and compiled a 31–33 record.

Holmgren faced two major problems in his dual role with Seattle. First, he appeared somewhat overmatched as a personnel evaluator. Earlier in this chapter, I discussed the fact that most outstanding coaches have been excellent judges of talent. Holmgren, however, seems to be one of the few who is not. After the 1999 season, he traded running back Ahman Green to his old team, the Green Bay Packers, in return for cornerback Fred Vinson and an exchange of late-round draft picks. Vinson barely played for the Seahawks and was released in 2001. Green has since developed into one of the best backs in the NFL. In his first three seasons with the Packers (2000–2002), Green gained 3,802 yards while averaging 4.5 yards per carry. Holmgren also miscalculated when he chose not to re-sign defensive tackle Sam Adams—a former first-round pick of the Seahawks in 1994—whose contract expired after the 1999 season. Adams was subsequently signed by the Baltimore Ravens as a free agent. He became the most dominating run stopper on a Ravens' defensive line that was part of a record-setting unit that allowed the fewest points ever (165) in a sixteen-game season. Baltimore won the Super Bowl in the 2000 season and Adams made the Pro Bowl. Meanwhile, Seattle's defense finished thirtieth out of thirty-one teams in average per rush (4.9) that year and surrendered the most total yardage, by far, in the NFL (6,391).

Holmgren's second problem was his hectic schedule. Due to a rigid agenda and the numerous responsibilities he undertook when he assumed the GM's post—Holmgren even handled some of Seattle's contract negotiations—he was unable to dedicate the same amount of time to his coaching duties as he had in Green Bay. Naturally, the quality of his coaching declined.

Holmgren's saga in Seattle seems to create an interesting paradox of sorts. If great coaches ultimately win regardless of the talent or conditions that surround them, then how do I explain Holmgren's failure in Seattle? As we have just ascertained, he made poor personnel judgments as GM. Those errors forced him to spend even more time satisfying his already extensive front-office obligations at the expense of his on-the-field duties. Nevertheless, if the basic contention of this book is to be taken literally—as it should—then Mike Holmgren, the great coach, should have succeeded despite the fact that Mike Holmgren, the GM, failed.

Did you get that?

Holmgren—if he were indeed a great coach—should have won in Seattle despite his own deficiencies as a GM. And since he failed to win, then either he is not a great coach or my declaration is not completely valid.

So what gives?

The answer is that the Mike Holmgren who coached in Green Bay (1992–1998) was a great coach, while the Mike Holmgren who coached in Seattle (1999–2002) was not. I know, I know—more riddles. Let me explain.

As head coach of the Packers, Holmgren was only responsible for on-the-field business. All of his time was strictly devoted to coaching matters. Under those conditions, he prospered, earning seventy-five wins and a victory in Super Bowl XXXI. He was regarded as one of the NFL's best coaches of the 1990s.

In Seattle, Holmgren's obligations changed. As a head coach/GM, he was no longer free to spend all of his time preparing players to win. He had far too many other duties that required his scrutiny as compared to when he acted in the sole capacity of head coach. His ability to focus and his attention to detail—talents that helped make him the great coach he was—began to deteriorate rapidly when he attempted to burn the candle at both ends. As a result of stretching himself too thin, Holmgren lost his ability to function as the great coach he had been in Green Bay. He was, essentially, transformed into a mediocre coach. Consequently, without the "status" of great coach, there was no correlation to my proclamation, and its integrity would remain intact.

Had Holmgren not been encumbered with the multitude of responsibilities he had as GM in Seattle, he would not have encountered the time constraints and fatigue problems that mitigated against his awesome coaching prowess. He would have maintained his ability to perform as an elite coach. At that point, my theory would have predicted success for the Seahawks—even if Holmgren had Moe, Larry, and Curly for his GM triumvirate. Holmgren would have been able to apply *all* of his efforts in a coaching capacity and could likely have devised tactics and strategies that would have enabled Seattle to flourish despite deficiencies with personnel evaluation. As it was, he lacked the time to accomplish that feat due to his tremendous front-office requirements.

When a successful coach makes the determination that he needs total and absolute control over all football matters, there exists a very high probability that he will overload his schedule and push himself to the brink of exhaustion—creating diminishing returns for the team and taking away from the extraordinary coaching attributes that made him special in the first place. It seems this fate befell Mike Holmgren in Seattle. Since Seahawks' owner Paul Allen decided to relieve Holmgren of his GM duties after the 2002 season, Holmgren will now be free to concentrate on his coaching responsibilities full-time, like he was in Green Bay. As a result, we should have an opportunity to see the "real" Mike Holmgren coach Seattle in 2003.

Quarterback play can often make the difference between winning and losing in the NFL. The quarterback controls the ball more than any other player on the field after the snap and is clearly the most important player on the team. Entire franchises can be transformed by the emergence of an exceptional signal caller, especially when that quarterback is paired with a gifted head coach. The annals of the NFL abound with celebrated quarterback/coach tandems who collaborated to achieve extraordinary success: Sammy Baugh and Ray Flaherty, Otto Graham and Paul Brown, Bart Starr and Vince Lombardi, Roger Staubach and Tom Landry, Fran Tarkenton and Bud Grant, Bob Griese and Don Shula, Terry Bradshaw and Chuck Noll, Joe Montana and Bill Walsh, Jim Kelly and Marv Levy, Phil Simms and Bill Parcells, and John Elway and Mike Shanahan, among others.

Football fans often debate whether the quarterback or the coach has more influence on a team's success. Since quarterbacks usually receive most of the notoriety, many people are of the opinion that an outstanding signal caller is more crucial to victory. They believe that a club can win consistently with a great quarterback despite mediocre coaching and that coaches with outstanding records generally prevail due to superior quarterback play. How many times have you heard the remark, "He [the successful coach] only wins because he has so-and-so [a great quarterback]"? Well, if that pronouncement is true, it should be easy to prove. Let's take a look at applicable cases from the quarterback/coach list just profiled. Almost all of the men included in that example are, or will be, Hall of Famers—clearly establishing their abilities as "great" coaches and quarterbacks for the purposes of this examination. In order to determine the validity of the aforementioned assertion, we will compare the success of those particular individuals when they operated exclusive of the other's presence. If the declaration is accurate, the great quarterbacks should have realized success with almost every team or coach for whom they played, while the great coaches will probably have encountered difficulties when they functioned without a superb quarterback. The results of this investigation will go a long way towards proving which person is more consequential to victory.

Let's begin with Vince Lombardi and Bart Starr. As we know, Lombardi took over the Green Bay Packers in 1959. Starr's career, all sixteen years of which were played with Green Bay, began in 1956. That season (in which the Packers finished 4–8), Starr played sparingly and was not Green Bay's starting quarterback. Beginning in 1957, however, and continuing through 1971, he was the Packers' starter. Starr's aggregate record with Green Bay from 1957 to 1958 and from 1968 to 1971 (the pre- and post-Lombardi years) was 28–48–4 (.375), with no playoff appearances. With Lombardi as the coach, Starr's record was 89–29–4 (.746), with five NFL championships. I think it's safe to say that Lombardi had the greater impact on the Packers' achievements.

Hall of Fame quarterback Fran Tarkenton entered the NFL with the Minnesota Vikings in 1961. Norm Van Brocklin was Minnesota's head coach at the time. From 1961 to 1967, under Van Brocklin's direction and with Tarkenton at quarterback, the Vikings compiled a dreadful 29–51–4 record for a .369 winning percentage. Granted, Minnesota was an expansion team in 1961. Nevertheless, after amassing an 8–5–1 record in 1964—indicative of the team's "coming of age"—Tarkenton and Van Brocklin could muster only a .500 record in 1965 and slipped all the way back to a 4–9–1 mark in 1966. After the disappointments of those two seasons, Van Brocklin was fired, and Tarkenton was traded to the New York Giants.

In Tarkenton's five-year stint with New York (1967–1971), and from the ages of twenty-seven to thirty-one—the prime of his career—his record was 33–37 (.471). In four of those seasons, Tarkenton's passer rating was well into the eighties and ranked in the top five of the NFL (see table 13-3). Yet the Giants—under head coaches Allie Sherman and Alex Webster—were an ineffective team, making no playoff appearances despite the outstanding quarterback play.

For Van Brocklin in Minnesota (1961–1966) and Sherman and Webster in New York (1967–1971), Hall of Fame quarterback Fran Tarkenton accumulated a record of

Table 13-3. Fran Tarkenton's QB Ratings and Team Records, 1967–71

Year	Rating	League Ranking	Giants' Record
1967	85.9	3	7–7
1968	84.6	5	7–7
1969	87.2	3	6–8
1970	82.2	3	9–5
1971	65.4	out of top 10	4–10

Table 13-4. Minnesota Quarterback Passing Performance, 1967–71

Year	Att	Comp	Comp%	Yards	YPA	TD	INT	Rating
			Joe Kapp					
1967	214	102	47.7	1386	6.48	8	17	48.2
1968	248	129	52.0	1695	6.83	10	17	58.8
1969	237	120	50.6	1726	7.28	19	13	78.5
			Gary Cuozzo					
1970	257	128	49.8	1720	6.69	7	10	64.3
1971	168	75	44.6	842	5.01	6	8	52.2

62–88–4 (.416). Meanwhile, future Hall of Fame coach Bud Grant, who had taken over for Van Brocklin as head coach of the Vikings in 1967, was having great success despite the handicap of inferior quarterback play. From 1967 to 1971, while Tarkenton was with the Giants, Grant basically used two signal callers in Minnesota, Joe Kapp and Gary Cuozzo, both of whom possessed below-average ability (see table 13-4). Yet, somehow, despite horrific performances from his most important players (the quarterbacks), and despite employing many of the same athletes from the dismal Van Brocklin era, Grant's teams were quite successful (table 13-5).

Shortly after Tarkenton was traded back to the Vikings in 1972 and was teamed with Bud Grant, Tarkenton finally began to win football games—at an alarming rate (table 13-6).

Quite revealing, don't you think?

We all realize that current Broncos' head coach Mike Shanahan had nothing to do with the trade that brought quarterback John Elway from Baltimore to Denver in 1983—that was Dan Reeves's club. But Shanahan did take the franchise where no one, Elway and Reeves included, had ever gone before—to a Super Bowl victory—*twice* (1997 and 1998), mind you. If you asked fans about Denver's championship prospects back in 1994 (after the Reeves and Wade Phillips eras), they probably would have told you that the Broncos would *never* win a Super Bowl. The team had been crushed in its

Table 13-5. Minnesota Vikings' 1967–71 Record

Year	Wins	Losses	Ties	
1967	3	8	3	
1968*	8	6	0	
1969†	12	2	0	
1970*	12	2	0	
1971*	11	3	0	
Total	46	21	3	(.679)

* Made playoffs
† Lost in Super Bowl

Table 13-6. Minnesota Vikings' 1972–78 Record

Year	Wins	Losses	Ties	
1972	7	7	0	
1973†	12	2	0	
1974†	10	4	0	
1975*	12	2	0	
1976†	11	2	1	
1977*	9	5	0	
1978*	8	7	1	
Total	69	29	1	(.702)

* Made playoffs
† Lost in Super Bowl

four previous title game appearances (1977, 1986, 1987, and 1989). Shanahan, who took over in 1995, quickly changed all that. Then, two years *after* Elway's retirement (2000), Shanahan led the Broncos to an 11–5 slate and had them in position to make another run at the Super Bowl. Unfortunately for Denver, they encountered a Baltimore Ravens' defense in the playoffs that decimated every team in its path. In addition, the Broncos were forced to play the Ravens without their starting quarterback, Brian Griese, who was injured. Baltimore defeated Denver 21–3. That loss notwithstanding, Shanahan keeps winning regardless of his quarterback. And the Broncos have him to thank for their championship legacy.

In Miami, Don Shula engaged Bob Griese, Earl Morrall, David Woodley, and Dan Marino as his primary signal callers from 1970 to 1995. As previously documented in the chapter on Shula, Woodley was by far the least effective of the quartet. Take another look at Woodley's figures in table 13-7 and Shula's record in table 13-8 during those years.

Although Woodley's statistics are indicative of a youthful passer whose indiscretions often cost teams games—poor touchdown-to-turnover ratios and low yards-per-attempt figures—Shula led the Dolphins to two playoff appearances and one Super Bowl (albeit in a strike-shortened year) in a three-year span. Remarkable.

There are other, more recent examples of highly acclaimed quarterbacks and coaches whose career results are germane to this analysis. Quarterback Brett Favre led Mike Holmgren's Green Bay Packers to a Super Bowl victory in the 1996 season. In 1997, Favre guided Green Bay back to the Super Bowl, this time losing to the Denver Broncos. The following year (1998), after the Packers finished 11–5 and lost to the San Francisco 49ers in the playoffs, Holmgren resigned. Ron Wolf, Green Bay's GM, decided to hire Ray Rhodes as the new Packers' coach, even though Rhodes had just been fired from the Philadelphia Eagles' job, where he had a disastrous 3–13 season.

Table 13-7. David Woodley's 1980–82 Passing Performance

Year	Att	Comp	Comp%	Yards	YPA	TD	INT	Rating
1980	327	176	53.8	1850	5.66	14	17	63.1
1981	366	191	52.2	2470	6.75	12	13	69.8
1982	179	98	54.7	1080	6.03	5	8	63.5

Table 13-8. Miami's 1980–82 Record with Don Shula

Year	Wins	Losses	Ties	
1980	8	8	0	
1981*	11	4	1	
1982†	7	2	0	
Total	26	14	1	(.646)

*Made playoffs
†Lost in Super Bowl

In the three years prior to Rhodes's arrival (1996–1998), Green Bay's record with Brett Favre (three-time Associated Press NFL MVP, 1995–1997) and Mike Holmgren was 37–11 (.771)—never worse than 11–5 in any year. Under Ray Rhodes, however, the 1999 Green Bay Packers struggled to salvage an 8–8 mark. Green Bay ostensibly had the same team with the same players and the same GM as they did in 1998. Only the head coach was different. Nevertheless, Brett Favre, the great quarterback, could not manage a winning season.

Joe Gibbs won three Super Bowls with three different starting quarterbacks (Joe Theismann, 1982; Doug Williams, 1987; and Mark Rypien, 1991), the latter two of whom were average players at best. No doubt here that the coach was the instrumental factor in the team's success.

I believe a distinct pattern has emerged.

While there are certainly some examples of outstanding quarterbacks who have overcome the disadvantage of poor coaching to lead their teams to victory, there appear to be many more coaches than quarterbacks who have succeeded—even flourished—while lacking a great complement. Great coaches possess the amazing ability to win consistently despite inferior performance from their most conspicuous player. They somehow manage their strategies and schemes so as to counteract the shortcomings of a mediocre signal caller. Great quarterbacks, on the other hand, seem to have much less prosperity in the absence of a premier coach. Although the quarterback is the most consequential athlete on the field, and although an excellent signal caller can substantially boost a club's win total, the fact is that he never plays defense or special teams. As a result, his influence is limited. The head coach controls all aspects of the team and clearly has the more significant effect on a club's success. The proof is in the numbers. Great coaches win almost anywhere, anytime. Great quarterbacks do not.

Since many great coaches have demonstrated the ability to win despite mediocre quarterback play, it might prove a useful strategy for some well-coached teams—particularly in the salary cap era—to trim their expenses at that position in favor of fortifying other areas of their roster. If a club is able to acquire an adequate though unspectacular signal caller at approximately 40 percent of the cost of a star quarterback ($3–4 million versus $8–10 million in the year 2003), the savings ($4–7 million) would permit that team to fit an additional four or five talented players under their salary cap. If the head coach is then capable of negating some of the tactical disadvantages of a lesser signal caller, the extra athletes gained in the process could afford these clubs a clear edge over teams that have apportioned large sums of money to their prized quarterbacks.

In the coming years, there will be much debate as to the ideal method by which to maximize a team's talent base under the restrictive conventions of current salary guidelines. Some clubs may be able to retain their great quarterbacks without compromising the structure of their salary cap. Most, however, will not. They will be forced to decide between allocating as much as 15 percent of their funds for one player or dispersing that money among four or five other quality athletes. Every case is different, and no intelligent person can unequivocally support one system over the other given the disparate, fluctuating salary cap circumstances prevalent throughout the league. One thing, however, is certain. It is possible—especially for outstanding coaches—to prosper in the contemporary NFL without a high-priced starting quarterback. Since 1999, Tom Brady, Aaron Brooks, Trent Dilfer, Jeff Garcia, Tommy Maddox, and Kurt Warner—the latter five of whom were discovered by and/or played for coaches with lifetime winning percentages exceeding .575—have made enormous contributions to championship-caliber football teams while earning one million dollars or less per season. In fact, from 1999 to 2001, the aggregate salary of the three Super Bowl–winning quarterbacks (Warner, Dilfer, and Brady) was only $1.7 million. And there must be more bargain-basement signal callers still waiting for a chance to prove themselves.

Whether they are cultivating the skills of an inexpensive quarterback to help reduce their team's salary burden, overcoming a mediocre general manager, or eliciting intense effort and devotion from their athletes in the face of discouraging odds, the elite coaches of the NFL somehow surmount the obstacles to success. By combining masterful strategies with a commanding presence and relentless desire to succeed, these gifted leaders develop winning tactics, a confident atmosphere, and loyal, motivated players who will exhaust every ounce of energy in an attempt to accomplish victory. These decisive factors enable superior coaches to consistently outperform their opponents and win championships.

The most meaningful tribute to any such coach is realized when their players—many years later—fondly remember their interaction and frequently utilize the wisdom and perspective they gained from the relationship.

Herb Adderly, former Packers' Hall of Fame cornerback (1961–1969), cherishes his memories of head coach Vince Lombardi. Adderly offers a simple interpretation of the profound influence Lombardi had on his life. "I love my father, who is also deceased, but I don't think about my father every day," he said.

Jerry Kramer, Green Bay's Hall of Fame guard from 1958 to 1968, recalls his favorite and most motivating Lombardi quote: "You don't do things right once in a while, you do them right all the time." Said Kramer, "Of all the lessons I learned from Lombardi, from all his sermons on commitment, integrity, and work ethic, *that* one hit home the hardest. Whenever I'm tempted to screw off, or cut corners, I hear that raspy voice saying, 'This is the right way to do it. Which way are you going to do it, mister?'"

Whether we contemplate Adderly's or Kramer's reminiscences of Lombardi, Jim Jensen's thoughts relative to Don Shula, or George Martin's retrospections of his dialogues with Bill Parcells, the gist is the same. Each instance is signatory of youngsters learning and growing from the lessons of their masterful mentors, then sustaining the legacies of their instructors by applying that knowledge again and again throughout their lifetimes.

In closing, I would like to leave you with a statement attributed to Phil Bengston (Packers' assistant coach under Vince Lombardi): "If I were lost in the middle of nowhere with only one dime for the pay telephone, and needed a doctor, lawyer, priest, and a friend, I'd call Vince Lombardi."

This remark seems to characterize leadership and respect as well or better than any definition you would find in the pages of a dictionary.

Coaching matters. Believe it.

EPILOGUE

Much can be learned from a simple examination of the lifetime records of Super Bowl coaches. Although thirty-seven years of data in this vein does not necessarily constitute a valid sample for statistical purposes, it probably develops a fairly accurate representation of the facts.

Table 1. Super Bowl Coaching Roster

Year	Winning Coach	Lifetime Record after 2002	Losing Coach	Lifetime Record after 2002
1967	Lombardi	96–34–6	Stram	131–97–10
1968	Lombardi	96–34–6	Rauch	40–28–2
1969	Ewbank	130–129–7	Shula	328–156–6
1970	Stram	131–97–10	Grant	158–96–5
1971	Mccaferty	28–17–2	Landry	250–162–6
1972	Landry	250–162–6	Shula	328–156–6
1973	Shula	328–156–6	Allen	116–47–5
1974	Shula	328–156–6	Grant	158–96–5
1975	Noll	193–148–1	Grant	158–96–5
1976	Noll	193–148–1	Landry	250–162–6
1977	Madden	103–32–7	Grant	158–96–5
1978	Landry	250–162–6	Miller	40–22–0
1979	Noll	193–148–1	Landry	250–162–6
1980	Noll	193–148–1	Malavasi	44–41–0
1981	Flores	97–87–0	Vermeil*†	90–91–0
1982	Walsh	92–59–1	Gregg*	75–85–1
1983	Gibbs	124–60–0	Shula	328–156–6
1984	Flores	97–87–0	Gibbs	124–60–0
1985	Walsh	92–59–1	Shula	328–156–6
1986	Ditka	121–95–0	Berry	48–39–0
1987	Parcells†	138–100–1	Reeves†	187–155–2
1988	Gibbs	124–60–0	Reeves†	187–155–2
1989	Walsh	92–59–1	Wyche*	84–107–0
1990	Seifert	114–62–0	Reeves†	187–155–2

(continued next page)

*Losing career record at end of 2002 season
†Still active

Table 1. Super Bowl Coaching Roster (continued)

Year	Winning Coach	Lifetime Record after 2002	Losing Coach	Lifetime Record after 2002
1991	Parcells[†]	138–100–1	Levy	143–112–0
1992	Gibbs	124–60–0	Levy	143–112–0
1993	Johnson	80–64–0	Levy	143–112–0
1994	Johnson	80–64–0	Levy	143–112–0
1995	Seifert	114–62–0	Ross	74–63–0
1996	Switzer	40–24–0	Cowher[†]	109–66–1
1997	Holmgren[†]	106–70–0	Parcells[†]	138–100–1
1998	Shanahan[†]	89–59–0	Holmgren[†]	106–70–0
1999	Shanahan[†]	89–59–0	Reeves[†]	187–155–2
2000	Vermeil[*†]	90–91–0	Fisher[†]	76–58–0
2001	Billick[†]	37–27–0	Fassel[†]	54–41–1
2002	Belichick[*†]	61–67–0	Martz[†]	31–17–0
2003	Gruden[†]	50–30–0	Callahan[†]	11–5–0

Category	Winning Coaches		Losing Coaches	
Aggregate Record	2498–1670–47	.598	2457–1718–40	.588
Average record per 16-game season	9.57–6.43		9.41–6.59	
Average record per 160 games/ 10 current seasons	96–64		94–66	
Number of coaches with losing career record	2		3	
Percentage of coaches with losing career record (above number/37)	5.4%		8.1%	

NOTES:
   Playoff records not included in totals.
   Ties count as a half-win and half-loss in calculating winning percentages.
   Aggregate records include repeat coaches' records only once.
   *Losing career record at end of 2002 season
   †Still active

Two intriguing items piqued my curiosity while scrutinizing this data. First, as of the completion of the 2002 season (Super Bowl XXXVII), only four coaches (five years) with losing career records had Super Bowl berths to their credit—Dick Vermeil (twice), Bill Belichick, Forrest Gregg, and Sam Wyche. This calculates to five of seventy-four (6.8 percent) Super Bowl participants that are represented by "losing" coaches. That statistic, in combination with an aggregate winning percentage of approximately .600 for the entire group of Super Bowl coaches (winners and losers), offers strong evidence to support the theory that exceptional coaching is the principal factor in a team's advancement to a championship. Interestingly, before the 2001 season, there were *no* Super Bowl–winning coaches who had losing career records. At the conclusion of that year, however, Belichick captured Super Bowl XXXVI—as head coach of the New England Patriots—with a 52–60 lifetime record, while Vermeil (winner of Super Bowl

XXXIV) experienced a decline in his career winning percentage from .510 (76–73) to .497 (82–83) as a result of his team's (Kansas City) 6–10 performance in 2001.

The second item that caught my attention was that only five Super Bowl victories (13.5 percent) were accomplished by a coach whose lifetime winning percentage (upon his retirement) was less than .550 (Weeb Ewbank, Tom Flores, twice, Vermeil, and Belichick).

The Coach Quotient System was designed as a simple tool to assist organizations in ascertaining the suitability of head-coaching candidates. Prospective head coaches should be graded from one to ten (ten being best) in each of the following seventeen areas to establish an overall rating indicative of their potential as an NFL head coach. Categories were determined based on the research conducted for this book. The following compilation appeared to be the most recurring and consequential personality traits and characteristics attributable to the greatest coaches in NFL history. The qualities considered to be the most significant have been designated as triple strength (x3) classifications. All other categories have been assigned a double strength (x2) level. Scores should be tallied as indicated below.

When evaluating a potential head coach, it may be difficult to rate the individual accurately in all categories—such as his ability to adjust, for example. However, if teams perform in-depth investigations and ask both detailed and hypothetical questions during the interview process, realistic valuations should certainly be possible.

Coaches can be graded both before and after the interview process. The scores should be used as a guide to help clubs identify individuals who seem to fit the profile of a highly effective NFL head coach. Ratings for all candidates should be kept as reference material and can be used for comparative purposes at a later date. As each team's system evolves, the categories and rating strengths should be assessed and, if necessary, modified to produce the most beneficial results.

Table 2. Coach Quotient System

Rate coaches from one to ten (ten being best) in seventeen different categories. An average rating should be scored as a seven. Calculate and add subtotals. Then divide by forty-five for the Coach Quotient (CQ) rating.

Sample Rating for Coach: *Oscar Madison*

Categories	Rating	Strength	Subtotal
• Ability to adjust	5.0	X 3	15
• Aggressive/confrontational/intimidating demeanor	6.5	X 3	19.5
• Attention to detail	6.0	X 3	18
• Communicator	7.5	X 3	22.5

(continued next page)

Table 2. Coach Quotient System *(continued)*

Categories	Rating	Strength	Subtotal
• Disciplinarian	9.0	X 3	27
• Game-day management	7.5	X 3	22.5
• Intelligence	7.0	X 3	21
• Personnel evaluator	6.5	X 3	19.5
• Sell philosophy/gain allegiance of players	5.5	X 3	16.5
• Teacher	7.0	X 3	21
• Will to succeed	8.5	X 3	25.5
• Aura of invincibility/confidence	7.0	X 2	14
• Capacity to work with others	6.5	X 2	13
• Ego	8.5	X 2	17
• Motivator	8.5	X 2	17
• Tactician	7.5	X 2	15
• Charismatic personality	7.0	X 2	14
Total			318

Coach Quotient ("CQ" rating): 7.07

NOTES:
CQ = Total points ÷ 45
    11 Triple categories (33) + 6 double categories (12) = 45
The highest possible score is 450. A 10.0 is the highest possible CQ rating.

I would *hope* that a few NFL teams already utilize similar systems when interviewing and critiquing prospective head coaches. But I doubt whether any of them have precisely delineated their criteria—they never seem to have time for the "little things." Perhaps this book and its unique evaluation method will enhance the coach selection process and afford teams more knowledge, direction, and accuracy in their quest to appraise potential head coaches in the future.

After exhaustive research and painstaking analysis, one thing seems crystal clear: *Great coaches ultimately win regardless of the talent or conditions that surround them.*

INDEX

49ers. *See* San Francisco 49ers

Adams, Bud, 73
Adams, Sam, 331
adaptability, 25, 63, 101–2, 107, 232
Adderley, Herb, 51, 337
Aikman, Troy, 294, 323
Aldridge, Lionel, 66
All-American Football Conference (AAFC), 15, 17;
  merger with NFL, 2, 21, 70; records, 20–21
Allen, Ermal, 60
Allen, George, 3, 53, 65, 216–17, 241
Allen, Marcus, 228
Allen, Paul, 305, 332
American Football League, 73
Anderson, Donny, 58, 59, 60, 79
Anderson, Ken, 37
Anderson, Neal, 256
Anderson, Ottis, 255, 257
Anderson, Willie "Flipper," 255
Andrie, George, 58, 79
Arizona Cardinals, 316
assistant coaches, 313–14, 315, 324; input, 239; as
  managers, 317; responsibilities, 108
Atkins, Doug, 29
Atkinson, George, 158
Atlanta Falcons, 291–92, 316
authority, 320; asserting, 322; challenges to, 285;
  delegating, 330; need for, 15, 323, 327, 330.
  See also control

backups, 5
Baldock, Al, 128
Baltimore Colts, 36, 54; 1965 games, 101, 318;
  1968 record, 103; 1968 Super Bowl, 103–4;
  1970 Raiders game, 134; 1971 Dolphins game,
  106; 1971 Super Bowl, 87; 1977 Raiders game,
  156–57; under Shula, 98–104; Shula's addi-
  tions to, 99–100, 101
Baltimore Ravens, 177–78, 331, 335
Banaszak, Pete, 131, 152, 155
Banks, Tony, 178
Bankston, Warren, 152
Barnes, Mike, 156
Barry, Dave, 107
Baugh, Sammy, 332
Bavaro, Mark, 252
Beathard, Bobby, 217, 240
Bednarik, Chuck, 40, 50
Belichick, Bill, 252, 257, 340, 341; with Jets, 267;
  Testaverde and, 267, 268
Bell, Bert, 21, 27
Bell, Bobby, 56, 132
Bell, Ricky, 92
Bengston, Phil, 48, 64, 338

Bennett, Edgar, 287, 295, 298
Bennett, Woody, 205
Berry, Raymond, 24
betting, 53
Bidwill, Bill, 316
Biletnikoff, Fred, 134, 146
Billick, Brian, 178
Blaik, Earl "Red," 44, 67
Blanda, George, 134, 140, 149
Bledsoe, Drew, 266, 299, 300, 301; record, 263–64,
  265
Bleier, Rocky, 152, 178, 181, 183
Blount, Mel, 165, 166, 168, 171; on Steelers' suc-
  cess, 183
Bono, Steve, 277
Bowman, Ken, 59, 80
Braase, Ordell, 103
Bradley, Ed, 179
Bradshaw, Terry, 93, 109, 164, 318, 332; 1972 sea-
  son, 137–39; 1973 Raiders game, 147; 1974
  Raiders game, 149; 1978 Super Bowl, 169,
  dedication, 169; initial performance, 165;
  injury, 181, 182; partnership with coach, 241;
  problems, 168; record, 166–67, 171, 172, 174,
  179–80, 182; strike participation, 177
Braman, Norman, 283
Branch, Cliff, 141, 146, 148–49
Brandt, Gil, 92
Bratkowski, Zeke, 54
Breaux, Don, 232, 309
Breunig, Bob, 91
Brickels, John, 15, 17
Bright, "Bum," 93
Brodie, John, 87, 89, 189, 212
Brooks, Aaron, 337
Brooks, Robert, 290–91
Brown, Aaron, 56, 132
Brown, Allen, 55
Brown, Charlie, 224, 227
Brown, Jim, 32, 33–34
Brown, Mike, 316
Brown, Paul E., 3, 13–42, 65; AAFC coaching, 15;
  Bengals ownership/coaching, 36–37; champi-
  onships, 27; civility of, 326; coaching capsule,
  41–42; coaching philosophy, 37–38; defensive
  system, 18–19; drafting system, 16–17; educa-
  tion, 13; on errors, 24; firing from Cleveland,
  36; Graham and, 241; high-school coaching,
  13-14; influence on other coaches, 39–40, 98;
  innovations by, 31, 32; intimidation style, 322;
  military service, 14–15; Navy coaching, 14;
  new plays, 18; on Noll, 160; offensive philosophy, 16, 22, 24; Ohio State college coaching,
  13–14; operating method, 18; passing game,
  25, 191; photo, 23; player characteristics

343

ABOUT THE AUTHOR

Formerly a sports agent consultant, Brad Adler contributed to *Dominance: The Best Seasons of Pro Football's Greatest Teams* by Eddie Epstein. He lives in Owings Mills, Maryland.

$26.95

DATE			

NOV   2003